D1213165

CHURCHES AND THE WORKING CLASSES IN VICTORIAN ENGLAND

STUDIES IN SOCIAL HISTORY

edited by

HAROLD PERKIN

Lecturer in Social History, University of Manchester

THE OUTLAWS OF MEDIEVAL LEGEND	Maurice Keen
RELIGIOUS TOLERATION IN ENGLAND, 1787–1833	Ursula Henriques
LEARNING AND LIVING, 1790–1960: A Study in the History of the English Adult Education Movement	J. F. C. Harrison
HEAVENS BELOW: Utopian Experiments in England, 1560–1960	W. H. G. Armytage
FROM CHARITY TO SOCIAL WORK in England and the United States	Kathleen Woodroofe
ENGLISH LANDED SOCIETY in the Eighteenth Century	G. E. Mingay
ENGLISH LANDED SOCIETY in the Nineteenth Century	F. M. L. Thompson
A SOCIAL HISTORY OF THE FRENCH REVOLUTION	Norman Hampson
CHURCHES AND THE WORKING CLASSES IN VICTORIAN ENGLAND	K. S. Inglis
A SOCIAL HISTORY OF ENGLISH MUSIC	E. D. Mackerness

CHURCHES and the WORKING CLASSES in Victorian England

by

K. S. Inglis

Associate Professor of History,
Australian National University.

LONDON: Routledge and Kegan Paul

TORONTO: University of Toronto Press

First published 1963
in Great Britain by
Routledge & Kegan Paul Ltd
and in Canada by
University of Toronto Press

Second impression 1964

Printed in Great Britain by
Staples Printers Ltd

Contents

Acknowledgements

THE late G. D. H. Cole, my supervisor at Oxford, directed me to many useful sources, saved me from making a number of mistakes, and helped me in other ways. I have had valuable comments on earlier drafts from Asa Briggs, W. H. Dray, A. M. McBriar, J. M. Main, Harold Perkin and Hugh Stretton. Judy Inglis gave me much help. Among people who made sources available I am especially grateful to Jessie Keeble and G. W. Keeble. Margaret Ackrill kindly checked a number of references. I also offer thanks to the Australian National University and to Nuffield College for making study in England possible.

Men . . . think that if they form an organization which expresses the love which flows forth from God and returns to Him once more, they are also meeting the need of the social groups which make up humanity as a whole.

ERNST TROELTSCH

Introduction

A LISTENER to sermons, and even a reader of respectable history books, could easily think that during the nineteenth century the habit of attending religious worship was normal among the English working classes. That was not the opinion of contemporaries. From the beginning of the century, the 'spiritual destitution' of the lower orders was a commonplace of religious discussion. Engels was not exaggerating much when he wrote, in 1845: 'All the writers of the bourgeoisie are unanimous on this point, that the workers are not religious, and do not attend church.'[1] Only once was this judgment given anything like an adequate statistical test. In 1851, for the first and last time, questions about religious worship were asked alongside the ordinary decennial census. 'Even in the least unfavourable aspect of the figures,' said the official report, '. . . it must be apparent that a sadly formidable portion of the English people are habitual neglecters of the public ordinances of religion.' It was plain, moreover, that most of the neglecters belonged to 'the masses of our working population. . . . These are never or but seldom seen in our religious congregations. . . .'[2] Attendances were lowest in London and in large manufacturing towns. The areas in which worship was least popular included every large cotton town, the two greatest woollen towns Bradford and Leeds, every large coal town except Wolverhampton, the two great hardware towns Sheffield and Birmingham, and every large town in Lancashire except Wigan

[1] F. Engels, *The Condition of the Working Class in England in 1844* (1892) p. 125.

[2] *Religious Worship in England and Wales* (1854), p. 93.

and Rochdale. In a score of the largest towns in England fewer than one person in ten, according to estimates made in the report, attended any place of worship on census Sunday.[1]

The Hammonds are partly responsible for an impression that the working classes in the early part of the century were solidly devout. From their influential account of the town labourer's life during the industrial revolution it is possible to conclude that except by those whom the authors call 'a few independent spirits', evangelical religion was accepted universally and with enthusiasm.[2] Other writers have assumed that the alienation of the working classes cannot have preceded the loss of faith among the middle classes provoked by movements after 1850 in the natural sciences and in biblical criticism. Again, Protestant authors have made claims far beyond their evidence about the hold of evangelical religion, especially in its Methodist forms, on the new population; and they have gone unchallenged by radical historians happy to have support for the argument that 1848 passed without a revolution because evangelicalism had chloroformed the people.[3] There is in other accounts an assumption that since religious belief is irrational, it was to be expected both that the working classes would remain devout as long as they were ignorant, and that they would shake off superstition as soon as education opened their minds – a hypothesis which does not explain, among other things, why so many working-class people stayed away from public worship long before systematic secular education was available to all.

Some efforts, which will be surveyed in this introduction, were made between 1800 and 1850 to attract the working classes of the industrial civilization to worship. After 1850 these efforts became more strenuous, more widespread and more experimental as church leaders tried to adapt denominational machinery inherited from earlier times to the exigencies of a

[1] K. S. Inglis, 'Patterns of Worship in 1851', *Journal of Ecclesiastical History*, XI (1960), pp. 74–86.

[2] J. L. and Barbara Hammond, *The Town Labourer, 1760–1832* (1917).

[3] Inaccurate history is then innocently caricatured in the service of popular psychology: 'The Methodist revival . . . helped to condition the English of the early nineteenth century to accept social conditions which would have caused revolutions in most other European countries. Wesley had taught the masses to be less concerned with their miserable life on earth, as victims of the Industrial Revolution, than with the life to come; they could now put up with almost anything.' W. Sargant, *Battle for the Mind* (Pan Books, 1957), p. 201.

new society. Novel approaches were attempted in the last quarter of the century, when the working classes occupied a more prominent place in public discussion – in what G. M. Young has called 'the conversation of the people who counted' – than ever before. The belief among articulate people that the nation was now living through a crucial time in relations between 'the classes' and 'the masses' was as lively within the churches as elsewhere. It led some people to devise instruments which, they hoped, would supplement and supply the ordinary services of worship: such an instrument was the 'settlement'. It led others, most notably the founder of the Salvation Army, to discard normal forms of ecclesiastical organization altogether. It led others again – among them the founder of the Labour Church – to reject not only the methods of conventional religion but also its doctrines. It affected the manner in which church leaders spoke and acted on questions of social reform. These various enterprises, their presuppositions about society, and their results, are the subject of the chapters that follow.

If it is a mistake to imagine that the typical late-Victorian working man went to public worship for part of his life and then stopped, it may be almost as unwise to substitute a picture of his early-Victorian father or his Georgian grandfather worshipping for a time and then staying away. Before wondering why people stop doing something it is worth asking whether they ever started; and the social historian of religion in modern England could find a worse guide than the clergyman who remarked in 1896: 'It is not that the Church of God has lost the great towns; it has never had them. . . .'[1]

Between 1801 and 1851 the population of Great Britain almost doubled, from less than eleven millions to more than 21. The largest towns grew fastest of all, until in 1851 – for the first time in the history of any large nation – half the population was urban. The census of 1851 showed that in all towns (except Leeds) at least half the inhabitants were immigrants from the countryside, and that in 62 English and Welsh towns the immigrants made up two million of the three and one-third million inhabitants. Among the immigrants were many – we can only guess *how* many – who had worshipped in their

[1] A. F. Winnington-Ingram, *Work in Great Cities* (1896), p. 22.

village where religious practice was a familiar part of the weekly round. Joseph Arch described his father, an agricultural labourer in a village in early nineteenth-century Warwickshire, as a very regular churchgoer. 'I suppose he kept on going', Arch wrote, 'because he had been brought up to it. To church he had always been accustomed to go, so to church he went. And there were other working men like him in that.'[1] If a man like him pulled up his roots and went into a large town, however, the odds were against his maintaining the practice. Later in the century a bishop looked back on the migration into towns and observed:

> it is easy to see how the artisan and labourer fresh from the country villages where, at least, they might find room, and often sought it, in the House of God, should gradually lose the habit of worship and devotion, where there was neither place for them to worship nor pastor to lead them in the ways of God.[2]

It makes sense to speak of the churches *losing* such people, though it could be misleading to say simply that they stopped going to church. They worshipped in one environment where it was customary for people like them to do so; and when they were set down in new surroundings, where it was not customary for people like them to attend, they lost the habit. But among the masses of working-class people *born* in the large towns, many – perhaps most – had grown up from childhood attending no place of worship. Some had barely heard of the churches. What was St Paul's, Henry Mayhew asked one of his costermongers. 'A church, sir, so I've heard,' was the reply. 'I never was in a church.'[3] While Mayhew was writing about London the French social enquirer Le Play, preparing his pioneering survey of the European working classes, found among the English workers whom he studied neither devoutness nor hostility to religion, but an 'absence presque complète du sentiment religieuse.'[4] Evangelists among the town working classes knew only too well that they were dealing to a great extent with heathens, with 'families which, from infancy to manhood, have been unvisited by any message from Christianity

[1] J. Arch, *The Story of his Life* (1898), p. 21.
[2] W. D. Maclagan, *The Church and the People* (1882), p. 11.
[3] H. Mayhew, *London Labour and the London Poor* (1851), I. 21.
[4] P. G. F. Le Play, *Les Ouvriers Européens* (Paris, 1855), p. 193.

and on whose consciences the voice of Him that speaketh the word which is from heaven, has never descended. . . .'[1] So wrote Thomas Chalmers, an enterprising Scottish minister whose work in the slums of Glasgow and whose treatise *The Christian and Civic Economy of Large Towns* (1821) stimulated and guided many people in England. Chalmers distinguished between the commercial town, in which 'the great mass of the population are retained in kindly and immediate dependence on the wealthy residenters of the place,' and another sort of town in which 'the poor and the wealthy stand more disjoined from each other. It is true, they often meet, but they meet more on an arena of contest, than on a field where the patronage and custom of one party are met by the gratitude and goodwill of the other.' Although Chalmers called this second kind the 'manufacturing' town, the characteristics he described are social rather than technological: 'there is a mighty unfilled space,' he wrote, 'between the high and the low of every large manufacturing city. . . .' Chalmers was afraid that Christianity might not be able to cross this space. 'The atmosphere of towns,' he wrote, 'may at length become so pestilential, as to wither up the energies of our Church. . . .'[2] The notion that there was an essential hostility between the towns and the churches was a common one between 1820 and 1850. To the High Churchman the towns were areas wrested from God by Mammon; among the Tractarians and their secular allies of Young England, the hateful urban present was often contrasted with an imagined past in which the church helped to keep society firm, seamless and serene. 'The Church,' says one of Disraeli's characters describing a pre-industrial England, 'convened to its solemnities . . . the whole Christian population; for there, in the presence of God, all were brethren.'[3] Evangelicals talked less romantically, but they too believed that the towns offered a peculiar resistance to Christian ministry.

By 1800 a fear of the French Revolution, and a belief that the churchless poor were peculiarly exposed to the contagion of Jacobinism, made a concern for their souls more general and more acute than it might otherwise have been. It was on

[1] Quoted in B. Noel, *The State of the Metropolis* (1835), p. 28.
[2] T. Chalmers, *The Christian and Civic Economy of Large Towns* (1821), I. 27, 51.
[3] Egremont in *Sybil, or the Two Nations* (World's Classics, London, 1926), p. 113.

frankly secular grounds that Arthur Young begged parliament in 1798 to build new churches and to send more preachers where the lower classes were thickest. 'The true Christian will never be a leveller,' he wrote, 'will never listen to French politics, or to French philosophy.'[1] The revival of evangelical religion was another source of unusual anxiety about the spiritual condition of the poor. Embodied in the Wesleyan societies, spreading surely in the Church of England, and transforming Nonconformist sects, evangelicalism was inducing Christians to worry as they had not worried since the seventeenth century about what happened to people who died without Gospel truth in their hearts. The evangelical missionary to the heathen, whether in Africa or London, was driven hard by his conviction that if he stood idle for a moment, someone whom *he* could have saved might perish and begin to burn. In most efforts to reduce spiritual destitution between 1800 and 1850 Evangelicals were prominent, and even some of their opponents' zeal could be attributed to evangelical example. When E. B. Pusey set out in 1835 to interest Churchmen in what he called 'the spiritual starvation of the millions', he was no less anxious to dish the Evangelicals than to bring religion to the poor.[2] Evangelicalism not only helped to arouse a concern about the souls of the poor: it also affected the forms in which this concern was expressed. It made possible the active co-operation of people from different churches, for to the true Evangelical, faith and doctrine mattered more than denomination. Interdenominational societies formed to bring religion to the poor – such as the London City Mission (1835) – were evangelical enterprises.

Within the Church of England too, voluntary societies were formed to help fight the war against the towns. The Incorporated Church Building Society, founded in 1818 and incorporated by Act of Parliament in 1826, provided nearly £200,000 in its first twenty years for new churches, and drew out a larger sum by making it a condition of grants that local sources should also contribute.[3] In 1836 alone were established a Church

[1] A. Young, *An Enquiry into the State of the Public Mind amongst the Lower Classes* (1798), p. 25.

[2] H. P. Liddon, *Life of Edward Bouverie Pusey*, I (1893), p. 329.

[3] W. L. Mathieson, *English Church Reform, 1815–1940* (1923), p. 128.

Pastoral Aid Society to raise money for the Church of England in destitute areas, a Society for Promoting the Employment of Additional Curates in Populous Places, and a Bishop of London's Fund launched by C. J. Blomfield to build churches for 'the most ignorant and neglected of the population.'[1] The author of a survey of Church organizations in 1851 could observe that 'the poor . . . being, either from distaste or from necessity, in general absentees from public worship, are the objects of some dozen different societies. . . .'[2]

The Church of England had the peculiar advantage, in its efforts to gain working-class worshippers, that it was helped by the state. The crisis thrust on the Church by the growth and concentration of population was thought by politicians to be so urgent as to justify, for virtually the first time in history, grants of money from parliament – and large grants at that. Between 1809 and 1820 parliament voted £100,000 each year to endow and increase benefices in populous districts. In 1818 parliament gave the Church a million pounds, and another half million in 1824, to build churches in parishes of at least 4,000 inhabitants where there was Church accommodation for fewer than 1,000 worshippers.[3] When Grey and Peel began their campaign to reform the Church after 1830, they were not trying only to make the establishment defensible against the onslaught of moralists and radicals. The politicians wanted also to make the Church divert more of its wealth to centres of spiritual destitution.[4] The bishops and laymen who sat on Peel's Ecclesiastical Duties and Revenues Commission in 1835 became zealots for reform partly because their enquiry convinced them that the neglect of public worship in towns was vaster than they had known. Recommendations of this Commission about re-distributing certain Church revenues were embodied in legislation between 1838 and 1840. The fruits were modest. Between 1840 and 1843 the Ecclesiastical Commissioners who were appointed as a permanent body to administer this re-distribu-

[1] A. Blomfield, *A Memoir of Charles James Blomfield* (1863), I. 234.

[2] *Parliamentary Papers, 1852–3*, LXXXIX, Religious Worship (England and Wales): Report, p. xli.

[3] *See* M. H. Port, *Six Hundred New Churches* (1961).

[4] P. J. Welch, 'Contemporary Views on the Proposals for the Alienation of Capitular Property in England (1832–40)' *Journal of Ecclesiastical History*, V (1954), p. 192.

tion had only £30,000 a year to spread among poor livings. In 1843, therefore, Peel legislated to lend the Ecclesiastical Commissioners enough money to build 200 churches in districts where the Church had been virtually unrepresented.

It was not only poverty of rewards that kept clergymen out of the slums. When in 1829 Samuel Wilberforce, the future Bishop of Oxford, turned down an incumbency in industrial Lancashire, his father blessed the decision because in such a parish Samuel would have been unable to cultivate 'devotional feelings and spirituality of mind. . . .'[1] A generation later it would at least have crossed the mind of a young clergyman in Wilberforce's position that he might be *called* to serve the Church among the poor. The Tractarian movement helped to cause this change, by giving many clergymen a heightened sense of pastoral responsibility; and among these men some came to believe that they had a special mission to the multitude. The belief was encouraged by their leader Pusey, who had a church in working-class Leeds built at his own expense and who once wrote to a young clergyman: 'If I had no duties here [in Oxford], I would long ago have asked leave to preach in the alleys of London, where the Gospel is as unknown as in Thibet.'[2]

It was unfortunate for Churchmen who shared Pusey's anxiety about the alleys, that in them lived people against whom the power of the State – the Church's partner – was often exercised most severely. This was a disadvantage of establishment, to be set against its material benefits. Many clergymen, moreover, participated in suppressing radicalism – either by attacking social unrest in tracts and sermons or by frankly helping to put it down. In civil disturbances after 1815, magistrates who were also clergymen did not earn a reputation for more clemency than their secular colleagues. When the bishops – as members of the House of Lords – opposed the Reform Bill in 1831, it was they, not the Bishop of Rome, who blazed in effigy on many a bonfire on the night of November 5th; and when the first stone was laid for the first church to be built out of the Bishop of London's Fund, 'an infuriated ox was driven among the children, who were assembled to sing a hymn during the service. It indicated a very bad feeling on the part of a great

[1] A. R. Ashwell, *Life of the Right Reverend Samuel Wilberforce*, I (1880), p. 42.
[2] H. P. Liddon, *op. cit.*, III (1895), p. 32.

many. . . .'[1] Most of the obstacles before Churchmen who were trying to evangelize the working classes also confronted Christians in other denominations. The special difficulty of the Church of England lay in its close association with the act of governing and with the classes that governed.

Among the first generation of Methodists, doubtless a large proportion belonged to the working classes. Even in Wesley's own lifetime, however, there were signs that the Methodist societies were becoming predominantly middle class; and after his death the tendency went on. Methodism itself was partly responsible for the good fortune of its adherents. 'Methodists in every place grow diligent and frugal'; wrote Wesley, in a passage which for good reasons has been quoted widely, 'consequently they increase in goods'.[2] In 1856 the historian of a flourishing Methodist circuit declared that many a rich man would have been still in squalid poverty if Methodism had not taken him by the hand. 'It was she that saved him from rags – put him on his feet – gave him a character, and placed him in the path of industry in which he has found both affluence and position.'[3] Significantly the same writer said: 'we have not taken hold of the poorest – we have not reached the outcast and dregs of society.' A Methodist historian has concluded that in the early nineteenth century the movement drew 'its largest number of adherents' from among the middle classes who had made and been made by the industrial revolution.[4] Methodism was helping many people up the temporal ladder; but there is little evidence that in any form it was extending its ministry far into the great body of working-class people who attended no religious worship. Socially, the Church of England and Methodism were moving in opposite directions; the Church was turning slowly and clumsily to face classes which it had long ignored, and the Methodists, sprung from these same classes, were in many places shedding their humble associations.

[1] *Parliamentary Papers, 1857–8,* IX, Deficiency of the Means of Spiritual Instruction, Select Committee, H. of L.: Report, p. 6.

[2] Quoted from R. Southey, *The Life of Wesley,* in M. Weber, *The Protestant Ethic and the Spirit of Capitalism* (translated by Talcott Parsons, 1930), p. 175.

[3] J. B. Dyson, *The History of Wesleyan Methodism in the Congleton Circuit* (1856), p. 178.

[4] M. L. Edwards, *After Wesley* (1935), p. 145.

The roots of their evangelical faith were not so shallow as to make Methodists wholly content to be a comfortable and self-perpetuating club. Methodism had begun as a movement to revive English Christianity, and the local 'revival', or outburst of experiential religion, remained a characteristic event in the life of Methodist societies until well into the nineteenth century. Revivals helped both to heighten the zeal of those who were Methodists already and to gather new adherents. 'Some churches,' declared the Wesleyan Conference in 1840, 'regard revivals of religion as gracious singularities in their history; we regard them as essential to our existence.'[1] Among the converts made in these sudden waves of enthusiasm, many appear to have been labourers and their families. Miners were often mentioned by chroniclers of revivals. One writer noted that 'several persons in the middle class of society' were reached by a particular revival, as if this were a remarkable thing; and it may be that in so far as Methodism gained new adherents among the working classes between 1800 and 1850, revivals were mainly responsible.

It was perhaps in a certain type of village and smaller town that Methodism had its firmest hold on working-class people. In mining villages its success was often striking – partly, but not wholly, because many miners lived close to death. There was something about the social relations of a community neither agricultural nor urban that Methodism found congenial, and in the smaller industrial settlements working-class Methodists were often numerous. These places were unlike the traditional English village in that the inhabitants did not inherit feudal relationships, and unlike the large towns in that employers and employees lived fairly close to each other. 'Many advantages accrue,' wrote William Jessop, a historian of Methodism,

> both in social and religious life, from having the prosperous and intelligent residing in the midst of the population. The extremes of society are hereby brought into more frequent and intimate intercourse. Sympathies are developed which it would be extremely difficult to cultivate if these classes were entirely dissociated except for labour and business.[2]

[1] *Agency and Progress of Wesleyan Methodism* (1845), frontispiece.

[2] W. Jessop, *An Account of Methodism in Rossendale and its Neighbourhood* (1881), pp. 388–9.

Jessop, trying to explain the success of Methodism in the Rossendale valley of Lancashire, found a clue in the social and geographical distribution of the inhabitants:

> There are no large towns in the valley; and whatever advantages may be derived from concentration in large towns and cities, there is no evidence that town life tends to promote the moral and spiritual objects of the church. . . . In these smaller aggregations of population, there is less difficulty in realizing the family ideal of church life. . . .

He was saying of the industrial village more or less what Thomas Chalmers had said of the commercial town: that because relations between its employers and employees could be more personal than in a great manufacturing town, it was more likely than in a great town that the workers could be persuaded to embrace the religion of their masters. In a community of this sort the Methodist employer could perform roles undertaken in the agricultural village by the squire, and the Methodist chapel could become the resort of new-rich and poor, just as the parish church was still in many areas the resort of old-rich and poor.[1] Most Methodists, however, lived in other environments than the industrial village. So, of course, did most of the working classes; and those not reached by the churches were seldom regarded by Methodists as their responsibility. The Wesleyans, as a connexion, worried far less about the heathen at home than about the heathen abroad. When a fund was opened in 1839 to celebrate the centenary of Methodism, about one-third of the money raised was spent on foreign missions and not a penny on any kind of evangelism at home.[2] Yet in many places Methodism was still unrepresented, including areas in the great towns – especially London – which no church could claim. While foreign missions flourished, home missionary activity remained negligible until 1856. The uncrowned king of the Wesleyans, Jabez Bunting, did not share the anxiety displayed by leaders of other denominations about the neglect of religion in large towns. Almost Bunting's last advice to Methodists (at the conference of 1854) was that they should

[1] See G. D. H. Cole, *A Century of Co-operation* (1944), p. 55, for a suggestion that where employer and employee worshipped at the same Methodist chapel, class antagonisms were mitigated.

[2] G. Smith, *History of Wesleyan Methodism*, III (1862), p. 384.

cultivate country areas and remember that theirs was originally a rural system.[1]

The Wesleyans were by no means the only body of Methodists. In Wesley's own lifetime Whitefield had broken with him and begun the history of Calvinistic Methodism. In 1797 the first serious schism among the Wesleyan Methodists occurred and the Methodist New Connexion was formed. During the next fifty years there were other expulsions and secessions, until in 1850 the stream of Methodism flowed along many different channels. The Wesleyan Methodists of the original connexion remained by far the largest of these groups, in terms both of membership and of accommodation. Next in size came the Primitive Methodists, who had their origin in outdoor preaching of which the Wesleyan Conference disapproved. The Primitives were readier than others to seek the vulgar, and with vulgar methods. While the Wesleyans acquired the blessing and curse of respectability, the Primitives – travelling preachers (or ministers), local (lay) preachers, members and adherents alike – remained humble. It should be remembered, however, that in 1850 their total membership was only a little over 100,000. Even making a generous guess about the ratio of members to adherents, it is clear that the proportion of working-class people reached by Primitive Methodism was small. Moreover, as the first major historian of the moment observed in 1860, its strength did not lie in the large towns:

> Look at London, Portsmouth, Bristol, Plymouth, Liverpool, Manchester, Birmingham, Leeds, Bradford, Newcastle-on-Tyne, and several other large towns and cities! How little has the Connexion done for them compared with their pressing wants and its powerful resources! . . . Cannot the ecclesiastical system of the community be made to work with as much efficiency there as in smaller towns and villages?[2]

In a few large towns, he said, something had been done; but in too many, the Primitive Methodist societies were 'few and feeble . . . compared with the amount of population.' Without doubt the Primitive Methodists and some other Methodists bodies were more democratic than the Wesleyans of the original connexion in organization and atmosphere. By the test of

[1] T. P. Bunting and G. S. Rowe, *The Life of Jabez Bunting*, II (1887), p. 373.
[2] J. Petty, *The History of the Primitive Methodist Connexion* (1860), p. 386.

numbers, however, they were less popular – a paradox which none of the historians who have celebrated them appears to have considered. There were in 1850 more than three Wesleyan Methodists to every Primitive. The census showed that in the great towns, Methodism owed more of its strength to the Wesleyans than to any other group. It showed also that by far the majority of working-class people were absent from Methodist worship. The achievement of Methodism was a remarkable one; Wesleyan Methodist membership alone increased about twice as fast as the population between 1800 and 1850, and it may well be, as R. F. Wearmouth calculates, that 'the grand total under direct Methodist influence in 1850 would approximate to at least two million people.'[1] But when he adds that Methodism 'captured the affections of the common people', we must remember that his estimate represents about one-tenth of the population of Great Britain, that by no means all Methodists belonged to 'the common people', and that the largest Methodist body almost certainly had the lowest proportion of such adherents.

In some sections of Nonconformity, scarcely any effort was made before or after 1850 to reach the working classes. The elect were content merely to preserve their own fellowship. The Quakers, noted for the scarcity of poor people among them, were possibly the only religious body whose numbers actually declined during the century. 'It keeps out multitudes,' John Bright remarked of the Society of Friends.[2] The Unitarians, although not as exclusive, were similarly uninterested in evangelizing the masses; theirs, G. M. Trevelyan remarks, was a faith likely to be taken up by the mill-owner but not by his workmen.[3] Among Baptists the Particular (or Calvinistic) section included some keen evangelists; but even they had not much influence on the working classes except among spinners and weavers in Lancashire and the West Riding. In large towns the Baptists, whether Particular or General, were not a popular body. They had 'lost touch with the workers,' writes their

[1] R. F. Wearmouth, *Methodism and the Working Class Movements of England, 1800–1850* (1937), p. 16.

[2] A. G. Gardiner, *Life of George Cadbury* (1923), p. 195.

[3] G. M. Trevelyan, *British History in the Nineteenth Century and After* (1937), p. 155.

historian W. T. Whitley; 'they saw no problem in the rise of cities.'[1]

Even among Congregationalists there were people who believed that Dissenters were an élite, withdrawn from the world, who should never try to increase their adherents. But the evangelical revival affected the Congregationalists deeply enough to give many of them a new interest in aggression. The problem of spiritual destitution was considered from time to time at assemblies of the Congregational Union of England and Wales – a national body which was in no way authoritative but whose foundation in 1832 expressed an awareness among Independents that in a changing society some federal planning between their congregations was necessary. The committee of the Union declared itself in 1837 'impressed with the vast extent of ignorance and irreligion,' and observed two years later that Congregationalism was making little progress among the masses.[2] In 1840 the Congregational Union became formally associated with a Home Missionary Society which had been run mainly by Congregationalists since its formation in 1819.[3] The committee of the Union hoped that this Society would take the gospel to the godless working classes in towns, the ignorant and apathetic in country districts, and potential victims of Tractarianism. As a practical essay in evangelism it remained a token gesture, however, having an income of less than £8,000 a year.

When the leaders of Independency discussed the general problem of reaching the poor, they agreed that their own success was slight. In 1848 Algernon Wells, a highly respected minister who was secretary of the Congregational Union, read a paper to its autumn assembly called 'Thoughts on the need for increased efforts to promote the Religious Welfare of the Working Classes in England, by the Independent Churches and their Pastors.'[4] Wells did not think that any other body had

[1] W. T. Whitley, *A History of the British Baptists* (2nd ed., 1932), p. 171.

[2] A. Peel, *These Hundred Years, a History of the Congregational Union, 1831–1931* (1931), pp. 101–2.

[3] J. Waddington, *Congregational History, Continuation to 1850* (1878), pp. vi, 322–3.

[4] *Congregational Year Book* (1848), pp. 83–95. His definition of the working classes excluded the unskilled; but he was far from arguing that Independency or any other branch of English Christianity had recruited *them*.

succeeded where his own had failed; the working classes, he asserted, were 'not converted by Romish zeal, or any longer gathered by Wesleyan energy, or drawn by the more intellectual discourses of Independent and Baptist preachers.' He did think, however, that Congregationalism would have affected the working classes more, but for one peculiarity: 'the working of our church system casts itself too much into an aristocratic mould to present a pleasing aspect to the working classes.' In Mrs Oliphant's novel *Salem Chapel*, Mrs Brown of the Devonshire Dairy tells the new pastor that the congregation are 'all in the way of business, except just the poor folks, as is all very well in their place, and never interfere with nothing, and don't count. . . .'[1] Wells, though speaking in a different tone of voice, was describing a situation recognizably the same.

Although Wells wanted his brothers to approach the working classes more ardently, he was faced with a dilemma. The middle-class atmosphere of Independency seemed to him both a cause of reasonable resentment among poorer people, and a great source of strength 'that we must not alter, even did we know that the effect would be to gather to us great numbers of the artisan population. For in that case it would really be that we joined them, not they us.' What then was to be done? Perhaps God intended Congregationalists to preserve their ministry for the middle classes. 'If we are not, indeed, a body adapted to act powerfully on the working classes, that may not be our calling of the Lord.' This was not Wells' view alone: Thomas Binney, who was chairman of the Congregational Union when this discussion occurred, and whose moral authority among Congregationalists was comparable with Jabez Bunting's among Wesleyans, once declared: 'Our mission is neither to the very rich nor to the very poor, but to that great middle section of the community.'[2] In the speeches by Binney and others that followed Wells' address, many different causes were suggested for the alienation, but nobody denied it. At the end of the debate the assembly resolved merely to give five lectures to the working classes, in London, 'on subjects showing the dependence of their social interests on their religious and

[1] M. Oliphant, *Salem Chapel* (1863), p. 10.

[2] Quoted in A. C. Whitby, 'Matthew Arnold and the Nonconformists' (unpublished B. Litt. thesis, University of Oxford, 1954), p. 88.

moral character,' and to send letters to those ministers who knew the working classes best asking if they could suggest ways of reaching them. The lectures were duly given and printed. Not many ministers replied to their letters.

There were some Independents who denied that the social atmosphere of chapels had anything to do with the scarcity of poor worshippers. According to the *British Quarterly Review* (a mainly Congregational journal), the working classes deserved to be roundly chastised for neglecting religion.

> Let ministers of religion be men of honest speech, say we, whether addressing courts or crowds. . . . The great cause of the evil we deplore is, with the poor as with the rich, the repugnance of an earthly mind to the spiritual life enjoined in the gospel.[1]

The journal said that poor people would be more welcome in the chapel if they were cleaner, and it denied that Christians had too little sympathy with them. Such a view was very different from Wells'; but it revealed, even while it denied, that very acceptance of middle-class mores and manners which Wells had delineated. The one solid point of agreement between Wells and the *British Quarterly Review* was that the success of their sect in evangelizing the working classes had been so far slender.

The only body of Christians who could claim a steady increase of working-class adherents were the Catholics – an increase which they owed entirely to hideous economic facts in another country. Irish immigrants arrived in substantial numbers after 1800, and especially after the famine and epidemic of 1822. Most landed in Liverpool and went no farther than the manufacturing towns of Lancashire; thousands went on to London. When disease swept though the Irish potato crop in 1845, a wave of migration added several hundred thousands to the Irish population of England without much altering its distribution. Even before this new tragedy, the Catholic church in some parts of England was struggling hard to keep in touch with the Irish faithful. A priest in Manchester informed Rome in 1845 that although the twelve priests in the city were working as hard as they could, 'about 40,000 Catholics

[1] *British Quarterly Review*, XIX (1854), pp. 449–50.

have not made their Easter "duty" for sheer want of someone to hear their confessions.'[1] Priests were afraid that many immigrants would lapse from the faith unless more clergy and more churches were provided quickly. Few of them were likely to become Protestants: when Mayhew asked an Irish stallkeeper, irregular in attending mass, whether he went to any other place of worship, the man replied: 'Ave coorse not!'[2] The danger was rather that poverty-stricken newcomers to a strange society, forced into the most wretched parts of great towns, would abandon altogether the religious practice which had been part of their life in agricultural Ireland.

Between 1845 and 1848 the hard-pressed clergy in manufacturing towns were helped by a band of itinerant missionaries of a new Italian order, the Institute of Charity. After three missions in Manchester and Salford during 1846, the local clergy thanked their leader, Father Gentili, for reclaiming an 'immense multitude of degenerate Catholics,' and declared: 'the practice of giving missions, which you have recently introduced into this country, is one of the greatest blessings which has accrued to religion in modern times.'[3] When Gentili died of cholera in 1848, the author of a tribute in a Catholic paper wrote: 'From the beginning, members of this Order have spoken to the people; have endeavoured above all things to reach the heart of the masses. . . .'[4] A few men in a few years could touch only a small proportion of the Irish in England; but their presence, holding public meetings in English towns where the celebration of mass had for long been virtually clandestine, was one sign of a general stirring in English Catholicism. At the beginning of the century Catholics in England had been a tiny, proud, persecuted body. Even after the Roman Catholic Relief Act of 1829 removed almost completely the civil intolerance which Catholics had suffered for centuries, they were still reluctant as a body to evangelize their countrymen, rich or poor. When the Hon. and Rev. George Spencer, a convert, began in 1838 asking Catholics everywhere to pray for the conversion of England, the head of the clergy in

[1] D. R. Gwynn, *Father Luigi Gentili and his Mission (1801–1848)* (1951), pp. 208–9.

[2] H. Mayhew, *op. cit.*, I. 107.

[3] G. P. Pagani, *Life of the Rev. Aloysius Gentili* (1851), p. 255.

[4] L. C. Casartelli, *A Forgotten Chapter of the Second Spring* (1895), p. 24.

England ignored the campaign except to prohibit public prayer for it. A few years later, in the same month as Ireland's potatoes were ruined, Newman became a Catholic. These two events marked the end of an age in English Catholicism which Henry VIII had begun. Newman's conversion and those that followed it – above all, Manning's – brought to the leadership of the church men with a crusading zeal rare among 'old' Catholics. Refugees from famine in Ireland gave Catholicism an opportunity among the very classes which were the despair of other churches – if only the immigrants kept the old faith in the new land.

Most evangelistic activity between 1800 and 1850 rested on an assumption that millions of people were absent from worship simply because churches had become inaccessible to them, and that they would become willing worshippers as soon as the facilities for doing so were brought within their reach. Lord Vansittart expressed this assumption plainly in 1818 when, introducing the bill which gave parliamentary aid for church building, he said that:

> a very large proportion of those who did not now attend the worship of the established church, had not voluntarily forsaken the church; but that the church, from an unfortunate train of circumstances, which could not be too soon remedied, had shut her doors upon them.[1]

Nor was this view held only in the Church of England. The very phrase 'spiritual destitution' seemed to imply a hunger and thirst after righteousness that the churches had only to satisfy. Thomas Chalmers, for one, was doubtful. 'The less we have of it,' he said of religious instruction, 'the less we desire of it. It is not with the aliment of the soul, as it is with the aliment of the body.'[2] More specifically, he warned that church-building alone could never win the masses. Bishop Blomfield learned this truth when new churches which he provided for the London poor remained half empty.[3] The Rev. Charles Kingsley had a character in his novel *Yeast* (1849) say: 'After all the expense, when they've built the church, it's the tradesmen and the gentry and the old folk that fill it, and the working men never come

[1] *The Parliamentary Debates*, XXXVII. 1125.
[2] T. Chalmers, *op. cit.*, I. 90.
[3] A. Blomfield, *op. cit.*, I. 243.

near it from one year's end to another.'[1] There was little working-class demand for the tons of evangelistic pamphlets put out by such bodies as the Religious Tract Society; religious literature, said the historian of that body in 1850, circulated chiefly among 'professing Christians of the middle classes.'[2]

The most clear-sighted students of the matter were forced to realize that non-worshippers among the working classes were not just physically inaccessible to Christian ministry but were declining to accept it. The old approaches were continued; but they were accompanied, from the middle years of the century, by a growing number of enterprises whose authors saw that evangelism involved an encounter between ways of life. Thus a Congregational minister in Leeds said to a group of working men: 'You have a character and wants peculiar to the class . . . Religion is beginning to be conscious that she does not, with her present appliances, meet your requirements. . . .'[3] The Christian Socialists, who formed themselves together in 1848, were trying as Churchmen to be, in F. D. Maurice's words, 'mediators . . . between young England of the middle and upper classes, and the working people,' and to free Christianity from what Maurice called 'caste morality.'[4] When Edward Miall's journal the *Nonconformist* invited working men, also in 1848, to write letters on 'The Working Classes and Religious Institutions,' respondents denounced the social distinctions made within churches, their worship of respectability and contempt for the poor, the 'almost total want of sympathy manifested by the ministers of religion of every denomination with the privations, wants, and wastes of the working classes' and the 'aristocratic character of religious institutions.' Miall himself declared that Christians had a morbid horror of poverty. 'The service concludes, and the worshippers retire. Communion with God has not disposed them to communion with each other, beyond the well-defined boundaries of class.'[5] Mayhew found among poor Londoners a feeling that going to worship was an activity appropriate only among classes higher than their own.

[1] C. Kingsley, *Yeast* (1897 ed.), p. 144.
[2] R. K. Webb, *The British Working Class Reader, 1790–1848* (1955), p. 27.
[3] G. W. Conder, *Six Lectures to Working Men on Christianity* (1850), p. 4.
[4] F. Maurice, *The Life of Frederick Denison Maurice* (1884), I. 477–8; F. D. Maurice, *Social Morality* (1866), p. 453.
[5] E. Miall, *The British Churches and the British People* (1848), pp. 143–4.

'Religion is a regular puzzle to the costers,' a former coster-monger told him.

> They see people come out of church and chapel, and as they're mostly well dressed, and there's very few of their own sort among the church-goers, the costers somehow mix up being religious with being respectable, and so they have a queer sort of feeling about it. It's a mystery to them.[1]

Among the observers who insisted that social divisions discouraged working-class attendance was Horace Mann, who conducted the census of religious worship. He argued in the report that positive infidelity among the working classes was rare, and that the masses could be described better as 'unconscious Secularists,' having not philosophical grounds for rejecting Christianity but practical objections to the forms given it by the churches. When Mann gave a summary of opinion in the churches about the causes of popular hostility or indifference, he emphasized the lack of sympathy among Christians for the social burdens of the poor; a suspicion that ministers were secular and selfish; and the fact of poverty itself. He praised such devices as 'ragged churches' and special services for poor people in halls and lecture-rooms; 'the success of these proceedings,' he observed, 'seems to prove that multitudes will readily frequent such places, where of course there is a total absence of class distinction, who would never enter the exclusive-looking chapel.'

This report was published in 1854. It was widely read, quoted and written about. The statistical analysis and Mann's general observations made it a remarkable essay on the social pathology of English religion. It showed that well-tried approaches to the working classes were having little success. It helped church leaders to realize just how solid was resistance to their ministry, especially in the large towns; and it helped them to decide that if old methods were failing, new ones should be sought.

[1] H. Mayhew, *op. cit.*, I. 21.

1

The Church of England

Parish, Diocese and Nation

BETWEEN 1850 and 1900 there were people in the Church of England, including some of its leaders, who cared as little about the spiritual condition of the masses as the masses were supposed to care about religion. To them the first task was defending the establishment, meeting the intellectual challenge of secular thought, or taking a side in the struggle over ritual. Nevertheless, the Church's relationship with the working classes was one of a few issues which Churchmen in general believed to be crucial. When clergymen addressed or talked about working-class people in this period, they normally sounded unlike those of their fathers who had scolded the poor for neglecting public worship, blamed them for their poverty, and ordered them to obey their spiritual masters.[1] Clergymen were now more inclined to offer hand-shakes and smiles. Charles Kingsley and F. D. Maurice were men of influence who spoke in the new tone of voice; but it could be heard also in a sermon preached in 1858 by John Keble, the least socially-conscious of the Tractarians, on the subject: 'The rich and the poor one in Christ.' It was audible at a conference attended by Churchmen and Nonconformists on 'Working Men and Religious Institutions' in 1867, when the Dean of Westminster, A. P. Stanley, invited working men to suggest how services

[1] For all these attitudes see T. Gisborne, *Friendly Observations Addressed to the Manufacturing Population of Great Britain* (3rd ed. 1827).

in the Abbey might be made 'more available and more useful for them.'[1] The friendly and diplomatic approach was expressed in the custom, begun in 1866, of holding at the annual Church Congress – an institution whose purpose was 'to assist in forming and also in partially expressing the public opinion of the Church on the current Church questions of the day'[2] – a special meeting for working men. The meetings were begun by the Archbishop of York, William Thomson, who admitted to having a skilful way with a working-class audience. In 1878, addressing the working-men's meeting at the Church Congress in Sheffield, Thomson said expansively that at first the clergy had not hit quite the right note in these meetings.

> We began by saying, You are a working man and I am a working man, and now we have come to you as one working man to another. But I am afraid the working man saw through that. He saw a distinction between the position of a bishop and the position of a man who works day by day for his daily wages. . . . We are not working men addressing working men. . . . We have a stronger bond yet than that of being working men together. We are immortal souls together. . . .

Thomson went on, amidst Hear-Hears, to say that the future of England lay with the working man.[3] The archbishop agreed that this remark might sound like flattery. He was, however, in earnest. 'I see very clearly,' Thomson said once, 'that the Church of England must either come into closer contact with the working classes of the country, or else her national position will suffer, and her leading position perhaps be ultimately lost.'[4] This was one powerful reason for the changing tone of Churchmen towards the working classes, and it is significant that it can be seen at work in minds as different as those of this Archbishop of York and F. D. Maurice. It was a translation into ecclesiastical terms of the anxiety and the hope which led Disraeli to take his leap in the dark.

In the Church as in the nation, discussion of the working

[1] *Working Men and Religious Institutions* (1867), pp. 25–6.

[2] *Church Congress Report* (1895), p. 30.

[3] E. M. Thomson, *The Life and Letters of William Thomson* (1919), pp. 165–6. According to official reports these meetings were usually packed and enthusiastic. Whether many non-worshippers were reached, and what proportion of the audiences were working class, cannot be judged from the reports.

[4] C. Bullock, *The People's Archbishop* (1891), p. 39.

classes became more intense and more widespread during the last two decades of the century. In his opening address to the Church Congress of 1880 the Bishop of Peterborough, William Magee, described the religious condition of the masses as the 'one great Church question of our time, before which all others fade into insignificance.'[1] The Convocations of Canterbury and York each appointed a committee in 1883 'on the spiritual needs of the masses of the people', one bishop calling the subject 'perhaps the most pressing of the day.'[2] Concern about the working classes was now expressed at all levels of the Church, from the Convocations down to a journal produced by discontented curates which observed in 1882: 'there are large classes of the community which the Church does not attract or reach,' the writer concluded that she must 'untie her red-tape and unstarch her surplices.'[3] It was expressed in all parties, from the Evangelicals of the Church Pastoral Aid Society to the ritualists in the slums. The *Year-Book of the Church of England*, a publication which could commit itself to opinions only when they were outside controversy, said in its first issue (1883):

> the Church of England has but one plain and solemn duty which God seems to set so clearly before her now as the Church of the nation – namely, to multiply every force at her command, and by methods and with teaching of the simplest possible kind to go in and out among the masses lifting up the Cross of Christ as God's message of mercy to the world.[4]

This notion that it was the peculiar responsibility of the Church of England, as 'the Church of the Nation', to bring the masses to worship, had long been a popular one in sermons and pamphlets. Horace Mann expressed it in his report on the religious census of 1851. 'Without doubt', he wrote:

> the destitute condition of this vast proportion of our countrymen appeals to the benevolence of Christians indiscriminately; but the claim for sympathy is preferred with special force upon the Church of England, to whose care the spiritual welfare of these myriads is peculiarly entrusted, and whose labours for their benefit need

[1] *Church Congress Report* (1880), p. 26.
[2] Convocation of Canterbury, *Chronicle* (1885), p. 98.
[3] *Church Reformer*, Feb. 1882, p. 4. For a note on this journal, see pp. 273–4 below.
[4] *Year-Book of the Church of England* (1883), p. 83.

> not be limited by any courteous fear of trespassing on ground already occupied by other Christian agents.[1]

It was often said that this responsibility was formally expressed in the parochial principle, for the vicar was held to be charged with the care not only of his worshipping congregation, but of everybody in the parish. The Church, said one of George Eliot's clergymen, 'ought to represent the feeling of the community, so that every parish should be a family knit together by Christian brotherhood under a spiritual father.'[2] Most clergymen, of course, had to share their territory with other aspirants to spiritual fatherhood; many resented the competition, and some (especially in villages) let it divert them from the task of seeking those people who worshipped nowhere. The fiction that no rival pastor existed nevertheless had a high symbolic importance in the Church of England. The parochial principle was dear to Churchmen both because it gave the clergy a special position in relation to other ministers, and because it represented the Church as a living part of the whole community, having a mission at once spiritual and social.

The ideal community of parochial theory belonged to a rural, pre-industrial England. The urban Englishman today still dreams of the country; and three generations ago, when millions were alive who had known a time when most people lived outside large towns, memory as well as imagination fed this nostalgia. Nowhere was it stronger in the Church, and nowhere indulged with better reason. For in a stable, hierarchical, rural community, the parish church had an importance which it seldom gained in towns. The Church Pastoral Aid Society, which described its task as 'the maintenance of Curates and Lay-Agents in populous districts,' had on the front page of its monthly journal, *Church and People*, a sketch of a medieval church in a tiny village. Its unspoken aim was to reproduce in an urban environment the relationship between church and society which its members believed to have been characteristic of an earlier and happier England.

The difficulty of accommodating the parochial machinery of the Church to the new society was enormous. The parish had evolved in communities which were small and socially hetero-

[1] *Religious Worship in England and Wales* (1854), p. 73.

[2] Dr Kenn ,in *The Mill on the Floss* (1860), III. 259.

geneous. It had now to be adapted to areas in which not only was the population dense, and getting denser, but – as one Churchman put it – all who made jam lived in one place, and all who ate jam lived in another. 'The parochial system', observed Lord Shaftesbury in 1855, 'is, no doubt, a beautiful thing in theory, and is of great value in small rural districts; but in the large towns it is a mere shadow and a name.'[1] The Bishop of Manchester, James Fraser, whose office forced him to reflect as seriously as anybody about the problem of organizing the Church in a great city, said to his clergy in 1872:

> The parochial system, as ordinarily conceived, admirably efficient in rural parishes and among limited populations, where the pastor knows and is known by every one committed to his charge, breaks down in face of that huge mass of ignorance, poverty, and wretchedness by which it is so often confronted in the thickly peopled areas of our manufacturing towns.[2]

It was Fraser's generation which first used the word 'parochial' as a pejorative term. Yet few concluded that in an industrial society the Church should set aside the parochial structure, however nobly it had served in different circumstances, and should find more appropriate methods of organizing its energies. To those who loved her, a church without the parochial system would be no Church of England. They were proud that, unlike the Nonconformist chapel, the parish church belonged to its community at large. A greatly respected clergyman remarked at the Church Congress in 1881 that if the parochial system were destroyed in large towns, 'we at once become Congregationalists.'[3] In urban areas where churches of every denomination appeared to serve their own regular worshippers rather than the surrounding population, the difference between the two systems was already small enough; 'by sensible stages,' said another clergyman, 'there has been in many towns a substitution of the congregational system for the parochial system.'[4] But the instinct of every good Churchman was to

[1] *Hansard's Parliamentary Debates*, 3rd. series, CXXXIX. 500, quoted in O. J. Brose, *Church and Parliament: The Reshaping of the Church of England 1828–1860* (Stanford, California, 1959), p. 206 n.

[2] J. Fraser, *Charge* (1872), pp. 76–7.

[3] J. J. Hannah, in *Church Congress Report* (1881), p. 195.

[4] Archdeacon Blunt, in *ibid.* p. 209.

resist this tendency. 'Congregationalism is of foreign growth,' said the *Church Reformer* in 1882, 'and quite out of harmony with the mind of our Church.'[1] It was often asserted in the Church that a congregational system could never reach the masses. But could the parochial system reach them either?

When they discussed the place of parochial organization in large towns, Churchmen usually expressed both respect for the system and dissatisfaction with it. Walsham How, who was trying to bring the Church to life in East London, told a meeting at the Mansion House in 1880 that Churchmen 'could not set the parochial system aside if they would, and they would not do so if they could. (Hear, hear.) Their plan was to supplement it.'[2] This view was expressed plainly by a committee of the Canterbury Convocation on reaching classes of non-worshippers. The committee said in 1889:

> while the Parochial System offers a priceless organization for the work of the Church Pastoral and the Church Beneficent, it is inadequate for the purposes of the Church Militant and Evangelistic, among populations comprising multitudes who are but little accessible to ordinary agencies, and are constantly sinking into more complete indifference to their religious privileges.[3]

If and when the Church subdued these multitudes, agencies designed for her emergency could be allowed to wither away, leaving only the normal, parochial structure. In the meantime, the parish was to be merely a loose framework within which abnormal enterprises were conducted on behalf of the Church Militant. Which enterprises would best supplement the parochial system, and what their relation to the system should be, were among the main preoccupations of people in the Church who wanted to reach the millions who attended no place of worship.

Nobody imagined that parochial organization was proving inadequate in *all* urban areas. There were parishes in the poor parts of large towns where churches had hundreds of communicants, schools and clubs thrived, voluntary district visitors canvassed the neighbourhood, and dependent mission churches were maintained. It is likely that in the cities the Church of

[1] *Church Reformer*, Jan. 1882, p. 8.

[2] *Ecclesiastical Gazette*, 16 Aug. 1880, p. 26.

[3] Convocation of Canterbury, *Report of Joint Committee on Organizations to Reach Classes Now Outside Religious Ministrations* (1889), p. 7.

England attracted to worship, more than Nonconformity ever did, some of the very lowest class, 'the indiscriminate poor.'[1] There are scattered reports like that of A. Osborne Jay, a clergyman who provided for bodies and souls in Shoreditch and who believed that he was vicar of 'the only consecrated Parish Church in England upstairs.' On the ground floor, he wrote, 'is practised the feeding of the hungry, the clothing of the naked, the housing of the homeless. Here above continually ascends the glad incense of the people's praise, though their attendance is neither bought nor forced.' A hell on earth, he declared, had been transformed simply by his operating 'the common, worn-out, old fashioned Parochial System.'[2]

Many clergymen at first welcomed the division of large parishes into smaller ones, which was undertaken under church building Acts after 1850 and which was intended to make the urban population more accessible to parochial care. The fruits were disappointing, however. In the most crowded areas, mere division could achieve little. 'It is impossible,' said the vicar of St Pancras in 1858, 'so to divide the parish as to give each district that mixture of rich and poor which it is desirable there should be as an essential element in every parish. . . .'[3] The practice steadily lost support. Between 1868 and 1880, some seventy new parishes were constituted each year, usually in the most crowded dioceses. From 1880 to 1900 the average annual number of new parishes was only thirty-five. A clergyman told the Church Congress in 1889 that the division of new parishes was now 'in many eyes a lost cause, an exploded method.'[4] Committees of the Canterbury and York Convocations, reporting in 1889 and 1892, found that most of the clergy whom they asked about dividing parishes were opposed to it. The York committee reported a general opinion among the clergy that it was better to have resident curates in various parts of a large parish under the guidance of its incumbent, than to reproduce the entire parochial machinery several times over.

[1] The phrase is from E. R. Wickham, *Church and People in an Industrial City* (1957), p. 142. The author is writing of Sheffield between 1850 and 1900; but like many of his findings, this one is undoubtedly true of other cities.

[2] A. Osborne Jay, *Life in Darkest London* (1891), pp. 5, 68, 72.

[3] *Parliamentary Papers*, 1857–8, IX, Deficiency of the Means of Spiritual Instruction, Select Committee, H. of L.: Minutes of Evidence, p. 209.

[4] H. J. Tebbut, in *Church Congress Report* (1889), p. 51.

The Ecclesiastical Commissioners helped to sustain old and new churches in working-class parishes. After 1850 their revenues began to increase as cathedral offices scheduled for abolition by an Act of 1840 became vacant and were not filled; and by 1856 they had paid off the loan raised to form the Peel districts in 1843. Between 1857 and 1861 the Commissioners made grants of almost £400,000 to supplement poor livings. The distribution of these grants was criticized, however, by a select committee of the House of Commons which noticed that almost as much money was given to small, mainly rural, parishes as to crowded urban ones.[1] The Commissioners admitted in 1863 that there were many large and needy parishes to which they had given no help.[2] But they had increased 1,200 poor benefices in all, and endowed 300 new parishes in large towns. In the next twenty years another 4,000 benefices were supplemented, until by 1885 the Commissioners were making annual grants of £739,000, while some four and a half million pounds had been drawn from voluntary sources between 1840 and 1885 in the form of the benefactions which the Commissioners normally required before they made a grant.[3] It was steady, unspectacular aid; but without it the Church's witness would have been far less effective.

Another device intended to make crowded parishes more efficient was the provision of missionary clergymen, having no parochial responsibilities and instructed to help overburdened incumbents. A Clergy Mission College was established for this purpose, and in 1863 a meeting of 'Owners of Property and Employers of Labour in London, with other persons interested in the welfare of the Metropolis,' pledged itself to send mission clergy – 'living agents to labour in the living Church' – into the poorest parishes.[4] There were also clergymen who went into slum parishes, singly or in groups, to establish mission stations on their own initiative (though with the consent of the incumbent nominally responsible). Such a man was Charles Lowder, a young follower of the Tractarians

[1] *Parliamentary Papers*, 1863, VI, Ecclesiastical Commission, Select Committee' H. of C.: Report, p. iii.

[2] *Ibid.*, Minutes of Evidence, p. 12.

[3] *Year-Book of the Church of England* (1887), p. 35.

[4] A. C. Tait, *The Spiritual Wants of the Metropolis and its Suburbs* (1863), pp. 3, 5.

who in 1856 moved into a dockside neighbourhood in London and set up a mission church.[1]

The mission service was a device of growing popularity. Services in mission rooms were almost universal by 1885, according to a committee of the Canterbury Convocation.[2] In Liverpool an enterprising manufacturer offered, to clergymen who were trying to reach shifting populations, iron mission rooms 'tasteful in design, economical, durable. . . . Can be taken down, removed, and re-erected at a small cost.'[3] Mission churches in towns were supported by a number of public schools and university colleges. By 1887, at least sixteen schools and colleges were taking entire or partial responsibility for Church of England missions in working-class parts of London, and similar missions were supported by Clifton College in Bristol, by Rossall in Manchester, and by Winchester in Portsmouth.[4] Such help relieved clergymen of financial worry, and often provided them with the personal service of earnest young laymen. Some – like the Eton Mission in Hackney Wick – were intended to remain missions permanently. The Winchester Mission in Portsmouth was of a different type. Its committee believed that a mission should 'prepare the way for the more regular organization of a Parish with a Parish Church.[5] The mission church, opened in 1884, was surrounded by five thousand poor and crowded people (and 51 public houses), part of an enormous parish whose population of 27,000 had been served previously by one church, with a vicar and a curate. The clergyman in charge of the mission was Robert Dolling, an ardent ritualist who was forced to resign in 1895 because his bishop, Randall Davidson, suspected him of a popish view of purgatory. In his ten years at the mission, Dolling, helped by funds and senior boys from Winchester, built up a congregation; and by 1900 a separate parish was in sight. The purpose of a mission like this one was to divide a

[1] See C. Lowder, *Twenty-one Years in St George's Mission* (1887).

[2] Convocation of Canterbury, *Report of Joint Committee on the Spiritual Needs of the Masses of the People* (1885), p. 8.

[3] *Year-Book of the Church of England* (1889), advertisements, p. xxi.

[4] *Ibid.*, pp. 72–82.

[5] Winchester College Mission, St Agatha's Landport, Portsmouth, *Annual Report* (1893–4), p. 6. See also R. R. Dolling, *Ten Years in a Portsmouth Slum* (1896); C. E. Osborne, *The Life of Father Dolling* (1903).

large parish, but only after abnormal methods had secured sufficient income, and sufficient local demand for the church, to make parochial organization appropriate.

The word 'mission' was used also to describe a short evangelistic campaign intended to invigorate the spiritual life of a parish. Missions of this sort were conducted by George Body, a clergyman who began in 1869 a series of 'Ten Days' Missions' in large towns, aimed at non-worshippers; and by a Church Parochial Mission Society whose foundation was provoked by the visit of the American evangelists Moody and Sankey in 1875. These 'parochial missions' were held widely after 1880; by 1900 some 360 clergymen were offering to help lead them. As a device for widening the appeal of the Church, they seem to have been unsuccessful. 'The Parish clergy,' said Body, pioneer of the movement, 'use Missions as a means of raising the church life of their people, rather than of gathering in the ungodly.'[1]

Whether it remained large or was divided, whether it depended entirely on resident clergymen or employed visiting missionaries, the urban parish was commonly believed to be too narrow a unit for evangelistic purposes. 'I believe that our greatest need is to have more sympathy between rich and poor parishes', said the vicar of a working-class parish in Nottingham at the Church Congress of 1881.[2] This opinion, and the accompanying view that evangelism was best planned at the diocesan level, were at least as old as the Bishop of London's Fund established in 1836 by C. J. Blomfield. In 1863 A. C. Tait began a new Bishop of London's Fund because, he said, 'the original evil of a vast population inadequately cared for remains much as it was when Bishop Blomfield began his labour.'[3] The resources and needs of the diocese were plotted more thoroughly than in Blomfield's day; and the new Fund was spent to provide clergy, lay agents and schools, as well as new buildings. Church extension societies, now operating in every densely populated diocese, were an important means of distributing voluntary funds more fruitfully between parishes. At Birmingham a Church Extension Society was founded in 1865 'to relieve the spiritual destitution of the most crowded parts of the town,' and

[1] *Goodwill*, July 1898, p. 157.
[2] F. F. MacCallan, in *Church Congress Report* (1881), p. 218.
[3] A. C. Tait, *op. cit.*, p. 4.

in forty years from 1851 the number of churches in the parishes of Birmingham, Edgbaston and Aston more than doubled.[1] In Manchester, which became a separate diocese in 1847, the progress of building was even more rapid. When the first bishop, Prince Lee, was appointed, the Church had some fifty places of worship in the city, distributed without much relation to the density of population. A Diocesan Church Building Society was formed, which helped in the next 21 years to build 90 new churches and to enlarge or rebuild 61 old ones. Such activity strengthened the case for creating other new dioceses in crowded areas. In 1876 a meeting of clergy and eminent laymen in London resolved: 'That the spiritual necessities of England require a well-organized scheme for the increase of the Home Episcopate.'[2] Persuaded that this view was correct, Disraeli introduced a bill which made it possible to form the dioceses of Truro (1877), St Alban's (1877) and Liverpool (1880).

There was a considerable demand for more diocesan action. The bishop of an ancient diocese suggested in 1880 that missionary work among the inhabitants of great towns, as among navvies and miners, was best led not by a clergyman already occupied with parochial duties, but by a member of a cathedral chapter.[3] E. W. Benson, soon to be Archbishop of Canterbury, agreed. 'The same man,' he said, 'cannot be both pastor and evangelist in the same small area effectively, but in every pastor's sheepwalk much evangelizing has to be done.'[4] More diocesan activity, said many in the church, demanded more bishops. In 1885 the secretary of the Additional Bishoprics Fund told Gladstone that if the Church was to reach the masses in large towns, more new bishops were needed than the four lately provided under an Act of Disraeli's. Gladstone, never greatly interested in the religious condition of the masses, was not much moved by this appeal.[5] The advocates of new dioceses

[1] A. Briggs, *History of Birmingham*, II (1952), p. 3.

[2] *Year-Book of the Church of England* (1883), p. 307.

[3] E. H. Browne, Bishop of Winchester, in *Church Congress Report* (1880), p. 363.

[4] *Ibid.* p. 369.

[5] A. Jones to Gladstone, 13 Jan. 1885. British Museum, Add. MSS 44489, ff. 52–4. Jones was suggesting in particular a new diocese for East London. Gladstone wrote on the back of the letter: 'Thank. Recognize his title to express his views on subject of this kind relating as it does to cause in which he has devoted so much time and labour.'

nevertheless had some success between 1880 and 1890. Parliament allowed the creation of the new dioceses of Newcastle in 1882, Southwell (containing the counties of Derby and Nottingham) in 1884, and Wakefield (the south-west of Yorkshire) in 1888. The campaign continued. 'An increase of the Episcopate,' said Canon J. Allan Smith at the Church Congress of 1893, 'is indispensable if our vast teeming centres are ever to be efficiently worked.'[1] Funds were opened for several proposed dioceses, to meet parliament's demand that a considerable endowment should be raised voluntarily for any new creation; but no more appeared before 1900. An Act of 1888 permitted 'bishops suffragan' to be appointed as assistants for bishops. There were already four such officers, consecrated under an Act of Henry VIII, and by 1900 most other bishops had appointed suffragans.[2]

Although a suffragan bishopric, having no formal independence, income or rights of patronage, was no substitute for the creation of a new diocese, an energetic man in a neglected area could use the office to advantage. The best example of such a man is Walsham How, who from 1879 to 1888 was bishop suffragan of Bedford – in effect, of East London.[3] 'The Church is *nowhere* in East London,' How remarked when he was appointed.[4] Many new parishes had been formed in Bethnal Green, Spitalfields, Shoreditch and Stepney, but to little purpose. 'In parish after parish,' wrote someone who knew the area, 'the necessities of Church life were lacking or inadequately provided.'[5] How asked wealthy laymen to give to an East London Church Fund, which attracted £16,846 between June 1880 and the end of 1882. The money was used not to make new parishes, but to supply curates, mission clergy, deaconesses and lay helpers in established ones. By introducing militant evangelism in East London, How encouraged those members of the Church who believed that her past policy for the towns

[1] *Church Congress Report* (1893), p. 281.

[2] The four bishops suffragan in 1887 were those of Dover (in the diocese of Canterbury), Bedford (London), Nottingham (Lincoln) and Colchester (St Alban's). For a list of bishops suffragan in 1900 see *Crockford's Clerical Directory* (1900), p. lxvii.

[3] Why he had to take the title Bedford is explained in F.D. How, *Bishop Walsham How, a Memoir* (1898), p. 144.

[4] *Ibid.* p. 129.

[5] *Ibid.* p. 155.

was to rationalize and supplement the parochial system by episcopal planning.

The growing faith in diocesan initiative led Churchmen to hold regular diocesan conferences, at which clergymen and elected laymen met, under the ultimate control of their bishop, to discuss the condition of the Church. Between 1864 and 1874 such conferences were initiated in ten dioceses, and in another twelve between 1875 and 1881.[1] By 1885 every English diocese except Worcester had one. They were purely consultative bodies, but their resolutions often provoked diocesan action – to increase clerical stipends, for example, or to form a diocesan evangelistic society. In particular, the conferences were responsible for founding organizations to provide lay evangelists. In 1881 a Central Council of Diocesan Conferences was formed on the initiative of people who believed that the Church should make a concerted, national attack on the problems of the day, including the neglect of religion. Sir Richard Cross, a former Home Secretary, said at the Church Congress of 1881 that the parochial system was too inelastic, that the efforts of diocesan and central bodies were fine but inadequate, and that the Church should be able to supply her wants 'not as at present, somewhat haphazardly, but through authority, on a system, and with certainty.' The secretary of the Incorporated Church Building Society thanked Cross for pointing out 'a very great need.'[2]

Since 1830 the Church had been shedding ancient abuses and accommodating herself in many ways to the industrial society. Formal opportunities for discussions were greater, through the Convocations, the Congress and the diocesan conferences, than they had ever been. The Ecclesiastical Commissioners and voluntary donors had helped the Church to distribute her strength more evenly and to keep closer to the urban masses. But compared with a carefully planned young church like that of the Wesleyans, or with Rome, the Church of England was a chaotic institution. History had spread power in the Church irregularly between the crown, parliament, private patrons, bishops and incumbents of parishes. Alongside the normal machinery were scores of societies for particular purposes, representing opinions within a triangle whose extremes were

[1] *Year-Book of the Church of England* (1883), pp. 380–417.
[2] *Church Congress Report* (1881), pp. 192, 212.

close to Nonconformity, to scepticism and to Rome. Moreover, this chaos was necessary to the Church, whatever dreams anybody might indulge about a day when her resources could be directed like an army's. Only because power was diffused so widely in it could a church containing so rich a variety of belief and taste hold together. Any attempt to concentrate power, even in such a popular cause as increasing the efficiency of evangelism, could make little progress against the instinct which told Churchmen when it was dangerous to tamper with the basis of the Anglican compromise.

The impossibility of unified national action did not make Churchmen believe any less deeply that theirs was the church of the nation. When they thought about the special status conferred on the Church by the fact of establishment, it sometimes appeared to clergymen who were concerned about the spiritual condition of the common people that interest pointed the same way as duty, that the Church needed the working classes just as they needed her. 'We cannot do without "the masses,"' said the Bishop of Liverpool, J. C. Ryle, in 1882. 'The Church, whose adherents are a minority in the land, will not be long allowed to retain her endowments and her connection with the State in this age.'[1] At the Church Congress of 1880 another clergyman expressed this same apprehension with equal candour: 'If we in the Church of England do not deal with the masses, the masses will deal with us. We depend, as far as our organization goes at present, upon the popular vote of the country.'[2]

Clergy and Laity

In 1889 a committee of the Canterbury Convocation proposed, as the best response to the failure of the parochial system among the masses, that brotherhoods of clergy should be formed. The plan was that clergymen should live together, celibately, taking vows for as long as they remained in the brotherhood. They should undertake evangelistic and pastoral work at the invitation of incumbents, and the bishop should have final authority over them. It was generally assumed that

[1] *Ibid.* (1882), p. 77.
[2] J. H. Lester, in *ibid.* (1880), p. 460.

the author of this report was Canon F. W. Farrar, the rector of St Margaret's, Westminster, whose liberalism in theology made him about equidistant from the Evangelicals and the ritualists. When defending the committee's report, Farrar explained that he put his hope in brotherhoods because the Church had 'practically lost all effectual hold on the mass of the working classes,' and because he could see no other way to regain such a hold than to form communities of priests trained and dedicated to doing among the masses what the parish clergy could not do. Only clergymen in brotherhoods, he believed, could supply what the Church needed: 'a more burning enthusiasm, a more powerful and unencumbered organization.'[1]

Brotherhoods had been a dream of Pusey's. It was partly for this reason that the very word was enough to raise a holy fear of Popery in many Evangelicals. The report to Convocation was widely interpreted as a plot to revive the monastic system. The journal of the Church Pastoral Aid Society, whose illustrations normally showed deep-chested, square-jawed Protestant clergymen braving the irreligious slums, grew suddenly sombre with sketches of leering, tonsured men in cowls, who could have come straight from a Victorian edition of *Foxe's Book of Martyrs*.[2] Farrar wrote to the journal declaring his faith in the principles of the Reformation and insisting that his only motive was 'an earnest desire to add effectiveness to the existing organization of the Church of England.'[3] Evangelicals nevertheless remained suspicious. One of the most Protestant of bishops, J. C. Ryle of Liverpool, declared that the 'well-meant new machine' was not needed, and would never work; few of the right men would be found, and between brotherhood and parish there would always be friction. Moreover, the idea of clergymen taking vows displeased him.[4]

When Convocation considered the report, it was the Popish overtones that occupied speakers rather than the reasons for organizing clergymen in a new way. After seeking some euphemism for the phrase 'dispensable vows' and adding safeguards to the authority of the bishop and incumbents, both

[1] F. W. Farrar, 'Social Amelioration', a sermon reprinted in *Essays and Sketches, The Salvation Army* (1906), p. 16.

[2] *Church and People*, Oct. 1889.

[3] *Ibid.* April 1890, p. 3.

[4] *Church Congress Report* (1890), pp. 351–2.

upper and lower houses resolved in favour of brotherhoods.[1] The response in the Church at large was slight. The Community of the Resurrection (1892) was really the only body to appear by 1900 which corresponded closely with Farrar's ideal. At the end of the century this brotherhood had ten members and three probationers.[2] Despite Farrar's good intentions, his report stirred more partisan rancour than missionary endeavour. Not for the first time since Victoria came to the throne, some Churchmen were expending energy in attacks on other members of their communion which might have been directed towards reaching people who worshipped nowhere.

Churchmen might quarrel about how to train and employ clergy; but all parties agreed that there were not enough of them. Between 1811 and 1871, when the population of England and Wales increased from some ten millions to 23 millions, the numbers of active clergy rose only from 16,000 to rather more than 19,000.[3] Urban parishes suffered most. Trollope declared that *nobody* would be a town incumbent who could get a country parish offering a higher income and a better chance to marry the bishop's daughter.[4] A less ironic observer, W. F. Hook, vicar of Leeds, who was working as hard as any man in England to reach the poor, told a committee of the House of Lords in 1858 that because churches in great manufacturing towns were so poorly endowed, only inferior men were going to them.[5] This committee estimated that the Church of England needed, at once, 1,000 more clergymen in large towns. Such bodies as the Pastoral Aid Society and the Additional Curates' Society supported many curates in towns; each of these two was paying some 500 men in 1870. But the shortage remained acute. The inadequacy of stipends was certainly one cause; a private income, as well as a passionate pastoral zeal, was needed by any man who replied to an advertisement saying: 'Wanted, a young curate. Hard work and no pay.'[6] But a slum parish could never be made as attractive as a fat rural living to a Trollopian

[1] *Year-Book of the Church of England* (1891), p. 362; (1892), p. 366.
[2] *Ibid.* (1900), p. 154.
[3] J. Stoughton, *Religion in England from 1800 to 1850* (1884), II. 275.
[4] A. Trollope, *Clergymen of the Church of England* (1866), p. 67.
[5] *Parliamentary Papers*, 1857–8, IX, Deficiency of the Means of Spiritual Instruction, Select Committee, H. of L.: Appendix G, pp. 592–3.
[6] *Church Congress Report* (1881), p. 100.

clergyman. An appeal such as Pusey made, not to ambition but to sacrifice, was more likely to draw able and dedicated men to the towns. A number of clergymen, whose ability and social standing would have earned them a far more comfortable existence, worked instead in slums between 1850 and 1880. Arthur Chandler gave up an Oxford fellowship for Poplar. W. W. Champneys and Brooke Lambert in Whitechapel, Edward Stuart in St Pancras, John Richard Green in Stepney, Alexander Mackonochie in Holborn, Septimus Hansard and Stewart Headlam in Bethnal Green, and Llewelyn Davies in Marylebone, were clergymen who believed that they had been called to the poor as others had been called to China or Africa. Samuel Barnett was another, asking in 1872 for the parish in Whitechapel which the Bishop of London described as 'the worst parish in my diocese, inhabited mainly by a criminal population. . . .'[1] Out of Barnett's experience in that environment was to come the settlement movement. All the men named here, except Champneys, belonged either to the 'Broad' or to the 'High' groups in the Church. But Champneys, a moderate Evangelical, spoke for the slum clergy of whatever party when he defined his mission:

> We want a place of worship which the people shall feel to be *their own*; we want the sick to be visited; we want the poor to be specially cared for, and to be able to say amidst all their cares, 'Well, we have something in England, we have our own church and our own parson.'[2]

The supply of clergy, however, dedicated or otherwise lagged ever farther behind the growth of population, until in 1883 an official estimate put the shortage at 2,500 or more. The numbers of new clergy now began actually to fall: an average of 755 deacons were ordained each year from 1880 to 1889, and only 703 each year from 1890 to 1899. This decline was the subject of anxious discussion in the Convocations, at the Church Congress and in diocesan conferences. The *Year-Book* noted in 1900 that the clergy were becoming too few to maintain the present work of the Church, let alone to extend her ministry among the non-worshippers.[3]

[1] H. O. Barnett, *Canon Barnett, His Life, Work and Friends* (1921), p. 72.
[2] Islington Church Extension Society, *Report of Proceedings* (1857), p. 23.
[3] *Year-Book of the Church of England* (1900), p. 1.

One reason for this diminution was the decreasing social and intellectual respect which could be anticipated by young men entering the clergy. Secular professions – especially, as Halévy points out, the profession of teaching which was virtually created by the Education Act of 1870 – were drawing men who might otherwise have entered the Church.[1] The declining status of clergymen was perhaps too delicate a subject for free and open discussion. In public, Churchmen were more inclined to blame the level of clerical incomes for discouraging young men from taking holy orders. A speaker at the Church Congress in 1880 said that it would be a mistake to regard this problem as affecting only the interests of the clergymen themselves. The inadequacy of clerical incomes was strictly relevant, he declared, to the Church's 'mission to the freshly gathering masses of our home population. . . .'[2]

The Ecclesiastical Commissioners were now distributing some £150,000 a year to increase the stipends of clergymen. The Church Pastoral Aid Society was spending £66,000 a year by 1900, and helping 656 ill-endowed parishes. In the same year the Additional Curates' Society made grants of £57,000 towards the stipends of 1,217 curates in urban parishes. E. W. Benson, when Bishop of Truro, said of this last body that without its help, 'some of the most thorough and most spiritual work in our parishes would be impossible. . . .'[3]

Yet despite the subsidies provided for the working clergy by these societies and by other smaller ones, every second incumbent was getting less than £200 a year, while the stipends of thousands of curates were much nearer £100. Everybody in the Church deplored this situation, but what could be done about it? 'There is nothing that can be offered to draw men into the ministry more than is offered now,' concluded a committee of the York Convocation in 1882.[4] Within a few years, incomes began to drop farther. This most recent decline was explained by the Dean of Norwich in 1895 as the result principally of

> the ruin which has come upon the landed interest, by which farms are derelict, rents are reduced or unpaid, tithes have shrunk by

[1] E. Halévy, *A History of the English People in the Nineteenth Century*, V (1951), p. 171.

[2] J. J. Halcombe, *The Clergy, Too Many and Too Few* (1880), p. 8.

[3] *Ecclesiastical Gazette*, 15 May 1880, p. 177.

[4] *Year-Book of the Church of England* (1883), p. 15.

> twenty-four per cent, glebes have fallen one-half in value, while taxation increases, and the claims made in a hundred ways on the resident clergy are as numerous as ever.[1]

Clergymen helped by the Ecclesiastical Commissioners, as well as those whose stipends depended directly on revenue from land, were suffering on account of the agricultural depression.

Out of this crisis came in 1897 the Queen Victoria Clergy Sustentation Fund, for which it was hoped collections would be made in every parish to raise the incomes of small benefices, including those reduced directly by agricultural depression and those of clergymen in densely populated parishes. This was an attempt to make clerical incomes depend less than traditionally on the condition of the rural economy. 'The endowments of the past,' said a founder of the Fund,

> have been drawn mainly from real property; in the future they must largely depend on the personal property or accumulated wealth which has now largely been distributed through all classes of the community, especially in our large towns.[2]

Like many experiments designed to make religion popular in Victorian England, the Clergy Sustentation Fund drew attention to a problem without solving it. One of its objects was to convince everybody in the Church that it was his duty to take a part in maintaining the clergy. In its first year, however, only 2,500 people contributed. It became a useful addition to the agencies already at work, but the *Year-Book* observed in 1900 that additional income from all sources, including the new Fund, still left stipends far too low.[3]

In any case, the Fund was used to help beneficed clergy, not curates; and if the interests of the Church Militant were to be considered, then curates in large towns needed help just as urgently as incumbents. A clergyman wrote in 1882 that there were 'few positions in life more trying than that of an incumbent with small private means or with none at all, who is appointed to one of these poor town churches.'[4] One of the few positions more trying was surely that of a curate in the same

[1] W. Lefroy, in *Church Congress Report* (1895), pp. 225–6.

[2] Lord Egerton of Tatton, in *ibid.* (1896), p. 462.

[3] *Year-Book of the Church of England* (1900), p. 481. The Queen gave £1,000.

[4] A Priest of the Church of England, *The Church, the Census and the People* (1882), p. 16.

environment who was paid worse than the vicar of his parish and who had – through no fault of his own – little chance of preferment. For in its efforts to keep up with the population, the Church had engaged an ever larger proportion of unbeneficed clergy. As a committee of the York Convocation observed: 'the number of curates increases so much more rapidly than the number of benefices, that a constantly increasing number have to wait twenty or thirty years before obtaining preferment, while many have to remain curates all their lives.'[1] A Curates' Augmentation Fund was established to provide 'increased stipends for Curates who have served without reproach for not less than fifteen years. . . .'[2] There were 1,200 such men in 1888, and the Fund merely saved some of them from the hardship and humiliation of having stipends *reduced* as they grew older.

One drastic remedy suggested for the poverty of the town curate was that Parliament should interfere with the rights of private patrons, to give deserving but obscure men a chance of being appointed to livings otherwise reserved for well-born young clergymen who might be almost straight from Oxford or Cambridge. 'As long as patronage is free from any control, direct or indirect,' wrote one reformer,' . . . so long will social standing have the power to turn the scale against merit, ability and service.'[3] But private patronage was a time-honoured institution, built too solidly into the structure of the Church to be removed. If a rise in the town curate's prospects depended on such a radical reform, then they must remain low, even if men were deterred thereby from taking orders.

An equally bold means of getting more clergymen was proposed by a member of the committee of the Clergy Sustentation Fund. 'Are there no men from the lower classes who have received the call from God?' he asked. 'The need is imperative. No plea of social custom or convenience can weigh with us for an instant.'[4] Rarely and unconvincingly, it was said that the Church did offer a career to men from all social stations. When

[1] *Year-Book of the Church of England* (1883), p. 17.
[2] *Ibid.* (1888), p. 428.
[3] T. C. Fry in C. Gore, ed., *Essays in Aid of the Reform of the Church* (1898), p. 301.
[4] A. Riley, in *Church Congress Report* (1896), p. 466.

William Magee was elevated to the see of York in 1891, a provincial newspaper declared:

> The Church, after all, is a democratic institution, and the knowledge that it is possible for a Dublin curate to rise to one of the highest positions in a community wedded to aristocratic traditions may certainly form the fair subject of a proud boast.[1]

The journal forbore to add that this particular curate's path from rags to riches was made less stony by his having an education at Trinity College, Dublin, and a grandfather who was archbishop of that city. The social range from which clergymen were drawn was widened a little, it is true, by the ordination of men trained in theological colleges without having attended a university. But the tradition was tenacious that a clergyman, however badly paid, must be a gentleman. Trollope believed that the man who had been merely to a theological college, 'who won't drink his glass of wine, and talk of his college, and put off for a few happy hours the sacred stiffness of the profession and become simply an English gentleman – he is the clergyman whom in his heart the archdeacon does not love.'[2] The type remained in a minority: in 1878, 16,297 of the 23,612 clergymen in England and Wales had been to Oxford or Cambridge.[3] In any case, few among the remainder were of birth humble enough to approach the artisan or docker or miner without crossing a wide social gap. Although the theological colleges took men from lowlier homes than supplied the universities, they were still thoroughly middle-class institutions. They reduced the difference in rank between the clergyman and the Nonconformist pastor; but no serious effort was made in the Church of England, or in the larger Nonconformist bodies, to reduce the difference in rank between ministers of religion and the working classes. 'The Reformation,' wrote a French observer of England in 1867, 'desired to bring the priest nearer to the people, in order to bring men nearer to God; but birth, education and fortune still create a gulf between the Protestant minister and the most humble of his congrega-

[1] *Derby and Chesterfield Reporter*, 8 May 1891, p. 5.

[2] A. Trollope, *Clergymen of the Church of England* (1866), p. 48. For a list of theological colleges, four founded between 1816 and 1850 and ten between 1850 and 1880, see *Year-Book of the Church of England* (1887), p. 4.

[3] *Crockford's Clerical Directory* (1880), preface, p. viii.

tion.'[1] It was partly on account of this gulf that William Booth founded the Salvation Army. By 1900 few men from working-class homes had entered the ministry of the Church. 'This is more specially the case with the Anglican Church,' said a layman, 'than with any other branch of the Catholic Church.'[2]

Most people in the Church still preferred it that way. 'It will be a fatal day to the Church of England,' said one of her bishops, 'when she shall be obliged to recruit her ministry from men of lower education and social position.'[3] Churchmen held firm to this opinion despite the shortage of clergy, and despite the acknowledged difficulty of crossing the gap between classes in evangelizing the poor. In 1885 a clergyman who was secretary of the Christian Evidence Society confessed that when he was working in a very poor parish in London, he wished earnestly that he had been born a working man; for then, he said, 'I might have been able to feel that true sympathy with the working classes which otherwise it is difficult to acquire.'[4] But he did not suggest that the solution was to recruit working-class clergymen. Nor did the speaker at the Church Congress in 1881 who asserted that the clergy in mining districts were out of touch with working-class life. His remedy was that they should go down a mine with the men once a week. 'It would be a good piece of physical exercise,' he wrote, 'and give a capital appetite for dinner.'[5]

If it was impossible to improve professional conditions and undesirable to admit men of lower-class birth to the clergy, could the gaps in the Church's ministry nevertheless be filled with lay helpers? Scripture readers and lay evangelists had been employed steadily for many years. The slum clergyman encouraged agents of the London City Mission to work in his parish. 'I do very strongly think,' said one such clergyman in 1858, 'that they have the advantage wherever there is prejudice in any way existing against the parson, as such, which . . . is

[1] A. Esquiros, *Religious Life in England* (1867), p. 156.

[2] T. C. Fry in C. Gore, *op. cit.* p. 300.

[3] Quoted in J. R. Humble, '*Clergy and the Masses*': *the Curate Question* (1888), p. 8.

[4] C. Lloyd Engstrom in Church of England Working Men's Society, *Report of the Ninth Anniversary Meeting* (1885), p. 44.

[5] H. Wright, in *Church Congress Report* (1881), p. 158.

the feeling prevailing amongst many of the lower orders.'[1] A number of semi-professional revivalists were permitted to work for the Church after 1860.[2] Later in the century lay helpers were sought with more vigour, as a crucial support for an increasingly undermanned Church. Among new societies formed to provide lay help was the Lichfield Evangelist Brotherhood (1887), a body of laymen who were given a more thorough training than lay evangelists usually had, before being sent out to help incumbents. The founder and warden was H. A. Colville, who made the very rare spiritual pilgrimage from the Salvation Army (in which he was an officer) to the Catholic wing of the Church of England. Colville regarded his society as evidence of a 'wonderfully increased recognition of lay work in the Church.'[3] In 1889 the Society for Promoting Christian Knowledge established in Stepney a Church Training College for Lay Workers whose warden, a clergyman, described it as 'a theological college for those who wish to do Home Mission work as laymen.'[4] A society of American origin, the Brotherhood of St Andrew, was introduced to England in the 1890s. Its purpose was to be 'a mission of men to men, who, without leaving their daily occupations, are engaged as missionaries in purely spiritual and aggressive work.'[5] In 1900 it had about a thousand members.

One argument for employing lay evangelists was that they could move more freely than clergymen among the poor. 'Poor as the payment of most clergy is,' said a future Bishop of London in 1896, 'who can doubt that working people are apt to look on the parson's work as a business as much as their own?'[6] The vicar of Hanley, Staffordshire, observed that the lay missionary was respected more than the clergyman when it was known that his labour for the Church was voluntary.[7] If the only difficulty experienced by the evangelizing clergyman was on account of his profession, then the solution was simply

[1] *Parliamentary Papers*, 1857–8, IX, Deficiency of the Means of Spiritual Instruction, Select Committee, H. of L.: Minutes of Evidence, p. 127.
[2] W. G. McLoughlin, Jr., *Modern Revivalism* (New York, 1959), p. 184.
[3] *Church Congress Report* (1896), p. 129.
[4] E. R. Ford, in *ibid.* p. 121.
[5] *Year-Book of the Church of England* (1900), pp. 113–4.
[6] A. F. Winnington-Ingram, *Work in Great Cities* (1896), p. 105.
[7] T. P. Ring, in *Church Congress Report* (1888), p. 626.

to engage laymen of whatever social background to canvass the non-worshippers. But since the clergyman's class position was also an obstacle, there seemed to be a case for enrolling evangelists who could meet poor people as social equals. The hero of a novel called *John Brown, Working-man* put bluntly his view of clergymen and well-bred lay evangelists: 'Sure we all suspect these people, God knows of what; but the lowest one amongst us thinks the clergy and the Society people have something to gain by our reformation.'[1] Many Churchmen who opposed the admission of working men to the clergy were enthusiastic about having them as lay missionaries. The search for such an aid to aggression was approved by high authorities. In 1880 W. D. Maclagan, the future Archbishop of York, said that missionary activity by working-class laymen among their own class was perhaps the task of the age.[2] The Archbishop of Canterbury, E. W. Benson, told the Church Congress in 1887 that the Church needed many more representatives who could influence the masses. 'These people,' he said, 'must in anything like the numbers that are wanted, come out of the masses themselves.'[3]

The immediate context of the Archbishop's remark was a tribute to the Church Army. This organization was founded in 1882 by Wilson Carlile, a clergyman who believed that the Salvation Army, lately created by William Booth, had given the Church a lesson. Carlile had entered the ministry after sixteen years in a bank. As a curate in Kensington he conducted enthusiastic mission services, and it was out of these that the Church Army emerged: its earliest evangelists were men who had been trained to help Carlile in Kensington.[4]

Like the Salvation Army, the Church Army was attacked fiercely by mobs; Carlile himself once spent six months in hospital after being assaulted. Its journal, the equivalent of Booth's *War Cry*, began in 1883 with the even more bloodthirsty title of *Battleaxe*; but within three years it became, more decorously, the *Church Army Gazette*. In organization the Church Army was very different from the Salvation Army; for

[1] Anon., *John Brown, Working-Man* (1879), p. 57. The novel is set in the sixties.

[2] *Church Congress Report* (1880), p. 105.

[3] *Ibid.* (1887), p. 27.

[4] E. Rowan, *Wilson Carlile and the Church Army* (1905), pp. 116–7.

the Church was careful to avoid any possibility that it would become schismatic, or that any man would seize the power which William Booth held, or that an aid to the parochial system would become a threat to it. Authority was distributed between the headquarters committee which chose and trained candidates, the bishop who sanctioned any particular mission of the Army in his diocese, and the parish clergyman who directed its activity. Each evangelist employed by the Church Army was under a bond – at first £100, raised in 1887 to £500 – to move out of any parish when ordered, and never to return in any missionary capacity.

At first the Church Army was called a working men's mission to working men, and its first officers were working-class (if that is the term for a butler and a groom). Subsequently, however, Carlile appears to have recruited helpers of any social origin; and his army became a far less plebeian institution than Booth's. The difference went still deeper. 'The Salvation Army,' wrote Charles Booth, in his social survey of London ' . . . is before everything a religious community. The Church Army is not a separate religious body at all; it is merely a working association of members of the Church of England.'[1] Lacking thus the peculiar fellowship which nurtured the enthusiasm of the Salvation Army, the Church Army was bound to be less spectacular. According to a sympathetic observer in 1890 moreover, its work was impeded by 'want of sympathy between the Incumbent and the Church Army system,' and by a careless choice of officers.[2] When the Archbishop of Canterbury praised the Army in 1887, he added that its efforts 'must be multiplied a thousandfold' before the Church's work among the masses could be done.[3] There was no sign of that happening by 1900. Nevertheless it had by then an annual income of £110,000, a troop of 65 vans manned by travelling evangelists, and more than 600 evangelists and nurses helping the parochial clergy. For its work as a social rescue agency – which, by the end of the century, it was gradually becoming – it had nearly sixty labour and lodging houses in large towns.

[1] C. Booth, *Life and Labour of the People in London*, 3rd. series, *Religious Influences* (1902), VII. 345.

[2] W. E. Richardson, in *Churchman*, Aug. 1890, pp. 565–6.

[3] *Church Congress Report* (1887), p. 27.

'No Church party spirit' was a principle of the Church Army. The Church of England Working Men's Society, another body formed to provide working-class evangelists, was by contrast candidly ritualist. This Society was formed in 1876 under the wing of the English Church Union, the organization representing anti-Protestants in the Church. It grew out of a committee set up to defend Alexander Mackonochie, the ritualist vicar of St Alban's, Holborn, against evangelical persecution, and to campaign against the Public Worship Regulation Act. On paper the Society's first concern was to send out people who were 'working men themselves, acting unostentatiously, as missionaries to their fellow workmen.'[1] The first enemy named in the secretary's report for 1883, however, was not religious indifference but the anti-ritualist Church Association. A series of 'New Tracts for the Times,' published by the Society, was meant to answer Protestant doubts about ritualists rather than working-class doubts about the Church as a whole. Probably most people who joined the Society were convinced High Churchmen already. The membership of 9,500 in 1888 was made up of 1,228 'honorary' members who were 'not strictly working men in the ordinary sense of the word,' 6,816 working-men communicants, and only 1,446 'associate' members – working men who were not communicants. The Society was a sign that such ritualist clergymen as those of St Alban's, Holborn, could attract and hold a number of working-class worshippers. As a missionary instrument, however, its success appears to have been slight – too slight, certainly, to count as evidence for the opinion, sometimes expressed in this period, that the peculiarities of ritualism had a special appeal to the working classes. When a ritualist clergyman asked a number of his fellows: 'Are the working men influenced by the High Church movement, especially in regard to "Mass", "Confessional", and "Ritual"?' the answers suggested that where working-class people attended a 'High' service, it was more out of respect for the personality or secular opinions of the clergyman than out of appreciation for the doctrines or symbols of his party.[2]

Efforts to get lay evangelists, of whatever Church party or

[1] *Year-Book of the Church of England* (1887), p. 448.

[2] J. Adderley in G. Haw, ed., *Christianity and the Working Classes* (1906), pp. 248–51.

social class, were one part of a movement to persuade the laity to accept a greater responsibility for the condition of the Church and for its relationship to the nation at large. A committee of the Canterbury Convocation on the spiritual needs of the masses declared in 1885: 'the time has arrived for turning to account that large body of intelligent lay people, whether men or women, who have at heart the cause of Christ and His Church.'[1] 'Let the laity do their part,' said a layman at the Church Congress of 1886, 'and the Church's influence may be amazingly extended in a very short space of time. There is no other method I know of for bringing a large amount of influence to bear upon the lapsed masses.'[2] A year later the Congress had a session on 'The Priesthood of the Laity; its Privileges and Responsibilities.'[3] The very presence of laymen at these meetings was one formal means of concerning them in the problems of their Church. Other means were also sought. Houses of Laymen were added to the Convocations, first at Canterbury in 1886 and soon afterwards at York. Parochial church councils were approved in principle by the lower houses of both Convocations, the Canterbury body resolving in 1894 'that in populous parishes a voluntary Parochial Council is of great service in bringing the Clergy into closer touch with the people, and in interesting the Laity in the work of the Church. . . .'[4]

In every age the Church owed much to particular laymen, and in the nineteenth century her history would have been far less happy without the devotion of a Peel or a Shaftesbury. Great, too, was her debt to the rich men and women who endowed new churches; to the greater number of the less rich who subscribed to general funds for sustenance and extension; and to the thousands who voluntarily become district visitors, or lay evangelists, or helped to administer parochial charities. But the age resisted every effort of the Church to grapple with it. Among the clergy a feeling grew towards the end of the century that the national energy of the Church would be adequate only if a sense of responsibility such as moved the

[1] Convocation of Canterbury, *Report of Joint Committee on the Spiritual Needs of the Masses of the People* (1885), p. 21.

[2] J. Trevarthen, in *Church Congress Report* (1886), p. 260.

[3] *Ibid.* (1887), pp. 73 ff.

[4] *Year-Book of the Church of England* (1898), p. 458.

devoted minority of laymen could be spread among the laity as a whole, so that their minds, purses and personal efforts were dedicated to her. It was a large demand. 'The great majority of Church people,' said a group of anxious and eminent laymen in 1893, 'have a very inadequate idea of the spiritual wants of the nation.'[1]

Pews and the People

The actual forms of service employed in the Church of England seemed to some people to discourage working-class attendance. There were many clergymen in the cities who chafed, as Samuel Barnett did in Whitechapel, at the limits which the law set to imaginative experiment. Walsham How, reflecting on wide experience in East London, admitted that he had 'a sense of the unsuitableness of the Service to the needs of the people.'[2] He and others introduced simple mission services in the hope that they would draw people towards normal worship. Such devices could be defended as an adaptation to the needs and tastes of the poor; but they could also be attacked for avoiding the problem of relations between classes at worship. 'Why are "the working classes" to be treated in this way,' asked a clergyman in 1861, 'as a separate and distinct body apart from the common worship of the Church of Christ? What we really want is not "special" and exceptional services for the poor – but that all classes should be equally welcome to the ordinary and regular services of our churches. . . .'[3] Twenty-five years later, the Bishop of Peterborough, William Magee, spoke vigorously to the House of Lords against the institution of separate services for the poor, declaring that estrangement between classes ('one of the sorest and saddest evils of nineteenth-century life') was encouraged by their separation on Sundays. Lacking a common sanctuary with the rich, being denied 'at least one place on this side of the grave' where equality was granted to them, the outcast poor had formed the mobs lately smashing

[1] From two identical petitions to the upper house of the Canterbury Convocation, signed by J. G. Talbot, M.P., and others. Convocation of Canterbury, *Chronicle* (1893), p. 21.

[2] *Church Congress Report* (1883), pp. 434–5.

[3] E. Stuart, *Free and Unappropriated Churches* (1861), prefatory letter, p. 4.

windows in the West End.[1] Magee never liked to bridle his arguments, and sometimes – as on the immortal occasion when he declared that he would rather see England free than sober – they would gallop away with him. His remark about mobs in the West End was doubtless intended rather to attract their Lordships' attention (they were bored and talkative when he stood up) than out of any real conviction that mission services were the cause. But his rhetoric was dancing around a serious argument, offered by many other Churchmen: that if the Church wanted to gain ground among the working classes, she must treat all worshippers alike whatever their social station. In particular, she must abolish the pew system.

Magee was speaking on behalf of the Incorporated Free and Open Church Association, a body which had been working since 1866 to persuade the Church to abolish the custom of allowing worshippers to rent and appropriate pews. A corollary of this custom was that 'free' seats were set aside for the poor. Throughout the reign of Victoria reformers struggled against this system.[2] In his report on the religious census of 1851 Horace Mann set out their case clearly:

> Working men, it is contended, cannot enter our religious structures without having pressed upon their notice some memento of inferiority. The existence of pews and the position of the free seats, are, it is said, alone sufficient to deter them from our churches; and religion has thus come to be regarded as a purely middle-class propriety or luxury.[3]

Mann had been told by many clergymen, on the census forms which they sent to him, of potential worshippers whom the pew system excluded. 'This Church being unendowed,' wrote a curate in Whitechapel, 'and the District being poor, is practically useless to the vast majority of the 13,000 souls dwelling in the District. As they know that the Church is not endowed, and the Pews are to be let, they refuse to come because they are utterly unable to pay.'[4] From Sheffield,

[1] *Hansard's Parliamentary Debates*, 3rd. series, CCCIII. 934.

[2] E. R. Wickham, *Church and People in an Industrial City* (1957), is the only modern study to indicate the full significance of the pew system. As the author remarks (p. 42n.), 'It is of immense sociological value to know the exact practices that obtained.'

[3] *Religious Worship in England and Wales* (1854), p. 94.

[4] Public Record Office, Home Office Papers, 129 (Ecclesiastical Returns), 22.6.1.2.

Manchester, Liverpool and Birmingham, clergymen in working-class parishes reported in their census returns that they had *no* seats available for the poor. Moreover, people who subscribed towards building a church were often given pews in return as their private property. A clergyman in Leeds described a church in which the pews were owned by proprietors most of whom lived elsewhere. For the population at large, he said, 'it will continue to be very much the same thing as if there were no Church at all.'[1] Pew rents were supposed to be charged only where parliament specifically allowed them, which meant, on the whole, only in churches built since 1800. But in many older parish churches, pews were appropriated for the use of particular worshippers without a rent being asked. The practice was almost certainly illegal, but it flourished.

At the time of the census a campaign against the pew system had been under way in the Church for some ten years. In 1850, for the first time in modern London, a new church (St Barnabas', Pimlico) was opened in which no seats were rented or appropriated and which was open on week-days. Nine years later St Philip's, Clerkenwell, became the first church in London with rented pews to abandon the system. Piecemeal protests were drawn together after 1860 by two bodies – the National Association for Freedom of Worship, founded in Manchester, and the London (later the Incorporated) Free and Open Church Association. The Manchester body declared in 1869: 'Our "hobby" has become a "question", our question a "movement" and our movement will in its time be a "success".'[2] For some years relations between the two bodies were uneasy; but by 1875 they were amicably sharing the work of propaganda with each other and with an ally, the Chester Diocesan Open Church Association, based in Liverpool.

The campaign drew support from members of all parties in the Church. Its goal was equality in church, not outside. The patrons of the London Association included eight bishops. The National Association boasted in 1869 that only its activities could account for the satisfactory number of votes cast in the

[1] *Ibid.* 501. 3.3.24.

[2] *Church of the People, and Free Church Penny Magazine*, Jan. 1869, p. 1. On the earliest phase of the movement, see J. M. Neale, *The History of Pues* (3rd. ed., 1843); and on later stages see Incorporated Free and Open Church Association, *Free and Open Church Chronology* (1892).

recent election for 'the Church' – that is to say, for the Tories – in Lancashire.[1] The movement was just as respectable as the Primrose League, and its aim was similar. Shaftesbury expressed this purpose when he attacked the pew system in 1857. 'Unless you show them proper respect and admit that in the House of God at least there is equality,' he predicted, 'the vast proportion of the labouring population of London will never be brought to attend the worship of the Establishment.'[2]

When the crusaders were so many and so eminent, why did they not win at once? There were two main sources of opposition. First, many incumbents believed that pew rents were indispensable in ill-endowed churches. The reformers replied that an offertory would yield as much income as rents; but many clergymen were not convinced. The system tended to be financially necessary just where it was socially undesirable, as a clergyman in Liverpool observed on his census return: 'To make the Church fit for the poor and crowded District of 16,000, half of of it should be free, but where is the money to do this?'[3] Second, pew-holders were unwilling to surrender what seemed to them rights in worship. One clergyman even suggested that in trying to conciliate the poor, the reformers were inviting a revolt of the rich; there was, he said, 'a most tenacious feeling, on the part of occupiers of pews, as to their rights, which if rudely dealt with would cause a tremendous outburst, and lead to great alienation from the Church.'[4] A French writer described this obstacle more simply: 'The English love a *home*, even in God's house.'[5] Some defenders of the system added that the poor stank. A layman writing in 1865 said that worshippers must be protected against 'being placed too near, or even next, to those whose habits are wanting in the ordinary decencies of life'; he referred without details to 'an odious American habit, which is really distressing to people of delicacy, or even of common decorum.'[6] To an observer living in the hygienic twentieth century, this may sound like class prejudice;

[1] 'Why Lancashire Polled for the Church', *Church of the People*, Jan. 1869, pp. 5–7

[2] Quoted in *Free and Open Church Chronology* (1892), p. 31.

[3] Public Record Office, Home Office Papers, 129, 462, 1.1.1.

[4] E. Harland, in *Parliamentary Papers*, 1857–8, IX, Deficiency of the Means of Spiritual Instruction, Select Committee, H. of L.: Appendix S, p. 634.

[5] A. Esquiros, *Religious Life in England* (1867), p. 43.

[6] 'A Barrister', in the *Christian Observer*, May 1865, p. 420.

but a curate in Stepney who knew his people well, and liked them, opposed abolishing the pew system in 1858 because 'though it is a painful subject to mention, the dirt of some of the people, and the fleas that we see, would prevent many persons going. . . .'[1]

The attack on the pew system nevertheless made progress. Between 1870 and 1876, the proportion of churches in London without rented seats rose from 10 per cent to 30 per cent, and of churches having a weekly offertory from 20 per cent to 48 per cent.[2] By this time the system had few defenders among leaders of the Church, although it remained firmly, if defensively, entrenched among the rank and file of worshippers. After 1880 the campaign was conducted by tactics of three sorts: general propaganda, encouragement of reforms in particular churches, and an attempt to get the help of parliament. The Incorporated Free and Open Church Association tried to spread its principles both in print and by putting up speakers at the Church Congress. At diocesan conferences, resolutions were passed which showed either that the Association had sponsored them or that support for its crusade was diffused quite widely through the Church. Where particular churches ended appropriation and replaced rents by an offertory, the Association gave publicity to the change, especially if the church could report a consequent improvement in attendances without any loss of revenue. If efforts to free pews in a church were resisted by any of the parties affected – the bishop, the vicar, the churchwardens or the pew-holders – the Association would interpret for the benefit of the reformers the obscurities of the law relating to pews. Legal action was frequent. In 1885 alone, the Association defended three parishioners served with writs of trespass by a pew-holder, helped in a case in which a churchwarden tried to allot seats after a notice had declared them 'free to the parishioners for ever', and appealed on behalf of a lad who, attempting to sit where the churchwarden did not want him, to, was convicted of violent behaviour under a Brawling Act.[3]

[1] T. J. Rowsell, in *Parliamentary Papers*, 1857–8, IX, Deficiency of the Means of Spiritual Instruction, Select Committee, H. of L.: Appendix S, p. 634.

[2] London Free and Open Church Association, *Tenth Annual Report* (1875–6), p. 11.

[3] *Year-Book of the Church of England* (1887), p. 144.

Cases of this sort could be as important for the public interest stimulated in them as for the effect on the parties directly involved. The sturdy churchwardens of Beverley, in Yorkshire, enjoyed a brief national fame when in 1886 they refused to appropriate seats in the parish church although the vicar and the Archbishop of York instructed them to do so. The contest was reported throughout England, and several journals commended the churchwardens in editorial articles. The rebels' best thrust was a letter to *The Times* declaring:

> we rely upon our character, built up by long years (from forty-five to sixty-five years) of honest life and labour amongst our townsmen to support us against the rash and unverified charges and imputations brought against us by a Bishop whose face and voice we hardly know, and by a vicar who is almost a stranger amongst us, and whose comparative youth and inexperience may perchance be pleaded in extenuation of his temerity.[1]

The Incorporated Free and Open Church Association, though cheering for the churchwardens, doubted whether the law was on their side. The secretary of the Association declared that the law would be clearer and better if parliament passed the Parish Churches Bill, sponsored by the Association, which was now before it.

This was a private member's bill which had been before parliament since 1870 and remained so, nominally, until 1890. Its purpose was to prohibit absolutely the appropriation of seats and levying of rents, except where parliament had explicitly allowed it in church building Acts. In 1882, a house almost empty except for supporters of the Association agreed at 2 a.m. to a second reading. The bill disappeared for four years, until Magee moved its second reading in the House of Lords. By assuring members that it was 'not by any means the rash, revolutionary, and confiscatory measure which it was by many supposed to be,' and by poking[2] the Archbishop of Canterbury to his feet at the right moment, Magee secured the appointment of a select committee, of which nothing came except a statistical return. When another version of the bill was intro-

[1] Quoted in *Rank and Degree in Church* (1887), p. 36.

[2] The word is Magee's. J. C. Macdonnell, *The Life and Correspondence of William Connor Magee* (1896), II. 228.

duced into the Commons in 1890, it was read once and dropped.

The appeal to parliament failed not simply because it ran into all the traditional defences of the pew systems, but for two additional reasons. First, many Churchmen believed that the bill interfered too drastically with the authority of bishops, and through them churchwardens, over the affairs of a church. Second, many opponents of the pew system, even some members of the Incorporated Free and Open Church Association, were reluctant to call on parliament for aid under any circumstances, feeling that it was wiser to advance the anti-pew movement by piecemeal, voluntary means. As a piece of propaganda, however, the bill was not useless. A notice in the *Year-Book* on behalf of the Association remarked that it had 'brought the need of reform in this respect before the public in a way which could scarcely otherwise have been done.'[1]

The one concrete result of the appeal to parliament was the statistical account drawn up by the select committee of the House of Lords, which had questioned every incumbent in England and Wales about seating arrangements in his parish. At first glance it might have appeared that the abolition of pews was almost complete, for in 9,113 out of 11,155 churches no sittings were rented. But 7,703 of these 9,113 were ancient parish churches, predominantly rural. Of 3,121 new parish and district churches, seats could be rented in 1,410.[2] Moreover, the table published by the select committee gave no account of churches in which seats were appropriated without being rented. The Archbishop of York, W. D. Maclagan, had told the disobedient churchwardens of Beverley that it was their legal duty, as his officers, 'to assign seats in the church to the parishioners according to their degree.'[3] The Incorporated Free and Open Church Association said that this view rested only on the obsolete *obiter dictum* of one judge, but in 1895 the standard guide for churchwardens still instructed them that in the matter of seating they were subordinate to the bishop, who was

> presumed by law to be the properest person to be entrusted with the judging of different qualities and degrees of people, in order

[1] *Year-Book of the Church of England* (1887), p. 144.
[2] *Parliamentary Papers*, 1890, (9), Return, Free Seats in Churches, p. 1.
[3] *Rank and Degree in Church* (1887), p. 12.

> to the placing of them in the church, each according to his rank, so that there be no contention there about this matter.[1]

Whatever their legal duty, many churchwardens did not attempt the awkward task of seating worshippers 'each according to his rank', although an unofficial order of precedence was often maintained. There appear to be no estimates of the actual number of churches in which *formal* appropriation remained; but a critic of the practice in 1898 spoke of it as a major impediment to the Church in its mission to the working classes.[2]

A steady decline in the number of churches with rented pews was reported after 1890. At the end of the century the Incorporated Free and Open Church Association concluded that owing to its work, people were realizing at last that a church was 'a permanent mission to all living in the parish, and should be quite free and open to all.'[3] Was it then because the Association had virtually achieved its aims that its income and activities fell away after 1890?[4] Or was the explanation rather that in its wider object the movement had not succeeded at all, and that people who had put their faith in it could now see that it never would succeed?

By 1900, abolition of renting and appropriation had gone far enough for whatever effects it might have on the religious habits of the working classes to be discernible. Here and there, clergymen announced that poor people were attending church now who had never come while the pew system lasted; but nowhere was it claimed that a general flow of working-class people to worship had occurred as 'free and open' principles spread. Where measurement was possible, the usual opinion was rather that the slight hold of the Church among the working classes was relaxing. Yet in plea after plea for 'free' churches, it had been presupposed and even stated plainly that it was only, or mainly, the pew system that kept the working classes away from the Church.[5] In general statements of its objects the

[1] *Prideaux's Practical Guide to the Duties of Churchwardens* (1895), p. 288.

[2] T. C. Fry in C. Gore, ed., *Essays in Aid of the Reform of the Church*, p. 309.

[3] *Year-Book of the Church of England* (1900), p. 133.

[4] Income declined from £1,140 in 1885 to £698 in 1893 – the last year for which it was given in the *Year-Book*.

[5] E. Stuart, *The Pew System* (1851), p. 12; Anon., *The Church and the People* (1865), p. 3; C. Powell in *The Times*, 5 Oct. 1888; *Year-Book of the Church of England* (1890), p. 391. Many other examples could be cited.

Incorporated Free and Open Church Association made less extravagant claims. 'The principles of the Association,' said a statement made on its behalf in 1884, 'are by no means put forward as a remedy for all the ills under which a parish may be suffering . . . the freedom of a church is in no sense a substitute for diligent parochial visitation, nor a remedy for ministerial inefficiency.' Nevertheless, the statement continued, abolishing pews *would* attract 'the people.'[1]

Why did the people not respond? Was it that the freeing of seats was merely one of a number of changes necessary before working-class worshippers could be gained, and that the other changes were not made? Were the reformers right in thinking that the pew system was (wholly, or mainly, or partly) responsible for repelling working-class people; but that once repelled, they became so resistant to evangelistic pressure that the mere invitation offered by 'freeing' a church was not enough to win them back? The poor, Magee observed, 'soon lost the desire for the religion which was so persistently denied them.'[2] But there is a more persuasive explanation. A Unitarian discussing the pew system in his own sect wrote in 1865: 'I sorrowfully admit that in many of our chapels the poor are hardly to be found; I admit, too, the existence of the pew system; but I want facts to convince me that in this case the *post hoc* is also the *propter hoc.*'[3] Nonconformists and Churchmen who were anxious about the spiritual condition of the working classes found this slide from *post* to *propter* an easy one. One can sense in many of their discussions a determination to find a single, simple cause of working-class abstinence from worship which could be identified easily and removed without endangering the foundations either of the Christian churches or of English society. The pew system was such a factor. It was accepted almost eagerly as the cause, and its abolition was proposed as a fairly painless nostrum.

It could be illuminating to see the pew system as an impediment to working-class attendance at worship. It was a clear advance on the old theory that the working classes lacked only the opportunity to worship, and that the need was simply for

[1] *Year-Book of the Church of England* (1884), p. 121.
[2] *Hansard's Parliamentary Debates*, 3rd. series, CCCIII. 928
[3] *Theological Review*, 1865, p. 108.

more churches and clergy. It suggested to Christians that when working-class people did not respond to efforts to bring them to church, they might be making a gesture of social protest. But beyond this point, to blame the pew system was misleading. Pews were only a symbol of a social climate in churches, which was not much affected merely by having a carpenter make seating uniform throughout a church, by passing round a plate instead of making a quarterly charge, and by letting worshippers choose any unoccupied seat. 'Amongst the working classes,' said the Rev. J. F. Kitto, 'there is a feeling that they compromise themselves in some way by going to a church.'[1] The social distinctions which went so far to arouse this feeling were expressed in the pew system; but to think that they would be banished merely by ending the system was to mistake a symptom for a cause.

Church and Society

By the end of the century the Church of England was spending more than two million pounds a year on building and restoring churches, and the Ecclesiastical Commissioners were distributing over a million pounds a year to sustain the Church, most of it in thickly populated districts.[2] All this expenditure kept the Church moving more slowly, however, than its silent but unrelenting enemy, the rise of population. Each year the number of people in England and Wales rose by more than 300,000. A survey of the Bishop of London's Fund in 1900 showed that the efforts which it had made possible were quite inadequate in a diocese whose population had grown by 330,000 in the past ten years. In Manchester, despite all the energy thrown into Church extension for half a century, the proportion of church sittings to population declined. 'The fact is,' said the Archdeacon of London in 1899, 'that the population is increasing with such enormous rapidity that we are never able to overtake the neglect of 100 years ago.'[3] Neither he nor any other Church leader now imagined that their task was merely to bring the means of worship within reach of hungry millions; they were

[1] *Church Congress Report* (1881), p. 215.
[2] *Year-Book of the Church of England* (1900), pp. 19, 33, 574.
[3] W. MacDonald Sinclair, in *Church Congress Report* (1899), p. 37.

sadly aware of popular resistance to evangelism. But they knew, too, that quite apart from the non-worshippers who had been confronted by the Church's ministry and rejected it, there were more people every year who were quite out of its range.

Of those working-class abstainers who were within range, and who were articulate about their absence, it was generally believed in the Church that only a very small proportion entertained intellectual objections. 'Is secularism of the aggressive type on the increase among the working men of England?' asked Randall Davidson in 1883.

> Opinions differ, but I can see no evidence of any increase. If the circulation of its newspapers be larger than it was, I believe it may be fairly ascribed to the greater demand for cheaper periodicals of all sorts and kinds. . . . Count the numbers present at all the secularist halls in London upon any given Sunday, and I greatly doubt whether they would together equal the congregation of many a single parish church. Look at the advertised lists of secularist lecturers all the country over, and you will find about half a dozen names in all. Mr Bradlaugh's Parliamentary adventures have drawn an attention to his creed out of all proportion to the numerical strength of its adherents.[1]

This last assertion had the support of a clergyman who, after making an enquiry into the popularity of secularism, said in a report to the Archbishop of Canterbury that Bradlaugh and his friends greatly exaggerated the numbers of their supporters.[2] When clergymen throughout the province of Canterbury were asked to name what seemed to them the chief obstacles to the success of the Church among the masses, a very small proportion mentioned positive scepticism, and the report on their replies did not mention it as a factor.[3] A committee which put the same question to clergymen in the rest of England reported: 'Few have had experience of the open attacks of infidels.'[4] The infidelity of the age was a problem that distressed earnest Churchmen; but on the whole they did not think that it had infected many working-class people. A typical opinion was that

[1] *Year-Book of the Church of England* (1883), pp. 127–8.

[2] A. Hatchard, in *Church Congress Report* (1882), p. 101.

[3] Convocation of Canterbury, *Report of Joint Committee on the Spiritual Needs of the Masses of the People* (1885).

[4] Convocation of York, Lower House, *Report of Committee on the Spiritual Needs of the Masses of the People*, 1892, p. 7.

of the clergyman who believed that two sorts of people were cut off from Christian influences, 'the secularists on intellectual grounds, the masses on social grounds.'[1]

Different elements in the social atmosphere of the Church were blamed by different people for keeping out the poor. To some it was the pew system. Others believed that poor people were unwilling to come to worship on account of the clothes they wore: the working-man in shabby fustian, it was said, would not take himself to church alongside respectable broadcloth. 'God, it is true, does not look at clothes,' said a clergyman in 1880 who had had a wide home missionary experience,

> But congregations and guardians of the temple do, answer the working classes. Nowhere do the pomps and vanities of this wicked world assert themselves more strongly than in the House of God. 'Broadcloth and silk shrink from fustian and print in the church, as much or more than they do in the theatre,' writes a working man.[2]

When he was Bishop of Lichfield, W. D. Maclagan asked worshippers to show their reverence for God and love for the poor, and to risk the sneers of the fashionable world, by dressing plainly for Church so that working-class people would be coaxed along too.[3] In 1903, according to Robert Blatchford's *Clarion* (not the most sober of witnesses), a parson in Clerkenwell was holding special services for shabby parishioners 'in a dim religious light, almost in darkness, so that the people cannot see each other's looped and windowed raggedness . . .'[4] To others again, the trouble was that the Church offered working-class people no positive role in its life. This was one of Robert Dolling's conclusions from his experience at the Winchester mission in Portsmouth. 'For their fathers and for themselves,' he wrote, 'the Church of England has practically forbidden all

[1] An unnamed author of a reply to the enquiry reported in Convocation of Canterbury, *Report of Joint Committee on the Spiritual Needs of the Masses of the People* (1885), p. 4. For other denials, each by a bishop, that secularism was widespread among the working classes, see Walsham How in *Church Congress Report* (1880), p. 95; J. C. Ryle in *ibid.* (1882), p. 78; C. H. Bromby in *ibid.* (1884), p. 199; C. J. Ellicott, in the Convocation of Canterbury *Report* cited, Appendix, p. 25.

[2] Canon Money, in *Church Congress Report* (1880), p. 438.

[3] W. D. Maclagan, *The Church and the People* (1882), p. 9.

[4] *Clarion*, 6 Feb. 1903, p. 4.

work.'[1] 'The Church of England', said another of her clergy in 1895,

> gives the working man nothing to do. He feels he forms no integral part of her, that he is in no vital connexion with her, that he is not built into her structure, but is left, a loose stone, lying about for anyone to tumble over.[2]

The general conclusion common to such various assertions was that the Church was an institution belonging to and satisfying some social groups, but not others. The problem was stated simply by Walsham How, who had investigated it as closely as anybody, when he spoke of 'a terribly deep-rooted notion that the Church was for the rich and comfortable.'[3] It distressed many Churchmen that this notion had survived their efforts to nurture a parochial life in large towns, their novel missionary methods, their use here and there of working-class evangelists, their freeing most churches of the pew system, and the rest of their attempts to throw the mantle of the Church around the common people.

There were some in the Church, however, who believed that none of the gestures made so far were thorough-going enough to deserve success. Clergymen, even bishops, could talk as if they were recommending a leap in the dark. But Disraeli took a risk, and offering the working classes a share of political power. What risk was the Church taking? What was she offering except friendly chats about the unreality of social differences? The headmaster of Berkhamsted School, the Rev. T. C. Fry, was speaking for the socially radical minority in the Church when he wrote, in 1898:

> The Church is mostly administered and officered by the classes; her influential laity belong almost wholly to the class; she is doing a great and growing work among the masses; but the deep sympathies of the clergy with the poor are largely obscured to the eyes of the masses by the fact that social rank and social position secured by wealth and tradition still count for so much in her service, both amongst clergy and laity.[4]

[1] R. Dolling, *Ten Years in a Portsmouth Slum* (1896), p. 131.
[2] J. Foxley, *A Sermon on Church Reform* (1895), p. 6.
[3] *Church Congress Report* (1888), p. 662.
[4] T. C. Fry, in Gore, *op. cit.* p. 303.

To Fry and those who agreed with him, it appeared that the Church would attract the working classes only if her members showed, by expressing an active concern for social justice, that they were not tied in their thinking about social relationships to the prejudices and interests of the rich. Whether he was right it is perhaps impossible to know.

2

The Nonconformists

Nonconformity and the Time-spirit

SOME people in the Church of England, believing that the parochial system was an unwieldy means of reaching the masses, envied Nonconformists the fellowship built into their polity by such devices as congregational meetings and the election of members to offices of real responsibility. Yet Nonconformists, aware of their own deficiency as evangelists, could look towards the Church of England with envy. A conference of Nonconformists recommended 'the adoption, by the Nonconformist churches of Bradford, of a parochial system. . . .'[1] Some Nonconformists wished that Dissent allowed for the employment of curates, and others were convinced that their ministry to the poor was hampered by the principle of congregational autonomy. Methodists believed themselves hindered by the circuit system and the principle of itinerancy, which John Wesley had bequeathed to them. There was, in short, a tendency to see the peculiarities of one's own organization as impediments and those of others as advantages. As fishers of men in Victorian England, each body of Christians was sailing in a vessel designed for calmer waters; and to each the sea seemed roughest under its own boat.

The movement of population from the centre of cities to the suburbs, which accelerated momentously after 1850, was observed by Nonconformists as a force damaging to their churches.

[1] *Christian World*, 21 April 1892, p. 315.

An elderly Wesleyan minister said in 1898 that in London during the middle years of the century, not even the disastrous schisms and agitations had injured Methodism as much as 'the rush of the better-to-do-classes to new suburbs, ever increasing.'[1] When he began work in London in 1855, he recalled, the wealthier Wesleyan families – 'shipowners, manufacturers and merchants' had already left their chapels in St George's-in-the-East and Spitalfields, and later the shopkeepers followed them out. A Congregational minister remembered a time slightly earlier when 'Westminster and the opposite side of the Thames saw, on Sunday and week days, in the same neighbourhood both the poor and rich. Thus pious families exerted an immediate and constant influence where they lived. . . .'[2] It was a distant recollection when he wrote of it late in the century. A similar emigration went on in other cities. A Nonconformist journal noted in 1887 that for half a century the middle classes in all large towns had been moving 'from the centre and its close, confined streets and houses, to the circumference with its open spaces and more wholesome dwellings.'[3] The beneficent effects of piety, according to one Wesleyan minister, were themselves responsible for the movement:

> Godliness leads to sobriety and to additional power of mind, and so prosperity is secured. To the prosperous a great temptation is presented. Trams and railways invite a movement towards or into the suburbs, and thus the salt which once seasoned the thronging myriads extracts itself from them and goes where it is not nearly so much needed.[4]

The flight to the suburbs possibly affected the Nonconformists more severely than the Church; for their chapels, not being endowed, depended on wealthy local inhabitants for support, and when they left a district its chapel could be marooned in poverty. 'The tendency of dissent,' as a Wesleyan minister said in 1859, 'is to deal with the middle class, and when the middle class forsake a given neighbourhood, the chapel is re-

[1] T. M'Cullagh, in *Methodist Recorder*, 17 Feb. 1898, p. 12.

[2] J. Stoughton, *Recollections of a Long Life* (2nd. ed. 1894), p. 34.

[3] *British Weekly*, 25 Feb. 1887, p. 1. For a general account of the 'exodus of the well-to-do' from Manchester and its cultural effects, see K. C. Chorley, *Manchester Made Them* (1950), pp. 136–41.

[4] E. Smith, *The Great Problem of the Times* (1883), p. 3.

moved as the seat-holders are gone. . . .'[1] The problem was nevertheless not peculiar to Nonconformity. The cities also had Church of England places of worship with little or no endowment. Moreover, it was the separation of classes that distressed earnest Christians, not just the financial problems of the central churches. The 'mighty unfilled space,' as Thomas Chalmers had called it in 1821, 'between the high and the low of every large manufacturing city,' was made mightier by the rise of suburbs. In 1858 a clergyman who was secretary of the London Diocesan Church Building Society expressed the deepest cause of anxiety among Christians – Church of England or Nonconformist – who observed the phenomenon: 'the old associations which have so much weight with the English mind are almost entirely wanting now from the way in which those people congregated together, all of one class.'[2]

What could be done about it? Urge the wealthy, replied some, to visit the poor whom they had left behind. 'Each visit of sympathy', said the Bishop of London in 1871, 'breaks down some prejudice and clears away some misapprehension.'[3] The settlements which appeared in the 'eighties represented a systematic attempt at visits of sympathy. A less demanding suggestion to the emigrant rich, popular among Nonconformists, was that they should give money for Christian work in the regions they had quitted. Plans were made in various denominations to encourage such gifts, to distribute them, and to send missionary agents into the neglected centre. Some of these plans simply intensified efforts of a kind which had gone on for decades. There were also novelties, responses to changing circumstances and to the apparent failure of conventional evangelism.

One such novelty, sponsored by a committee of Nonconformists and Churchmen in 1851, was a series of Sunday services in Exeter Hall for people who lived in central London and normally went to no church. Four years later Charles Spurgeon, the Baptist minister who was to be hailed as the greatest preacher of his century, engaged the same hall, and the Surrey Music Hall, for religious services, and filled them for months. The

[1] Rev. J. Osborn, quoted in A. C. Whitby, 'Matthew Arnold and the Nonconformists' (unpublished B.Litt. thesis, University of Oxford, 1954), p. 93.

[2] T. F. Stooks, in *Parliamentary Papers*, 1857–8, IX, Deficiency of the Means of Spiritual Instruction, Select Committee, H. of L.: Minutes of Evidence, p. 57.

[3] J. Jackson, *The Parochial System, a Charge* (1871), p. 37.

organizers of these services, and of similar ones in St. James' Hall, said that the people who crowded them were habitual neglecters of worship. An evangelical journal doubted, however, whether the audience at Exeter Hall was made of such people at all.[1] Even if it was, the proportion of London's non-worshippers among those present cannot have been large. What were two halls, asked an officer of the London City Mission, for a population of three millions?[2] A further innovation was to hire popular theatres in London for 'special services for the working classes' which could be described by 1861 as 'a part of the recognized machinery employed for the evangelization of the masses.'[3] The most celebrated of such meetings were held by the American evangelist Dwight L. Moody, who came to London in 1875 and preached at the Agricultural Hall, the Royal Haymarket Opera House, and elsewhere, accompanied by his singing colleague Ira D. Sankey. Nonconformists and evangelical Churchmen were grateful to the Americans for attracting large and enthusiastic audiences, among whom it was generally thought many were not ordinarily churchgoers. But as the superintendent of a small mission remarked: 'If the masses of London are to be reached, not only does there need such labourers as the highly honoured Mr Moody, but a vast increase of stationary, plodding, mission agency. . . .'[4] At best the services in secular buildings could prepare people for attending normal public worship. It was up to the enterprise of particular churches to gather whatever fruits were produced. The fruits, moreover, may have been few. A clergyman wrote to *The Times* saying that whenever he attended Moody's meetings he 'saw but very few of the working class'; and Moody himself, according to an early biographer, realized 'that he was failing to attract a suitable proportion of the poor and wicked into his meetings.'[5]

[1] *Record*, 6 Jan. 1856, quoted in J. W. H. Molyneux, *A Letter Addressed to the Lord Bishop of Ely* (2nd. ed. 1856), p. 6.

[2] C. W. Sawell, quoted in E. Hodder, *The Life of Samuel Morley* (1887), p. 145. He was referring to Exeter Hall and St James' Hall.

[3] W. Tuckniss, introduction to H. Mayhew, *London Labour and the London Poor*, IV (1861), p. xx.

[4] *Great Arthur Street Mission Echo*, Dec. 1874. Moody had been in Britain since 1873, and arrived in London on 9 March 1875 after more than a year's planning. W. G. McLoughlin, Jr, *Modern Revivalism*, p. 196.

[5] *Ibid*, p. 203.

From time to time Nonconformists co-operated with evangelical Churchmen in a common assault on the neglect of worship. Some rich laymen on both sides, and some clergymen and ministers, supported in the 'sixties an association of evangelists, the Conference of Christian Workers, which tried to preserve the missionary energy generated in a 'revival' of 1859–60.[1] F. D. Maurice and other clergymen conferred with Nonconformist ministers and with some working men in 1867 to ask why the churches were less effective among the working classes than elsewhere.[2] In 1876 the Archbishop of Canterbury himself discussed with a group of leading Nonconformist ministers the possibility of united efforts against atheism and against 'the lamentable ignorance and indifference as to religion which prevails among the masses of the community.[3] Nothing came of this particular meeting except a reminder that the obstacles to formal co-operation between the Church and Dissent had deep roots. A common anxiety made joint activity seem urgent to many people; but even if the traditional grounds for hostility had been overcome, the mounting strength of 'ritualism' in the Church of England would have prevented any close alliance.

Within Nonconformity, however, a movement towards common evangelistic action was encouraged by this growth of what Nonconformists liked to call 'sacerdotal practices'. A necessary condition for any such movement was that Wesleyans should think of themselves as Nonconformists, rather than as a people set apart from both Church and Dissent. This more and more Wesleyans tended to do after 1850, until Gladstone could count on them voting not Tory, as an earlier generation did, but Liberal, like most Nonconformists in the older sects.[4] The phrase 'the Nonconformist conscience' was invented and wielded most fiercely by a Wesleyan minister, Hugh Price Hughes.[5] Co-operation between dissenting bodies for particular evangel-

[1] On this 'revival' see *ibid.* pp.183–4. There is a fuller account, which considerably exaggerates its effects, in E. Orr, *The Second Evangelical Awakening in Britain* (1949).

[2] *Working Men and Religious Institutions: Full and Extended Report of Speeches* (1867).

[3] Quoted from the official record of the meeting in J. Stoughton, *op. cit.* p. 260.

[4] See H. Broadhurst, *The Story of His Life* (1901), p. 38. For the part of the education question in this change, see E. Halévy, *A History of the English People in the Nineteenth Century*, V (1951), p. 174.

[5] M. L. Edwards, *Methodism and England* (1943), p. 155.

istic works was not new. Until late in the century, however, each sect tended to have its own climate of opinion, its own rhythm of activity. Only an unusual event like the census of religious worship shook all of them into a simultaneous concern. By the late Victorian years, Nonconformist responses were more often in step with each other. The case of *The Bitter Cry of Outcast London* (1883) was one sign of this greater uniformity.

This famous pamphlet was the work of the Rev. Andrew Mearns, secretary of the London Congregational Union, and two other Congregational ministers.[1] Its title was so often on the lips of social reformers that its religious origin and purpose were commonly forgotten – an oversight encouraged by W. T. Stead, editor of the *Pall Mall Gazette*, who first brought it to general notice by a digest in his paper which played down its evangelistic portions.[2] *The Bitter Cry* was indeed a plea for parliamentary action, especially to provide decent cheap housing; but it was also a report on the rarity of church-going among the poorest Londoners, a criticism of the churches for devoting so much wealth and effort to the spiritual care of the well-to-do, and an appeal on behalf of missionary and philanthropic work by the London Congregational Union in slum districts.

On other Nonconformist bodies *The Bitter Cry* had a direct impact and a more diffused one. Soon after its publication, and

[1] No author was named in the pamphlet, but on the last page appeared the advice: 'All Communications should be addressed to Rev. Andrew Mearns, London Congregational Union, Memorial Hall, Farringdon St, E.C.' The *British Museum Catalogue* names W. C. Preston (another Congregational minister) as author, and so does Halkett and Laing's *Dictionary of Anonymous and Pseudonymous English Literature*, giving no reason but the precedent of the Liberal Club's *Gladstone Library Catalogue*. The following remarks by Mearns, in *Contemporary Review*, Dec. 1883, p. 933, seem fairly conclusive: 'I ought to explain that I have no wish to be described as the author of "The Bitter Cry of Outcast London", but having seen printed statements to the effect that two others who acted as my assistants are credited with the pamphlet, it seems necessary that I should say that the inception was entirely mine, the investigation was carried out under my direction, and the pamphlet was prepared according to my instructions and subject to my revision. I was greatly helped in the investigation by the Rev. James Munro, formerly of Limerick, and in the literary work by the Rev. W. C. Preston, formerly of Hull, and acknowledge my indebtedness to both. Others helped, but to a lesser degree.' R. C. K. Ensor, in *England, 1870–1914* (Oxford, 1936), p. 127, attributes the pamphlet to G. R. Sims, presumably by a slip of memory. R. F. Wearmouth, in *Methodism and the Struggle of the Working Classes, 1850–1900* (Leicester, 1954), p. 155, attributes it to James Clark.

[2] *Pall Mall Gazette*, 16 Oct. 1883.

provoked by it, a conference representing Wesleyans, Baptists, Presbyterians and Congregationalists was held in London to discuss the spiritual and social condition of the London poor. The wider effect may be seen in the increased attention which the Wesleyans gave to London and to the general problem of the poorest people in large towns. In 1884 the Methodist Ministers' Meeting in London heard a paper from one of its members on 'Outcast London'.[1] The Wesleyan Conference noted in the same year that the 'temporal and spiritual interests of the dense populations of our large towns, more especially of London, have excited much public attention through the year,' and announced that it was considering special methods for London.[2] 'If any place under heaven should be made truly Christian, London is the place,' said the committee of the Wesleyan Metropolitan Chapel Building Fund in its report for 1884.[3] A year later the annual address of the conference, citing *The Bitter Cry*, took up this theme that London had a peculiar importance:

> this great centre of national, imperial world-life is the prize, the citadel, for which the powers of light and darkness must contend. . . . We can use no language strong enough to express our sense of the responsibility of English Christians in respect of the great city, its sin and sorrows.[4]

If London had an unusual share of sins and sorrows, they were not newly acquired. The concern expressed here showed not that poverty and irreligion were spreading, but that the Wesleyans had been infected by the mood of *The Bitter Cry*.

The infection was not limited to Nonconformists. Both the appearance of this pamphlet and its public reception were evidence of a general sensitivity to the condition of poor people which was characteristic of England in the 1880's. Despite what has been said of *The Bitter Cry* by its contemporaries and by some historians, it did not *arouse* a new interest in social distress. The housing of the poor was being discussed publicly, in the weeks before the pamphlet appeared, by Chamberlain and Salis-

[1] R. B. Thompson, *Peter Thompson* (1910), p. 33.
[2] *Wesleyan Conference Minutes* (1884), p. 310.
[3] *Ibid.* p. 346.
[4] *Ibid.* (1885), p. 300.

bury.[1] *The Bitter Cry* was not even a very original document, for much of its evidence was taken straight from a more vivid tract by G. R. Sims, called *How the Poor Live.*[2] Mearns' pamphlet owed its fame to its arresting title, to its exploitation by W. T. Stead in the *Pall Mall Gazette*, and to its timing. People usually quoted the title, not any of the contents; it expressed exactly that mood of corporate guilt and apprehension which stirred some members of the comfortable classes after 1880 to lend a hand to their poorer brothers. Stead, who had just become editor of the *Pall Mall Gazette*, always knew exactly how and when to strike his readers. He took up *The Bitter Cry* at a moment when the condition of the poor, and especially their housing, was being discussed in the monthly reviews, and threw the subject to the middle-class public at large, among whom many were prepared to feel uneasy about the plight of the outcast. A pamphlet by a Congregational minister on behalf of an evangelistic scheme thus became for a time a symbol for the general mood.

Translation of common sentiment into common action was attempted on other occasions. Local councils of Free Churches were formed in Midland towns in the early 'eighties. In 1886 a section of the Congregational Union of England and Wales was urging 'an agreement ... between the Congregational and other Evangelical bodies, with a view to preventing overlapping in Church and Mission Work. . . .'[3] In 1891 the Nonconformist *British Weekly* said of an unofficial census of religious worship taken in Liverpool: 'Questions of proselytising become monstrous here, in view of the vast multitude untouched.'[4] Nonconformists in Birmingham drew a similar conclusion from a house-to-house enquiry about religious habits. They formed a Free Church Council under the presidency of George Cadbury, who lamented that Christians whose only serious disagreements

[1] See J. Chamberlain, 'Labourers' and Artizans' Dwellings', *Fortnightly Review*, Dec. 1883, pp. 761–6; J. L. Garvin, *Life of Joseph Chamberlain*, I (1932), p. 406; Lady G. Cecil, *Life of Robert Marquis of Salisbury*, III (1931), pp. 68–71.

[2] *How the Poor Live* (1883) was reprinted from the *Pictorial World*. It sold at a shilling, *The Bitter Cry* at a penny. Mearns denied the *Pall Mall Gazette*'s assertion that 'most of the cases' he cited were taken from Sims. But he acknowledged that eight of them were, he allowed that Sims had been 'first in the field', and occasionally he quoted a phrase directly from him (for example, 'Marriage, as an institution, is not fashionable in these districts'.).

[3] *Congregational Year Book* (1888), pp. 5–7.

[4] *British Weekly*, 29 Oct. 1891, p. 3.

were over church government should compete so wastefully when the spiritual darkness was so vast. At Birmingham in 1895 on Cadbury's initiative and with his money to support it, a National Council of the Evangelical Free Churches was formed. The first national activity inspired by the Council was a mission arranged in 1900 of Nonconformist churches to 'the masses of the people.'[1]

Among both Congregationalists and Wesleyans, towards the end of the century, a sense of mission to the masses was expressed by a number of young ministers who had in them a discontent with old forms of thought and action, a reforming energy which they shared with many contemporaries in other churches and outside organized religion. In Wesleyan Methodism the leader of such men was Hugh Price Hughes, who launched a weekly newspaper in 1885 to give, as the first page of the first issue proclaimed, an organ to the younger generation of Methodists. This journal, the *Methodist Times,* was constantly urging Wesleyans to throw greater effort into seeking allegiance among the working classes. 'Methodism has reached the parting of the ways', Hughes announced in an early number, 'We must either go back into the obscurity of a class religion, and the impotence of a moribund sect; or we must go forward into the blessed opportunities and far reaching beneficence of a national religion, which preaches the Gospel to the poor.'[2]

Hughes came to stand for what he and others called the Forward Movement. It was a vague concept, made no less vague by Hughes' own attempts to clarify it, but not a meaningless one. The Forward Movement was an attempt to awaken Nonconformists to duties which the young believed that their elders had neglected – especially the duties to think out Christianity freshly in the light of new secular knowledge and opinion, and to grapple with a changing society. Although the phrase was Wesleyan in origin and was at first used mainly by Wesleyans, the spirit which it described was at work in other Nonconformist bodies. Among the Baptists John Clifford embodied it. In Congregationalism the *British Weekly*, a journal founded in 1886,

[1] C. S. Horne, *Nonconformity in the Nineteenth Century* (1905), p. 153. The phrase quoted is from *Wesleyan Conference Minutes* (1900), p. 341. See also A. G. Gardiner, *Life of George Cadbury* (1923), pp. 174–9.

[2] *Methodist Times*, 19 March 1885, p. 177.

expressed attitudes very like those of the *Methodist Times.* Its founder, W. Robertson Nicoll, called it privately 'a paper for Christian Radicals.'[1] The first issue reported results of a census of religious worship in London conducted on behalf of the journal, and the problem of spreading evangelical religion among the working classes was always one of its main concerns. The actual term 'Forward Movement' appears not to have become current among Congregationalists until 1893, when R. F. Horton, whose place among Independents was very similar to that of Hughes in Methodism, used it to describe his plans for an effort 'to bring the vast uncared-for masses back to God.'[2] Another Congregational minister, J. Guinness Rogers, was soon complaining that the term was 'likely to become a cant phrase', capable of covering a great variety of methods, some valuable and others not; but he agreed that it had a meaning: 'What I understand ... by a Forward Movement is some action inspired by devoted loyalty to the Master, for bringing men to faith in Him.[3] Another leading Congregational minister said a few years later that he understood by the Forward Movement those enterprises which showed 'a serious resolve on the part of the Nonconformist Churches to keep pace with and even to gain upon the growth of population.'[4] Supporters of the Forward Movement had in common a belief – perhaps highly articulate as in Hughes or perhaps vaguely felt – that Nonconformity was facing what might be its final intellectual and social challenge.

The sensitivity of men like Hughes and Horton to currents of secular thought and social change was part of a general lowering of the barriers between Nonconformists and English society. In so far as it made some people responsive to the challenges of the age, the change was possibly for the good of Nonconformity. But the old separation had also given Nonconformity some of its virtues. 'There is not in these days,' wrote a Congregationalist in 1891, 'the extraneous pressure which makes every [Congregational] church a compact and heroic phalanx.'[5] One great strength for Nonconformists had been their adherence to the ideal which has been called the sect-type, their sense of being

[1] T. H. Darlow, *William Robertson Nicoll, Life and Letters* (1925), p. 69.

[2] *British Weekly*, 9 Feb. 1893, p. 259.

[3] J. G. Rogers, *The Forward Movement of the Christian Church* (1893), pp. 4, 8.

[4] C. A. Berry, in *Sunday Magazine*, June 1898, p. 399.

[5] J. B. Aitken, in *Congregational Monthly*, Oct. 1891, p. 267.

a special people, apart from the world. 'The old seclusion and separateness are broken down,' said Wesleyan ministers to their rank and file in 1900, 'You are in the world, brethren, steeped in its affairs, conversant with its ideas, and affected by its fashions and maxims to a degree that would have shocked your fathers.'[1] The Congregationalist leader R. W. Dale asked anxiously: 'are we mastering the world by the power of God and making it what God meant it to be, or is the world mastering us?'[2]

A conformity with worldly standards was widely noticed among Nonconformists in the late Victorian years. 'Those who only know what Methodist society is now,' wrote the Congregationalist John Stoughton in 1884, 'can have no conception of what it was sixty years since. Neatness and order were the rule, but no extravagance, no waste.'[3] A Congregational deacon remarked in 1886 that respectable Nonconformists now preferred not to attend worship in the evenings, 'the morning being considered more stylish, less democratic. . . .'[4] The 'chapel' had become the 'church' in name and in design.[5] A guide to Manchester in 1888 spoke of

> Dissenting ministers in the place who enjoy incomes which sound almost fabulous to those who believe the tradition of the Dissenting clergyman's dependence upon the hardly-extracted contributions of the tradesman and the artisan. When it is mentioned that on one chapel alone the Independent body expended £26,000, and that the income of one popular Dissenting preacher is stated to be some £1,500 a year, it will readily be understood that 'the dissidence of Dissent' in Manchester does not imply sitting and waiting upon Providence.[6]

Would it not be a wiser policy, in the interests of evangelism, to build more austerely and devote more money to home missions? The answer was partly that if congregations wanted

[1] *Wesleyan Conference Minutes* (1900), p. 404.
[2] R. W. Dale, *The Old Evangelicalism and the New* (1889), p. 36.
[3] J. Stoughton, *Religion in England from 1800 to 1850* (1884), I, 351.
[4] E. M. Smith, in *British Weekly*, 10 Sept. 1886, p. 322. He was speaking of Yorkshire. For similar evidence about Nonconformists in Manchester, see K. C. Chorley, *Manchester Made Them*, p. 172.
[5] R. Stanley Morgan, 'Some Victorian Chapel-Builders', *Congregational Quarterly*, July 1955, p. 237.
[6] *Manchester Today* (1888), pp. 39–40.

handsome buildings and were willing to pay for them, they could not be stopped; partly that people were prepared to give money for a new chapel to sit in who would not have given so much for reaching the distant poor; and partly that it was prudent to let well-to-do worshippers build to suit themselves: 'We are told,' wrote a Congregationalist in 1890, 'it is a matter of policy to build fine chapels. Thus and thus only shall we be able to let out sittings to the wealthier classes whose well-filled purses will guarantee us against deficits.'[1]

To understand this last reason one must remember that although Nonconformists suffered no longer any serious discrimination at the hands of the law once the Burial Act of 1880 was passed, there were still social disabilities attaching to Dissent. 'Nonconformity has not the weight with the educated classes of the country which it has with the commercial classes,' wrote a minister in 1885. 'It fills but a small place in public life. Some of its greatest leaders are comparatively unknown. . . . Its social importance is vastly inferior to its political importance.'[2] For Nonconformists who had prospered, membership of a dissenting sect could seem a link with a more plebeian past which, like a raw provincial accent, must be discarded if they were to move easily on social levels which their wealth now made accessible.

Late in the century remarks about the drift of rich people from Nonconformity to the Church were so common as to suggest that it was increasing. The *London Quarterly Review*, a Wesleyan journal, observed in 1899: 'The Society of Friends, the Congregational Church, and Methodism in a still larger degree, are ever losing their wealthier members and the children of such members, who find their way into the Anglican communion.'[3] However the individual recruit to the Church might explain his translation, his former brethren had no doubt about the motive: 'it is the social position of the Church that draws,' said a Congregational minister, expressing the general opinion. '. . . Those who go over are in the vast majority of cases the worldly and

[1] B. P. Neuman, 'The Weaknesses of Congregationalism', *Nineteenth Century*, Oct. 1890, p. 63.

[2] Dr Hatch, in *Methodist Times*, 11 June 1885, pp. 369–70.

[3] *London Quarterly Review*, April 1899, p. 352. See also *Congregational Review*, July 1888, p. 595; K. C. Chorley, *op. cit.* pp. 172–4; J. S. Leatherbarrow, *Victorian Period Piece* (1954), p. 179.

those who seek a higher status in society than Nonconformity offers to give them.'[1]

Nonconformists who said that fine chapels were 'a matter of policy', then, meant that they satisfied a desire for display and dignity among those people whose wealth made them possible deserters to the Church of England, and whose defection would mean – apart from any other consideration – a serious financial loss. But if handsome buildings did induce many rich people to remain Nonconformists, their allegiance may have been bought at a price. For it is likely that each gesture intended to suit the tastes of the rich made the spirit of Dissenting worship a little more uncongenial to the poor.

The Problem of Pleasure

The compromise between Nonconformity and the world alarmed those dissenters to whom the world, the flesh and the devil were a dreadful trinity. 'Love not the world', Wesleyans were exhorted in 1855 by the Conference which had 'observed, with sincere regret, the existence, in some quarters, of a disposition to indulge in and encourage amusements which it cannot regard as harmless or allowable.'[2] The middle-class Nonconformist family in late Victorian England may appear, from our vantage point, to have been severely ascetic in its habits; but older Nonconformists could see a clear trend in their lifetime towards frivolity. In 1887 R. W. Dale, now an old man, measured the church-going middle classes of the day against those of fifty years earlier. 'There are many amusements which our people now take delight in without any scruple', he said, 'which were then altogether avoided, on the principle that it was desirable to surround the moral life with a certain environment favourable to the development of the graver and more serious virtues.'[3] The problem of worldly amusements was a common theme in Nonconformist discussion. 'We are living in the midst of a great reaction from Puritanism', said the Wesleyan Conference in 1890.[4] The reaction was seeping into the churches. In an ad-

[1] W. Jones, in *British Weekly*, 25 Aug. 1888, p. 275.

[2] *Wesleyan Conference Minutes* (1855), pp. 78, 182.

[3] From a sermon given in 1887 and printed in *British Weekly*, 23 May 1895, p. 66.

[4] *Wesleyan Conference Minutes* (1890), p. 353.

dress on 'The Secularisation of the Church', the chairman of the Congregational Union in 1894 said:

> Christian parents no longer forbid their children to read novels or to learn dancing; some of them accompany their sons and daughters to the theatre and the concert; in many Christian homes billiards and cards are allowed, and both in occupation and amusement the line that once divided the world from the Church is tending to disappear.[1]

Growing indulgence in worldly pleasures offered both a practical and a spiritual threat to the churches. Practically the problem was that amusements were competing with public worship for the patronage of people on Sunday. The first railway excursion had been organized in 1841 by a young Midland carpenter for a temperance society. The young man, Thomas Cook, was an earnest Baptist; but he had invented (to his own good fortune) an institution which the churches soon came to regret. By 1858 a clergyman in London was reporting that 'in the summer months, when there are Sunday excursion trains, . . . there is consequently great temptation, and a very great tendency to desert the church, and to spend the Sunday as a holiday.'[2] Before long there was an even easier way of getting into the countryside on the Sabbath. 'That innocent machine, the bicycle,' said a clergyman in 1898, 'is, I believe, doing more to abolish church-going, and so, it may be said, to undermine Christianity, than any other social force.'[3] Cycling, railway trips, concerts, and – if the National Sunday League had its way – art galleries, parks and museums, were all tempting alternatives to church in a society whose members were tending to look on pleasure with tolerance.

The spiritual threat was more insidious. Its operation was described by the chairman of the Congregational Union in 1885, who laid it down that

> those amusements are not innocent which, when seriously reflected upon, naturally raise a doubt in one's mind – which are connected

[1] G. S. Barrett, in *Congregational Year Book* (1895), p. 47.

[2] T. F. Stooks, in *Parliamentary Papers*, 1857–8, IX, Deficiency of the Means of Spiritual Instruction, Select Committee, H. of L.: Minutes of Evidence, p. 87.

[3] Canon Wollaston, quoted in *Great Thoughts*, 19 Nov. 1898, p. 121. For a similar Wesleyan view see D. Young, quoted in *British Weekly*, 13 Aug. 1896, p. 259.

> with matters that are sinful – which unfit a man for spiritual work, and tend to estrange his mind from spiritual realities. Certainly such amusements are perilous to spiritual religion.[1]

This suspicion of pleasure was not, of course, peculiar to Nonconformists in Victorian England. It was an evangelical Churchman, Sir James Stephen, who according to his son Leslie 'once smoked a cigar, and found it so delicious that he never smoked again.'[2] Bishop Blomfield, a genial man and not an Evangelical, would allow no card-playing in his house, disapproved of the theatre, and disliked dances 'on account of the unwholesome excitement too often inseparable from them.'[3] Even on spirits who had shaken off religious orthodoxy, the puritanism of the age could act powerfully: Herbert Spencer gave a very solemn apology for the pleasure of playing billiards.[4]

The puritan discipline was a concomitant not merely of Dissent but of respectability. The waning of its power, however, imperilled Nonconformity most of all. Competition from Sunday amusements affected all churches; but the corrosion of spirituality by participation in worldly pleasures was a special danger to the sects which in every generation had kindled their communal life from the flame of the puritan tradition. Could the heirs of Paul, Augustine, Luther, Calvin, Milton, Bunyan and Wesley afford to return the world's smile? The question had great relevance for evangelistic as well as pastoral activity. Nonconformists had to decide both how their own members ought to respond to the invitation of worldly amusements, and what to say and do about the pleasures of the masses.

When the pleasures were agreed to be vicious, it appeared to many Nonconformists that the problem was simply how best to suppress them. Against the pleasure or solace of drunkenness they became the most active crusaders. Early in the century the temperance movement was on uneasy terms with the leaders of Nonconformity, who feared that it might be a rival sect. After 1850 they embraced it with ever-increasing ardour. Ministers were total abstainers, opposition to alcohol was expressed in missions among the poor, and the representative organs of Non-

[1] J. Thomas, in *Congregational Year Book* (1886), p. 52.
[2] N. Annan, *Leslie Stephen* (1951), p. 14.
[3] A. Blomfield, *A Memoir of Charles Blomfield* (1863), II. 198.
[4] H. Spencer, *An Autobiography* (1904), II. 225.

conformity lent their authority to the campaign for teetotalism. Many Nonconformists also supported the closing on Sundays not only of public houses but of other possible alternatives to worship. Although Nonconformists were by no means unanimous on the question of opening museums, art galleries and libraries on Sunday, the energy of the Lord's Day Observance Society and the Working Men's Lord's Day Rest Association was drawn largely from among them.[1] The Congregational millionaire Samuel Morley was for many years a vice-president of the former society, which led the campaign against allowing the working classes to have public secular temptations on Sunday.

Morley himself had, in his biographer's words, 'a Puritan dread of what are termed "worldly amusements".'[2] Not alone among the puritans of his day, he overcame this dread when it occurred to him that negative opposition to the evil pleasures of the poor was not enough. In 1880 the Victoria Theatre, or Old Vic, in Waterloo Bridge Road, notorious among the pious, was taken over by a committee of reformers who re-named it the Victoria Temperance Music Hall and put on programmes which, although still full of clog-dancers, comic singers, acrobats, nigger minstrels and performing dogs, were purged of lewdness. At first Morley disapproved, on the ground that even a clean music hall was a music hall. In 1882 he changed his mind, convinced that if Christians deprived the working classes of opportunities for vicious amusements, they must provide purer forms. He joined the committee running the Hall, saved the enterprise by giving it money, and went so far as to justify his own amusement at a performance, observing: 'I believe in good hearty laughter, it tends to health.' The great object of the entertainment, Morley said, was to win people from the public house. 'Can people conceive', he asked,

> what is meant when told that husband, wife, and six children are living in a single room? These people will go somewhere in the evening to seek amusement. I hold it to be a Christian duty to give them amusement.[3]

[1] On the former society see S. Maccoby, *English Radicalism, 1886–1914* (1953), p. 482; on the latter see *Great Thoughts*, 19 Nov. 1898, pp. 120–2.

[2] E. Hodder, *The Life of Samuel Morley* (1887), p. 430.

[3] *Ibid.* p. 437.

Soon services were being held at the Hall on Sunday evenings. Although mission services in theatres, as we have seen, had been held since the 'fifties, this was probably the first time that a Sunday service was organized in a theatre by the people who were also responsible for its programmes during the week. The whole enterprise was an attempt to enlist pleasure in the service of religion. A similar motive inspired ministers to organize sporting activities in association with particular places of worship. 'The pastor who cares for the healthy recreation of his young people', wrote the *British Weekly* in 1896, 'will not find that they desert him on Sunday.'[1] Some Wesleyan churches had their own cycling clubs, and in North Finchley a Baptist minister set apart a special pew for visiting cyclists. Many churches and chapels ran football teams, several of which eventually became leading members of the Football League.[2]

Some Christians believed that amusement should not only be associated with a church but admitted inside its doors, at special services intended at least partly to entertain. They were encouraged towards this belief by the example of the Salvation Army, which offered what one member called in 1882 'a religion of enjoyment.'[3] 'How far is it the duty of the Church to provide amusements for the people?' asked the chairman of the Congregational Union in 1885. It was now one of the questions of the day for Nonconformists. His own answer was tight-lipped: 'I look with a very suspicious eye upon every movement tending in that direction.'[4] When the *British Weekly* held an essay competition on the subject in 1891, it set out clearly the most common practical objection:

> Those who come to church because there is amusement to be found in connection with it, remain only as long as this attraction lasts for them. You do not find such persons eager to attend the services that are held for worship and purposes of spiritual communion.

But opposite this argument the journal set what seemed, to the advocates of holy amusement, a more powerful consideration. 'If amusements are regarded by the Church as contraband, the young will be repelled, and the masses of the people whose lives

[1] *British Weekly*, 7 May 1896, p. 35.
[2] M. Marples, *A History of Football* (1954), p. 167.
[3] Frank Smith, in *War Cry*, 21 Sept. 1882.
[4] J. Thomas, *loc. cit.*

are so much in want of being brightened, will be confirmed in their indifference to public worship.'[1] People who took this view did not necessarily deny the danger to spirituality of giving amusements an unbridled welcome into church. They were saying rather that when newspaper proprietors, railway companies, publicans and theatrical entrepreneurs were so keenly offering entertainment to the masses, it was more dangerous to perpetuate the division between religion and amusement. They were recommending that the churches take pleasure and consecrate it.

Some of the experiments in this cause were not meant specifically to attract working-class people: cycling, for example, was mainly a middle-class diversion. Others were directed at the poor. The Wesleyan minister in Liverpool who began in 1875 to urge drinkers out of pubs and into cocoa rooms, had many successors.[2] The most systematic attempt to attract new working-class worshippers by offering them consecrated pleasure was the Pleasant Sunday Afternoon movement, which some Nonconformists hailed as being more likely than any other method to bring the common people into the churches.

The Pleasant Sunday Afternoon was invented in 1875 by John Blackham, an Independent deacon in West Bromwich.[3] Blackham made no effort to persuade anybody to copy the system, and at first it was adopted only in the neighbourhood of West Bromwich. In 1885 he explained the work to a group in Derby who founded a P.S.A. Society there and invited him to open its first meeting. From Derby the movement spread to Birmingham, Hanley, Wolverhampton, Nottingham and several other midland towns; to Sheffield and Leeds (where a Yorkshire Union of P.S.A. Societies was formed in 1892); to Sunderland, to Manchester and to parts of London.[4] In some towns there were several separate P.S.A. Societies. In Wolverhampton the Society had over 1,000 members in 1891. The Society at Hanley, described as one of the largest, had 1,680 members in the same year.

[1] *British Weekly*, 31 Dec. 1891, p. 158.

[2] *Ibid.*

[3] S. Lees, 'The P.S.A. Movement', *Christian World*, 7 April 1892, p. 276. See also A. H. Byles, *The P.S.A., What It Is, and How to Start It* (1891).

[4] This list is probably far from complete. Its sources are *P.S.A. Magazine*, Dec. 1891; J. W. Dixon, *Pledged to the People: a Sketch of the Rev. Richard Westrope* (1896), p. 15; *Labour Leader*, 19 May 1894, p. 7.

The organization of a P.S.A. Society was modelled on that of the Adult Bible-Classes which Joseph Sturge had begun in Birmingham. Members enrolled, made a nominal weekly payment, elected a committee of management, and agreed to come every Sunday if possible. Non-members were welcomed, and encouraged to become members. A few Societies were for women only, some admitted men and women, and many – perhaps most – were for men only.

'The title "Pleasant" ', wrote a sympathizer in 1892, 'was to some an offence. It was gratuitously supposed to present an entertainment. And some of the objections went far to sustain the opinion which Mr Blackham believed working men to hold – that pleasantness and religiousness in meetings were incongruous, if not contradictory terms.'[1] The president of the Hanley P.S.A. Society admitted that the word 'suggests claptrap, it savours of sensationalism, it has provoked in some a feeling of aversion and called forth ridicule. . . .' But he believed that the word had paid its way: 'It is drawing the masses, and in larger numbers, probably, than they would have been drawn by any other name.'

> The great desire of all who are taking part in this movement is to make these services 'pleasant', in order to distinguish them from those that have been very unpleasant; but that they may be really 'pleasant', and not merely amusing, they have given foremost place to that 'greatest tidings of joy' which falls with as pleasant a sound on the ear of the artizan of the nineteenth century as it did on that of the shepherds of the first.[2]

Nobody today inspecting the agenda of a P.S.A. meeting would call it frivolous. Since each society was autonomous, the form of the meetings could vary; but procedure at the Nottingham Society in 1889 was fairly typical. This Society was for men only, and met in a public hall. At 2.30, after 'welcomers' had shaken hands with each man and shown him to a seat, a hymn was sung from the Sankey book with which each man was issued.[3] A reading from the Bible was followed by another hymn. A short prayer was led by 'a working man'. A lady

[1] S. Lees, *loc. cit.*

[2] A. H. Byles, *op. cit.* pp. 5–6.

[3] In 1892 a special Song Book was complied for P.S.A. meetings, which was believed to be more robust than Sankey's. *Christian World*, 12 April 1892, p. 295.

delivered a sacred solo, 'The Better Land', and was cheered. the leader gave – for ten minutes only – a religious or moral address. Then came a sacred duet or quartet and another short address. Another solo, or perhaps a chorus, was sung. Finally there were announcements, a closing hymn and a benediction. The whole meeting took just over an hour.[1]

Believing that conventional services were too long, too dull, and encouraged fellowship too little, the conductors of P.S.A. Societies designed for their movement the motto 'Brief, Bright and Brotherly'. An emblem used by the Societies showed these words around two clasped hands and the words 'A helping hand.' This last phrase referred to activities which most P.S.A. societies conducted alongside the religious meeting – a benevolent and sick provident fund, a savings bank, a poor man's lawyer, a temperance society.

Most P.S.A. Societies were associated with particular Nonconformist bodies. By 1890 the movement had been taken up by so many Wesleyan churches that the Conference discussed it in the annual address to members, saying: 'Pleasant Sunday Afternoon Services meet the needs of working people, but they are not substitutes for Senior Bible-classes.'[2] Three years later the Conference called for a special report on the movement, which showed it to be 'a conspicuous feature in Church life today.'[3] The thriving Society at Hanley was founded by a Congregational minister, A. H. Byles. Another Congregational minister, Richard Westrope, brought the system to Leeds in 1890 and was first president of the Yorkshire Union of P.S.A. Societies. A committee of the Congregational Union in 1895 described P.S.A. services as common in Independency. John Clifford, a leading Baptist minister, conducted P.S.A. meetings at his church in Paddington.[4]

The Nottingham Society, which probably had more members than any other, was run not by any one denomination but by a 'United Gospel Mission' with which the sects refused to cooperate because they believed that the P.S.A. was stealing some of their people. This, at any rate, was the explanation offered

[1] 'Pleasant Sunday Afternoons' (1889), in *Adults and the Sunday Schools* (n. d.), pp. 3–5.

[2] *Wesleyan Conference Minutes* (1890), p. 349.

[3] *Ibid.* (1895), p. 380.

[4] *Congregational Year Book* (1896), p. 78; *British Weekly*, 26 April 1894, p. 9.

by the founders of the Nottingham Society, to whom the attitude seemed typical of a sectarianism which had helped the churches to lose the masses. The group running the Nottingham P.S.A. wanted the movement to have no link whatever with particular sects. 'To our mind', said the *P.S.A. Magazine*, published in Nottingham,

> the connection of the P.S.A. with any denomination, tends to limit, to a great extent, its sphere of usefulness in attracting the lower classes. Distressing as it may be for us to acknowledge in the face of our boasted civilization, it is no use disguising the fact that there is a large class who cannot be induced to connect themselves, even indirectly, with a place of worship.[1]

It was implied here that P.S.A. Societies should not try to recruit worshippers for the churches, but should rather provide permanently an alternative form of worship suitable for the non-churchgoing classes.

Congregationalists or Wesleyans could easily agree that a P.S.A. Society must not appear to be the agent of a particular sect. A. H. Byles, the Congregational minister in charge of the Hanley Society, insisted on this point:

> There must be absolute freedom from all suspicion of any sectarian purpose . . . if we would gather in the outsider we must drop our denominationalism and even our church names, and speak to them only about 'the Kingdom of God and His righteousness'.[2]

At Leeds, Richard Westrope said that a P.S.A. Society, although affiliated to a local church, would not succeed unless it was 'autonomous in constitution'.[3] But the Nottingham group were right to say that Byles saw P.S.A. work 'from a denominational standpoint.'[4] He preferred P.S.A. meetings to be held in churches rather than public halls, so that going inside a place of worship would become a familiar activity to members: the unsectarian atmosphere was part of the bait. Similarly Westrope's opinion that the P.S.A. Society should be separate from a church was offered in the course of a paper on 'The P.S.A. Movement: how best to gather its fruits'.

[1] *P.S.A. Magazine*, Dec. 1891, p. 4.
[2] A. H. Byles, *op. cit.* pp. 33–4.
[3] J. W. Dixon, *op. cit.* p. 15.
[4] *P.S.A. Magazine*, Dec. 1891, p. 4.

Unless the fruits could be gathered, the dalliance with pleasure could not easily be justified in many Nonconformist minds. Advocates of the P.S.A. principle said that the meetings were winning people – especially men – outside the normal social range of churches.[1] Byles declared that

> thousands of our working men, who belong to what are called 'the lapsed masses', are being drawn Sunday after Sunday . . . they are not ashamed to come in such clothes as they have, because they know that they will only meet with men, and men of their own class.[2]

A correspondent in the *British Weekly* in 1892 found in the movement 'a practical answer to the question that is now vexing the minds of our Churches – how to reach and influence the working men of our country.'[3] But was it *the churches* that were reaching them? One critic said that 'the sight of well-filled chapels, halls, or meeting rooms must indeed be an inspiration to those taking part in the entertainment – I beg pardon, *service*.'[4] The Congregational minister J. Guinness Rogers warned: 'it does not follow that everything which attracts the people is Divine. The question comes, "To what are they attracted, and what is the effect on them?" '[5] Was the P.S.A. movement a consecration of pleasure in the service of religion, or a corrosion of religion by pleasure?

When Byles and other leaders of the movement were challenged about the fruits of membership, they said in general terms that people attracted to their meetings often passed on to attend formal worship. But lacking direct evidence that P.S.A. meetings supplied many recruits for normal services, and believing that the mixture of entertainment and undenominational uplift given by the societies was no satisfactory substitute for worship, the leaders of Nonconformity were never quite able to look on the experiment without suspicion. The Wesleyan Conference warned members in 1895 that 'as popular services, they

[1] A Congregational minister in London, however, abandoned a P.S.A. service when he found that all who attended it came from other churches. C. Booth, *Life and Labour of the People in London*, 3rd. series, *Religious Influences* (1902), VII. 154.

[2] A. H. Byles, *op. cit.* pp. 3–4, 9.

[3] C. K. Sykes in *British Weekly*, 17 Nov. 1892, p. 60.

[4] *P.S.A. Magazine*, Dec. 1891, p. 6.

[5] J. G. Rogers, *The Forward Movement of the Christian Church* (1893), p. 4.

[Pleasant Sunday Afternoons] are not without dangers, against which we bid you to be on your guard. It is possible to attempt to brighten the hours of the day of rest at the expense of its sacredness.'[1] Wesleyans were directed by the conference to encourage P.S.A. Societies so long as Wesleyans led them and they followed forms of organization prescribed to keep them safely close to the church.[2] Behind this advice was the twofold wish that the P.S.A. meeting would be made like a religious service and that its members would graduate to attending ordinary Wesleyan worship. The people who conducted the Nottingham P.S.A. believed this impossible. The Wesleyans were replying that on no other terms could the movement earn the support of Methodists.

In 1894, the year before this declaration of policy, G. S. Barrett discussed the P.S.A. movement in his chairman's address to the Congregational Union. He expressed both a fear that it might 'degenerate into mere amusement of the people', and an anxiety, not mentioned by the Wesleyans, that 'the addresses delivered may be so secularized as to become political or socialistic. . . .'[3] There was some evidence to justify his concern. A leader of the Nottingham P.S.A. Society said: 'sometimes temperance, or thrift, or good habits will form the theme; never politics.'[4] Elsewhere this ban was not always applied: the socialist orators Tom Mann and Caroline Martyn spoke at P.S.A. meetings on such subjects as 'Social Teachings of Christ'[5]. A suspicion that some of the societies were becoming vehicles for socialist propaganda hardly distinguishable from Labour Churches would not raise the P.S.A. movement in the eyes of Nonconformists who were uneasy about it already for other reasons.

As an attempt to attract working-class non-churchgoers by relaxing the puritan temper and by surrounding a mildly religious meeting with agencies for philanthropy and mutual aid, the P.S.A. movement had a number of local successes, especially in Midland towns. To the people who ran it – mostly Nonconformists – these successes appeared to depend on the Societies being free of formal association with any church. The

[1] *Wesleyan Conference Minutes* (1895), p. 380.
[2] *Ibid.* pp. 257–8.
[3] G. S. Barrett in *Congregational Year Book* (1895), p. 43.
[4] 'Pleasant Sunday Afternoons', *loc. cit.* p. 5.
[5] *Labour Leader*, 19 May (1894, p. 7.) *Labour Annual* (1896), p. 212.

more they insisted on this point, the more it seemed to leaders of the largest Nonconformist bodies that the movement, which could be justified only as a feeder to their worship, might become instead a rival to it. It is not profitable to ask whether the P.S.A. Societies would have had a wider and more durable success if more Nonconformists had supported them; for this support could have been won only by sacrificing the independence, the difference from conventional religion, which the leaders of the movement believed necessary for enlisting working-class members.

The Wesleyans

From the middle years of the century, according to a Wesleyan historian, Wesleyan Methodism entered its mahogany age. In these years, he writes, 'we got our mahogany pulpits and the preachers found their way to the mahogany tables of wealthy laymen.'[1] It was a common opinion at this time that the Wesleyans as a body were getting richer. 'Methodists,' said a leading Wesleyan minister in 1855,'. . . have gratefully to acknowledge their full share in the steady prosperity of the country. . . .'[2] The rich laymen who gave largely to their church were given large respect by their fellows. In 1856 one of the leading ministers of his generation, James Rigg, went to the Stockport circuit, which his biographer described – because it contained such rich people – as 'the most important to which he had yet been appointed.' His mother said that he was now working 'among the elite of Methodism,' including some whom the biographer called 'Methodist princes'.[3] By 1880 there were Wesleyan baronets, many Wesleyan members of parliament, and even a Wesleyan Lord Mayor of London.[4] Some of Wesley's successors worried, as he had, about the effect of riches on his people. 'What a host of noble lay members,' wrote a minister in 1866, 'have proved that "godliness is profitable to all things" . . .' but he doubted whether this was wholly gain:

[1] A. W. Harrison in A. W. Harrison and others, *The Methodist Church* (1932), pp. 68, 72.
[2] C. Prest, *The Home-Work of Wesleyan Methodism* (1855), p. 19.
[3] J. Telford, *The Life of James Harrison Rigg* (1910), p. 107.
[4] William McArthur. He was knighted in 1882.

'Gold comes in at one door, and Grace is driven out at another.'[1] This minister blamed the 'style of worldly conformity and worldly bearing' among Wesleyans for the absence of poor people from their worship. But as a body the Wesleyans were proud of their prosperity. 'No church,' said a semi-official Wesleyan publication in 1879, 'possesses a more liberal and a more active body of laymen. With their munificence they combine intelligence, zeal, and activity in relation to the agencies of the Church.'[2] In the previous year, laymen had been admitted for the first time to a place in the Conference which governed the Church. At the end of the century a Wesleyan baronet looked around him and said with satisfaction: 'The Methodist people are said to be a thrifty, saving, and sober people; we know that many of them are captains of industry in the great commercial life of the land. Some of them are millionaires. . . . Methodist laymen now have their mansions, equipages, and domains in various parts of the land.'[3] This news might not have pleased the founder of Methodism. But the reformers in the Forward Movement were less troubled about the great riches of a few than about the moderate comfort of the many. 'It is evident at once,' said Hugh Price Hughes' paper the *Methodist Times* in 1886, 'that Methodism has been much too exclusively the sect of the lower middle class.'[4] In 1897 Hughes' journal deplored the rule of 'shopocracy' in Methodism, and declared: 'we make the pulpit and the pew too much a middle-class monopoly.'[5]

When the report on the census of religious worship was published in 1854, Wesleyans were exhorted to help their ministers 'penetrate the neglected masses of the heathenish population of our large cities.'[6] The Wesleyan Conference resolved upon 'reviving and sustaining the Home Missionary spirit of Methodism,' and to this end established a 'Home Mission and Contingent Fund, for the SUPPORT and SPREAD

[1] 'A Wesleyan Minister', *Temporal Prosperity and Spiritual Decline* (1866), pp. 16, 18.

[2] *Methodism in 1879* (1879), p. 161. A list of some thirty prominent laymen follows.

[3] Sir Robert Perks, in *Methodist Recorder*, 3 Feb. 1898, p. 4.

[4] *Methodist Times*, 19 Aug. 1886, p. 557.

[5] *Ibid.* 4 Feb. 1897, p. 65.

[6] *Wesleyan Conference Minutes* (1854), p. 180.

of the Gospel in Great Britain and Ireland'.[1] The minister in charge of this fund, Charles Prest, believed that 'to meet and remove the spiritual destitution and distressing apathy of the population' was 'the first and *greatest* duty of our times . . .' and held this to be a more pressing duty than the quest for heathen converts abroad.[2] The work conducted by him was not, however, pioneering. He laboured simply to stir in Wesleyans, and to organize efficiently, the sort of energy for evangelizing the multitude which had been aroused already among other groups of Christians. The home missionaries, most of whom were ministers freed from circuit work, were instructed to do what agents of similar bodies had long been doing. They were to visit every house in their district. They were to read the scriptures to people and pray with them, emphasizing in prayer and conversation the doctrines of sin and salvation. They were to hold regular public worship, preach in the open air, hand out tracts, visit the sick and dying, and give what philanthropic aid they could. Although controversy must be avoided, sin should be reproved 'faithfully, but prudently and affectionately . . . especially profaneness, intemperance, and Sabbath-breaking.'[3] A historian of Wesleyan Methodism reported in 1862 that the efforts of the home missionaries had been 'great and praiseworthy', but he did not pretend that they had yet got far. 'The heathenism of our home population has never yet been adequately exposed,' he wrote. The Wesleyan response was 'as yet in its infancy, and requires considerable improvement before it can be regarded as a permanent institution in Methodism.'[4] As president of the Conference, Charles Prest warned his brothers that the rise of population was outstripping all the efforts of home missionaries.[5] Certainly the scale of work was not spectacular. By 1866, when there were 53 home missionaries at work, the total expenditure of the Home Mission and Contingent Fund (which served several other purposes as well as home missions) was just under £21,000.

[1] *Ibid.* p. 179; *ibid.* (1856), p. 266. The Contingent Fund was over a century old. On its purpose see H. W. Williams, *The Constitution and Polity of Wesleyan Methodism* (1881), p. 125.

[2] C. Prest, *Fourteen Letters on the Home-Work of Wesleyan Methodism* (1856), p. 5.

[3] *Wesleyan Conference Minutes* (1878), p. 224.

[4] G. Smith, *History of Wesleyan Methodism*, III (1862), pp. 495, 517–8.

[5] C. Prest, *A Charge* (1863), p. 33.

A minister who disliked the ecclesiastical style of the new chapels – or churches, as they were now likely to be called – rising in the suburbs of every city, calculated that for the cost of one new tower or spire, five home missionaries could have been supported for a year.[1] A survey of Methodism in 1879 admitted frankly that 'the home missionary machinery is not adequate to the crying necessities of the time.'[2] Its resources were not only slender; they were also being diverted in large part to arrest the decline of Methodism in villages rather than to attack the neglect of worship in large towns. In 1880 the district around Oxford received a grant from the home missionary fund equal to those given for Manchester, Bolton and Liverpool together. 'Our Home Missionary operations are conducted with vigour, so far as the funds at disposal permit,' said the Conference in 1884.[3] Had the Conference wished, money for this purpose might have been taken out of the Thanksgiving Fund, launched in 1878, to which nearly £300,000 was contributed by 1883. But although the task of reaching the masses was given verbal blessing in annual addresses, the Home Mission and Contingent Fund received only £21,000 from the Thanksgiving Fund, of which at most £9,000 was used for evangelistic work, including £4,000 set aside for activity among soldiers and sailors. The work of the Home Missionary Committee was hardly affected by the mood of *The Bitter Cry* or the energy of the Forward Movement. It was never more than a token gesture towards 'the spiritual destitution and distressing apathy' which it was supposed to help remove.

Nor, until 1885, were the Wesleyans confronting the unchurched masses by any other systematic means. The Conference, as always, blessed all efforts at 'revival'; but revivals in the old Methodist manner, spontaneous and contagious waves of enthusiasm, had become rare among the Wesleyans when, as a minister put it, 'what was once a living, glowing mass of individual activities crystallized into a vast ecclesiastical organization.'[4] Moody's crowded meetings were welcomed and

[1] 'A Wesleyan Minister', *Temporal Prosperity and Spiritual Decline*, p. 124.

[2] *Methodism in 1879*, p. 129.

[3] *Wesleyan Conference Minutes* (1884), p. 310.

[4] 'A Wesleyan Minister', in *British Weekly*, 8 April 1887. R. F. Wearmouth, *Methodism and the Struggle of the Working Classes, 1850–1900*, pp. 126–7, mentions several Wesleyan revivals of the old type after 1850, but none after 1860.

imitated by the Wesleyans, who held 'revival missions' in Halifax, Bradford, Birmingham and Liverpool. These were not unforeseen outpourings in the old style, but calculated drives – 'combined and well-organized efforts,' the Conference called them, 'to bring the Gospel to bear upon the unsaved multitudes. . . .'[1] The Wesleyans had no machinery in the cities, however, by which such activity could be maintained and its fruits, if any, reaped.[2] To Hugh Price Hughes and his friends, who became vehement on the matter in the 'eighties, it seemed that their church was conducting a mere guerrilla campaign against the neglect of worship. They tried to persuade the ministry at large that the polity of Methodism was inadequate to the facts of urban life.

The pastoral and evangelistic organization of Methodism rested first on the circuit, a unit comprising a number of societies and congregations and served by several ministers under a superintendent; and secondly on the itinerancy – the custom, which Wesley made binding on his successors, by which no minister could be appointed to the same place for longer than three years.[3] The circuit was a device for distributing the services of a given number of ministers throughout a much greater number of congregations. When a minister could not be present, a local lay preacher took the service. One task of the superintendent minister in each circuit was to draw up his circuit plan so that every body of worshippers was visited as often as possible by an ordained preacher. The system also expressed Wesley's belief that no minister should strike roots in one particular place and thus forget that the world was his parish. The itinerancy was an institution with this same purpose – one dear to Wesley, whose own life was one long itinerancy.

Ministers carrying the gospel among non-worshippers in great cities found that the circuit and the itinerancy hindered them. In Liverpool a minister dismissed both in one sentence: 'No man can win the confidence and love of poor fallen people

[1] *Wesleyan Conference Minutes* (1876), p. 227.

[2] Before 1880 the only missionary organization in London recognized by the Wesleyan Conference was a small body known as the Metropolitan Lay Mission.

[3] See H. W. Williams, *op. cit.* pp. 51–5. There were certain exceptions of long standing, such as the provision (1836) that ministers in connexional offices could remain for six years.

who only appears in the same pulpit once a month in the morning, and once a month in the evening, and that for the short space of three years.'[1] A Wesleyan with experience in Spitalfields said that the inhabitants of such a district 'care next to nothing for the ministerial office – their regard is almost purely personal'; and that a minister should therefore stay among them for at least ten years so that he and the people could get to know each other.[2] Ministers who had seen large central chapels decline as members left for the suburbs often suggested that they should be detached from ordinary circuits and organized as mission stations. It was even alleged that some circuit officials in London discouraged the missionary activity of their own denomination when in their judgment it came too near existing chapels.[3]

Wesleyans critical of the circuit and the itinerancy found a ready vehicle for their views in Hugh Price Hughes' weekly, the *Methodist Times*. 'The circuit system,' said that journal in 1886, 'has, for purposes of effective aggression, completely broken down in all the great cities.'[4] When arguing that the principle of triennial itinerancy should be relaxed in special cases, Hughes pleaded 'that Methodism was not now a rural system, as England was not now a rural nation.'[5] Only forty years earlier Jabez Bunting had insisted that Methodism *was* a rural system. He was here contradicted by the minister who was as clearly the natural leader of the Wesleyans by 1900 as Bunting had been in his own prime.

Hughes' proposal to modify the three-year rule was resisted strongly by James Harrison Rigg, a late and formidable representative of the Bunting tradition, who feared that unless the old institutions were preserved intact, the Methodist system might fall to pieces.[6] But men younger than Rigg who had a more direct knowledge of conditions in large towns agreed with Hughes that however adequately the itinerancy and the circuit served areas where Methodism was thriving, it had to be amended where their work was missionary.

[1] Charles Garrett, in *Methodist Times*, 29 April 1886, p. 278.
[2] W. A. McArthur, in *ibid.*, 1 Jan. 1885, p. 4.
[3] *Ibid.*, 27 May 1886, p. 341.
[4] *Ibid.*, 30 Sept. 1886, p. 653.
[5] *British Weekly*, 8 Aug. 1895, p. 243.
[6] *Ibid.*

Like Churchmen dissatisfied with the parochial system, they were saying that the machinery of the church pastoral was not adequate for the work of the church militant.

In 1885 the Wesleyan Conference permitted certain densely populated areas in London to be exempted from the circuit and itinerancy rules. Five years later the conference rejoiced that in a number of large towns, ministers and laymen from different circuits had formed committees 'for the purpose of united action in such evangelistic and aggressive work as can best be carried out by a union of the forces of several Circuits.'[1] This was simply an attempt to co-ordinate the activities of different circuits, involving no interference with the orthodox disposition of ministers within a circuit. Even in allowing such a cautious change, the Conference reminded Methodists that the circuit remained the primary factor in their church organization, on which all other institutions depended. In 1895 Hughes' proposal for relaxing the itinerancy rule was accepted by the Conference, but with a rider which showed a wide sympathy among the Wesleyans for Rigg's conviction that the general principle of itinerancy must be protected.

In 1885 the Conference authorized the first of several missionary innovations which embodied, as Home Missionary operations did not, the spirit of the Forward Movement. The foundation of the London Wesleyan Mission was described by Hugh Price Hughes' paper as 'probably the most significant and important event in the modern history of Methodism.'[2] The journal had urged such a mission from its first issue. Its appearance was a triumph for Hughes and his supporters over those who believed that the experiment was a slight to Methodists already at work in London and a threat to existing home missionary activity in villages and elsewhere.

The official object of the London Wesleyan Mission was 'To carry the Gospel to such regions of London, and especially of Central London, as are most spiritually destitute and degraded.'[3] Announcing the plan in 1885, the Conference agreed to raise £50,000 for the Mission – far more than had ever been available for the entire home missionary activity of the church.

[1] *Wesleyan Conference Minutes* (1890), p. 243.
[2] *Methodist Times*, 12 March 1885, p. 161.
[3] *Wesleyan Conference Minutes* (1885), p. 228.

By means of abnormal, missionary organization, it was hoped to make the services in central chapels more attractive to poor people. The small respectable congregations in such chapels, hanging on after most of their kind had left for the suburbs, did not always like their places of worship being taken over for missionary purposes: the residue of a middle-class congregation in St George's-in-the-East so resented their chapel being put under the authority of the London Mission that they left for more fashionable chapels farther out.[1]

The methods of the London Mission may be illustrated by a glance at one of its four parts, the Central London section, situated in Clerkenwell. It was conducted by Edward Smith, a minister with a long experience of preaching to the poor and an orthodox evangelical view of the world. 'In preaching,' wrote Smith, 'my great aim is to help the Divine Spirit to produce conviction of sin among the ungodly.' His services were simpler than ordinary Wesleyan services; and bolder devices – tickets handed around gin shops, advertising boards carried by lay helpers – were used to announce them. Smith approved the movement to offer consecrated pleasure to the poor, and ran weekly 'Pleasant Evenings for the People' at which lectures and sentimental ballads alternated with more solemn items, 'arranged,' he said, 'with the idea of sandwiching the educational between the interesting, the sacred between the secular.'[2] The Pleasant Evenings came into a category of activities which Smith described as social, and which included a brass band, a temperance meeting, and societies intended to keep working-class people out of mischief, to civilize them, and to coax them towards worship. No free food or charitable aid of any other sort was offered. None of the Mission's techniques was really original, and some had been anticipated by the Salvation Army, whose example after 1880 affected most evangelistic work in large towns. But much that was done at the London Mission was novel for Wesleyans. It was carried out by means of an organization in which the circuit system had no part, and led by ministers exempt from the itinerancy rule.

Just before the Conference authorized the London Mission, it expressed concern also about the problem of central chapels

[1] R. B. Thompson, *Peter Thompson* (1910), p. 40.
[2] E. Smith, *Three Years in Central London* (1889), pp. 73, 81.

in other large towns which had been deserted by their seat-holders and which were surrounded by 'dense populations living in vice and indifference. . . .'[1] Outside London, Manchester was the first large town in which the Wesleyans acted on their new concern about the plight of central chapels. The chapel in Oldham Street, the oldest Wesleyan chapel in Manchester, had long been deserted by the 'many families of wealth and intelligence' whom a minister had found there early in the century.[2] Its last service was held in February 1883. It was then pulled down, and in 1887 a new building, called a Central Hall, was opened on the site. This hall had no pews. It was planned to accommodate secular, week-night clubs and meetings as well as Sunday worship. The word 'Wesleyan' did not appear in its name, nor was it called a church. 'It shows,' wrote the *British Weekly*, 'that the Wesleyans are alive to the necessity of adapting means to ends, and going forth, as it were, heart and soul to the masses, who do not and will not attend ordinary "church" or "chapel" services.'[3] The Central Hall was made the base for a mission which operated throughout working-class Manchester.

The central mission system was adopted for several other large towns after 1890, and by the first years of the new century Wesleyans accepted it as the appropriate response to the challenge of urban working-class districts. By 1909 there were 41 central halls and mission centres in England. Gifts of money from interested laymen had helped to promote this extension. One man gave £5,000 towards a central hall in Bolton; the special interest of Joseph Rank, a Wesleyan millionaire, was given in *Who's Who* as 'erecting mission halls'; and the rich Wesleyan solicitor Sir Robert Perks, proposing a special fund to greet the new century, suggested that a large proportion of it should be spent on central halls.[4]

Lay help was important for the central missions, as for all

[1] *Wesleyan Conference Minutes* (1884), p. 282. The composition of the committee set up on this subject shows which towns the Conference had in mind. It represented the following Wesleyan Districts: first, second and third London, Bristol, Birmingham and Shrewsbury, Liverpool, Manchester, Bolton, Halifax and Bradford, Leeds, Hull, Sheffield, and Newcastle-on-Tyne.

[2] T. Jackson, *Recollections of My Own Life and Times* (1873), p. 176.

[3] *British Weekly*, 25 Feb. 1887, p. 2.

[4] *Wesleyan Conference Minutes* (1900), p. 514.

the work of a church which in 1900 had (in Great Britain) 2,152 ordained ministers and 19,956 lay preachers. In London and Manchester the missions each absorbed an older lay mission. The Bermondsey Settlement, opened in 1892 and responsible to the Wesleyan Conference, invited young educated laymen to live among the London poor. The habit of 'slumming', for which the Bermondsey Settlement gave a formal opportunity, was also indulged elsewhere on local initiative: in Sheffield a historian of Methodism described 'the eager spirits of consecrated men and women' making their way on behalf of the church 'into the purlieus of poverty, vice, and crime. . . .'[1] For lay women Hugh Price Hughes invented a new Methodist institution, the sisterhood – 'the term "Sister",' as Mrs Hughes explained carefully, 'being used in its human and democratic sense, and not with an ecclesiastical signification.'[2] By 1891, fifty sisters were working for the London Mission.

It was characteristic of Wesleyan missions that Hughes and his wife should have recruited their sisterhood from women who were ladies. 'Without any thought of disparagement for the services rendered by humble women in the past as Bible-women, city missionaries, etc.,' wrote Mrs Hughes,

> we felt the time was come when women who had received the inestimable privileges of education and culture, were called to devote those great gifts to the service of the Church, and that they would be able to do a kind of work impossible to others.[3]

Edward Smith, of the East London Mission, was quite emphatic that he did not want to make a working-class church. 'To attract and keep middle-class families was part of my design,' he explained, 'They are valuable in performing functions which working-class people could not manage.' The humble poor, he believed, were 'best reached by those who are slightly superior to them in social life.'[4] A writer in the *Methodist Times* spoke similarly of East London, where he believed a minister should 'aim not only at the working classes, for if he is to have success

[1] J. J. Graham, *A History of Wesleyan Methodism in Sheffield Park, Sheffield* (Sheffield, 1914), p. 173.
[2] D. P. Hughes, *The Life of Hugh Price Hughes* (1904), p. 201.
[3] *Ibid.*
[4] E. Smith, *op. cit.* pp. 45–6.

with them, he must have success with their natural leaders.'[1] It was no part of the Wesleyan theory of urban missions to build up – as some in the Church of England were trying to do and as the Salvation Army did – a body of evangelists from the same social strata as the non-worshippers. The Wesleyans assumed that working-class people were incapable of finding satisfactory leaders from among themselves. It was an assumption which came easily to people many of whom were themselves removed by only a couple of generations from the ruck, and who could conclude from a study of their own family history that the natural leaders born among the working classes had lifted themselves by now to higher rungs of the ladder, leaving behind the naturally led.

The central missions made Wesleyan aggression among the urban working classes more lively than it had been at any time during the century. By 1900 it was claimed that the Manchester mission was attracting to its twelve branches more than 14,000 people, 'mostly of the non-churchgoing class.'[2] In Birmingham, a Congregational minister said in 1896 that the new Wesleyan mission was touching 'a class of population which no other religious body, with the exception of the Salvation Army, has ever reached.'[3] The London Mission was said to have recruited 7,000 new members by 1898, and to be attended by some 20,000 other people.[4] Nobody imagined, however, that these achievements had reduced the proportion of non-worshippers in England. Moreover, the most ambitious of the missions, in London, scarcely expanded its work between 1890 and 1900, despite the appointment of a commission to plan a more systematic Wesleyan attack on the city. An appeal for £100,000 on behalf of the mission was set aside in 1898 in favour of the connexional Twentieth Century Fund. Nor had the London mission anywhere built up the self-supporting churches which the minister in charge in East London believed to be its ultimate aim.

While Hughes and his friends were building the central missions they were also trying to abolish the renting of pews,

[1] G. Lidgett, in *Methodist Times*, 4 June 1885, p. 354.
[2] J. F. Hurst, *The History of Methodism* (1901), III. 1438.
[3] J. H. Jowett, in *British Weekly*, 13 Feb. 1896, p. 282.
[4] J. F. Hurst, *op. cit.* III. 1441.

which despite John Wesley's vehement opposition was as normal among Wesleyans as in the Church of England.[1] Jabez Bunting believed the custom inevitable for a church without endowments. 'Voluntaryism,' he said, 'cannot, or will not, dispense with pew-rents. . . .'[2] William Booth, the future creator of the Salvation Army, learned as a young lay preacher for the Wesleyans in Nottingham during the 'forties how the pew system divided worshippers according to their station. When he rounded up a band of slum youths and led them to chapel, he was rebuked for taking them in the front door and sitting them in the pews; next time, he was told, he should bring them by a back door (invisible behind the pulpit) and sit them on the benches reserved for the poor.[3] Not until the 'eighties was there a campaign against the practice among Wesleyans comparable with the one being waged in the Church of England. When the designers of the London Mission in 1885 urged that mission chapels should be seated throughout with open benches, the Conference resolved merely that in old central chapels, 'a larger number of free seats, comfortable and easily accessible, should be provided. . . .'[4] In chapels where the inhabitants were poor, the Conference said in 1887, pew rents should be reduced as far as possible, and good free seats marked 'For visitors.' If a building was used entirely as a mission chapel, the Conference suggested that it might be as well to free all seats. Rents were in fact retained at the Central London Mission on the ground that they were financially necessary. Some reforms were made, however. The doors to pews were removed, the tariff was reduced by a quarter, and pews were declared open if the seat-holders had not arrived when a service was due to begin. In the new central halls at Manchester and elsewhere, which had no established pew-holders to placate and which were financed out of special funds, all seats were free and unappropriated. A weekly offering was collected in some chapels. The Conference appointed a committee to study the system in 1887, and two years later expressed cautious approval – but as a method of supplementing

[1] For Wesley's opposition see his *Journal*, 21 and 24 Dec. 1787.
[2] T. P. Bunting and G. S. Rowe, *The Life of Jabez Bunting*, II (1887), p. 122.
[3] H. Begbie, *The Life of William Booth* (1920), I. 71.
[4] *Wesleyan Conference Minutes* (1885), p. 265.

pew rents, not as a substitute. At the same time the Conference gave mild encouragement to Wesleyans who wanted to abandon rents, by rescinding an old rule that no chapel without pew rents could have an interest-free loan from the connexional Chapel Fund. But in chapels belonging to the circuit system as well as in some mission chapels, pew rents were still customary in 1900. There was far more tolerance of the system among Wesleyans than in the Church of England, and more than in Congregationalism.

It may be that Wesleyans were more anxious than Churchmen or Congregationalists not to antagonize seat-holders. Wesleyans always had a more precise and comprehensive statistical picture of their own strength than did either of the other bodies. Each year the Conference knew how membership figures compared with those of twelve months ago; the Church of England had only annual confirmation figures, which were not nearly as useful, and Congregationalists had no accurate knowledge of membership until the very end of the century. Probably Wesleyans were losing no more supporters than their rivals; but they alone knew just how large was the loss. It reminded their leaders that the fate of Methodism depended on keeping the people already within the fold as well as on attracting outsiders. The two tasks might demand conflicting policies, especially on such an issue as pew rents.

The Wesleyans' numbers, reduced by schism in 1849, rose from the 'fifties to the 'seventies and then stopped. Between 1877 and 1880 the number of members in Great Britain fell from 382,289 to 376, 678. The Conference spoke grimly of these ominous figures in its annual address. The president, Ebenezer Jenkins, expressed dismay. 'If our system will not admit of the freest evangelical action,' he said, 'if it so hedge up our way as to impede our direct access to the masses . . . then either we are building unwisely, or, with the old designation of Methodism upon us, we are becoming something else and allowing other people to do Methodist work for us.'[1] By 'other people' he may have meant the Salvation Army, now enjoying its first burst of success. To all Christians William Booth's Army was a challenge, but to Methodists it was a rebuke: for Booth was a man who had found that Methodist organization and manners

[1] *Ibid.* (1880), p. 275.

imprisoned his evangelical ardour, and early triumphs of the Army up and down England encouraged in Methodist leaders a mood of self-criticism in which they questioned not only the zeal of individuals but the efficacy of institutions. Wesleyan membership rose in the 'eighties, but more slowly than the population. In 1890 it was officially reported that 131,754 members had fallen away (in addition to those who had died or emigrated) in the previous five years.[1] The losses were easier to count than to explain. One cause recognized by the Conference was internal migration. Methodism in villages was declining as the inhabitants drifted to large towns, and like many rural-born immigrants before them the newcomers often failed in the town to join the church to which they had previously belonged. Possibly, as some believed, too few chapels were being built to keep up with an expanding and moving population; but the rate of building was considerable. In London the Metropolitan Chapel Building Fund helped to provide 78 new chapels between 1861 and 1885. It was calculated in 1909 that over the whole country an average of more than two new chapels every week had been built in the past fifty years, and that more than £200,000 a year had been spent on new chapels in the same period.[2] Although a local demand for accommodation may occasionally have gone unmet, a group of Wesleyans who wanted a chapel could usually afford to build it.

The health of Methodism rested in the long run on the ability of its members to find fellowship together. Methodists met not only as congregations on Sunday but as societies during the week; and a Methodist society, John and Charles Wesley had said, was

> a company of men having the form, and seeking the power, of godliness; united in order to pray together, to receive the word of exhortation, and to watch over one another in love, that they may help each other to work out their salvation.[3]

The special means for nurturing this fellowship was the weekly class meeting into which members of each society were divided under leaders. But was the class meeting always

[1] *Ibid.* (1890), p. 349.

[2] W. J. Townsend and others, *A New History of Methodism* (1909), I. 468.

[3] The first rules, 1743, quoted in H. W. Williams, *The Constitution and Polity of Wesleyan Methodism* [1881], pp. 1–2.

what it purported to be? In debates about the loss of members, some Wesleyans were arguing by 1880 that it was not, and that regular attendance at a class meeting should be no longer required as a condition of membership. Such a change in the rules was always resisted by a majority in the Conference. When James Harrison Rigg, one of the most respected men in the ministry, defended the class-meeting late in his long life he spoke of the church as 'a contexture, a web of such class-meetings', each of them not only preserving the zeal of established members, but sealing, fixing and perpetuating the awakening and converting influence of preaching to the masses.'[1] The class-meeting was thus supposed to foster fellowship in general and to help bind working-class recruits into the Wesleyan community. It was an eloquent account, but not, at the end of the nineteenth century, a very accurate one. Many Wesleyans were nevertheless reluctant to lower the status of the class-meeting not because they imagined it to be working satisfactorily but because they believed that a church without it would not be truly Methodist. Like Churchmen determined not to discard the parochial system, they feared that radical change could threaten their denominational identity. As a committee appointed by the Conference to consider the class-meeting said in 1889, it was 'not a limb which can be removed without endangering the vital organs, but is the very heart of the system. . . .'[2]

Many people in fact stayed away from class-meetings for long periods without being expelled. A minister who believed that many class-meetings were incompetently run and 'marked by formality and routine' observed in 1898 that 'multitudes ceased to meet in class because they do not find it helpful.'[3] The places where Wesleyans now claimed success in reaching the working classes were those in which special missionary organization, not including the class-meeting, was used.

In 1898 the Conference admitted that despite the efforts of the new missions in large towns, 'the mass of irreligion and indifference at our doors shows little sign of disintegration and

[1] J. H. Rigg, *The Class-Meeting Fellowship of Wesleyan Methodism* (1907), pp. 11, 18.

[2] *Wesleyan Conference Minutes* (1889), p. 407.

[3] T. F. Rawlings, *The Leakage of Methodism* (1898), p. 10.

abatement. . . .'[1] The leaders of Wesleyan Methodism did not believe that their hold on the working classes was strong. It could nevertheless appear a great opportunity for Methodism that other churches had done no better. In 1899 the editor of the Wesleyan *London Quarterly Review,* who had been editor of the *Wesleyan Methodist Magazine* and a president of the Conference, declared: 'the supreme question is, Who shall capture the unconverted millions, the seventy-five per cent of the population outside any place of worship?' The Church which could gain 'the suffrage of the outside population' would, he believed, be the victorious one. 'Which of the religious denominations will secure this suffrage by bringing the godless multitude into the fellowship of Christ? . . . Has not God fashioned Methodism for this hour?'[2]

The Congregationalists

The leaders of Congregationalism were proud of having firm roots in middle-class prosperity. 'We regard it as a significant and cheering fact,' said the Rev. Eliezer Jones in 1852, 'that we number in our ranks so large a proportion of the middle classes of this country, the backbone and sinew of its strength and probity, of its intelligence and industry.'[3] Independents were prominent among the people into whose hands the industrial and commercial wealth of England was flowing. A Nonconformist writing of Lancashire in 1869 noted that 'in the more important towns they have collected larger and more influential congregations.'[4] In Manchester as a young pastor, Joseph Parker preached in 1858 to a congregation in which, he remembered later, 'every man seemed to be looking at me over the top of a money-bag.'[5] These, 'the Congregational millionaires of Cavendish Street Chapel', were unusually rich for their sect; Parker believed that his salary of £425 was higher than any Independent minister had ever before received. But money-bags were common enough equipment for Independents elsewhere; 'as a community,' said a speaker to an

[1] *Wesleyan Conference Minutes* (1898), p. 427.
[2] 'The Mission of Methodism', *London Quarterly Review*, April 1899, pp. 355–6.
[3] *Congregational Year Book* (1853), p. 85.
[4] R. Halley, *Lancashire, its Puritanism and Nonconformity* (1869), II. 497.
[5] J. Parker, *A Preacher's Life* (1899), p. 143.

assembly of the Congregational Union in 1878, . . . our resources are mainly derived from trading transactions. . . .'[1] Three years later the chairman of the Union said that his own people were probably the wealthiest among English Nonconformists.[2] At Wolverhampton in 1891 the secularist lecturer F. W. Foote could raise a laugh by suggesting that the advice 'sell what thou hast, and give to the poor' was not followed by the leading Congregational minister in the town and the rich in his chapel.[3]

The princes of Independency gave generously to their churches. Profits from Joshua Wilson's silk, Francis Crossley's carpets, the Wills' tobacco and Titus Salt's alpaca found their way to the architects and builders of new chapels and the ministers who preached in them, and sometimes to Congregational and other evangelists among the poor. King among these princes was the knitting millionaire Samuel Morley. He was a Victorian Christian employer, tough but scrupulous; a proud embodiment of what he called 'the perseverance, the industry, the intelligence, and, I add unhesitatingly, the integrity, which, for the most part, distinguishes the trading and mercantile classes of England;[4] a Liberal, willing to allow the working classes to take part in politics and expecting them to remain upright and deferential; a campaigner for Nonconformist rights, insisting firmly but without bitterness that a gentleman was a gentleman whether a Churchman or not; and a devout Evangelical quite as anxious to spread gospel truth as to sell clothes. Before joining the campaign to consecrate pleasure at the Old Vic he had supported Moody and Sankey and helped William Booth when the founder of the Salvation Army was still struggling to run a mission in Whitechapel. There were deputations at his funeral in 1886 from nearly a hundred religious, philanthropic and political bodies. In his own denomination, which elected him to the chair of its Union the year he died, nobody worked more keenly to carry evangelical religion to the working classes.

A patriarchal employer of Morley's stamp might worship

[1] H. Lee, in *Congregational Year Book* (1879), p. 101.
[2] H. Allon, in *ibid.* (1882), p. 66.
[3] *Midland Wednesday News*, 3 June 1891, p. 4.
[4] E. Hodder, *The Life of Samuel Morley* (1887), p. 259.

together with the workmen whom he knew, without the difference of class between them causing any uneasiness. When James James died in Birmingham in 1852, his workmen, fellow-worshippers at the Carr's Lane Chapel, paid for a tablet to be set in the chapel wall 'as an expression of their gratitude and respect for his justice and kindness and considerateness as a master and as a proof that the operatives know how to acknowledge the excellence of their employers.' A gesture of such warmth was perhaps rare even in Birmingham, where relations between business men and working men were closer than in most other great towns; but there were doubtless many Congregational chapels like the one in Ashton-under-Lyne where J. Guinness Rogers was minister, and where the worshippers, he said, included 'working people', 'employers', and 'what may be regarded as the middle class,' each amicably represented among the deacons.[1] Where working people did attend Independent worship, they tended to be of what a visitor to a chapel in Birmingham called 'the better class'.[2] When the chairman of the Congregational Union in 1893, Albert Spicer, surveyed the social spectrum of Independency, he said: 'Our Churches . . . consist . . . for the most part of sections of the working, the lower middle, and middle classes, and they represent very largely the comparatively well-to-do side of these classes; they consist, if I may say so, of the "haves". . . .'[3] Most Independent chapels between 1850 and 1900 had no patriarch and few if any working men. 'Our congregations,' said a minister in 1872, 'belong for the most part to the *middle* middle classes.'[4] At an assembly of the Union in 1852 the Rev. Eliezer Jones expressed 'deep regret . . . that the artisans and working men of England are so rarely drawn within our circles.' He disagreed with people who spoke nostalgically about them. 'We question, indeed, if we have *lost* them,' he said, 'because it can hardly be said that *we* ever had them.'[5] Was the gap between the working classes and the kind of people sitting in Congregational churches nevertheless *widening*

[1] J. Guinness Rogers, *An Autobiography* (1903), p. 112. On class relations in Birmingham see A. Briggs, *History of Birmingham*, II. 6.
[2] J. A. Hammerton, in *Sunday Magazine*, Nov. 1898, p. 743.
[3] *Congregational Year Book* (1894), p. 37.
[4] J. Kennedy, in *ibid.* (1873), p. 86.
[5] E. Jones, in *ibid.* (1853), p. 85.

after 1850? Some thought so. The committee of the Union in 1865 could speak of 'working men and other classes of persons beyond our denominational line. . . .'[1] It appeared to some that increases in prosperity and in the physical separation of classes had made the obstacles to evangelism larger, and that although Independent leaders might be anxious to reach the masses the atmosphere in congregations was making it harder to do so. This was the opinion of the minister who addressed an assembly of the Union in 1876 on the 'tendency of Congregational churches to assume a sectional or class character.' Rich and poor Independents, he said, were tending to worship separately, so that the markings of social strata, far from being destroyed by a common church life, were made more obtrusive. This 'triumph of frost over fire, the power of the world over the spirit of the Gospel,' he could see most strikingly in towns with several Congregational churches; but he detected it also where there was only one church.

> The one community may show signs of separation into coteries. There may be the gallery and floor pews; the middle seats and the side aisles; the occupants of which, fellow-worshippers, declared 'members of one body' though they be, may be almost as far dissociated as if they never saw each other's face. That which would under other circumstances operate to the separate clustering of the people under different roofs, shows itself in the division of the one community into graduated sections.[2]

To gain new adherents for such churches from the social groups least disposed to attend worship would be no easy task.

Earlier in the century some Congregationalists had believed that God might wish them to minister to the middle classes, leaving poorer people to others. After 1850 this conviction was rarely expressed at assemblies of the Union. Discussions in that forum about the spiritual condition of the working classes became more frequent, and took place in a more sustained mood of self-criticism. Special meetings for working-men were instituted alongside the annual assembly of the Union, following the example set by the Church Congress. At the annual assembly in 1875, five of the addresses were about ways of reaching non-worshippers. 'Is it not, alas, far too true,' asked one speaker,

[1] J. Waddington, *Congregational History, 1850–1880* (1880), p. 480.
[2] D. J. Hamer, in *Congregational Year Book* (1877), pp. 148–9.

'that most distantly we have resembled Him whose tender eyes looked out upon the uncared-for multitude, and whose whole nature yearned over them with infinite compassion?'[1] This uneasiness arose in part from the knowledge that however vigorous the local and national life of Independency might appear, the denomination was really doing no more than hold its own. 'Concerning Congregational churches,' a minister said to the Union in 1873, 'our judgment must be based on the general confession of our pastors, that the work of genuine conversion is of slow and irregular occurrence.'[2] This anxiety and this earnest interest in evangelism were part of a general movement of opinion in the churches. Like Disraeli and Lowe, like Gladstone and Chamberlain, religious leaders were seeing now a new challenge in the working classes. 'Other classes,' wrote J. B. Paton a few years before Disraeli's Reform Bill, 'need equally to be evangelized, but the chief concernment of the Churches of Christ must ever be how to appeal most winningly and secure most safely that class which forms the great majority of every community.'[3] This was a normal theme in Independent oratory between 1870 and 1900, and especially in the sermons and writings of the men who contributed to the *British Weekly*.

Such men were shocked when R. W. Dale, the most honoured of Congregational ministers, revived the notion that the mission of Independency was not to the poor. In his younger days Dale had preached about the need to attract humble worshippers, and as chairman of the Union in 1869 he had expressed the hope of seeing 'a great army of preachers rise up among the working people themselves. . . .'[4] Now, in 1891, he surprised many of his brethren by agreeing with an American Independent who remarked in London that it had never been, and never would be, the special province of the Congregationalists to reach the lower classes. Like all Christians, Dale said, Congregationalists had a duty to the lowest; but this was not their special mission.

> The vigorous and the cultivated need salvation as well as the ignorant and the wretched. The intellect as well as the heart has to

[1] J. P. Allen, in *ibid.* (1876), p. 187.
[2] W. A. Essery, in *ibid.* (1874), p. 118.
[3] J. B. Paton, *Evangelization of Town and Country* (1863), p. 4.
[4] *Congregational Year Book* (1870), p. 66.

> be claimed for Christ, and it is the special duty of Congregationalists so to present the Christian gospel as to draw to Christ those who are never likely to be reached by the Salvation Army, and so to discipline them to the highest intellectual and ethical perfection.[1]

Dale had looked forward to a working-class army of evangelists, and now William Booth, so he thought, had provided one. Since the Salvation Army was ministering to the poor, Independency could devote itself with a clearer conscience to higher classes. A Wesleyan writer, agreeing that the mission of Independency was to the understanding, said that Dale himself had not been very successful as an evangelist to the poor, and that he was therefore 'an unconscious witness to his own contention touching the limitations of the ecclesiastical system in which he so fully believed.'[2] That was debatable. But Dale was certainly convinced that the passion to assault the unconverted, which the evangelical revival had stirred in Congregationalism, was now dead, and could not be resurrected because God did not repeat Himself.

To the *British Weekly*, representing a younger generation of Independents, what Dale said was monstrous:

> Our contention is that the policy recommended is directly anti-Christian; that the distinction on which it is based is fallacious; that the estimate of the Salvation Army on which it commits itself is at variance with the most notorious and glaring facts; and that finally the truth is one for all men. . . . The Congregationalist ministers of the future are not called to any apostolate of prigdom.[3]

The chairman of the Union in 1889, F. J. Falding, took a view like that of the *British Weekly*. 'As an assembly of our churches,' he said, 'we must consider if we are taking our part in evangelizing our population. . . . Have we not been too quiet, too respectable, too cold and conservative in our methods?'[4] Dale's own successor at Carr's Lane Church in Birmingham, J. H. Jowett, spoke similarly about the danger of Independency of becoming 'a middle-class and suburban denomination. . . . There has been a certain stiffness in our methods which will have to be relaxed before we can be in the truest sense a church of the

[1] A. W. W. Dale, *The Life of R. W. Dale* (1898), p. 613.
[2] *London Quarterly Review*, April 1899, p. 344.
[3] *British Weekly*, 27 Aug. 1891, p. 1.
[4] *Congregational Year Book* (1890), p. 34.

people.'[1] Morlais Jones, chairman of the Union in 1896, urged his brothers that they should 'let no one be able to say, when wealth recedes from a neighbourhood, "Congregationalism can live no longer here". . . .'[2]

In 1890 the most widely circulating monthly review, the *Nineteenth Century*, printed articles on 'The Weaknesses of Congregationalism' by a layman, B. P. Neuman, and a minister, T. H. Darlow.[3] As seen by these writers, Independency was fettered by the classes whom Dale wanted it to claim for Christ. Neuman asserted that 'the prevalence of the commercial spirit' was a cardinal weakness of Congregational communities, which often tried 'to apply to the Church of the living God precisely the rules and principles that govern a well-ordered retail business'. The harsh portrait of an Independent deacon, 'Tozer', in Mrs Oliphant's novel *Salem Chapel* (1863), seemed to Neuman lifelike. 'We can hardly help shuddering at Tozer,' he wrote, 'for do we not recognize him? Is he not the incarnation of our commercial system of church management?' Darlow expressed 'profound sympathy with both the spirit and substance' of Neuman's essay. To him if not to Dale the 'Congregational fondness for middle-class respectability' was a blight. Both men denounced the pew system. 'The building is not Christ's house,' said Neuman, 'but theirs who pay for a share of it.'

As in other churches, Congregational opinion on pews varied from the view that it protected the clean against intimacy with the dirty to the conviction that it was 'a disgusting arrangement.'[4] The most solid argument in favour of pew rents, as among the Wesleyans, was their inevitability in a voluntary church system. Another possible defence, which might appeal to laymen, was that under the pew system a minister could be paid by results. When Joseph Parker went to Manchester he was promised a bonus above his handsome salary if he could preach well enough to let all the pews. He did so.[5] Not until the 'seventies did the leaders of Congregationalism indicate as a body that they were unhappy about seating arrangements.

[1] *British Weekly*, 13 Feb. 1896, p. 282.
[2] *Congregational Year Book* (1897), pp. 30–1.
[3] *Nineteenth Century*, Oct. 1890, pp. 627–39.
[4] *British Quarterly Review*, 1854, p. 445.
[5] J. Parker, *A Preacher's Life*, p. 147.

Compared with the reformers in the Church of England, whose campaign provoked them, they were starting late; but they were well ahead of the Wesleyans. Among Congregational leaders there was support for the view that in new churches, weekly offerings should be relied on entirely to maintain the ministry and public worship, and that in existing churches, having pew rents 'which could not be altered without a conflict of opinion which it may not wish to provoke,' weekly offerings should be substituted as far as possible.[1]

Motions of the Congregational Union were not binding on particular churches. In the Church of England, opponents of pews might invoke points of law; but the Congregationalists could only plead. The articulate, the evangelistic, were convinced that rents should go; but they knew also that many of their adherents enjoyed the comfort and the proprietorial sense which renting a pew gave them. One opponent of the practice begged such people, if they were determined to hang on to their pews, at least to go out and 'lay violent hands morally' on some among the outcasts from worship and put them in their own seats; for 'to gather together the perishing and the lost, that they may be brought within reach of the bread of life and of the water of life, is a far loftier act of worship than any praying or psalm-singing. . . .'[2] But praying and psalm-singing, and listening to a sermon, were what the ordinary, unheroic adherents of Victorian churches understood by religious worship. The minority among the Independents, or in any other church, who were trying to bring in the multitude, would need unusual aid from Providence if their plans depended on first leavening the whole lump of their own worshippers.

Renting was attacked by Congregational leaders for the rest of the century, but remained normal practice. In particular chapels, ministers who believed that the pew system had driven away the workers persuaded congregations to abolish all appropriation of seats and to accept an offertory instead. Elsewhere, as at Carr's Lane, Birmingham, under J. H. Jowett, the custom was relaxed a little and all seats were declared vacant unless the holders arrived by a certain time. As on many other questions, Congregational statistics were silent about the

[1] *Congregational Year Book* (1875), p. 92.

[2] A. Common, in *ibid.* (1876), p. 130.

tenacity of the pew system; but in 1906 C. S. Horne, who knew Independency as well as anybody, could say: 'Nearly every chapel in the country is the victim of a mortal malady. . . . Shall I make myself understood if I say at once that the disease is – Pews? . . . Indeed, Congregationalists will boast of a church without creeds but a chapel without pews offends every sense of propriety.'[1]

The more conventional work of the Congregational Home Missionary Society did not conflict with any preference among members at large, and could be directed by an energetic few. In the 'fifties it was spending some £6,800 a year to keep agents in the field – most of them, however, at work in villages.[2] Samuel Morley, deciding that the Society was doing too little to win the masses, stepped in to stir it up and was appointed treasurer in 1858. He canvassed rich laymen to help its funds, and made it co-operate more closely with county and local Congregationalism. In Manchester and Bristol, institutions were opened in the 'sixties to train lay missionaries. Much of its resources, however, still went to help rural Independency, which like Methodism was suffering as the population ebbed from the countryside. 'In our English towns,' wrote a minister, J. B. Paton, in 1863, ' the establishment of Mission Churches is, alas! but seldom attempted.'[3] Church building went along for the most part independently of home missions. Thanks to the work of four building societies associated with the Congregational Union, to building done on local initiative and finance, and to a special fund in 1862 which raised £150,000, most of it used for building, several hundred new churches were opened between 1850 and 1880. Normally, however, they went up where congregations awaited them, not where they would be spearheads of evangelism. Even if they were quite near a population of poor non-worshippers, the members in a new church might ignore these neighbours; 'in close proximity to some of our largest churches,' J. B. Paton said, 'you will find haunts of heathenism that are little troubled by the missionary or purifying spirit of the Church.'[4]

[1] C. S. Horne, *The Institutional Church* (1906), pp. 21–3.

[2] A. Mearns, *England for Christ: a Record of the Congregational Church Aid and Home Missionary Society* (1886), p. 109.

[3] J. B. Paton, *op. cit.* p. 18.

[4] *Ibid.* p. 14.

The Home Missionary Society, on the other hand, appeared to act on the assumption that in the working-class territory of large towns its agents would be always invaders, without ever settling down to occupation. In the 'seventies some people decided that the assault on heathenism would be more effective if church building were undertaken as a missionary activity and if the work of home missionaries were directed towards making new churches. In 1878 both sorts of work became the responsibility of a single new body, the Congregational Church Aid and Home Missionary Society. Its foundation was greeted as a long step towards the union of separate congregations into a single national church. The impulse to overcome the Independent's traditional suspicion of central organization was explained in the Society's first report:

> The accord and the union of sporadic and isolated agency to which we have attained were not sought at the bidding of the spirit of centralization by which the age is said to be haunted, or out of envy of the elaborate ecclesiastical organizations which are around us, but solely with the view of making English Congregationalism more effective as a means of extending the kingdom of Christ in England.

Like Churchmen amending the parochial system and Wesleyans modifying the rules about circuits and itinerancy, the Congregationalists believed that they had been forced to take unusual measures by the 'abstention of multitudes from public worship.'[1]

The formal objects of the new Society were to help weaker churches, to plant and foster new churches where needed, and 'To provide for the preaching of the Gospel and other evangelistic work in spiritually destitute places.' The paint did not long stay fresh on this body. By 1882 its annual report was warning Congregationalists to expect only 'quiet, steady perseverence' from it, not 'any startling achievements'. Three years later, modesty had become disappointment: the committee of the Society declared that it had 'not been supported by the Churches as it ought to have been, and as, when it was founded, it was firmly believed it would be'.[2]

In 1895 the Church Aid and Home Missionary Society had

[1] J. Waddington, *op. cit.* p. 588.

[2] *Congregational Year Book* (1879), p. 29; (1883), p. 27; (1886), p. 33.

an income of £23,487, which it distributed thinly over 742 churches and 228 mission stations, in 36 counties. For evangelism in large towns the Society did almost nothing. The Committee admitted in 1893 that its work was mainly with village churches. 'The Society, through lack of resources, cannot yet to any great extent initiate movements of church extension in the densely populated districts of our large cities. . . .'[1] Nobody would have guessed from the Society's reports that it had been established to co-ordinate church extension and home missions. Despite statements of aggressive intention, the limited resources available for home missionary purposes were absorbed almost entirely in the countryside. The churchless multitude might have a great need of salvation, but they were unaware of it; the village churches, on the other hand, were importunate, and their plight was discussed whenever Congregationalists met to consider common problems. As J. B. Paton pointed out in 1897, the only permanent solution would be a national agricultural policy which reversed the drift from the land of the small farmers among whom the backbone of rural Congregationalism had been found.[2] The help given by the Church Aid and Home Missionary Society was no more than token, but it was enough to exhaust its funds.

In 1895 the committee of the Congregational Union confessed: 'the entire expenditure on Home Missions by our churches is inadequate to their claim upon us.'[3] After long negotiations it was now agreed to amalgamate the Church Aid and Home Missionary Society with the Congregational Union, and the committee of the latter expressed the hope that home missions would consequently prosper. It was tacitly accepted, however, that the Church Aid and Home Missionary Society would go on supplying mainly villages and small towns. Like the Wesleyan Home Missionary Committee, the Society never became a vigorous force in large towns.

As among the Wesleyans, there were individuals and bodies working outside the normal pastoral machinery of the church to reach non-worshippers. Their assumptions and methods pro-

[1] Church Aid and Home Missionary Society, *Fifteenth Annual Report* (1892–3), p. 23.

[2] *Congregational Year Book* (1898), pp. 78–86.

[3] *Ibid.*, 1896, p. 53.

bably differed more widely than within Methodism; for Congregationalism, essentially a federation of local communities, accommodated a greater variety of ideas and tastes. In Birmingham the Rev. Charles Leach claimed to draw 3,000 working-class people every Sunday afternoon at the Town Hall to hear sermons which were biblical and wholly orthodox, but were advertised sensationally and illustrated with novelties of technique which he described proudly in a pamphlet, *How I reached the masses* (1887). Leach believed (though his mind was to change later) that popular indifference could be overcome by salesmanship.[1] A very different approach was taken by the minister who concluded from his experience of special Sunday evening services for working men in Anerley, Kent, that it was wise to keep the sermon on secular affairs, and that the church most likely to attract the masses would be one free from all doctrinal tests.[2] In Bolton a minister and congregation pursued this belief even further and in 1892 constituted themselves a Labour Church.[3] Between these extremes of orthodox evangelism well-advertised, and innovations so drastic as to threaten the Congregational identity of a church, many ministers tried with more or less originality to attract the working classes. One notable example was R. F. Horton, the first Nonconformist ever to be elected to a fellowship at Oxford, who was minister at a church in Hampstead between 1884 and 1893. In his own church he set aside one Sunday a month for working-class people. Believing that missions like those of Moody and Sankey were valuable but too temporary in their effect on outsiders, and convinced that every minister should be his own missionary, Horton opened mission stations in Kentish Town and Cricklewood which he persuaded his congregation to pay for. Horton was once described as the man Matthew Arnold would have been if he had become a captain in the Salvation Army. With his zeal to convert the multitude went a sympathy for plans to improve their social condition. Both attitudes were part of a general resolution to make Independency a more vigorous force in the life of England.[4]

[1] See below, pp. 296–7, 301.
[2] *Christian World*, 10 March 1892.
[3] See below, pp. 227, 230.
[4] R. F. Horton, *An Autobiography* (2nd. ed., 1918), passim.

The problem of the urban working classes was discussed earnestly at assemblies of the Congregational Union between 1892 and 1895. In the latter year the Union received a report from a committee which it had authorized to map the strengths and weaknesses of Independency and to make recommendations about church extension. Since there were no figures of membership, the committee plotted carefully the distribution of accommodation. It found that over the whole country the proportion of sittings to population had dropped only slightly since 1851. Their distribution, however, was much less satisfactory. Congregationalists usually reckoned that they should supply a number of sittings equivalent to 5 per cent of the population. In large towns the figure was now well below 5 per cent; but near the centres of these towns the want was worshippers, not accommodation. The deserted central churches worried Congregationalists as they worried Wesleyans. This committee noted that these churches had decayed 'through an alteration in the quality of its residents, and through our failure to attract the later arrivals.' It was said that many of the central churches had now been sold and turned into business premises. The assembly of the Union greeted this report with a resolution affirming it 'a primary and imperative duty of the Churches of Jesus Christ to bring the Gospel within reach of all our fellow-countrymen', urging both local and national action, and directing that a central fund be launched for church extension.[1] By 1900 the grants from this fund amounted only to some £5,000 a year, and no attempt had been made to deal nationally with the problem of the empty central churches.

Congregationalists as a whole were less active than the Wesleyans in efforts during this period to evangelize the working classes. In both sects the ordinary machinery for home missions did little more than maintain village preachers; but in large towns the Wesleyans were far more active in devising abnormal methods for attracting the outsiders. Why should this have been so? One difference was that while the Wesleyans thought of themselves as a people who had risen since Wesley's day from poverty to middling prosperity, the Congregationalists saw their ancestors right back to the Commonwealth as continuously middle-class. A sense of responsibility towards the non-

[1] *Congregational Year Book* (1896), pp. 13–4.

worshipping poor was perhaps more likely to appear in a group which carried an image of its own plebeian past than in one for which a large proportion of working-class adherents would be a novelty. No Wesleyan leader ever dared to suggest, as Dale did, that the poor should be left to others. But this leaves evidence unexplained. Although many a comfortable worshipper doubtless agreed with Dale that Independency could carry on its middle-class tradition with a clear conscience, there were other Congregationalists who believed nothing of the sort. A passion for the souls of the poor moved many Congregationalists as well as Wesleyans and members of the Church of England. Most leading ministers and laymen believed – some ardently – that their church should play its part in reaching the masses; and they did not temper this belief by reflecting that their fathers were yeomen and burghers. Denominational indifference to the working classes is only a part of the story.

'Independency leads to isolated action on the part of local Churches', wrote a minister, John Stoughton. 'It is unfriendly to cohesion and co-operation. It provides for freedom, and nothing else.'[1] Each congregation was separate and self-governing. The deep Independent suspicion of central organization prevented the Congregational Union of England and Wales from gaining any real authority. When Horton tried in 1898 to draw the 250 Congregational churches of London closer together, 'so that they might feel and act as one' and especially to plan church extension, he failed entirely to overcome this suspicion.[2] Yet local initiative was quite inadequate for systematic aggression. An early report of the church extension committee gave these results of an enquiry among local churches:

> To the question, 'In your judgment are the churches in your district able, separately or collectively, to undertake further Church Extension?' only twelve positively answered 'Yes'; three answered, 'if needed'; one replied 'if united'; one 'not now'; while forty-two blankly answer, 'No'. And this negative answer comes from districts, many of them, where vigorous action is most urgently called for.[3]

How then was local activity in building churches, in employing

[1] J. Stoughton, *Recollections of a Long Life*, p. 125.
[2] R. F. Horton, *op. cit.* pp. 181–3.
[3] *Congregational Year Book* (1894), p. 69.

missionaries, in paying to maintain chapels, to be supplemented? 'The root ideas of Independency', said the *British Weekly*, 'do not encourage central funds from which weak churches can draw.'[1] Nor did they encourage any of the central activities which Churchmen and Wesleyans found necessary in attempts to adapt their ministry to the neglect of religion. In the Church of England, ill-endowed churches in large towns were assisted out of a number of national and diocesan funds. The parochial ministry was supplemented by such bodies as the Church Army, the Church of England Working Men's Society, and national or diocesan societies of lay evangelists. The Church's efforts in working-class districts tended more and more to be planned on a higher than parochial level. Among the Wesleyans, the London Mission was controlled by the Conference, and the central missions in other large towns had been founded after canvassing and discussion at the Conference. Congregationalists still lacked in 1900 a unity of organization, a focus for planning, to make possible the internal co-operation which Churchmen and Wesleyans could take for granted. The Congregational Union was not a governing body, and it could not become one until Congregational churches developed a stronger sense of community. Throughout the century, leaders of Independency had recognized the weakness, especially for evangelistic purposes, of a church with little central organization. But the movement towards federation was slow. Independency remained in 1900 primarily a series of self-governing congregations, whose discreteness was never more obvious than during financial appeals on behalf of Congregationalism at large.

After 1900 the Congregationalists moved cautiously towards denominational unity. In 1904 a new constitution for the Congregational Union was adopted, giving the central body for the first time a direct responsibility for home missions and church extension. The wish to seek non-worshippers more efficiently was one of the motives persuading Congregationalists to modify the principle of independency. But the principle still had adherents, and even after the changes of 1904 the Congregational Church was still far less capable than the Wesleyan Methodist Church of concerted, national action for any purpose. In trying to reach the working classes, Congregationalists were familiar

[1] *British Weekly*, 14 Dec. 1893, p. 115.

with all the problems confronting other Nonconformists, and with one problem which could not arise in a severe form under the connexional system devised by John Wesley.

Nonconformity and Respectability

When Nonconformists tried to explain why they were not having more success among the working classes, they tended to blame above all else the social atmosphere in which religious worship took place and the attitudes to social questions believed to be characteristic of ministers and church-goers. Wesleyans and Congregationalists appeared not to believe that positive infidelity had infected the working classes deeply. In general statements of the Wesleyan Conference and the Congregational Union, as in comparable statements from the Church of England, it was said that most working-class non-worshippers were indifferent rather than hostile to religion, and that where hostility was found it was to the churches rather than to Christianity.

Working-class people, it was noticed, were rarely elected to any of the offices filled by the laity. 'Many Nonconformist Churches are democratic only in name', said Richard Westrope, a Congregational minister in Leeds.[1] Within the ministry Westrope was an unusually severe critic of the social conservatism of Dissent; but the *British Weekly*, a reputable if radical journal, agreed with him so far as to ask, of Nonconformists in general: 'What can be done to give working-men place and influence in the government of our churches?'[2] A Congregationalist, Morlais Jones, gave one answer: 'you must abolish the unwritten law that the first qualification to be deacon is that the man should possess a cheque-book.'[3] A Baptist deacon, writing in the *British Weekly*, denied that anything could be done. 'For official position in most Churches,' he said, 'a higher measure of education is desirable than is usually possessed by working men. Business ability, tact in dealing with men, knowledge of affairs, all come in as requisites.'[4] 'What a calumny of my brother workmen!' exclaimed a working-class correspondent

[1] *Ibid.*, 17 Nov. 1892, p. 60.
[2] *Ibid.*, 3 Nov. 1892, p. 19.
[3] *Congregational Year Book* (1897), p. 32.
[4] *British Weekly*, 17 Nov. 1892, p. 60.

a week later. Had the Baptist writer never heard of trade unions or co-operatives run by working men? Faith and common sense, the writer declared, were sufficient qualifications for church government; if more were required, then the Church had forsaken Christ's principles for the world's.[1]

The problem of clothing was blamed by some Nonconformists, as by some Churchmen, for abstention from worship. When the *Methodist Times* invited working men to contribute essays on 'Why the Working Classes Do NOT go to Church', one writer said that a section of working-class people 'give as a reason . . . that they cannot dress respectably as they should like, for they feel that there is a marked distinction made between those who dress well and those who wear meaner clothing.'[2] A writer in the *British Weekly*, responding to a request for the opinions of working men about churches, made a similar but more astringent observation: 'There are three unwritten laws, unchristian but yet held by many church-members, which run thus – (1) whosoever goes to church must go well dressed, (2) whosoever goes well-dressed to church is respectable, (3) whosoever is respectable is a worthy church-member.'[3] A campaigner for mission halls said that the poor liked special services where they had not to worry about their dress.[4] 'To start a mission hall,' said the *British Weekly*, 'is to say to the working classes of the district, "You have churches around you, but they are unsuited to your needs. . . . We have provided this hall specially for yourselves. Here you may come in your working clothes . . ." '[5] Yet on another occasion the journal had seen the mission hall as an adjustment to evil social conditions instead of an effort to overcome them, as a sign of 'a condition of society fatal to pure, simple Christ-religion,' as an institution 'maintained by the rich for the poor because distance and mutual shyness make it well nigh impossible for them to sit together in their Father's house. Sad is the burlesque of the great uniting Gospel . . .'[6]

Pew rents, the rarity of working-class stewards and deacons, and the silent demand for middle-class dress were admitted by

[1] *Ibid.*, 24 Nov. 1892, p. 76.
[2] J. Davies, in *Methodist Times*, 4 Feb. 1897, p. 83.
[3] P. Anderson, in *British Weekly*, 10 Nov. 1892, p. 34.
[4] W. Olney, in *ibid.*, 21 Oct. 1887, p. 400.
[5] *Ibid.*, 29 March 1894, p. 361.
[6] *Ibid.*, 14 Oct. 1887, p. 376.

some Nonconformists to be signs that worshippers were unwilling to accept artisans and labourers and their families among them on terms of social equality. Richard Westrope declared this fatal to evangelism because the working classes would no longer tolerate an inferior status: 'slowly and yet surely men have come to believe that the old idea of a class or section of the community subject to another class is untenable. . . .'[1] A plumber who wrote to the *Methodist Times* in 1897 paraphrased thus the call of Christians to the non-worshipping masses:

> We want you, the working 'classes', to attend our church; but you must forget that you *are* the working 'classes', and you must not on any account presume to be on an equal footing with ourselves, as you don't belong to our 'set', and you should be grateful to us for our condescension in asking you to come at all.[2]

Nor was this judgment on Nonconformity made only by its extreme critics. In an editorial assessment of essays received from working men, the *Methodist Times* concluded: 'Above all, they are indignant at class distinctions in the House of God.'[3] Beside an iconoclast like Westrope one can quote the eminent Congregationalist A. M. Fairbairn, who blamed the churches for having tended 'to grow into societies for the demarcation and consecration of class. And the more they have done so, the more distasteful have they become to working men.[4]

It was also observed by Nonconformists who were introspective about the condition of their faith that the churches accepted the existing social order uncritically, and that the opposition of Christians to schemes for social reform contributed powerfully to keeping working-class people away from worship. This opinion was offered by such a thoroughly respectable leader of Dissent as J. Guinness Rogers, who said that at the root of working-class indifference lay 'a belief on the part of the people that they have not the sympathy from the churches and their ministers which, from the teachings of Christ, they had a fair right to anticipate; that, on the contrary, their leanings, like

[1] *Ibid.*, 17 Nov. 1892, p. 60.

[2] C. Barton in *Methodist Times*, 3 Feb. 1897, p. 86.

[3] *Ibid.* p. 65.

[4] A. M. Fairbairn, *Religion in History and Modern Life* (New York, 1894), p. 34.

those of the world outside, are to the wealthy, the influential, the successful classes. . . .'[1] Similarly, Fairbairn said from the chair of the Congregational Union: 'the English working-man . . . thinks religion helps him but little in the struggle for life; thinks it hinders him rather, being mostly on the side of privilege and capital.'[2] The 'social Christianity' propagated by Hugh Price Hughes and others, like the revived Christian socialism in the Church of England, was inspired partly by a conviction that working-class non-worshippers would come to church only if Christians showed a practical sympathy with their social aspirations.

In the Church of England and in Nonconformity, the mission of English Christianity to the urban working classes was treated between 1850 and 1900 as an urgent question. It was generally agreed that a majority in these classes attended no place of worship in 1850, and that at least as high a proportion stayed away at the end of the century despite all the efforts made to win them. The efforts were more various than has been indicated in this survey, in which attention has been given only to the activities of the largest denominations. No other Protestant body, however, whether the Baptists, the Unitarians, the Quakers or the more democratic of the Methodist sects, enjoyed a conspicuous evangelistic success. If we excluded all those people in large towns who were attending service provided by Nonconformists other than the Wesleyans and Congregationalists, the pattern of working-class behaviour would not be strikingly distorted. 'The battle of Christianity must be fought out in these vast towns', wrote a clergyman in 1882.[3] If the counting of heads at worship was a fair test, it could not be said in 1900 that Christianity, in either its Anglican or Nonconformist version, was winning the battle.

[1] Editorial in *Congregational Review*, July 1888, p. 603. Rogers edited the ournal.

[2] *Congregational Year Book* (1884), p. 91.

[3] A. L. Oldham, *The Church and the Census* (1882), pp. 15–6.

3

The Catholics

The Irish

CATHOLICS in England formed a social pattern almost exactly the opposite to that made by Nonconformists. Among shopkeepers and tradespeople – the solid core of Dissent – Catholics were few. In the nobility and landed gentry, groups virtually closed to Nonconformists, Catholics were a minority, but it was the steadfastness of these few that had kept the faith alive down the centuries. Unskilled urban labourers and their families, acknowledged by Nonconformists to be rare in their ranks, made up the vast majority of Catholic worshippers. The pattern changed very little from decade to decade, for the classes in which Catholicism had most support were those having least social mobility, while its recruits by conversion and immigration were drawn from groups where it was already strong.

Converts were usually from what the Catholic weekly the *Tablet* called on one occasion 'the affluent class', and on another 'the more intelligent classes'.[1] 'To the upper classes we have the easiest access', wrote an English Jesuit in 1892 in the Jesuit journal the *Month*. The middle classes seemed to him, as to many other Catholics, the seat of bigotry. 'How are we to get at them, how to secure a hearing, how appeal to their common sense?'[2]

[1] *Tablet*, 6 Jan. 1883, p. 6; 19 April 1884, p. 602.

[2] J. Morris, 'Catholic England in Modern Times', *Month*, May 1892, p. 42. For a similar comment on the middle classes see E. H. S. Escott, *England* (1879), II. 303.

Nor did Catholics claim to be gaining many converts among the working classes. 'Without the Irish', said the same writer, 'we should have had, comparatively speaking, no poor.'[1]

The Irish arrived steadily in the decades after the great famine. 'Wherever employment is active the Irish flock,' said the report on the census of population in 1861, 'and they abound in the large towns, – in London, Liverpool, Manchester, Birmingham, Leeds, Bradford and Sheffield. . . .'[2] At the census of 1881 there were 109 Irish-born people in England and Wales for every 1,000 still in Ireland – a higher figure than ever before or after. 1878 was the last year in which the number of Irish immigrants exceeded 10,000; in 1880 fewer than 8,000 arrived, and in the twenty years from 1879 to 1898 an average of fewer than 4,000.[3] In 1881 there were 562,374 Irish-born people in England and Wales, and in 1901 only 426,565. We do not know how many Irish people came to England and stayed there, or how many people of Irish *descent* were living in England at any time; but it is clear that the numerical strength of Catholicism depended more and more after 1880 on the loyalty of people born in England of Irish stock, and less and less on that of people born in Ireland.

In the 'fifties they generally occupied particular quarters of the cities. The Irish, said one Catholic, 'are congregated together in the poorest, the most squalid, the most neglected, and the most destitute corners of our cities . . .' and were 'considered even by the lower classes of the English population to occupy a still lower grade in the social system than themselves. . . .'[4] Later in the century the Irish immigrants and their descendants were distributed a little more evenly. In 1892 an alert Irish observer noted that the Irish quarters of large towns were tending to disappear.[5] But despite this diffusion the Irish remained almost entirely in manufacturing and mining areas. In 1881, of every 1,000 Irish-born people in England and Wales, 378 lived in Lancashire, 176 in and around London, 101 in Yorkshire, 54

[1] *Month*, April 1892, p. 521.

[2] *Parliamentary Papers*, 1863, LIII, part I, Census of England and Wales, 1861: General Report, p. 40.

[3] Calculated from Emigration Statistics of Ireland in *Parliamentary Papers* annually, 1879–98.

[4] 'The Irish in England', *Dublin Review*, Dec. 1856, pp. 472–4.

[5] J. Denvir, *The Irish in Britain* (1892), p. 398.

in Durham and 42 in Cheshire. The barrier between unskilled and skilled labour was still formidable, and especially so for Irishmen; at the census of 1891 most of them were described as 'engaged in the rougher kinds of unskilled labour, the proportions of artisans and of dealers of all kinds and grades being very small.'[1] The immigrants and their children seldom acquired the income, the skills or the manners to lift themselves out of the lowest stratum of English society.

They carried from Ireland the habit of going to church regularly. Worship with their fellows, led perhaps by an Irish priest, was one of the few familiar and comforting things available to them in ugly industrial England. 'Their most striking characteristic', said a writer in the *Fortnightly Review* in 1880, 'is their unexampled religious fidelity' – a fidelity forged generations ago when the oppressed Irish had found a solace in the Catholic church.[2] It occurred to some Catholics in England that the coming of the Irish might be providential. In the authoritative Catholic quarterly the *Dublin Review*, one writer in 1856 said that everybody interested in extending Catholicism in England should devote himself to 'bringing into shape, and order, and discipline, that vast body of Catholics which is comprised within the Irish poor', because through them the Church might become more genuinely popular in England than she had been for more than three centuries. 'It is very well to have rich people . . .' he said; 'but after all, it is the poor who constitute the real bulwark of the Church.'[3]

By 1850, when the English hierarchy was restored, some Catholics were dreaming of a converted England. The new cardinal, Wiseman, supported a crusade of prayer for the purpose; and when he received into the church the man who was to succeed him at its head in England, Wiseman said to Manning: 'Go forth, my son, and bring your Brethren and fellow countrymen by thousands and tens of thousands into the one true fold of Christ.'[4] A few months earlier Pope Pius IX had expressed an even higher hope when he exhorted the English

[1] *Parliamentary Papers*, 1893–4, CVI, Census of England and Wales, 1891: General Report, IV. 697.

[2] J. O'Connor Power, 'The Irish in England', *Fortnightly Review*, March 1880, p. 411.

[3] *Dublin Review*, Dec. 1856, p. 484.

[4] E. S. Purcell, *Life of Cardinal Manning* (1895), I. 633.

faithful to 'pray insistently that the Lord may remove all the obstacles and bring to the new Church a million, three million, indeed all your compatriots who at one time were torn from the Church.'[1] Although the most sanguine Catholic could not imagine that this was likely to happen suddenly, it was not just the tactless phrasing of Wiseman's first pastoral letter that made it reasonable for Protestants to speak of 'papal aggression'. There was indeed an aggressive mood within English Catholicism by 1851. The conversion of Newman and Manning contributed most to its making; the Irish immigration had played little part so far. But when Catholic leaders, and above all Manning, turned their minds to the strategy of converting England, it occurred to them that, thanks partly to the Irish, their church was in some ways better placed than any other to win sympathy among the English working classes. The conversion of England was a less pressing matter, however, than the retention of those who were already Catholics.

The Leakage

In 1885 a well-born Catholic layman, Edward Lucas, said in the *Month* that since 1841 a vast number of souls – perhaps 750,000, perhaps a million or more – had fallen away from the faith in England and Wales.[2] His was one of several warnings issued to English Catholics in the 'eighties against waiting complacently for Providence to bring about the conversion of England. For as long as the Irish had been arriving in large numbers 'the leakage' had been a familiar phrase to English Catholics. The problem was now taken more seriously than ever. James Britten, who was probably the most prolific lay writer on the affairs of his church, said in 1887 that since Lucas' essay appeared, a remarkable change had come over Catholic opinion in England. Until recently, Britten believed, Catholics in England had assumed that the spiritual progress of the faith was satisfactory; but now they realized that leakage was vast.[3] According to Britten, Catholics were thoroughly if tardily aware that the losses being suffered by the church in Britain were greater than her gains.

[1] E. E. Y. Hales, *Pio Nono* (1954), p. 141.
[2] E. Lucas, 'The Conversion of England', *Month*, July 1885, p. 310.
[3] J. Britten, 'The Work of the Laity', *Dublin Review*, July 1887, pp. 151–2.

Although Lucas' estimate that a million Catholics had been lost since 1841 was generally accepted, it was based on statistical assumptions which could not really be verified. The number of English and Welsh Catholics in 1885 varied according to the method of estimation and the definition of a Catholic. Calculations based on school attendances, on baptisms, on marriages, and on the estimate of local priests gave different results. The Registrar-General's criterion for a Catholic – a person married in a Catholic church – was more exclusive and more precise (though not necessarily more just) than the criteria among Catholics, who usually counted 'those who have their children baptized in the Catholic church and send for the priest when they are ill.'[1] Estimates of Catholics in England and Wales in the 1880s varied from just over a million to nearly 1.7 million.[2] For 1841, the earlier year in Lucas' calculation, estimates disagreed wildly. When *The Times* asserted that as late as 1854 there were fewer than 200,000 Catholics in England and Wales, it was certainly being mischievous.[3] But the figure which Lucas took for 1841, 800,000, was simply a compromise between two contemporary guesses, neither firmly based. The intermediate calculations were no less risky, since nobody knew the number of permanent Irish immigrants, or their fertility, or their death-rate. 'For our own part,' the *Month* said in 1874, 'we do not believe that any one can tell the exact number of the Catholic population of England, Wales, and Scotland at any two given periods of our recent history. . . .'[4] This was a thoroughly safe assertion, and it would still have been so in 1885, when Lucas made his calculations.

His estimate would not have been accepted, however, unless the experience of responsible Catholics had made it appear plausible to them. Lucas offered descriptive as well as statistical evidence for his pessimism.

> It is the experience of almost every priest with whom I have conversed on the subject that, in all of our great towns, there is a large body of people, beyond and above those of whom the local

[1] J. Morris, *loc. cit.* p. 33.

[2] For a discussion of several different estimates see C. G., 'The Leakage of the Catholic Church in England: Its Remedy', *Month*, Feb. 1887, pp. 117–8.

[3] *The Times*, 10 Jan. 1854.

[4] 'The Measures of Catholic Progress', *Month*, Aug. 1874, p. 472.

> clergy have personal cognizance, who ought to be Catholics, and who might be brought within the Church, were it possible to look after them. But the work of hunting them up, in addition to the other labours of keeping their acknowledged parishioners to their duty, visiting the sick, administering the sacraments, and collecting funds for various purposes, is altogether beyond the physical powers of the clergy.[1]

James Britten agreed. 'The overworked priest of the courts and alleys of our large towns,' he wrote,

> as well as the pastor of a handful of souls in remote country districts, knew too well the other side of the brilliant picture held up for our admiration.[2]

'It was but the other day', Britten wrote,

> that I was told of a family of three generations, numbering forty-seven in all: of these only the original father and mother are faithful to their religion, which has been entirely abandoned by the remaining five-and-forty.[3]

The *Catholic Times* believed that it was a general tendency for English-born children of Irish immigrants to neglect the practice of their religion, and a priest estimated that in London, three-quarters of the Catholic labouring classes were absent from mass.[4]

Although national figures were not reliable, particular statistical enquiries suggested that the leakage was considerable. When the Bishop of Salford, Dr Vaughan, realized in 1884 that many poor Catholics were being lost, he appointed a board of enquiry which reported that the Catholic population of Manchester and Salford was 75,000 including almost 10,000 children whose faith was in danger on account of the spiritual condition of their parents.[5] Vaughan's previous experience – Stonyhurst, Downside and a Jesuit school in Belgium, study in Rome, educa-

[1] E. Lucas, *loc. cit.* p. 311.

[2] J. Britten, *loc. cit.* p. 152.

[3] *Catholic Times*, 30 Oct. 1891, p. 4.

[4] *Ibid.*; Canon McGrath, in Catholic Truth Society, *Conference Papers* (1891), p. 62. On London see also *Month*, Feb. 1889, p. 154; *Blackwood's Magazine*, July 1901, p. 133. On great towns in general, see *Month*, May 1895, p. 106; P. Thureau-Dangin, *The English Catholic Revival in the Nineteenth Century* (1914), I. xxvii–xxviii.

[5] A. Oates, 'The lost, strayed and stolen of our Catholic poor children', *Dublin Review*, Jan. 1887, p. 161; J. G. Snead-Cox, *The Life of Cardinal Vaughan* (1910), I. 403–8.

tional work in England and a mission to negroes – had left him unaware until now that poor Catholics had any special problems. 'Why have I not known all this before?' he asked in 1886. 'Why have I been so long blind and deaf to the misfortunes of my people?'[1] A Catholic analysing the figures which provoked these questions concluded that the situation was similar in a number of other large towns.[2] In Liverpool an official census of attendance at Catholic worship was ordered by the bishop in 1881 and another in 1891. The *Catholic Times* found in the results proof that negligence had grown during the decade.[3]

The sudden invasion of the late 'forties had almost overwhelmed the Catholic clergy in some places. At Gateshead in 1851 there was only one priest, who had three thousand Catholic parishioners and a derelict warehouse, which could hold 300 people, for all his services.[4] On census day in that year the priest in charge of St Wilfrid's, Preston, reported 6,000 worshippers at three masses; at St Patrick's, Manchester, which could hold 1,250 worshippers, 6,000 were said to have attended at five masses; and at St Anthony's, Liverpool, the number at five masses was set down as 7,200.[5] For the priests it was heavy work simply ministering to people who came to church; seeking out the less ardent was often impossible. Priests came from Ireland to help. Churches were built: in Liverpool, ten went up between 1850 and 1856 alone.[6] But as Lucas, Britten and others observed, resources did not increase fast enough.

Nor was it simply a matter of supplying priests and churches. There was also the task of combating a hostile environment. 'Every class, order, and rank of Catholics in these islands . . .', wrote a priest in 1865, 'is brought into situations of difficulty, because into practical relations of some kind or other with the great non-catholic majority; and is thwarted, or embarrassed, or tempted, or tried, in consequence, according to his characteristic liabilities.'[7] The Irish poor had their special trials and

[1] J. G. Snead-Cox, *op. cit.* I. 413.
[2] A. Oates, *loc. cit.* p. 163.
[3] *Catholic Times*, 30 Oct. 1891, p. 4.
[4] Public Record Office, Home Office Papers, 129, 551.2.1.15
[5] *Ibid.*, 482.2.2.24; 473.5.1.3; 461.1.18.
[6] *The Catholic Family Annual* (Liverpool, 1886), p. 101.
[7] F. Oakeley, 'The Position of a Catholic Minority in a Non-Catholic Country', in H. E. Manning, ed., *Essays on Religion and Literature* (1865), pp. 138–9.

temptations. In 1883 the *Tablet* set out what it believed had been the history of many Irish families in England since Queen Victoria came to the throne:

> They . . . have clung to the faith once delivered to the saints: they come with the virtues of a Catholic peasantry and with the feelings of an impetuous, generous, warm-hearted race. Poverty has driven them from their native soil. In our large towns and cities they hope to find a livelihood. And they do find it. But the atmosphere in which it is to be gained is surcharged with moral poison. Drunkenness, dishonesty, impurity surround them on every side in the lanes and alleys in which they are huddled together. Their lot is cast among those who jeer at their religion, who scoff at their virtues, who make a mock at sin.[1]

The first Archbishop of Westminster, Cardinal Wiseman, resolved to give the poor his immediate attention; but his energy went less into directing the pastoral care of the Irish than into settling disputes within the church and trying to quieten English fears about its ambitions. Manning, who succeeded him in 1865, did more to protect the faith of poor Catholics. In 1866 and 1868 he secured legislation enabling Catholic children in work-houses to be brought up as Catholics and permitting all Catholic inmates to attend their own places of worship and to be visited by their own clergy. In 1866, having discovered that Catholic schools in London could accommodate only half the poor Catholic children in the city, he opened a diocesan education fund, out of which many new schools were built. In a predominantly non-Catholic country, denominational education is always crucial for the Catholic church. It was because Manning believed that the allegiance of the poor must be maintained by education that he refused to allow the building of the cathedral in London which had been planned before his accession. 'Could I leave 20,000 children without education,' he asked, 'and drain my friends and my flock to pile up stones and bricks?'[2]

Manning's battle against drunkenness was waged in the same cause as his campaign for Catholic education. Christians in many denominations were now giving ardent support to the temperance movement. But Churchmen and Nonconformists were trying to remove an obstacle to evangelizing the masses outside

[1] *Tablet*, 10 Feb. 1883, p. 201.
[2] E. S. Purcell, *op. cit.* II. 355.

their reach; for Catholics, the problem was rather to stop alcohol from causing their own members to lapse. 'Talk about leakage!' said one Catholic of drunkenness. 'It is scuttling the ship.'[1] Manning took a personal pledge of total abstinence, and founded in 1872 the Total Abstinence League of the Cross, a body through which he hoped to make the Catholic working classes sober, and more likely on that account to remain devout. Sobriety was made as attractive as possible. Banners, sashes and brass bands brightened the League's processions, and a sense of participation was encouraged by para-military organization. The Pope granted indulgences to members who abstained from alcohol during the feast of St Patrick. Manning was pleased with the work of the League. If it had been started twenty-five years earlier, he said once, it would have saved the faith of 100,000 Catholics in London alone.[2] Drunkenness among the Irish nevertheless remained a great source of anxiety to the church in England. Even the rallies of the League, it appeared, were not wholly abstemious affairs: in 1891 a Catholic journalist reported 'scenes of drunken brawl and depravity' among men returning home from the League's annual rally in the Crystal Palace (where there was a licensed bar), and said that the same happened every year.[3]

Some Catholics believed that the faithful – especially children – leaked away through holes bored by Protestant philanthropic agencies. But Dr Barnardo, sometimes suspected of capturing Catholic children into his homes, in fact wrote to Manning offering to hand over all Catholics sent to him if their church could look after them.[4] The general charge against Protestants was dismissed in 1900 by Lady Elizabeth Talbot, a Catholic engaged in voluntary work among children:

> The workers of the various denominations do not want our girls and boys – they have enough to do in looking after their own; we cannot accuse them of any direct desire of proselytizing; but their clubs are filled in many cases with our Catholic youth, simply because we have so few clubs of our own.[5]

[1] Canon Murnane, 'The Temperance Movement', Catholic Truth Society, *Conference Papers* (1890), pp. 82, 87.

[2] *Month*, April 1887, p. 467.

[3] *Catholic News* (Preston), 22 Aug. 1891, p. 5.

[4] R. F. Clarke, 'Our Waifs and Strays', *Month*, Feb. 1889. p, 154.

[5] Lady E. Talbot, *Rescue Work* (1900), p. 6.

It was no use merely exhorting Protestants to leave Catholic children alone: more energy was demanded on the part of Catholics themselves. A writer in the *Month* in 1887 called for 'the rescue of our poor children from the power of the devil and from the perversion and corruption to which they are exposed in all the large centres of England.'[1] James Britten urged Catholics to open homes for boys, to distribute tracts and conduct educational activity among the Catholic working classes, and in general to copy the missionary and philanthropic example lately set by Christians of other denominations.[2] From other Catholics, both priests and laymen, came suggestions for Catholic reformatories, more temperance work, sewing classes for girls and clubs for boys.

A number of organizations intended to stop leakage had been formed before 1880, of which the Society of St Vincent de Paul, introduced to England 1844, was the most ambitious. This was a body of laymen pledged to visit the Catholic poor, and in particular boys, instructing them in the faith and performing charitable works. Preserving the faith of children was a concern of several other bodies formed after 1880. In Liverpool a Catholic Children's Protection Society was founded in 1881, and the first fruit of Vaughan's enquiry into the spiritual state of Manchester and Salford was the Salford Catholic Protection and Rescue Society, whose object was to have poor and neglected children of Catholics brought up in the faith. In London there were boys' clubs, a home for waifs and strays, and a society for protecting girls in domestic service. Other societies helped adult Catholics. Often these bodies were copies of non-Catholic organizations: a prisoners' aid society, a night-refuge, and some working-men's clubs were inspired by the efforts of Protestant philanthropists. Orphanages, benevolent homes and hospitals staffed by nuns belonged more directly to the tradition of Catholic charity.[3]

These aids to pastoral activity were welcomed by leading priests and laymen, but the church remained ill-equipped to resist the pressures of English society. Active hatred of Popery

[1] C. G., in *Month*, Feb. 1887, p. 189.

[2] J. Britten, in *Dublin Review*, July 1887, pp. 162–7.

[3] See *The Handbook of Catholic Charities, Associations, Etc., in Great Britain* (1894).

was only one of these pressures. 'The natural forces in operation,' wrote Edward Lucas, 'apart altogether from intentional proselytism, are amply sufficient to absorb our small band, unless some principle of resistance able to cope with those forces exists among us.'[1] Mere poverty sapped the habit of worship in slum-dwelling Catholics without any help from Protestant fanaticism, by forcing them to destructive solaces and by setting them down among people who cared nothing for any church. Marriage with non-Catholics was a constant source of loss, for even if the Catholic partner remained loyal the children might not. According to Vaughan's survey of Manchester and Salford, mixed marriages were responsible for one in every four children whose souls were in danger.[2] This was an inevitable threat in a country where Catholicism was the religion of a tiny minority not protected by linguistic or racial barriers from contact with the surrounding society. It was not absurd for a Catholic to conclude, as one did, that the conversion of England was the one real insurance against loss:

> the only ultimate method of preventing leakage is to convert the multitude of non-Catholics amongst whom our own people dwell. So long as a few Catholics are scattered amongst a large population of non-Catholics, nothing will prevent a large leakage, especially in these busy industrial days.[3]

Short of awaiting the conversion of England, what could Catholics do more than they were doing already to prevent the leakage of the poor? A Catholic peer answered that the Church's resources could be used more efficiently, and alleged that large chapels were being built for rich worshippers with money which should have been spent on chapels for the working classes.[4] James Britten suggested that the custom of charging for seats in church was a hindrance.[5] This practice, though possibly not as widespread as in other denominations, was common enough for Britten to believe that it prevented many of the poorer Catholics from worshipping. A priest, writing in the *Month* in

[1] *Catholic Times*, 16 Jan. 1891, p. 5.
[2] A. Oates, *loc. cit.* p. 161.
[3] L. A. H. Cuthbert, *The Working Man's Apostolate* (1902), p. 1.
[4] Lord Braye, *The Present State of the Church in England* (1884), paragraph vii.
[5] *Month*, Oct. 1886, p. 158. On the pew system in Catholic churches see also Catholic Truth Society, *Conference Papers* (1891), pp. 70–1.

1889, recommended that as the miserably poor did not go to mass, mass should be taken to them. His reason for this radical proposal was expressed in a dialogue which he offered as more or less typical of affairs in all large towns in England.

> 'What, not been to Mass for six months?'
> 'No, your Reverence: we've got no clothes.'
> 'Why, but you go all about the town in the clothes that you have, why don't you come to church in them?'
> 'Oh, we don't go out on Sundays at all: we just stop quiet in bed in the morning, and in the evening the little ones crawl about in the court below, and we stay inside: we don't want to be laughed at among well-dressed people.'[1]

The writer believed this situation to be peculiarly English. 'In other lands,' he said, 'either the people are all poor together, or the superstition of "Sunday clothes" is less potent; or (as in Ireland) there is a second communion-rail for the poor.' Other Catholics had noticed the problem. An Italian missionary in the 'forties observed that many Catholics in England were 'ashamed to appear in Church with their ragged apparel.'[2] A priest in Walsall held a very early service each Sunday 'for people who from want of proper clothes do not like to appear out of doors at a later period of the day.'[3] The Irish, said a writer in 1856, 'cannot do in England what they were used to do at home. The women cannot go to mass with caps in place of bonnets, with broken shoes, or perhaps with no shoes at all. The odious goddess of "respectability" reigns supreme in this civilized land, over Catholic and Protestant, over rich and poor alike.'[4] English society threatened the church not only as an external enemy but as a fifth column within, affecting the relationships of the groups who made up the laity, setting up tensions of class within the religious community. 'There can be no doubt', wrote the *Catholic Times* in 1891, 'that our poverty and our want of social union are very serious sources of weakness.'[5] By 'social union' the journal meant harmony between rich and poor.

[1] J. Rickaby, 'The Great Clothes Question', *Month*, Oct. 1889, p. 248.
[2] Father Pagani, *Life of the Rev. Aloysius Gentili* (1851), p. 188.
[3] Public Record Office, Home Office Papers, 129, 380.3.1.4.
[4] *Dublin Review*, Dec. 1856, p. 503.
[5] *Catholic Times*, 17 April 1891, p. 24.

The Laity

In discussions about the leakage, no internal cause was mentioned as often as the neglect by wealthy Catholics of their poorer brothers and sisters. When he raised the alarm in 1885, Lucas said it was certain

> that lay activity is not very pronounced, that of lay organization there is very little worthy of the name; that our work among the poor is trifling compared with what is within our power; while the spirit of poverty is hardly mentioned out of the pulpit, our chief aim seeming to be to rise in social position. . . .[1]

The upper-class laity were accused by one writer of being 'strangely, if not even blamably, apathetic' to the need for money to build and run churches; by another, of neglecting clubs founded to rescue boys from 'wholesale loss of their faith;' and by another, of leaving the priests to conduct Sunday schools alone.[2] A group of Catholics said in 1900 that the charities of the church were supported only by a generous few, and according to one critic those Catholics who undertook philanthropic work often did so not gladly but as a penance, and soon found more congenial ways of reducing the time to be spent in purgatory.[3] A priest described a neighbourhood he knew well, in a manufacturing town. Some 2,800 of the 60,000 inhabitants were Catholics, most of them unskilled Irish labourers and their families and three-quarters of them not attending worship. The one priest in the district began a temperance society to resist the influence of the 120 public houses, but in this and other social activities he had to work quite without the help of laymen from outside the area; 'the clergy alone', said the writer, 'cannot do this work . . ., it depends on the laity themselves whether the leakage and the wreckage shall continue.'[4]

Many wealthy Catholics, according to Lucas, shrank from helping the poor because they were too fastidious to mix with any-

[1] *Month*, July 1885, p. 305.

[2] St G. Mivart, 'The Conversion of England', *Dublin Review*, July 1884, p. 86; cf. J. Britten, 'The Loss of Our Boys', *Month*, April 1887, p. 467; Dean Richardson, 'Catholics and Sunday Schools', Catholic Truth Society, *Conference Papers* (1891), p. 73.

[3] *Annual Report of Catholic Social Union* (1900), p. 10; 'Catholica', 'Catholic Women and Night-work', *Dublin Review*, Oct. 1887, pp. 299–300.

[4] Dr Barry, in *Catholic Times*, 3 Jan. 1891, p. 5.

body except their own social equals or superiors. Another writer observed that 'the chatter of uncharity' was familiar to Catholic ears, directed against all who were not gentlemen. 'Not all the learning and piety of one Bishop will atone, in the estimation of some, for the insecurity of his *h*'s.'[1] Manning himself spoke tartly about the apathy of the comfortable laity. 'What are our people doing? Oh, I forgot; they have no time. They are examining their consciences or praying for success in finding a really satisfying maid.'[2]

In a mission country like England, the church had special need of an energetic laity. 'It is all very well,' an American archbishop remarked,

> in a Catholic age, in a Catholic country, for priests only to preach and defend the Church. . . . But where we are, so to speak, in a state of war, we need the whole army; and priests and bishops alone are like officers alone on the battlefield, they can achieve very little.[3]

But in England the officers, undermanned though they were, had to undertake tasks which might have been left to the ranks. A bishop said in 1899 that the priest

> had not only to perform the sacred offices of the holy Liturgy, to instruct, and to hear confessions, but to beg his own bread, to keep a roof on his church, to visit and relieve his poor, to seek out the children, to find means for his schools, to conciliate or to fight the public bodies and the non-Catholic world in general, to keep hold of the young people of both sexes by clubs and guilds, and to visit and watch half-a-dozen public institutions.[4]

Although leaders of all denominations were always urging their laity to take a greater share in the spiritual care of the poor, the complaints of Catholics on this score were more than conventional exhortations to do better. James Britten documented his charges of apathy by showing that the Society of St Vincent de Paul – which more than any other organization gave laymen an opportunity to meet, instruct and help poor Catholics – had in 1886 only 1,200 active members in the whole of England.[5]

[1] Anon., *We Catholics* (1885), p. 10.
[2] M. Reckitt, *Faith and Society* (1932), p. 101.
[3] Catholic Truth Society, *Conference Papers* (1891), pp. 160–1.
[4] J. C. Hedley, *The Public Spirit of the Catholic Laity* (1899), p. 8.
[5] *Dublin Review*, July 1887, p. 159.

Five years later he observed that in London the society had only 336 members, many of them not active, and that it was doing very little to stop the leakage.[1] A convert writing in the *Dublin Review* about the loss of working-class Catholics found the indifference of laymen 'astounding', not only when measured against the scale of the problem, but also by comparison with the activity of the Protestant laity in supporting Christian organizations among the working classes.

> If we had a small proportion of the energy which is expended by the sects in these matters of detail, we should indeed be impregnable. We were ourselves, when we came straight from the centre of life in the English Church, the University of Oxford, into the fold of the Church, simply astonished at the comparison.[2]

There were several reasons why it was peculiarly difficult to arouse wealthy members of the Catholic laity to help in the pastoral activity of their church. It was not simply a matter of numbers. Compared with the hundreds of thousands of working-class Catholics, the rich and even the comfortable were certainly few. This their critics knew well, and it could be given as an excuse for the laity's avoiding *evangelistic* works. 'The paucity of Catholics in a Protestant country,' wrote the editor of the *Month*, 'and the primary importance of ministering to those who are the children of the Church, prevents any attempt at wide-spread missionary activity.'[3] But Catholics who begged for lay co-operation in *preserving* the faith in England believed that many who could help were idle. The traditions of English Catholicism had not prepared the laity for the kind of enterprise now being asked of them. True, the civil intolerance from which Catholics suffered for centuries had now gone almost entirely. But it was not long since they had been (in Newman's words) 'cut off from the populous world around them, and dimly seen, as if through a mist or in twilight, as ghosts flitting to and fro, by the high Protestants, the lords of the earth.'[4] Old habits from those days survived among Catholics. 'The social exile in which they have lived,' wrote a Catholic in 1863, 'and their exclusion,

[1] *Catholic Times*, 30 Jan. 1891, p. 5.

[2] H. D. Harrod, 'Catholic Boys' Clubs', *Dublin Review*, Jan. 1885, p. 117.

[3] R. F. C[larke], in *Month*, Dec. 1890, p. 469.

[4] J. H. Newman, 'The Second Spring', in his *Sermons Preached on Various Occasions* (n. d.), p. 9.

if not by statute, yet by traditional prejudice, from public and even private employment, have seriously diminished their capacities of usefulness.'[1] Generations of exclusion from the life of the nation had induced what a Catholic journal called 'want of heart' in the English laity.[2] Some became too timid to make so public a gesture as working among the Catholic poor. 'The temptation that even now besets many Catholics,' said the editor of the *Month*, 'is that it is more prudent to keep their religion always in the background, and to be a little ashamed, not of it, God forbid, but of its accidental circumstances, and of the people who belong to it.'[3] Social exclusiveness and spiritual introversion, the natural deposit of history on English Catholics, made it difficult for them to remember that they and the Irish newcomers were one body in Christ. The head, a priest remarked, had forgotten its duty to the feet.[4]

Manning hoped that the enforced isolation of Catholics from public life would prove an advantage to the church: having exercised no authority, Catholics alone among the wealthy might escape the charge of oppressing the people. But isolation had other, less fortunate consequences. Many of the wealthy laymen in the Church of England who gave money and energy to the task of winning the poor were moved by social guilt as well as by Christian zeal. They believed that their church and their class were responsible for letting the urban poor grow up in an uncivilized, unchristian environment. Such a sense of guilt was less likely to stir English Catholics. Like the masses, they had suffered at the hands of English society. Was it their fault that England had become two nations? Had there been a suffering industrial proletariat when the country was Catholic?

It was at Oxford and Cambridge, and especially at Oxford between 1875 and 1890, that many young gentlemen heard the call to make the poor civilized and Christian. Perhaps some Catholics would have been affected by this atmosphere too, if their Cardinal Archbishop had not declared his old university and its ancient rival out of bounds. 'If the laity had gone to

[1] Unsigned article, 'The Work and the Wants of the Catholic Church in England', *Dublin Review*, July 1863, p. 159.

[2] *Weekly Herald*, 14 June 1889.

[3] R. F. Clarke, 'The Missionary Church', Catholic Truth Society, *Conference Papers* (1891), p. 117.

[4] Canon McGrath, 'Catholic Organization', *ibid*, p. 64

Oxford there would have been no laity now', wrote Manning to a Catholic peer. 'It has been disastrous to the Catholic body in this country', remarked the peer, 'that so prominent an ecclesiastic holding this view (with which many may still agree) should never have been able to suggest any compensating method of higher education.'[1] James Britten pointed out to Catholics the example of university and public-school men in large towns on behalf of the Church of England. 'Like the men of Oxford and Cambridge,' said a priest, referring to Catholic laymen, 'they must not fear to go down to the submerged Catholic tenth, and bring what they can to the surface.'[2] There was a further obstacle to lay participation, also peculiar to Catholicism. The laity of every other denomination in England were more actively involved by custom and constitution in the affairs of their churches. The Catholic gentleman who chose a priest for his private chapel may have corresponded roughly to the lay patron in the Church of England, but he was a less typical figure by 1900 than he had been before 1850. The church-warden, the deacon, and the class-leader had no Catholic equivalents. Still less were there Catholic opposites to the Nonconformist lay preacher or the Church of England scripture-reader.

Many priests appeared to *want* laymen to be inactive. 'What is the province of the laity?' wrote a responsible clergyman to Manning. 'To hunt, to shoot, to entertain. These matters they understand, but to meddle with ecclesiastical matters they have no right at all.'[3] This was an extreme statement of a clerical opinion which was widely believed to be discouraging members of the laity from offering to help priests in their ministry to the poor. 'There are two views on this point,' wrote Britten; '... the clergy say the laity won't work, and the laity say they're not allowed to work.'[4] In support of the lay view he quoted a work on the leakage by a priest who said that 'voting supplies is the the proper work of the laity, their duty, and their glory.' This,

[1] Lord Braye, preface to T. Murphy, *The Position of the Catholic Church in England and Wales* (1892), p. 27n.

[2] Canon McGrath, *loc. cit.* p. 65. He was not making any precise estimate of the proportion of Catholics who were very poor; he was simply alluding to William Booth's phrase 'the submerged tenth'.

[3] Mgr. Talbot, quoted in D. R. Gwynn, *One Hundred Years of Catholic Emancipation (1829–1929)* (1929), p. xvii.

[4] *Dublin Review*, July 1887, p. 156.

Britten suggested with respect, was taxation without representation. Lady Elizabeth Talbot thought that 'a fear of having tactless district visitors in the parish', interfering with parochial routine, might account for clerical suspicion of lay interference.[1]

This reluctance among the clergy to accept help was noticed by priests as well as by laymen. One priest agreed that some of his brothers were to blame for not being readier to allow ladies to visit the poor.[2] Another admitted that some priests 'think that the layman belonging as he does necessarily to the Church taught, must be kept in his place, or he will try to constitute himself before long into the entire voice of the Infallible Church teaching . . .'; he believed that the clergy, as a body, were eager for lay help – so long as it was obedient help.[3] In 1898 some priests were considering a plan to draw the laity more actively into the pastoral life of the church by allowing them some of the local administrative responsibility exercised by laymen in a parish of the Church of England. The future Cardinal Gasquet defended the scheme by arguing that the vestry and churchwardens were older in England than the Reformation; but the *Month* reported an opinion among the clergy, hardly surprising, that the proposal was 'fraught with danger'.[4]

Organizing the Laity

To such men as Lucas and Britten the problem of lay participation seemed profound and complex, but soluble. They hoped much from a fresh organization of Catholic resources, a calculated effort to make English Catholics one community in fact as well as in theory. In 1885 Lucas began to campaign for a new organization by which the Catholic body could be 'welded into an homogeneous whole' – a body which would supply the corporate sense forged in harsher days by persecution, and which unlike previous formal associations of English Catholics would enfold the poor as well as the rich.[5] From the list of activities proposed by Lucas it was clear that his first interest was in getting help for the clergy to arrest the leakage. The idea caught

[1] Lady E. Talbot, *Rescue Work* (1900), p. 10.
[2] Canon McGrath, *loc. cit.* p. 63.
[3] Dean Richardson, *ibid.* p. 73.
[4] *Month*, Oct. 1901, p. 403.
[5] E. Lucas, 'The Organization of a Catholic Union', *Month*, April 1885, p. 472.

on, and in 1891 a Catholic Association was formed at a meeting in which Lucas occupied the chair. The impulse towards formal organization led also to the foundation of local bodies in which lay committees under clerical leadership helped mission priests among the poor.

The Catholic Association fathered by Lucas achieved less than he had wished. Any Catholic could see that its aims were worthy, but they were also vague. The ends which Lucas believed important were served rather better by the Catholic Truth Society, a body with more precise objects founded by James Britten in 1884. Its objects were:

1. To disseminate among Catholics small and cheap devotional works.
2. To assist the uneducated poor to a better knowledge of their religion.
3. To spread among Protestants information about Catholic truth.
4. To promote the inculcation of good, cheap, and popular Catholic books.[1]

At first Catholic journals and booksellers were cool towards the Catholic Truth Society, despite the support of Vaughan, then Bishop of Salford; but by 1890 it had the approval of the entire English hierarchy, the blessing of the Vatican, and the co-operation of a large body of priests and laymen.

As the list of its objects suggests, many publications of the Society were intended for Protestant rather than Catholic eyes. But Manning's part in the dock strike of 1889 probably did more to diminish popular antagonism towards Rome than all the literature of the Society, whose importance lay rather in helping to sustain the faith of Catholics. A writer in the *Month* said that the Catholic Truth Society had 'stepped in just at the very nick of time, when the spread of education has rendered literature a far more important means of influencing the masses than it ever was before.'[2] The Irish were among the groups most newly touched by education, and it was therefore timely of the Society to publish material intended to protect the faith of working-class Catholics. There were pamphlets replying to common criticisms

[1] *List of Publications of the Catholic Truth Society*, 1889. For evidence that Britten was the founder, see *Report of the Catholic Conference* (1897), p. 18.

[2] *Month*, Nov. 1892, p. 333.

of the church, and such devotional literature as lives of saints and meditation books. Prayer books, rosaries and pictures were supplied by the Society and distributed free to poor Catholics in workhouses and elsewhere. At first it operated in London only, but in 1892 branches were opened in the two provincial dioceses – Salford and Liverpool – where Catholics were most numerous.[1]

Beside these direct efforts to stop the leakage, the Society gave those Catholics who were most anxious about it a useful platform. In 1888 its leaders organized the first of a series of annual conferences which were soon acknowledged to be the most representative gatherings of English Catholics. In 1893 the conference was attended by some 1,500 priests and laymen. It was not, of course, an authoritative meeting like the Wesleyan Conference, or even a deliberative one like the Congregational Union. It was more like the Church Congress in that no resolutions were passed but prominent laymen and priests were given an opportunity to discuss publicly the pastoral and missionary work of the church. The leakage was a frequent subject at these conferences. Some speakers exhorted the faithful in broad terms to prevent it, others canvassed particular ways of protecting the faith of the poor: Sunday schools, social clubs, benefit societies, a campaign against mixed marriages, and special missionary drives were all proposed by one speaker or another.

While he was Bishop of Salford, Vaughan was president of the Catholic Truth Society and an earnest supporter of its activities. From 1885, when the danger from leakage first alarmed him, until the end of his life as Archbishop of Westminster, Vaughan encouraged his people, and especially the laity, to combat the effects of urban life on working-class Catholics. At Westminster (where he became Archbishop on Manning's death in 1892), Vaughan's own special concern was providing educational and philanthropic facilities for children. The collections which Vaughan ordered the clergy to make for such purposes did not increase his popularity among working priests who resented his remoteness and his failure to appreciate the hardships of a struggling mission; but he knew what he was doing.[2] Like Manning, he saw that the instruction of children

[1] G. E. Anstruther and P. E. Hallett, *Catholic Truth Society: the First Fifty Years* (1934), pp. 28–9.

[2] J. G. Snead-Cox, *op. cit.* II. 385.

was the Church's most economical and most durable protection against loss.

Vaughan was better able than Manning to enlist lay sympathy and service. At various times in his remarkable life Manning had antagonized those Catholics who did not like to see a convert rise like a rocket at the expense of 'old' Catholics, those to whom his ultramontanism seemed a break with English Catholic traditions, those who thought him irresponsible to support Home Rule, and those unable to share his passion for social reform. It was this last source of hostility that his biographer Purcell blamed for Manning's being 'in his latter years . . . out of touch with the leading Catholic laity.'[1] A French Catholic heard some upper-class English Catholics say when Manning died, 'At last we shall have a Cardinal of our own.'[2]

Vaughan came from an old Catholic family of landed gentry. His enthusiasm to lose no sheep from the fold was not mixed with any ambition to make the Catholic church an ally of social radicalism at large. Priests and laymen who had discussed the leakage during Manning's regime appeared not to be looking towards him for inspiration or advice, and the cardinal himself was far more absorbed by the task of winning the English people. One of Vaughan's first acts at Westminster was to launch a new organization for maintaining the faith of the poor. The purpose of this body, the Catholic Social Union, was to enlist 'the rich, the educated, and the refined' to help mission priests preserve the faith of poor Catholics in cities.[3] It represented the most authoritative effort so far to induce in Catholics, and to organize, the impulse which led other groups of Christians to found settlements and missions. When the Catholic Social Union was formed there was already one settlement, Newman House, which had been established in Southwark in 1891. Several other small settlements were opened in London under the auspices of the Union by 1900.

In its report for 1900 the Union claimed that 'ladies and

[1] E. S. Purcell, *op. cit.* II. 714. Purcell was not the most reliable of writers, but this part of his account was not challenged by Catholic reviewers who disagreed with him fiercely on other scores.

[2] J. E. C. Bodley, *Cardinal Manning, The Decay of Idealism in France, The Institute of France, Three Essays* (1912), p. 35.

[3] H. Vaughan, *The Work of the Catholic Laity* (1899), p. 10.

gentlemen have steadily come forward, with untiring energy and zeal, and have devoted themselves, night after night, to one great aim, namely, that of winning back to God and His Church those whom He has particularly chosen as His friends – the poor.'[1] Vaughan even said that the organization signified 'the bringing back of English society to the Catholic Brotherhood, in which every man is his brother's keeper.'[2] This was grand language to use about a few settlements, a Catholic Boy's Brigade begun in South London in 1896 on the model of a similar non-Catholic body, ten clubs in London, and some help to priests in Sheffield.

Ladies had supported the movement, as they did all pastoral activity among the poor, more readily than gentlemen.[3] Some of them were said to be freer with their well-filled purses than was good either for the church or for the poor, pauperizing Catholics instead of toughening their faith. 'It is hopeless', said a friendly critic of the Catholic Social Union,

> to put a band of kind-hearted, inexperienced ladies fresh from the ease and luxury of their West End homes and having at their command the means of giving *unrestrictedly*, face to face with the distressing misery of the East End, and expect them to give wisely.[4]

For a few years the Union, benefiting doubtless by Vaughan's association with it, had some success in engaging lay energy against the leakage. But the helpers were still far from adequate. 'If only we could have more, many more, such helpers, especially in large cities,' said the *Month* in 1901, 'what a difference it would make in our power to promote the welfare, spiritual and temporal, of our Catholic poor. . . .'[5] The achievement of this particular body, moreover, was temporary. The Catholic Social Union died early in the twentieth century, and the task of overcoming the forces making for an apathetic laity was taken up by the Catholic Social Guild, an organization with wider social aims founded in 1909.[6]

[1] *Report of the Catholic Social Union* (1900), p. 9.
[2] H. Vaughan, *op. cit.* p. 10.
[3] J. Norris, *The Help of the Laity* (1900), p. 12.
[4] *Month*, Nov. 1895, pp. 324–5.
[5] *Month*, Oct. 1901, p. 401.
[6] G. P. McEntee, *The Social Catholic Movement in Great Britain* (1927), pp. 164–5.

Catholicism and England

More than Christians of any other denomination, Catholics could anticipate high rewards merely from an increase in the facilities for direct spiritual instruction among the working classes. Most of the non-worshippers among these classes had not 'leaked' from any church: they had never been attached to one. But because Catholicism was more popular in Ireland than Protestantism in England, the Catholic church could rely on a reserve of loyalty, among the immigrants, to the faith of their old land. When the problem was not to initiate the habit of worship but to preserve or revive it, it was reasonable to see a better supply of clergy and a better provision of denominational schools as fruitful responses. The most extensive essay on the situation of Catholicism in England written before 1900 concluded: 'Our hope for the future is based on the increase of missions in large towns, so that the people may all be brought under the personal influence of the priesthood.'[1] The author, writing in 1892, believed that the worst of the leakage was over because the shortage of priests and churches and schools was no longer appalling. The number of priests in England, just over 800 in 1850, more than trebled by the end of the century. The number of children in Catholic schools in England increased greatly, thanks to the energy of priests, the generosity of some laymen, and grants from parliament. Until 1880 or so, this growth in the means for spiritual instruction was outpaced by the flow of immigrants; but when the flow slackened, the fruits of expanding pastoral and educational activity began slowly to be visible. The leakage was never again the source of extreme alarm which it had been in the 'eighties.

At the upper levels of English society, Catholicism was regarded more acquiescently in 1900 than it had been at the restoration of the hierarchy fifty year earlier. At the Queen's second jubilee in 1897 Catholics expressed loud gratitude to England for its liberality.[2] Some believed that tolerance had filtered generally through society: the arch-Protestant Bishop of Liverpool, J. C. Ryle, lamented in 1897 that 'aversion to

[1] J. Morris, 'Catholic England in Modern Times', part VI, *Month*, May 1892, p. 41.

[2] Catholic Truth Society, *Queen Victoria: Sixty Years of Catholic Progress* (1897), p. 14.

papistry', part of the nation's heritage, had gone and that Romanism was seen now as simply one of the many forms of religion in the country.[1]

It is possible that the neighbours of a working-class Catholic in 1900 were less hostile to him on account of his alien religion than were similar people fifty years earlier. Certainly many political leaders of the working classes took a not unfriendly view of Rome, owing largely to Manning's social activities.[2] The old hatred of Rome nevertheless persisted among many people at all social levels, and a dislike of Irishmen remained widespread, especially among labourers with whom they competed for employment. The conversion of England was still a very distant goal in 1900. The English people were either too loyal to Protestant traditions, too suspicious, or too stolid, to follow the trickle of converts into the Roman fold. In the long run it was the Irish famine, not the converts, that made Catholicism numerically significant for the first time in modern English history. Except for the leakage, the numbers would doubtless have been much greater. On the other hand, the fecundity of those families who remained loyal helped to make up for the loss of the rest. It was the prevalence of large families among working-class Catholics which, more than any other factor, produced during the twentieth century a gradual increase in the proportion of Catholics in England.[3]

[1] P. Thureau-Dangin, *The English Catholic Revival in the Nineteenth Century*, I. xxviii.

[2] See below, pp. 308–20.

[3] D. R. Gwynn, *op. cit.* p. xxv.

4

Settlements

Jacob and Esau

TOYNBEE Hall and the other 'settlements' which followed it were experiments in religious and social action, conducted by people who accepted a responsibility as Christians and gentlemen to live for a time among the urban working classes. The founders of settlements believed that clergymen alone would never succeed in the slums without the partnership of squires. 'The dwellers in the East end of our towns,' wrote a clergyman,

> will not be converted by missionaries and tracts sent by dwellers in the West End. The dwellers in the West End must go to the dwellers in the East themselves, share with the East those pleasures which give interest and delight to the dwellers in the West, and make up the fulness of their life. When the dwellers in the West go thus to the dwellers in the East they will be themselves converted, for they will have turned to Christ and accepted His yoke of personal service, and the dwellers in the East, recognizing the true helpfulness of the Christian life, will be converted too.[1]

The settlers hoped by their presence both to civilize working-class people and to make them Christians.

Among the many public comments on *The Bitter Cry of Outcast London*, the pamphlet produced by London Congregationalists in 1883, was an essay by the Rev. Brooke Lambert in

[1] W. Moore Ede, *The Attitude of the Church to some of the Social Problems of Town Life* (1896), pp. 102–3.

the *Contemporary Review.*[1] Lambert, who was now vicar of Greenwich and who had been a vicar in Whitechapel for some years, agreed with the authors of *The Bitter Cry* that the problem of the urban poor was a solemn one; but he dismissed their idea that mission halls and philanthropy would help to solve it. The gap between classes, he believed, yawned dangerously wide now, and could be closed only if members of the educated classes went among the poor and helped them back to humanity, becoming a Jacob in Esau's need. The path had already been shown, he said, by men like his friend Edward Denison, the son of a Bishop of Salisbury, who had gone to live in Stepney just before 1870 because he was convinced that East London needed a 'resident gentry'. Denison once explained his motive to a friend in these words: 'as I have both means, time and inclination, I should be a thief and a murderer if I withheld what I so evidently owe.'[2]

A sense of missionary duty had taken Lambert himself to working-class London, as it took many young clergymen whose family, education and acquaintance could easily have won them cosy rural livings. At Whitechapel he had been active in local administration and had formed several secular clubs and societies. The historian J. R. Green, a mutual friend of Denison and Lambert, was doing similar work as a vicar in Stepney when, in 1869, the three men met at John Ruskin's invitation to discuss plans for a colony of university men in London to carry on the kind of work which each had been doing independently. They agreed that men of culture should live among the poor in London, sitting on local boards, guiding education, and in general performing a social function complementary to the religious work of missions. Nothing came immediately of this meeting. Denison soon left for Australia and died on the way. Green, also seriously ill, gave up clerical life to write his *Short History of the English People.* Lambert remembered their plans, however; in 1881 he addressed a group of undergraduates in Merton College, Oxford, apparently urging them to come to help in Whitechapel.[3] By 1883 no general plan had been launched,

[1] B. Lambert, 'The Outcast Poor: I – Esau's Cry', *Contemporary Review,* Dec. 1883, pp. 916–23.

[2] Sir B. Leighton, ed., *Letters and Other Writings of the Late Edward Denison* (1884), p. 48.

[3] H. O. Barnett, *Canon Barnett, His Life, Work and Friends* (1921), p. 305.

but a number of young men from the universities had made individual decisions to live for a time in the slums. Theodore Talbot, a Christ Church man whose father was a landowning member of parliament and whose grandfather was a peer, worked as a lay assistant to the clergy of St Alban's, Holborn, shortly before he died in 1876.[1] Edmund Hollond, a friend of Denison's, and the son of a prominent Evangelical Churchman, followed Denison to Stepney in 1869.[2] Several undergraduates from Oxford, including Alfred Milner, R. L. Nettleship and Arnold Toynbee, spent vacations in the 1870s working in Whitechapel at the invitation of Samuel Barnett.[3] As vicar of St Jude's, Barnett was running the decrepit parish as experimentally as the conventions of the Church of England permitted. When Arnold Toynbee died in 1883, Barnett planned and built the first settlement as a monument to him and as a place where men of Toynbee's spirit could approach the poor by a novel route.

In September 1884 Brooke Lambert wrote again in the *Contemporary Review*, announcing that Jacob had answered Esau's cry.[4] With high excitement he suggested that just as war, and more recently commerce, had been the great outlet for human energies, so now 'the enthusiasm for humanity' might have its turn. He reported that Barnett and young friends from the universities, displaying this quality, were preparing to bring a leaven of culture and religion to the urban masses.

The first clear step towards Toynbee Hall was taken in November 1883, when Barnett read a paper to a group in St John's College, Oxford.[5] Barnett argued at this meeting that the college missions lately formed in parts of London were not an adequate expression for the desire of university men to help the poor. A mission, he said, lasted only until its district could become an independent parish; then the Eccesliastical Commissioners would take over financial responsibility, the bishop would probably acquire the patronage, and the college's

[1] G. W. E. Russell in *Commonwealth*, June 1896, pp. 217–8.

[2] R. A. Woods and A. J. Kennedy, *The Settlement Horizon* (1922), p. 21n.

[3] S. A. and H. O. Barnett, *Practicable Socialism* (new series, 1915), pp. 112–3.

[4] B. Lambert, 'Jacob's Answer to Esau's Cry', *Contemporary Review*, Sept. 1884, pp. 373–82.

[5] S. A. Barnett, *Settlements of University Men in Great Towns* (Oxford, 1884).

connexion would end. Nonconformists, moreover, were excluded from helping a college mission. Although he admitted that a mission could do good, Barnett suggested that what he called a settlement was fitted better to receive the spirit of the universities. His idea was that graduates and undergraduates should live together in East London, some working in London as curates or professional men and living permanently at the settlement, while others, working elsewhere or still studying, spent their vacations as residents. A clergyman, maintained by university subscriptions, would be in charge. The residents would co-operate with surrounding clergy, and they would be active in charitable activities, clubs, local government and university extension teaching. Although no resident would be required to pass any test of orthodoxy, the settlement would indeed be religious. 'The true religious teacher,' said Barnett, 'is he who makes known God to man. God is manifest to every age by that which is the Best of the age.' The special need of this age, he implied, was a restoration of intimacy between classes – a task as truly Christian as the most direct evangelism. The uplifting of the poor, as Barnett described it, was also religious; the inhabitants of settlements would be preparing a future 'when the disinherited sons of God shall be received into their Father's house. . . .'

In the rooms of Cosmo Lang, the future Archbishop, a meeting of undergraduates pledged itself to support Barnett's plan.[1] By February 1884 enough money was in hand to buy an old building in Whitechapel for the settlement, and prospective residents were being canvassed. In London, a committee including A. J. Balfour and the Duke of Westminster was appointed to buy and maintain the building and raise more money. Later in 1884 Toynbee Hall's first residents moved in, with Barnett as their warden.

The Mood of Oxford

Some of Barnett's audience at Oxford in November 1883 may have been drawn by reading or hearing about the *Bitter Cry*, published a few weeks earlier. If they attended morning service in St Mary's a fortnight before Barnett spoke, they saw

[1] H. O. Barnett, *op. cit.* p. 310.

the Head Master of Harrow, Dr Butler, flourish the pamphlet during a sermon and heard him pray that it would rouse the best to grapple 'with this supreme question of moral and physical destitution. . . .'[1] But as Barnett remarked: 'Undergraduates and graduates, long before the late outcry, had become conscious that social conditions were not right, and that they themselves were called to do something.'[2] His address in November was only an expansion of a letter written in June, in reply to some members of St John's College, Cambridge, who had asked him for suggestions about helping the poor. In May he had addressed a meeting in Oriel College, Oxford, appealing for money and men to help remove misery in East London. Barnett later attributed the response to his call for settlements to a general dissatisfaction in the universities with social and religious institutions. Men at the universities, he wrote,

> were conscious of something wrong underneath modern progress; they realized that free trade, reform bills, philanthropic activity, and missions had made neither health nor wealth. They were drawn to do something for the poor. . . . The chief machine, the Poor Law, seemed to have increased pauperism. Societies had become empty shells, missions seemed sometimes to corrupt men.[3]

In Barnett's view, a new uneasiness stirred Oxford and Cambridge, seeking new forms of social and religious service in which to express itself. Alfred Milner, an early resident of Toynbee Hall, described similarly a change of mood in Oxford between 1873 and 1883, a change 'which restored freedom of thought to economic speculation and gave a new impulse to philanthropy. . . .[4]

During 1883 and 1884 Oxford's interest in social problems was high. Well-known social radicals were giving addresses to large audiences. Joseph Arch spoke at the Town Hall early in 1883 on behalf of the Agricultural Labourers' Union, supported by several senior dons on his platform. When Frederick Rogers, bookbinder from Whitechapel, spoke to more than fifty men at St John's on social reform, the *Oxford Magazine*

[1] *Oxford Magazine*, 31 Oct. 1883, p. 334.
[2] S. A. Barnett, *Settlements of University Men in Great Towns*, p. 3.
[3] W. Reason, ed., *University and Social Settlements* (1898), pp. 12–3.
[4] A. Milner, *Arnold Toynbee: a Reminiscence* (1895), p. 49.

observed: 'it has been recognized, especially at this last meeting, that Oxford has much to learn from the working classes as well as the working classes from Oxford.'[1] A lecture from Henry George was given a stormy hearing, which the same journal put down not to his social doctrines but to two unfortunate assumptions by the speaker: that the audience had read his works, and that they were ignorant about the conditions of the poor. 'To us in Oxford,' said the journal, 'in whose ears has been ringing for this past year or more the exceeding bitter cry of the outcast, it seemed superfluous and almost impertinent to insist upon this fact.'[2] William Morris, far more radical than the rhetorical American but more congenial to Oxford, was applauded at a crowded meeting in the hall of University College when he declared himself a socialist. 'Great interest was with reason aroused by Mr Morris's lecture . . .' said the *Oxford Magazine*.

> Apart from its own merits, the fact of its being given, and the manner in which it was received, . . . emphasize a new phase of feeling in Oxford. The question has been asked, 'Is the new Oxford movement to be a Socialistic one?' and if this be interpreted to mean 'Is the most living interest of Oxford now that in social questions?' the answer must be distinctly Yes![3]

Respectable preachers in college chapels, as well as heretical visitors, talked to Oxford men about the gravity of the social question and their duty towards the victims of social disorder. The Master of University College, J. F. Bright, disliked what William Morris said; yet in the week of Morris' visit he preached a sermon deploring that the poor should live so squalidly while property-owners flourished on their misery. Was this not the work of the Devil? Had not eighteen centuries of Christianity produced a dismal failure?[4] A visiting preacher

[1] *Oxford Magazine*, 5 Dec. 1883, p. 432. This journal first appeared on 24 Jan. 1883 (and not in 1882, as its present conductors assert). It was fairly described in a prospectus as 'a periodical which shall include among its contributors and readers both Graduate and Undergraduate members of the University, and which shall represent every side of Oxford life'.

[2] *Ibid.*, 7 March 1884, p. 150. The words 'this past year or more' suggest that this phase of interest in poverty had begun more than six months before *The Bitter Cry* appeared.

[3] *Ibid.*, 21 Nov. 1883, p. 384.

[4] *Ibid.* p. 398.

in Balliol College chapel told his congregation that true charity required a man not merely to relieve his neighbours' wants, but to enter sympathetically into their feelings, 'bearing their woes and carrying their sorrows, in order that he may be able at once both to supply their needs and elevate their characters.[1] A sermon by F. W. Farrar struck a similar note. 'Old Oxford could afford to stand still,' Farrar said,

> or could decorously attend only to religion, or to the quiet needs of country parishes. Young Oxford must move forward, must grapple with modern town-life, must regard philanthropy to be comprised in the sweep of its Christian efforts.[2]

In 1883 and 1884, about half the sermons reported in the *Oxford Magazine* (no radical organ) referred at least partly to social problems. Many of them exhorted undergraduates to make the kind of effort which Barnett was designing Toynbee Hall to accommodate.

Arnold Toynbee embodied exactly Barnett's idea of a resident in a settlement, and his early death just before the first settlement was founded made the use of his name in its title an appropriate gesture. As Beatrice Webb recorded in *My Apprenticeship*, Toynbee knelt to the masses in the name of the upper and middle classes. His social theory presupposed that the rich as a whole could be persuaded to repent for making the poor suffer, and to accept voluntarily a redistribution of wealth.[3] The Slade Professor of Fine Art, John Ruskin, also believed that social reform could be achieved by plucking at the conscience of the rulers. It is not clear whether Toynbee learned much from Ruskin. At least he respected him enough to join Oscar Wilde and others in the digging party which in 1874, under Ruskin's direction, tried in vain to make a road to Hinksey.[4]

In religion Toynbee was one of those who, though dissatisfied with many teachings of the Church of England, believed that it could be reformed from within. His friend Alfred Milner

[1] *Ibid.*, 14 Feb. 1883, p. 76.

[2] *Ibid.*, 5 Nov. 1884, p. 381.

[3] A. Toynbee, *Progress and Poverty: A Criticism of Mr Henry George* (1883), pp. 49–50; A. Toynbee, 'Are Radicals Socialists?', in his *Lectures on the Industrial Revolution* (1884), pp. 231–2, 237.

[4] J. Evans, *John Ruskin* (1954), pp. 351, 364, 381.

said that Toynbee kept a faith in personal immortality.[1] Toynbee himself wrote in a letter a few months before he died: 'you could, I think, consider me a Christian, though I do not hold a great many of the doctrines of Christian Theology.'[2] He saw it as a profoundly religious task to improve the condition of the masses. 'Any attempt to preach a purer religion must go along with attempts at social reform,' he wrote; '. . . progress will never be organic until the religious spirit breathes through every act and institution.'[4] Any of these remarks might have been made by Barnett himself. As an undergraduate and a tutor at Balliol, Toynbee influenced many of his contemporaries. According to Milner,

> it was a distinguishing mark of those who came under Toynbee's influence, that they were deeply impressed with their individual duty as citizens, and filled with an enthusiasm for social equality, which led them to aim at bridging the gulf between the educated and the wage-earning class.[4]

A year before he himself died, Toynbee had been shocked deeply by the death of T. H. Green, who was then Professor of Moral Philosophy and who had been since 1866 a tutor at Balliol. Both directly and through Toynbee, who acknowledged a considerable mental and moral debt to him, Green's teaching and his example helped to make Oxford men think about living in a settlement. A passage in Mrs Humphrey Ward's novel *Robert Elsmere* describes the hero attending the funeral of 'Henry Grey' (T. H. Green) and musing about his dead teacher and friend:

> fresh from his own grapple with London and its life, what moved him most was the memory of the citizen, the friend and brother of common man, the thinker who never shirked action in the name of thought, for whom conduct had been from beginning to end the first reality.[5]

A pupil and friend, Henry Scott Holland, said of Green that he

[1] *Commonwealth*, March 1897, p. 105.

[2] G. Toynbee, *Reminiscences and Letters of Joseph and Arnold Toynbee* (n. d.), p. 165.

[3] A. Toynbee, 'Notes and Jottings' in his *Lectures on the Industrial Revolution*, p. 244.

[4] A. Milner, *Arnold Toynbee: a Reminiscence*, p. 27.

[5] Mrs H. Ward, *Robert Elsmere* (Nelson's Library, n.d.), p. 515.

had identified the interests of the ideal imagination with the common affairs of living men and women, and charged Holland and others

> with the democratic ardour which made him always the active champion of the poor and the preacher of the obligations of citizenship. . . . For us all he wore something of the prophetic air, and his too early death gave power to his prophecy.[1]

Green's emphasis on conduct, on the duties of citizenship, was displayed both in action and in writing. He was the first don to become a member of the Oxford Town Council; he spoke on public platforms for the Oxford Reform League; he was elected to the Oxford School Board; and he was president of the Oxford Band of Hope Temperance Union.[2] None of these activities was very important in itself: they were made, and taken, as the symbolic actions of a philosopher who believed in being involved in the affairs of society. According to an anonymous writer in the *Oxford Magazine* in 1883, the most important parts of his *Prolegomena to Ethics* were

> those parts where he attempted to discuss such a practical question as this, 'In relieving a beggar was I not merely compounding with conscience for shirking the trouble, which a more judicious exercise of charity would have cost me?' . . . It was in the attempt to get some light on these questions of actual life, and to point the way amid a collision of duties by reference to the spirit which gives them all their binding force, that the most practical effect of his teaching can be found.[3]

The most sensitive and sympathetic of his pupils were stirred by the dedicated humanism of Green's thinking, and by his social conscience. 'Lead a useful life,' he said to his wife as he died;[4] and in effect this was what he said to the young.

Whether Green's philosophic idealism and radical liberalism were connected as logically as he believed is a question best left to members of his own profession. What matters in the present context is that a man esteemed as he was should have deliber-

[1] H. Scott Holland, *A Bundle of Memories* (1915), pp. 145–6.

[2] On these and other activities, see R. L. Nettleship, *Memoir of Thomas Hill Green* (1906).

[3] *Oxford Magazine*, 7 Feb. 1883, p. 58.

[4] E. Abbott and L. Campbell, *The Life and Letters of Benjamin Jowett* (1897), II. 470.

ately set out to stir the civic conscience of people in Oxford, should have blessed unionism and the co-operative movement, advocated universal suffrage and asserted that the old universities had social responsibilities to the rest of England, and in particular to poorer citizens. His following was not vast. But the people whom he did affect were often affected profoundly, and they were a remarkably mixed band. Although his attitude to Christianity was even less orthodox than Arnold Toynbee's ('He could not be a clergyman,' said Robert Elsmere), much of his teaching was assimilated by Christians who thought themselves the guardians of orthodoxy: his honey, as Mark Pattison observed, was carried off to the hives of sacerdotalism.[1] Some Nonconformists also found him inspiring. Samuel Barnett noticed that the uneasiness which made young university men eager to come to Toynbee Hall was especially strong among those who had felt the influence of Green.[2]

Toynbee Hall also owed something to what Mrs Barnett called 'the constant, kindly sympathy' of Benjamin Jowett, the Master of Balliol.[3] It was even said after his death in 1893 that the settlement was founded largely under Jowett's inspiration.[4] Once, in 1875, when Barnett was addressing a meeting in the hall at Balliol, Jowett turned up unexpectedly, blessed the proceedings, and advised everybody present to 'make some of his friends among the poor.'[5] With this exception, however, it is hard to find any particular action by which Jowett contributed to the foundation of Toynbee Hall. Despite their close association Jowett did not really approve of Green, and did not share his dissatisfaction with the older liberalism.[6] His social consciousness was far less acute than Toynbee's, and he believed some of Toynbee's thinking callow and utopian.[7] He once remarked that in theory he had a great love for the poor; he believed that workers had the right to strike, until masons

[1] M. Pattison, *Memoirs* (1885), p. 167.

[2] W. Reason, ed., *op. cit.* p. 12.

[3] S. A. and H. O. Barnett, *Practicable Socialism*, p. 116.

[4] *Toynbee Record*, Dec. 1893, p. 37.

[5] H. O. Barnett, *op. cit.* p. 305.

[6] E. Abbott and L. Campbell, *op. cit.* II. 199; M. Asquith, *Autobiography* (Penguin, 1936), I. 37; L. E. Elliott-Binns, *English Thought, 1860–1900. The Theological Aspect* (1956), p. 126.

[7] B. Jowett, 'Memoir', in A. Toynbee, *Lectures on the Industrial Revolution*, pp. xiii, xviii.

struck at Balliol.[1] Twice he visited Toynbee Hall, but Mrs Barnett recalled that he found Whitechapel

> rough and noisy, the number of interests confusing, the freedom of equality too apparent, and everybody perhaps over-anxious to please him. . . . The Master referred more than once to all he had seen during his visits to the East End, but he evidently preferred to see us amid the dignity of Balliol.[2]

Jowett resented any enterprise which distracted his young men from their climb towards the summit of society. An ironic reporter of a sermon he preached on 'The Causes of Success and Failure in Life' said:

> Only occasionally . . . did there gleam across the fine-spun thread of the discourse a consciousness of the fact that men may be looked upon as something other (if not higher) than embryo Lord Justices or Bishops.[3]

Jowett confessed candidly to Mrs Barnett after Toynbee Hall had been open for some years: 'I used to be afraid of sending my men to you, not knowing what you would do to them; but now I safely send them for you are ambitious *for* them. A man's career should be his first concern.'[4] Perhaps Jowett's main contribution, then, was to assure his young men that by going to Toynbee Hall they could do good both to others and for themselves. Moreover, any word of blessing from a man with Jowett's prestige would probably win Barnett some support. He had the Barnetts to stay with him in Balliol when they were at Oxford recruiting. 'It is not possible to exaggerate,' wrote Mrs Barnett, 'what the hospitality of the Master of Balliol meant to us and through us to the Settlement movement.'[5] Jowett's attitude to religion also helped the enterprise. 'Balliol religion', a mixture of dogma and doubt concocted largely by Jowett, was summed up nicely in his remark to a young friend in 1892: 'My dear child, you must believe in God in spite of what the clergy tell you.'[6] It involved a scepticism about miracles and about scriptural inerrancy, a tendency to regard God as a spirit expressed in man, and Christ as the ideal

[1] E. Abbott and L. Campbell, *op. cit.* I. 343–4; II. 101–2.
[2] H. O. Barnett, *op. cit.* p. 439.
[3] *Oxford Magazine*, 12 Nov. 1884, p. 393.
[4] H. O. Barnett, *op. cit.* p. 415.
[5] *Ibid.* p. 414.
[6] M. Asquith, *op. cit.* I. 117.

human being; it involved, above all, an emphasis on practical morality. In religious matters Jowett was the teacher of Green and Toynbee, though Green went further than his master towards heresy. Green was expressing 'Balliol religion' when he spoke of an age in which the religious needs of man would be 'rather met by the sympathies of a society breathing the Christian spirit than by the propositions of an anthropomorphic theology.'[1] So was Toynbee when, according to Milner, he demonstrated the rationality of his faith 'by being as sober, as practical and as effective as any so-called Rationalist or Utilitarian.'[2] In a religion so purged of ritual and theology, benevolent action was the most satisfying form of worship. Indirectly therefore, Jowett provided an incentive to social service; and Barnett offered an opportunity for it.

The appeal of Barnett himself, preaching his gospel of settlements, was an important ingredient of his success. Scott Holland described him as a quiet, unexciting but convincing prophet, who came to Oxford just when a prophet was needed.[3] Another in Barnett's audience in 1883 spoke of him as 'a gentle and powerful spirit.'[4] At a time when English consciences were stirring uneasily over the condition of the urban masses, Barnett spoke in just the right tone of voice to some privileged young members of his own university (he had been at Wadham from 1862 to 1865) in whom the ideal of service had been planted by their teachers. 'He caught the ear of the Universities,' wrote a clergyman, James Adderley,

> especially of Oxford. 'Do you realize,' he would say, 'that all our social system is arranged on the tacit assumption that there is a leisured class in every locality who will see that the laws are carried out and generally keep the social life going? Do you also realize that there is no such class in East London, where it is most wanted? Come and be that class, not in a patronizing spirit but in a spirit of neighbourliness.[5]

Adderley observed that Barnett was exactly the man to teach the rich how to repent.[6]

[1] R. L. Nettleship, *op. cit.* p. 159.
[2] A. Milner, *op. cit.* p. 37.
[3] H. Scott Holland, *op. cit.* p. 92.
[4] T. Hancock Nunn, quoted in H. O. Barnett, *Canon Barnett*, p. 309.
[5] J. Adderley, *In Slums and Society* (1916), p. 48.
[6] H. O. Barnett, *op. cit.* p. 649.

The mood of social concern which Barnett exploited was far from universal in Oxford. There were common rooms where Home Rule and Disestablishment were the staples of controversy during the 'eighties; and as in every generation, there were staircases which no question of the day penetrated: 'a large proportion of Oxford undergraduates,' lamented a writer in the *Oxford Magazine* in 1883, 'come and go without ever becoming aware that there is a teacher or an influence in the University at all.'[1] Nor, of course, was the new social consciousness peculiar to Oxford. The settlements were nevertheless a very Oxonian response to the problem of social relationships. Cambridge had a part in the campaign for settlements. A Cambridge committee for Toynbee Hall, elected in June 1884, included Professors B. F. Westcott, J. R. Seeley and James Stuart – men who influenced Cambridge as much as Toynbee, Green and Jowett affected Oxford.[2] But Oxford was plainly the leader in the settlement movement, just as Cambridge, under Stuart, led the campaign for university extension. The members of St John's College, Cambridge, who in June 1883 invited Barnett to advise them about social service, were a group dissatisfied with their own college's plan for a conventional mission. Believing that Barnett's was a better approach to the urban poor, they came in behind the Oxford scheme to found Toynbee Hall.[3]

Toynbee Hall and Other Settlements

The distinction which Barnett drew between a settlement and a mission appeared to him a very important one, and in later years he described it more elaborately. 'A Mission exists to proselytize,' he wrote in 1897.[4] As a member of the Church of England he wanted to see people adopt certain principles, but as an Englishman he wished above all to see the islands of class joined by bridges of goodwill. The settlement, he believed, was a better base than the mission on which to build such bridges.

[1] *Oxford Magazine*, 7 Feb. 1883, p. 45–6.

[2] *Ibid.*, 4 June 1884, p. 281. See also J. A. R. Pimlott, *Toynbee Hall* (1935), pp. 35–7; H. O. Barnett, *op. cit.* pp. 425–7.

[3] A. Amos and W. H. Hough, eds., *The Cambridge Mission to South London* (1904), pp. 8–9.

[4] S. A. and H. O. Barnett, *Towards Social Reform* (1909), p. 271.

On local boards the rich could learn what the law can and cannot do for the poor; managing a school they could see the gaps in the educational system; in workmen's clubs they could learn how narrow are the pleasures of the mass; and by living among the poor they could help to pass on to the many the habits and refinements of the few. The visitors would be trusted more when it was known that they were not out to convert anybody. 'A sense of unity – like other good things – wears better when it comes unconsciously.'[1]

To Barnett, to other admirers of *Ecce Homo* and *Essays and Reviews*, and to people who had followed even less orthodox masters like T. H. Green, a settlement as described here might appear quite as religious as a mission. But Christians with a more conservative theological outlook could not be expected to agree. Although Barnett assured such Christians in 1883 that the tone of Toynbee Hall would be religious 'in the best and broadest sense,'[2] there were many, in Oxford and elsewhere, who denied that the broadest sense of religion was the best. A satirical novel about Toynbee Hall made the 'Broad' parson, who was plainly meant to be Barnett, send out invitations which ran: 'DEAR FRIEND, – Will you come to tea with Mrs Flux and me next Tuesday at half-past four, seeing that there are many religions but only one morality. – Yours earnestly, SIMEON FLUX.'[3] Toynbee Hall's religion was syncretic, undogmatic and humanitarian. Some men were attracted to it on that account. Others, though approving the general principle of settlements, looked for one which was more rigorously Christian.

Toynbee Hall expressed the spirit of Balliol. The next settlement to be established, Oxford House in Bethnal Green, came out of Keble College and represented the party associated with Keble's name. Its creators were among the leaders of what Mark Pattison, writing in 1884, sourly described as 'a clerical reaction' in Oxford; although influenced by the secular teachers of Oxford and especially by Green, they were still proud to identify themselves with the Tractarian tradition.[4]

[1] *Ibid.* p. 285.
[2] *Oxford Magazine*, 5 Dec. 1883, p. 438.
[3] C. R. Ashbee, *The Building of Thelema* (1910), p. 173.
[4] M. Pattison, *Memoirs*, p. 242.

They were frank, indeed vehement, about the overtly religious task of Oxford House. At the meeting which inaugurated it, the Bishop of Bedford, Walsham How, declared that the purpose of the settlement should be missionary; 'as I long that on the one hand the foundation of your work should be faith in our Blessed Lord,' he said, 'so I long, too, that the outcome of the work should be the true acceptance of that fundamental doctrine of the Incarnation, by which God and man are brought together. . . .'[1] Appealing on behalf of Oxford House, the Warden of Keble College, E. S. Talbot, who had been chairman at the inaugural meeting, said: 'one object animates the whole movement – the preparation of character for . . . the reception of the religion of Christ, for the advancement of which the Oxford House alone exists.[2] An early head of the settlement, H. Hensley Henson, contrasted its spirit with that of Toynbee Hall and asserted that a settlement should 'bear a Christian character and utter a Christian witness.' If the pagan East End was to believe in the Christianity of a settlement, he said, then the settlers must show a 'loyal intimacy' with the official Church in East London.[3] A few years after Henson made this remark, Oxford House became formally associated with the parochial work of St Matthew's, Bethnal Green.[4]

Although its residents, like those of Toynbee Hall, were laymen under a clerical head, Oxford House seems to have had a higher proportion who intended to become clergymen. Some of its lectures were meant to convert East End listeners, and in particular to defend the most vulnerable aspects of the Church of England. The ecclesiastical atmosphere attracted at least one resident from Toynbee Hall. Cosmo Lang, finding Toynbee Hall too academic and disinterested, went across to Oxford House, where, he said, 'they were rather loyally accepting something old and tried and sure and bringing it as a gospel, a good gift, to the people.'[5] In the view of A. F. Winnington-Ingram,

[1] *Work for University Men among the London Poor: Speeches* (1884), p. 10.

[2] *The Times*, 21 Jan. 1891, p. 13.

[3] H. Hensley Henson, 'The University Settlements in the East End', in *Some Urgent Questions in Christian Lights* (1889), p. 259. Henson was not a High Churchman, but at Oxford House he found that he had to seem one. See his *Retrospect of an Unimportant Life*, I. (1942), p. 27.

[4] *The Oxford House in Bethnal Green, 1884–1948*, (1948) p. 33.

[5] J. G. Lockhart, *Cosmo Gordon Lang* (1949), p. 50.

head of Oxford House from 1889 to 1898 and later Bishop of London, the point of having laymen as residents was itself apologetic; 'the very existence of a body of laymen,' he wrote, 'working in the cause of Christianity for the people is a protest against the idea that it is only the clergy who believe in Christianity.'[1]

The men at Oxford House gave Barnett the credit of having inspired them, and relations between supporters of the two schemes in Oxford were fairly cordial.[2] But as Mrs Barnett revealed after her husband died, the rival campaign distressed him. 'That men should think it necessary to start another settlement because Toynbee Hall was not in their opinion religious,' she wrote, 'was a deep, a very deep pain to Mr Barnett.'[3] She alleged that the High Church party tried to poach some Toynbee Hall men, and she said that antagonism was avoided only because Barnett bore disparagement so meekly. But their differences over religion should not obscure the similarity of purpose between these first two settlements. Especially under Winnington-Ingram, residents of Oxford House provided clubs for recreation, formed a sanitary aid committee, and agitated for improvements in housing. They took just as seriously as men at Toynbee Hall their responsibility to overcome bitterness and misunderstanding between classes. 'The resident settlers are designed to take the place of the fugitive natural leaders,' wrote one head of Oxford House. 'They ask the East End not to judge the educated classes by the absentees to whom they pay rent and render work, but to accept them as their truer representatives.'[4] On undergraduates with High Church sympathies, Winnington-Ingram had an effect rather like that of Barnett on young men with liberal theological views. A resident who heard him speak at Oxford said that he 'made us proud of Oxford House, and of its head, and most of us wished we could accept his invitation, and settle in the East End of London for a time.'[5]

[1] A. F. Winnington-Ingram, 'The Classes and the Masses', in *The Church of the People* (1894), p. 180.

[2] H. Scott Holland, *op. cit.* p. 93; W. Picht, *Toynbee Hall and the English Settlement Movement* (1914), p. 106n.

[3] H. O. Barnett, *op. cit.* p. 421.

[4] H. Hensley Henson, 'University Settlements in the East End', *loc. cit.* p. 256.

[5] *Sunday Magazine*, Feb. 1898, p. 110.

Of the settlements in London which followed these two, most were like Oxford House and unlike Toynbee Hall in being connected (some formally, some not) with a particular denomination and in undertaking evangelistic as well as social and educational work. Among the Nonconformists, in fact, there was a reluctance to approve of settlements unless they made a directly evangelistic approach to the surrounding population. When Scott Lidgett was trying to get support for a Wesleyan settlement he found that many suspected him of becoming a social reformer rather than an evangelist; and when the Conference gave formal authority to the Bermondsey Settlement in 1890, it specified that the work of the institution was to be 'Religious, Educational and Social.'[1] As warden of the settlement Lidgett was responsible for running two churches. He gave talks in and around the settlement expounding the Christian faith, and said later that 'the primary activity of the Bermondsey Settlement consisted in its religious work.'[2] The *British Weekly* kept a careful eye on two settlements run by Congregationalists, the Browning Settlement in Walworth and Mansfield House in Canning Town, for signs of any lapse towards the creedlessness of Toynbee Hall. When Browning Hall opened in 1895 the journal noted it as a reassuring thing that the settlement was to be connected with a local Congregational chapel and would offer religious teaching, non-sectarian but evangelical.[3] Mansfield House, which opened in 1890, pleased the *British Weekly* less. At a ceremony in 1896 to lay a stone to the memory of T. H. Green, the journal found a 'studious ignoring of the religious side of the Settlement,' and was apprehensive that the place might become a second-rate Toynbee Hall. 'Every settlement worth the name,' the leaders of Mansfield House were told, 'must be in a real sense a Christian mission.'[4]

Of the Nonconformist settlements, Mansfield House was certainly nearest to Toynbee Hall in religious atmosphere. The

[1] J. Scott Lidgett, *My Guided Life* (1936), p. 141; *Wesleyan Conference Minutes* (1890), p. 298.

[2] J. Scott Lidgett, *op. cit.* p. 141. On its evangelistic work see also P. Ashley, 'University Settlements in Great Britain', *Harvard Theological Review*, 1911, p. 179.

[3] *British Weekly*, 28 Oct. 1895, p. 89.

[4] *Ibid.*, 24 Dec. 1896, p. 183.

first warden, Percy Alden, was a Congregationalist who believed in uniting around him people inside and outside the churches who would pledge themselves to the service of humanity in the spirit of Jesus. An official account of the settlement spoke of its having 'a deeply religious aim, seeking to bring the teaching of Christ to bear upon all the problems of a poor man's life.'[1] But its members were more concerned in practice to carry out Christian works themselves than to try to convert the inhabitants of Canning Town. The classes they conducted were mostly vocational and wholly secular. This was one of the few settlements in London or elsewhere which on Barnett's definition was not in some aspects a mission.

Catholics regarded settlements as a device to help stop the leakage from the faith. St Philip's House in Mile End, the first Catholic settlement in East London, was the fruit of Cardinal Vaughan's anxiety about the abandoned Catholic poor.[2] Newman House in Southwark, which opened in 1891, was hailed by James Britten as answering a plea he had made for a positive gesture from Catholic university and public school men towards poorer Catholics in cities.[3] Another settlement with a missionary purpose, preaching a faith far from Rome's, was University Hall, formed in 1890 to carry on the social and religious message contained in *Robert Elsmere*, the novel by Mrs Humphry Ward which provoked an astonishing amount of discussion and which sold millions of copies. The hero had attained a kind of agnostic theism which, he believed, not only reconciled the need for a faith with the demands of modern intellect, but also had the power to make rich and poor care for each other. Surrounded by a group of mainly Unitarian friends – including Philip Wicksteed, who was about to bless, in the Labour Church, another social and religious experiment – Mrs Ward set about making a settlement which might embody her opaque message.[4] This was another hive into which the honey of T. H. Green passed: Mrs Ward said that one point of

[1] *Mansfield House Settlement in East London* (*Canning Town*) (1892). (A brochure.)

[2] D. Gleeson, 'The Decade of an East End Settlement', *Month*, Dec. 1904, pp. 598–9.

[3] Catholic Truth Society, *Conference Papers* (1891), pp. 98–9.

[4] Mrs H. Ward, *A Writer's Recollections* (1918), p. 290; J. P. Trevelyan, *The Life of Mrs Humphry Ward* (1923), pp. 82–5.

University Hall was to show that the faith of Green and Martineau and Stopford Brooke was viable. Its residents were also to perform acts of social service similar to those in settlements elsewhere. The missionary and practical activities ran uncomfortably in harness and before long came quite apart. In Gordon Square a middle-class audience heard lectures, and at Marchmont Hall in St Pancras a group of residents lived and worked in slums. This segregation of activities distressed Mrs Ward and disappointed Wicksteed, who had been warden of the enterprise and who now resigned. In 1898 the attempt to propagate neo-Unitarian religion was virtually abandoned, and the Passmore Edwards Settlement was formed to continue the social work.[1]

Whether missionary in purpose or not, whether run by Churchmen, Nonconformists, or Catholics, each of these institutions represented a gesture, by a group who held certain religious views in common and who came from the classes which had the largest share of education and wealth, to the classes which had the least. The Nonconformist settlers no less than the residents of Toynbee Hall and Oxford House conceived their role as a squirely one; indeed, many of the Nonconformists were themselves from the older universities. The first warden of Mansfield House, Percy Alden, was a graduate of Oxford, and so was its secretary Will Reason; the residents were mainly Oxford men, with a few from Cambridge. The initiative in founding it came in the first place from Mansfield College, the new Congregational establishment in Oxford.[2] Plans for the Bermondsey Settlement were laid first before Methodists at Oxford and Cambridge, and then before those at the University of Edinburgh and the University College of Wales.[3] According to the *Wesleyan Methodist Magazine*, this settlement also attracted 'medical students from Guys, business men from the city, and leisured men of means with no fixed occupation, all desirous of engaging in the social service of the poor. . . .'[4]

[1] J. P. Trevelyan, *op. cit.* pp. 90, 121; C. H. Herford, *Philip Henry Wicksteed, his Life and Work* (1931), pp. 99–100.

[2] *Life at Mansfield House* (1892), pp. 6–7; *Mansfield House Magazine*, Dec. 1893, p. 4.

[3] J. Scott Lidgett in *Wesleyan Methodist Magazine*, Jan. 1890, p. 75.

[4] Quoted in R. F. Wearmouth, *Methodism and the Struggle of the Working Classes, 1850–1900*, p. 152.

There were many other settlements. An unsectarian Women's University Settlement was founded in Southwark in 1887; an opposite number of Oxford House, called Cambridge House, appeared in Camberwell Road in 1897; and one of the settlements best known outside London, at Ancoats in Manchester, was opened in 1895. How many settlements existed at any time depended on one's definition; for the more evangelistic its work, the more reason was there for calling an institution a mission. In 1913 a student of the movement counted twenty-seven settlements in London, twelve in the rest of England, five in Scotland and one in Belfast; thirty-two of these were religious and twelve were not, with one doubtful case in Scotland; eighteen were directly associated with a university, and others had university men working in them.[1]

Settlements at Work

Around Barnett as warden, the first thirteen residents moved into Toynbee Hall in 1884. By 1889, 54 men had been in residence for periods varying from three months to four years. In local affairs, many of them began to act as Barnett said members of the leisured classes should. 'Toynbee men serve on the Local Boards,' he wrote in 1888, 'and take with them the wider views they have gained by education.'[2] Of the fifteen residents in that year, six were school managers, six were on committees to provide recreation, four were on committees of the Charity Organization Society, two were almoners for the Society for the Relief of Distress, one was a Poor Law guardian, and five worked in the summer for the Children's Country Holiday Fund. When Barnett decided that Whitechapel should have a public library, his young men canvassed ratepayers and gained an overwhelming vote in its favour in 1890. Residents conducted a campaign against the East London Waterworks Company in 1896 for not carrying out its contract, and after a conference at Toynbee Hall followed by a deputation to the President of the Local Government Board, the government intervened and the water supply improved.[3]

[1] W. Picht, *op. cit.* p. 99.
[2] H. O. Barnett, *op. cit.* p. 486.
[3] *Ibid.* pp. 451–2.

The line between philanthropic and political activity was bound to be crossed, as it was in this case, if the settlers were to carry out earnestly the civic role which Barnett had prepared for them. On occasions Toynbee men crossed the line more boldly. In the dockers' strike of 1889, despite Barnett's statement that the settlement was not *identified* with the strikers' cause, a number of residents were active in helping them to hold out.[1] In 1891 a busmen's strike was organized by two residents, A. P. Laurie and Llewellyn Smith, at the request of John Burns.[2] The study of unemployment conducted at Toynbee Hall may also be described as a political activity, since its purpose was reformist. In 1892 a 'Toynbee Commission' was organized by the settlement to report on the effects of trade depression on East London; and as a result of the report two hundred dockers were set to work on waste land in West Ham.[3] Ten years later Barnett devised a similar though more ambitious scheme of relief work outside London for the unemployed. The men began to drift back to London and William Beveridge, now sub-warden of Toynbee Hall, who with R. H. Tawney and others had been administering the plan, began to ask questions from which emerged (he said later) 'the theory of under-employment and the reserve of labour, as I developed it later in articles and lectures and in *Unemployment: A Problem of Industry*.'[4]

Although Toynbee Hall had officially no politics, and although the residents did include people of various opinions, there is little doubt that a large majority of them, and of the non-resident helpers and visiting speakers, were Liberal voters. Anybody who attended meetings at the settlement regularly from 1890 to 1900 would have heard many of England's leading Liberals and moderate socialists, talking on problems of social and imperial policy: some lecturing, others introducing debates, and many taking more than a passing interest in the institution by becoming 'associates', or sympathizers unable to become residents.

The core of Toynbee Hall's work was educational. The University Extension Society, whose teachers (among them

[1] *Toynbee Record*, Oct. 1889, p. 7; B. Tillett, *Memories and Reflections* (1931), p. 137.

[2] J. A. R. Pimlott, *op. cit.* pp. 86–7.

[3] H. O. Barnett, *op. cit.* p. 632.

[4] Lord Beveridge, *Power and Influence* (1953), pp. 23–4.

T. H. Huxley, George Goschen and the historian S. R. Gardiner) had been coming to Whitechapel at Barnett's invitation before 1880, based its activities in the district on Toynbee Hall from 1884. The settlement also ran its own classes. More than 130 different subjects were taught, and in 1896–7 alone the teachers included Arthur Sidgwick, Leslie Stephen, Frederic Harrison, A. V. Dicey, Sir Walter Besant, Augustine Birrell and Andrew Fairbairn.[1] One of Barnett's dreams was a University of East London, and it was in the light of this ideal that he saw the teaching work of Toynbee Hall. He was one of those liberals whose only article of dogma was a passionate faith in the cleansing and uplifting power of education. 'The social problem,' he wrote in 1893, 'is at root an edu cational problem . . . without more knowledge, power might be a useless weapon and money only a means of degradation. . . .'[2] In perhaps the last letter he wrote, Barnett said: 'The only thing which Liberals can compel is education, because till people are educated they cannot be free or use freedom.'[3] Toynbee Hall gained a name for vocational and cultural education. 'Toynbee Hall stands most for culture,' wrote Charles Booth, 'leading the way, teaching the teachers, lifting and ennobling all. . . .'[4] Some of this teaching was in a general sense religious, within the limits set by Barnett's determination not to make Toynbee Hall evangelistic. There were Sunday lectures on religion, but while some of the lecturers were clergymen and others Christian laymen, others again were not Christians at all. Prayers were conducted every morning by Barnett for those residents who wanted to attend them; but there was no pressure on them to come, and few did.[5]

What education was to Toynbee Hall, clubs were to Oxford House. Apart from the religious question, this was the main difference between the two settlements. Charles Booth, assessing the work of the three large clubs intended to attract inhabitants of Bethnal Green, particularly men and boys, observed that Oxford House had 'accomplished the difficult feat of club

[1] W. Reason (ed.), *op. cit.* p. 56.
[2] H. O. Barnett, *op. cit.* p. 340.
[3] *Ibid.* p. 734.
[4] C. Booth, *Life and Labour of the Poor in London*, 3rd. series, *Religious Influences* (1902), VII. 380.
[5] H. O. Barnett, *op. cit.* p. 490.

management without beer and without betting, or any of the other evils which are ruining so many of the great social and political working men's clubs, and causing them to be regarded as curses to the community.'[1] The political views of residents of Oxford House possibly varied even more than those of men at Toynbee Hall. During the dock strike of 1889, however, James Adderley saw to it that the radicals made the pace by collecting money for the strikers. One resident, Cosmo Lang, may have given unwitting aid in the same cause. When he lectured on Napoleon's strategy some time before the strike, he had in his audience Ben Tillett, who had a particular interest in Bonaparte because he was exactly the same height, and who learned from Lang's lecture, so he said, moves that proved useful when he came to run the great strike.[2]

The Congregational institutions, Mansfield House and Browning Settlement, were involved in activity for social reforms. The public campaign for old-age pensions which began at the end of 1898 was launched at Browning Hall, the home of the Browning Settlement; the National Committee of Organized Labour, a body created to work for pensions, was founded at Browning Hall; and in 1909, when the Act for pensions had been passed, Herbert Samuel paid a tribute to 'the splendid educational work which the Settlement had done' towards it.[3] The Browning Settlement also offered the usual study groups and recreations, and distributed some charitable relief. Its members were active on local public bodies, and declared their sympathy with Labour:

> We stand for the endeavour to gain for Labour not merely more of the good things of life, but most of the best things of life. Come and join us in the service of Him who is the Lord of Labour and the soul of all social reform.[4]

This conviction that settlers should engage in social reform for religious reasons was strong at Mansfield House. 'To carry out Christ's teaching fully,' wrote one of its leaders, 'we felt that a vigorous attack must be made on the evil *conditions* of life in

[1] C. Booth, *op. cit.* II. 88.
[2] B. Tillett, *op. cit.* pp. 112–3.
[3] F. H. Stead, *How Old Age Pensions Began to Be* (1909), p. 316.
[4] W. Reason, ed., *op. cit.* p. 181.

the district.'[1] To this end committees were set up on public health, education, the Poor Law, and other matters on which local initiative could be exercised. Representatives of the settlement gained election to the West Ham School Board, the Town Council and the Board of Guardians. A lodging house with beds at threepence to sixpence (and hymns on Sundays) was opened in 1893, and provided some 50,000 beds a year. The first 'poor man's lawyer' gave his services at Mansfield House from 1891. An associated Women's Settlement, formed in 1893, opened a hospital and a convalescent home. In national politics Mansfield House was solidly Liberal. Its vice-presidents included C. S. Horne and R. W. Dale, two leaders of the alliance between Nonconformity and Liberalism. Among its visiting speakers, however, were some more radical, including Ramsay MacDonald, Tom Mann and Keir Hardie. Such speakers presumably went down well among the inhabitants of Canning Town, who included Keir Hardie's electors. The warden, Percy Alden, described it as 'undoubtedly the most Radical district in England.'[2]

Despite their doctrinal and tactical differences, the leaders of settlements felt that they were parts of a single movement. Occasionally they joined forces. A conference on settlements was held in January 1895 on the initiative of Sir John Gorst, who now represented the University of Cambridge in parliament, and who had recently become an ardent convert to the principle of settlements.[3] The sponsors of this conference explained that they wanted to discuss what had been done so far in university settlements, and to encourage more people to reside in them. A number of clergymen and aristocratic laymen sat on the platform with representatives from most large English towns. 'The discussion was admirable if saddening,' wrote Mrs Barnett, 'for all seemed to agree as to the increasing separation of rich and poor in towns.'[4] One new settlement seems to have emerged from the conference.[5]

[1] W. Reason, *A Week at Mansfield House* (1893), p. 4.

[2] *British Weekly*, 5 Dec. 1895, p. 111. Keir Hardie was elected M.P. for South West Ham in 1892.

[3] Sir John Gorst in J. M. Knapp, ed., *The Universities and the Social Problem* (1895), pp. 6–9.

[4] H. O. Barnett, *op. cit.* p. 441.

[5] *Toynbee Record*, April 1895, p. 100.

Later in 1895, when the new Prime Minister, Lord Salisbury, made a speech about the need for social reform, a group of settlement leaders (from Toynbee Hall, Oxford House, the Browning and Bermondsey Settlements, and Mansfield House) greeted his remarks with delight and urged him to do something about the problems he had recognized. A similar joint statement was drawn up by Barnett in 1904 and signed by fourteen past or present heads of settlements, urging the rich to give up luxury in the spirit of Christ and the interest of national stability.[1] This was an old cause of Barnett's. Twenty years earlier he had said that the unemployed in East London were 'simply the reverse side of the unemployed who crowd West End clubs and drawing-rooms.'[2] He had faith that social problems could be solved when the wealthy showed some of the self-sacrifice which led the most dedicated among them to live in settlements. If Barnett or any of the other settlement leaders had lost this faith, it is unlikely that the movement would have continued for long.

The Practice of Neighbourliness

Of all the activities undertaken by settlers, possibly the most practical was their participation in local government and administration. They were often able to arouse local bodies to take notice of responsibilities which, though clearly defined on paper, were ignored in fact. Becoming members of Town Councils, Guardians of the Poor, school managers and so on, people from settlements – whether they called themselves Conservatives or Liberals, moderates or progressives – helped a little to humanize the local environment.

As teaching centres the settlements did two things, neither of which can be measured at all precisely. First, at a time when secondary education was denied to most people and when many still had little or no primary education, some of the settlements gave a wide range of practical and liberal instruction to those who were not too tired or too indifferent to accept it after a day's work. What they offered was no substitute for a proper education; but to workmen with a zeal for self-improvement who happened to live within range of an active settlement, it

[1] H. O. Barnett, *op. cit.* p. 649.
[2] *Ibid.* p. 654.

was better than nothing. Second, the settlements helped to spread liberal and socialist political ideas. They gave to Liberals a platform highly convenient at a time when their party needed to enlist working-class support. To trade unionists and moderate socialists they gave a respectable platform and a friendly audience, at a time when they were making articulate their views on the responsibility of the state for social legislation, and when they were beginning to seek parliamentary seats themselves. This was of course by no means the main role of settlements, and settlements were by no means the most important platform for radical speakers.

On the residents themselves, life at a settlement could have a powerful effect. It was even suggested by some observers of the movement that its most valuable function was to show the sons of the privileged what it was like to be a denizen of Ancoats or Whitechapel. 'We are witnessing a process of conversion,' Andrew Fairbairn said of the settlements in 1894,

> but it is of the missionaries at the unconscious hands of those they were sent out to convert; and this is a process which may have the most momentous results for the future of society and religion in England.[1]

When Barnett looked back across the movement after two decades he found much to disappoint him in its progress, but one claim he made with confidence. 'It is certain, at any rate, that the individual members who have lived among the poor have changed.'[2] Experience in a settlement led some residents to discard the social principles on which the movement rested for more radical ones. Others came out with their principles basically unchanged but with a fresh perspective on them. 'Toynbee Hall,' wrote William Beveridge in 1904, '. . . doesn't necessarily lead all men to one particular view.' Men might leave it, he said, aristocrats or *laissez-faire* liberals or violent socialists. But in each case I think they would at least understand their own views better.' They learned to make 'a protest against taking the structure of society for granted.'[3] Both Beveridge and E. T. Cook went from editing settlement magazines and seeing poverty close at hand, to writing knowledge-

[1] A. M. Fairbairn, *Religion in History and Modern Life*, p. 6.
[2] S. A. and H. O. Barnett, *Practicable Socialism*, p. 122.
[3] Lord Beveridge, *op. cit.* pp. 130–1.

ably about social problems for national newspapers. It may be inferred that residence in a settlement also left its mark on such men as Ernest Aves, E. J. Urwick and R. H. Tawney. In Mrs Barnett's view the frequent visitors to Toynbee Hall, as well as its residents, were affected with consequences important for the nation:

> they came into touch with the poor and ignorant and thus into their large and influential spheres carried the knowledge of the Esaus of the earth, and translated the cry of 'Hast thou not reserved a blessing for me? . . . Bless me, even me also, O my father,' into Acts of Parliament and codes of education.[1]

If effects of this sort are hard to document, it is still more hazardous to judge how successful the settlements were in decreasing hostility between classes. 'It has tended to mitigate class suspicion,' wrote Barnett of Toynbee Hall just before 1900:

> It would obviously be absurd to expect that twenty men living in Whitechapel should make any evident mark on the public opinion of half-a-million people, but for my part I am convinced that, as a result of their settlement, there is an increase of good will.[2]

Similar cautiously favourable assessments were made by others associated with the movement. The judgment of Charles Booth about the London settlements, as about so many other social and religious institutions, is worth attention; he knew them well in the 1890s, and he was not a man to let sympathy overrule candour. 'Settlements are still experimental,' he concluded in 1902,

> They are far from having reached the clear waters of an assured position; but are a success, if only because they have widened out the idea, and given new form to the practice of neighbourliness, and have thus made for social solidarity. They are few in numbers and financially weak, and even as to those with whom they come in touch can show no large totals; but raze them from London and London would be noticeably poorer.[3]

Fraternizing with poorer neighbours could be a more difficult task than it had appeared when first a young man at

[1] H. O. Barnett, *op. cit.* pp. 429–30.
[2] W. Reason, ed., *op. cit.* p. 22.
[3] C. Booth, *op. cit.* VII. 381.

Oxford or Cambridge was stirred by Barnett's call. Esau was a hairy man. 'It is strange,' wrote a resident of Mansfield House, 'that some Londoners will say *i* when they mean *a*.'[1] 'There was a time,' wrote a lady settler who had served in clubs for girls, 'when I thought of working girls as a class. Now I am inclined to think of young ladies as a class and the working girls as individuals. . . .' But in a sentence or two she was saying: 'The working girl . . . does not object to a "jawing", if you can strike straight home. . . .'[2] She could not cast off the habit of believing that there were two kinds of young female, 'young ladies' and 'working girls.' In cultural terms she was right, and some of the methods by which the two classes were supposed to become friends must only have emphasized their separation. Few social occasions can have been grimmer than the polite tea parties which the Barnetts held in Toynbee Hall, having sent off invitations East and West.[3]

Settlements were oases from which it was hoped to fertilize the surrounding desert. 'Toynbee Hall,' wrote a sympathetic American visitor,

> is essentially a transplant of university life in Whitechapel. The quadrangle, the gables, the diamond-paned windows, the large general rooms, especially the dining-room with its brilliant frieze of college shields, all make the place seem not so distant from the dreamy walks by the Isis or the Cam. But these things are not so much for the sake of the university men as of their neighbours, so that they may breathe a little of the charmed atmosphere.[4]

In 1914 another visitor, Stephen Hobhouse, found the charmed atmosphere choking, and felt that the comfortable, academic air of Toynbee Hall shut one off from the drab poverty of most of the humble homes around. 'It was the same with two or three other Settlements I visited – Oxford House, the Cambridge and Eton missions, and the Browning Settlements.'[5]

These two observers saw much the same facts. They carried away different impressions because they arrived with different

[1] *Mansfield House Magazine*, April 1894, p. 71.

[2] Emmeline Pethick in W. Reason, ed., *op. cit.* p. 100.

[3] See J. A. R. Pimlott, *op. cit.* pp. 74–5, C. R. Ashbee, *op. cit.* ch. xvi: 'A Tea Party with the Rev. and Mrs Simeon Flux.'

[4] R. A. Woods, 'The Social Awakening of London', in R. A. Woods, ed., *The Poor in Great Cities* (1896), pp. 19–20.

[5] S. Hobhouse, *Forty Years and an Epilogue* (1951), p. 133.

social attitudes. It was no part of the social theory behind settlements that the difference between classes should be ignored or removed. Settlements were intended to show that respect and friendship were possible between people in different classes. They were not supposed to foreshadow a classless society. Samuel Barnett, who launched the movement and expressed most articulately the principles embodied in its practice, hoped to see social harmony, but not social equality. He wished to see social justice done, through sanitary reforms, relief work (under severe discipline) for the unemployed, public feeding of school children, garden suburbs and universal old-age pensions. These reforms would restore the right relations between classes, not abolish the differences. 'Classes must exist', he declared:

> A body in which every member is a hand could do no work, and a city of one class would have no life. The classes in our great cities are many, but the terms 'rich' and 'poor', if not exact definitions, represent clearly enough the two great classes of society. Their unity means strength, their division means ruin.[1]

It was by no means lamentable that poverty should remain:

> Poverty is a relative term. The citizen whose cottage home, with its bright housewife and happy children, is a light in our land, is poor in comparison with some stately mansion. But his poverty is not an evil to be cured. It is a sign that life does not depend on possessions, and the existence of poor men alongside of rich men, each of whom lives a full human life in different circumstances, make [sic] up the society of the earthly paradise. The poverty which has to be cured is the poverty which degrades human nature, and makes impossible for the ordinary man his enjoyments of the powers and the tastes with which he was endowed at his birth.[2]

The cause of this second sort of poverty was the sin or selfishness of rich and poor, and its cure was to raise all men to the level of Christ. Residents of settlements could help to overcome such poverty by their example to other rich people and their service to the poor. But their main task was elsewhere. 'The important thing surely is not that the poor shall be exalted, but that rich and poor shall equally feel the joy of their being, and,

[1] S. A. and H. O. Barnett, *Towards Social Reform*, p. 26.
[2] S. A. and H. O. Barnett, *Practicable Socialism*, p. 143.

living together in peace and goodwill, make a society to be a blessing to all nations.'[1]

In the context of social philosophy the settlements may be seen as a late expression of the conviction, held by Disraeli, by Carlyle, by F. D. Maurice and Charles Kingsley, by Ruskin and by Toynbee, that the good society would be achieved by beneficent gestures from the leaders to the led. Like each of these men Barnett believed in the distinction between the masters and the rest. 'Universal experience goes to show', he wrote in 1896, 'that without a master the ordinary man does not work. It seems as if it were necessary that a man should be under authority.'[2] Barnett saw the settlement as, among other things, a training ground for the future rulers of England.

This did not escape George Lansbury, the socialist politician who was, like Barnett himself, a devoted and rebellious member of the Church of England. One of the sternest passages in Lansbury's autobiography deals with Barnett and Toynbee Hall. 'I yield to nobody in my respect for Canon Barnett and his wife,' he wrote, 'but I am more convinced than ever that their whole philosophy of life was all wrong'. To Lansbury, the purpose of Toynbee Hall was 'to bridge the gulf between rich and poor by the use of smooth words and ambiguous phrases. . . .' He implied that many of the residents were careerists seeking experience which would get them jobs, and he believed that the one solid achievement of Toynbee Hall was

> the filling up of the bureaucracy of government and administration with men and women who went to East London full of enthusiasm and zeal for the welfare of the masses, and discovered the advancement of their own interests and the interests of the poor were best served by leaving East London to stew in its own juice while they became members of parliament, cabinet ministers, civil servants . . .[3]

No settlement, Lansbury asserted, had had any permanent influence on the life and labour of the people.

The bitterness of Lansbury's attack makes it all the more interesting. His belief that the settlers were young men on the make was rather a sign of this bitterness than a cause of it. The

[1] *Ibid.* p. 122.
[2] *Commonwealth*, May 1896, p. 169.
[3] G. Lansbury, *My Life* (1928), pp. 129–30.

real complaint was that the settlement idea presupposed 'that the rich were as necessary as the poor – indeed, that nothing must ever be done to hurt the good-hearted rich who keep such places as Toynbee Hall going out of their ill-gotten gains.'[1] His was the voice of a new generation of social reformers to whom Barnett's social theory was merely a programme for repairing an unjust system instead of replacing it. The voice of Lansbury and his friends was becoming loud by 1900. Barnett was disturbed at the rise of people who wanted to improve society by manipulating national and municipal government, instead of attempting what appeared to him more sensible tasks, like 'democratizing the old Universities or . . . humanizing the working-man.'[2]

The hardiest settlements, including the first of them, still survive as fossils of a Victorian attitude to social relationships. Sir Walter Besant remarked at Mansfield House in 1897:

> 'The new teaching concerning the relations of the cultured and uncultured classes, which has taken shape and expression in the University Settlements, is very peculiarly the creation and growth of our own time . . . of the later Victorian age.'[3]

Only four years later, Charles Masterman concluded that the creative impulse of the movement was already exhausted. 'The wave of enthusiasm which created the modern settlement', he wrote, 'has ceased to advance; the buildings remain and a few energetic toilers, and the memory of a great hope.'[4] As a living force the settlement did not really survive the generation which devised it. Perhaps it was a prophetic apprehension of this fact that made Hensley Henson write in a diary, about 1889: 'The O.H. [Oxford House] is an impossible scheme, and must in the long run fail.'[5] In another twenty years a reformer of the next generation, speaking at St John's College (where Barnett had launched Toynbee Hall), said brusquely to his young listeners whom he was supposed to be encouraging to join a settlement in East London: 'if you cherish the illusion that you are going to do any good to your own soul or to anybody else's by this sort of benevolent picknicking, you had better not go at all.'[6]

[1] *Ibid.* p. 130.
[2] S. A. and H. O. Barnett, *Practicable Socialism*, p. 121.
[3] W. Reason, ed., *op. cit.* p. 1.
[4] C. F. G. Masterman, in *The Heart of the Empire* (1901), p. 35.
[5] H. Hensley Henson, *Retrospect of an Unimportant Life*, I. 31.
[6] M. Reckitt, *Faith and Society* (1932), p. 98n.

The speaker was H. G. Wells. 'Benevolent picknicking' is unfair, as rebels always are to the ideas of their elders. But the ideas of people like Wells were now more exciting than Barnett's to the socially-conscious young.

The settlements were religious in impulse, Toynbee Hall was run by a clergyman, and most of the others were connected officially or unofficially with a particular denomination. Did they alter attitudes among the working classes to the churches? This is perhaps an unreasonably large question to ask about what was, on the map of England, a small movement. Barnett himself said that the people of East London had 'less idealism' in 1906 than thirty years earlier; 'less superstition' some may interpose – yes, but the superstitions represented a grasp on the unseen and a consciousness of Divine relationship.'[1] He was not, of course, blaming the settlements for this trend. But neither he nor anybody else could plausibly argue that the settlement movement had seriously interfered with it.

[1] G. Haw, ed., *Christianity and the Working Classes* (1906), p. 96.

5

The Salvation Army

Founding the Army

WHEN Toynbee Hall was established in 1884 the Salvation Army was a little more than four years old. Like the settlements it had grown out of an experiment in Whitechapel, and like them it evangelized the urban poor. To William Booth and his followers, however, the ideas and the strategy of people like Samuel Barnett appeared mistaken. The attempt to bring the culture of the educated classes to the poor seemed to them a misreading of God's will. Booth's wife Catherine remarked in her last address that Christ came to save the world, not to civilize it; and she said of those people who put any hope in education: 'you cannot reform man morally by his intellect; this is the mistake of most social reformers. You must reform man by his SOUL!'[1] William Booth often joined issue with reformers who tried, as residents of settlements did, to improve the environment of the working classes. The world needed salvation alone, he said. 'You don't need to mix up any other ingredients with the heavenly remedy.'[2] When he wrote to the *Pall Mall Gazette* during the controversy over *The Bitter Cry of Outcast London* in 1883, it was to warn against faith in 'social arrangements', against 'the attempt to deal with the great social difficulty as though it had no deeper cause than a want of bricks and mortar. The first and great thing to be done by those who would improve the con-

[1] F. de L. Booth-Tucker, *The Life of Catherine Booth* (1892), II. 422.
[2] W. Booth, *Salvation Soldiery* (n. d.), p. 16.

dition of the wretched is to get at their hearts.'[1] His wife made this point more starkly when she cried, in 1881:

> Oh! how I see the emptiness and vanity of everything compared with the salvation of the soul. What does it matter if a man dies in the workhouse? If he dies on a doorstep covered with wounds, like Lazarus – what does it matter if his soul is saved?[2]

This indifference to temporal circumstances could be overcome only if it occurred to Booth that destitution might so corrode a man as to put him beyond the reach of salvation. In the first years of his holy war, such a thought was far from Booth's mind. There was a difference even more obvious between the settlements and the Salvation Army. The Booths believed that the divisions in English society made it impossible for envoys from the rich to reach the masses for Christ. They created the Salvation Army because they were convinced that the poor could be made Christians only (as Mrs Booth put it) 'by people of their own class, who would go after them in their own resorts, who would speak to them in a language they understood, and reach them by means suited to their own tastes.'[3]

This conclusion was reached by the Booths only after wide experience in several Methodist sects. William Booth gave his first sermons as a Wesleyan lay preacher at Nottingham in 1846, when he was seventeen. Later he preached for the Wesleyan Reformers, and then for the Methodist New Connexion, in which he became a minister in 1858. His wife was a Wesleyan before their marriage, until expelled for attending services run by the Wesleyan Reformers. Much in the history of the Salvation Army becomes intelligible only when it is seen as the creation of dissatisfied Methodists.

When Booth preached for the Nottingham Wesleyans it was as a layman, whose intended vocation was not to save the people but to exploit them as a pawnbroker. His father was a poor and illiterate man who dreamed nevertheless of riches, and William was supposed to attain through commerce the respectability which his family worshipped. Practically speaking, it was their only god. Despite an official legend in the Salvation

[1] *Pall Mall Gazette*, 22 Nov. 1883.
[2] *War Cry*, 7 July 1881.
[3] F. de L. Booth-Tucker, *op. cit.* II. 234.

Army that Booth was 'brought up in the Church of England', the adherence of his parents to the Church was merely nominal.[1] His own religious experience appears to have begun at the age of thirteen, when he first attended the Wesley Chapel in Nottingham. Two years later, in 1844, he was converted, and attained that conviction of salvation which he was to bring to his legions, and which was the source of their fighting spirit. For a time, according to a semi-official biography, he was drawn to Chartism by the oratory of Feargus O'Connor and the spectacle of bitter poverty.[2] In the Nottingham of his youth, handloom weavers and stockingers were suffering terribly; but if their plight moved the young Booth to sympathize with radical reform, his conversion gave him a view of poverty which soon put an end to any secular notions about it. The poor remained always his special concern, but it was now their lack of religious faith, not their physical hardship, that stirred him.

In 1851 Booth abandoned for ever his career in petty commerce, and the aspiration to gentility with which his family had saddled him. Many years later the idea of shopkeeping could make him shudder. 'Katie says you are gone shopping,' he once wrote to his wife, 'I dread the sound of the word shop.'[3] As a preacher in the 'fifties he left to others the established congregations of respectable Methodists, and engaged in roving evangelism. His power to arouse revivalist enthusiasm was remarkable, and to his future wife a little frightening. 'Watch against *mere animal excitement* in your revival services . . .' she warned him in 1853.[4] Before their marriage in 1855, however, she was persuaded that the violence and noise which her lover induced in his congregations came from God. 'I believe in revivalism *with all my soul*', she could tell him.[5]

It was becoming plain that Booth could never work for long in an organization devised by others. He left the Wesleyan Reformers after a quarrel in 1854 and his membership of the Methodist New Connexion was doomed from the day in 1857 when the Conference ordered him to stop touring the country-

[1] H. Begbie, *The Life of William Booth* (1920), I. 54–7.
[2] *Ibid.* I. 49–50.
[3] *Ibid.* I. 426.
[4] *Ibid.* I. 174–5.
[5] *Ibid.* I. 223.

side and work in a regular circuit. For the time being he obeyed; but in 1861, having reined his energy and ambition long enough, he resigned and went off to Cornwall as an undenominational preacher. The chapels were not cordial to the wild visitor. The Wesleyans and the Methodist New Connexion often closed their pulpits to him, and thus pushed the Booths one stage nearer to deciding that they would work outside churches altogether.

When this decision came, however, it owed no more to the hostility of the chapels than to the Booths' own discontent with the relation between the sects and the masses. Although Booth was now preaching, where he could, in chapels, the conviction grew on him (and more strongly on his wife) that this association was hindering the work. *'We can't get at the masses in the chapels'*,[1] wrote Mrs Booth in 1864. She had always been more articulately dissatisfied than her husband with the condition of English religion, more certain that the churches were rendered impotent by conformity with the ways of the middle classes. 'The more I see of fashionable religion,' she said once, 'the more I despise it; indeed, how *can* fashionable religion be other than despicable?'[2] Finally, despairing of ever opening the churches from within to admit the Holy Spirit, she urged Booth to set them an example from outside.[3] Booth needed little persuading, so overwhelmed was he by a sense of the urgency of saving the heathen masses, so disappointed by the lethargy of the churches and by the antipathy he had aroused in them, and so serenely confident that the hand of the Lord was upon him. The Booths put up a tent in Whitechapel in 1865 and launched the 'Christian Mission to the Heathen of our Own Country'. This mission became the Salvation Army by no sudden decision but by a steady expansion – first to other parts of London and later to the provinces – and by piecemeal adaptation as Booth's converts increased, and as he and his followers thought up new devices for attracting sinners.[4]

[1] F. de L. Booth-Tucker, *op. cit.* I. 379.

[2] *Ibid.* II. 219. See also her letter in H. Begbie, *op. cit.* I. 194.

[3] Booth often gave his wife credit for starting him thus on the way to the Salvation Army. See M. Asquith, *Autobiography*, I. 190.

[4] On the Mission, see R. Sandall, *The History of the Salvation Army*, I. *1865–1878* (1947); R. Gout, *William Booth et le Monde Ouvrier* (Geneva, 1955), pp. 81–209.

Who were his followers? His earliest assistants, according to Booth's own account in 1870, were all

> genuine working men. One has been a blacksmith, another a navvy, another a policeman, another a sailor, and the remainder have been engaged in similar callings. Consequently, they can speak to the working man as belonging to the same class, illustrating their exhortations with their own experience.[1]

Some of his supporters were the sons and daughters of not very fervent Nonconformists, and others were from families indifferent to religion. Many said they had experienced close shaves with death (granted by Providence, they would explain, to remind them that hell was close). In early or late youth, after a life of crime, vice, drunkenness – one leader claimed to have been drunk at six – or just 'mischief', they had seen suddenly that they were full of sin and drifting towards damnation. In some, the triumph of faith had occurred after hearing a travelling revivalist preacher; others had been converted by Booth himself or by one of his missionaries. They were young, many of them in their twenties, full of old-fashioned religious enthusiasm, and determined to save their brothers and sisters from hell. None believed that they could reach the heathen within the cold walls of churches, and none doubted that Booth's was the way, and he the man, to beat the devil.[2]

The people Booth attracted were typified by Elijah Cadman and George Railton, two men who later gained as much authority in the Army as anybody else outside Booth's own family. Cadman was a chimney sweep and professional boxer, illiterate until his wife taught him to write, who suffered a dreadful period in his early twenties when he was certain that he was damned. He joined a Hallelujah Band which toured the countryside in red shirts, and from one of his own converts heard in 1876 of Booth's mission. 'I've seen a people in London who live and serve Christ,' this man told him, 'and they're our class.' Off he went to London, where Booth impressed him overwhelmingly. According to a biographer, Cadman shouted: 'I'm in love

[1] W. Booth, *How to Reach the Masses with the Gospel* (1872), p. 77.

[2] See biographical sketches in early issues of the *War Cry*, and R. Gout, *op. cit.* pp. 287–93.

with him! He's a MAN!'[1] The Salvationist biographers of George Railton record, without appearing to think it remarkable, that he wrestled with God for some years before being born again in 1859, at the age of ten.[2] Railton, who was the son of a Wesleyan foreign missionary, worked briefly for a firm of merchants before being dismissed for scruples about the morality of commerce. At the age of fifteen he determined to give his life to God – but not to the churches, which in his view hindered the Lord's work. Once, he was convinced that the Lord intended him for Morocco; but when he landed without specific inspiration, or money, the British consul had to ship him home. Next he became a Methodist local preacher, despite his qualms about the churches. In 1873 he joined Booth's mission and at once became Booth's secretary.

After 1875 Booth began to move towards founding his Army. Encouraged by his son Bramwell and by Railton, Booth took control of the mission in 1877 from the hands of the council with which he had so far shared power. 'Confidence in God and in me are absolutely indispensable both now and ever afterwards', he announced simply.[3] 'I am determined', he told a correspondent, 'that Evangelists in this Mission *must hold my views and work on my lines.*'[4] This coup lost him a few supporters and exhilarated the rest.

About the same time Booth conducted a series of 'holiness meetings', which expressed both the sense of spiritual community now strong in the mission, and its leader's conviction that, having converted sinners, he must now go on to make saints. 'Big men, as well as women', said the mission's journal, reporting one of these meetings,

> fell to the ground, lay there for some time as if dead, overwhelmed with the Power from on High. When the gladness of all God's mighty deliverance burst upon some, they laughed as well as cried for joy, and some of the younger evangelists might have been seen like lads at play, locked in one another's arms and rolling each other over on the floor.[5]

[1] H. Wallis, *The Happy Warrior: The Life Story of Commissioner Elijah Cadman* (1928), p. 47.

[2] E. Douglas and M. Duff, *Commissioner Railton* (1920), pp. 6–9.

[3] H. Begbie, *op. cit.* I. 408.

[4] *Ibid.* II. 132.

[5] *Ibid.* I. 412–3.

At another 'holiness meeting', one of Booth's sons reported,

> every one was overpowered by the Spirit. . . . One young woman shook her head, saying, 'No, not tonight,' but soon was seen on the ground pleading mightily with God. . . . One brother said, 'Oh, oh! if this ain't heaven, what'll heaven be?' Another brother said, 'I must jump'. I said, 'Then jump,' and he jumped all round.[1]

Such scenes had been common enough fifty years earlier in the heyday of Methodist revivals; but they were very rare now. These accounts help one to understand the hostility which the Salvation Army aroused at first among the respectable. They show the mood of Booth's people on the eve of their war, sharing an ecstasy – 'the rapture of spiritual drunkards', their own journal called it – which was to sustain them in battle, making them indifferent to persecution and unawed by the scope of their campaign against the devil. Booth was purifying his followers for this campaign, making them into an army of saints. In September 1878 the journal of the mission referred to Booth as 'the General' (and not, as previously, 'the General Superintendent') and said that the Mission had organized 'a Salvation Army to carry the Blood of Christ and the Fire of the Holy Ghost into every corner of the world. . . .'[2] Booth was by no means the first crusader in Victorian England to dress his followers in a uniform and organize them as an army. The 'Shakespearean Association of Leicester Chartists' under Thomas Cooper, the Hallelujah Bands from which Booth had gained some recruits, and the temperance organization known as the Blue Ribbon Army, all preceded the Salvation Army and may each have helped to inspire it. Military discipline, moreover, now appealed to many people in England – owing partly to the rise of the volunteer movement – as admirable and even exciting. 'Out of fiery and uncouth material,' wrote John Ruskin, 'it is only soldiers' discipline which can bring the full force of power.' Quoting this remark, Samuel Smiles exclaimed: 'Wonderful is the magic of drill!'[3]

There were ample precedents in the Old and New Testaments, as Booth observed, for the use of military imagery in Christian

[1] *Ibid.* I. 414–5.

[2] *Ibid.* I. 437. The term 'the General' had been used occasionally before this time. So had 'the Salvation Army'. See R. Sandall, *op. cit.* I. 286.

[3] A. Briggs, *Victorian People* (1954), pp. 137–8.

endeavour. The notion of the Church Militant was an ancient one, and even those Christians who disliked the Salvation Army sang such hymns as Baring-Gould's 'Onward, Christian Soldiers.' Was it not a grave fault of ordinary Christians that they pretended to be soldiers without ever firing a shot? 'How long have we been singing, "I am a soldier of the Cross"?' asked Catherine Booth. 'And yet how little hand-to-hand fighting with sin and the devil!'[1] Booth himself was delighted by military organization and language. As a child he had loved to play soldiers and as a youth he had been 'captain' of a secret society. In his days as a young lay preacher he wrote to a fellow-evangelist an encouraging letter that was full of the imagery of warfare. When he seized power at the mission, during the Russo-Turkish war, he justified the action by saying: 'Fancy the Russians having a committee to carry on their war!' He explained that the task of a council was simply to inform and advise the commander-in-chief.[2] The rules and regulations of the British army, he once remarked, had helped him more than all the constitutions of the churches; and he kept a copy of them by his bed.[3] The uniform which he designed for his followers had a tactical purpose, given his judgment about the relations between evangelism and the social structure: in a society where dress normally recorded the wearer's status, the clothing worn by a Salvationist was classless.

Booth believed passionately in dictatorship. In this faith he was supported by his lieutenants, George Railton and Bramwell Booth.[4] If he had been tempted to take seriously the principles of liberalism, the younger men would have dissuaded him smartly. He suffered no such temptation, however. Was the military organization of the Salvation Army consistent with true Christian liberty? Yes, for liberty must be abridged if doing so would secure the greater good; and since the world was a constant battlefield between God and the Devil, liberty must always be abridged. Had not Christ laid down his own liberty

[1] Catherine Booth, *The Salvation Army in relation to the Church and State* (1883), pp. 37–8.

[2] H. Begbie, *op. cit.* I. 407–8.

[3] W. T. Stead, *The Salvation Army and its Social Scheme* (1890), p. 13.

[4] See [G. S. Railton], *Heathen England* (1877), p. 179; B. Booth, *These Fifty Years* (1929), p. 145.

on the altar?[1] Although Booth lived in a century when even men of natural intolerance might *learn* to be liberals, he had no time for the world's learning. Nor was he ashamed of his ignorance of profane subjects. The intellect was to him 'a mere human thing; human and nothing more.'[2] This was a damning epithet from a man with Booth's contempt for the things of this world. The common charge of Jesuitry against the Army was inaccurate, except in so far as Booth may have admired the Jesuits as organizers. For Jesuits believe in the power of argument; what their critics say is that they use it dishonestly. Booth did not believe in it at all. The saved had no need of it; and as for the rest of mankind, he instructed his officers: 'Argument never opened the eyes of the blind. Do not argue, but pray.'[3]

There was one thinker of his own century for whom Booth did have a good word. In 1890 he was shown passages from *Past and Present* (which he had never read) by a friend who was impressed by the similarity of Booth's ideas to Carlyle's. The extracts so pleased Booth that he added them as an appendix to his book *In Darkest England*. 'Despotism is essential to most enterprises', ran one of these passages. It was the view of W. T. Stead that admirers of Carlyle (among whom he counted himself) should support Booth. 'The Army is established on principles Carlylean,' he wrote, 'in exact opposition to the ideas prevalent in parliamentary circles.'[4] Booth's love of power, then, could have a free play. No qualm of mind or conscience struggled to restrain it. While being wholly true to himself he could exercise absolute authority over great and tiny affairs. He could order an officer to Africa or India, forbid him to marry except inside the Army and then only with permission, tell him how he must light the gas in meeting-halls, and ordain that a small theatre needs eleven collection boxes. And because Booth was a man of integrity and kindness, he could do all this without being uncharitable.

Although he disliked arguing, there was one defence of his autocracy which he enjoyed making – that it worked. 'Despite the alleged unpopularity of our discipline,' he wrote in 1890,

[1] *The Doctrines and Discipline of the Salvation Army* (1881), section 31:7.
[2] *War Cry*, 27 Dec. 1879.
[3] Unsigned article, certainly by Booth, in *ibid.*, 20 Oct. 1880.
[4] W. T. Stead, *op. cit.* p. 15.

'perhaps because of the rigour of military authority upon which we have insisted, the Salvation Army has grown from year to year with a rapidity to which nothing in modern Christendom affords any parallel.'[1] Stead believed that the practice of obedience was 'the very foundation of all the fighting power of the Army.'[2] As Booth pointed out to those who called him a tyrant, nobody was conscripted into his forces. Why did his followers submit so joyously? A glimpse of the answer may be had from Booth's remark that his Army made 'every soldier in some degree an officer, charged with the responsibility of so many of his townsfolk. . . .'[3] This was to take the Reformation's doctrine of the priesthood of believers with unusual literalness. To every willing and worthy recruit Booth offered not only fellowship, but a task – the salvation of their heathen brothers and sisters. From its first years the Salvation Army was both a religious community and an evangelistic agency. These two functions can be distinguished, but it is misleading to see them as separate. The internal spirit of Booth's community was forged by hatred and respect for the enemy.

Evangelical Religion and Vulgarity

The doctrines of the Salvation Army were simply those of the evangelical revival. An official catechism explained that the Army accepted exactly what was accepted by all the orthodox people of God:

> Utter ruin through the fall; salvation *alone*, from first to last, through the atonement of Christ, by the Holy Spirit; the great day of Judgment, with its reward of heaven for ever for the righteous, and hell for ever for the wicked.[4]

For an officer, however, it was not enough merely to assent to these doctrines. They must possess him. 'To believe as Salvationists believe, without feeling as Salvationists feel – if that were possible – will not be enough.'[5]

[1] W. Booth, *In Darkest England, and the Way Out* (1890), pp. 242–3.
[2] W. T. Stead, *op. cit.* p. 15.
[3] W. Booth, 'What is the Salvation Army?', *Contemporary Review*, July 1882, p. 178.
[4] *All about the Salvation Army* (1883), p. 16.
[5] *Orders and Regulations of the Salvation Army* (1886), p. 3.

The experience of conversion was required of officers and ordinary soldiers alike, and it had to be sudden: a person not converted suddenly, Booth believed, would never be converted at all. Conversion was no mere formality, but an escape from hell. Only to people who do not believe in the flames of hell do the physical phenomena associated with revivalist religion appear barbaric and repellent. 'Of course there is a Hell', said Booth

> – a lake that burns with fire and brimstone. . . . Everybody who has been converted knows there is a Hell, because they have themselves . . . trembled and groaned and gasped on the brink of the awful gulf, and have been snatched from the jaws of the destroyer by the Almighty hand . . . and breathed the first free, happy breath of life on the sure foundation of the Rock.[1]

Once safe on the Rock, Salvationists were as joyous as they had formerly been tormented. A secular journal suggested the atmosphere of an early meeting in the nice phrase 'pious jollity.'[2] The pleasures of the world, of course, contributed nothing to the Army's rapture. Since secular joys and comforts were not of God they were of the Devil, for there was no neutral ground in the war for souls. As a symbol of these sinful pastimes, smoking was prominent in accounts by Salvationists of their life before conversion. The Army's leaders were deeply shocked when Charles Spurgeon, the eminent Baptist preacher, not only arrived at one of his meetings puffing a cigar, but declared that he smoked to the honour and glory of God.[3] Drink was of the Devil not only because, like smoking, it encouraged self-indulgence, but because it poisoned and impoverished. When religion drove Chartism from his youthful mind, Booth at once attributed the wretched condition of people in Nottingham to their individual sins, and in particular to their use of alcohol.[4] In the early publications of the Army, drunkenness appeared often alongside 'neglect', 'misconduct', 'backsliding' and similar faults, as a cause of poverty.

The conviction that he was sanctified made a Salvationist wish not to draw away from a contaminating world, but to rush in and cleanse it of sin. Without arrogance, he marched forward

[1] *War Cry*, 2 Oct. 1880, reprinted from *Christian Mission Magazine*, July 1878.
[2] *Saturday Review*, 5 July 1879, p. 19.
[3] B. Booth, *Echoes and Memories* (1925), p. 35.
[4] H. Begbie, *op. cit.* I. 65, 100.

to rescue his fellows from the damnation which, he believed, he had so narrowly escaped himself. But the heathen masses, being heathen, did not *want* to be saved. Booth attributed much of his success to a frank awareness of this fact. 'We have recognized the antagonism in which we find unsaved men to the living God', he told a rally of his troops:

> When we go fishing, we bait our hooks with the most enticing bait we can find. If one bait does not take, then we try another, and another, and another, and if they won't take any, then, as one of our Officers said the other day, *we go down and hook them on* . . .[1]

One sort of bait was the brass band. It was first used to drown the roar of hostile mobs, but its more permanent task was to announce and brighten Army meetings, leading and sustaining the voices that sang simple, bouncing hymns, many of them by Salvationist composers. 'To whom does all the music of earth and heaven belong,' asked Catherine Booth, 'if not to Him? I contend that the devil has no right to a single note; and we will have it all away from him yet.[2] The ingenious advertising devised by William Corbridge was another form of bait thrown to the curious. His 'Hallelujah Railway Ticket', his pamphlet 'The Up Line to Heaven and the Down Line to Hell', and his little book offering 'Shares in the Salvation Mine . . . 100 per Cent guaranteed in this life, and in the world to come life everlasting', were examples of vivid, homely prose displayed by imaginative typography. Their use of topical secular images was typical of Army propaganda and preaching. 'There are in heaven,' William Booth would say, 'ever so many angels ready with copy books to enter the names of the reclaimed the moment they are announced through the telephones of the Celestial home.'[3] He would describe a shipwreck lately in the news, and make it a terrible symbol for eternal destruction. He would compare the Army's work with the cleaning of the street filth. The characters of the Bible were conscripted into the ranks: Booth said that David was the true type of the Salvation Army cadet, and one of his followers declared that the first Salvationist was Captain Abel, son of Mr Adam and Mrs Eve.

[1] *War Cry*, 25 May 1882.
[2] Catherine Booth, *op. cit.* p. 53.
[3] *Age* (Melbourne), 21 Sept. 1891.

The language, song and gesture of the Army's evangelism were not translations made to accommodate the authors' principles to the tastes of the masses. Certainly Salvationists believed that their bands and hymns and homely imagery were strategically necessary as advertisements to attract the heathen; what made these devices so lively, however, was that the Salvationists thoroughly enjoyed them. Long before Booth had decided that the spiritual condition of the masses demanded new methods, he had been preaching exactly in his later manner. He dropped his aitches and spoke in a rough Midland accent not because that would get him a better hearing from working-class audiences (though he may well have thought that it did), but because that was the way he talked. The simplicity of many in his ranks was even less calculated than his own. Elijah Cadman's tactics for winning souls were an unrehearsed expression of the plain enthusiasm which had made him announce his own salvation by running into a Methodist meeting and shouting the news.[1] William Corbridge's literary novelties were merely a sanctified version of the conjuring tricks which he had performed as a boy in his Leicestershire village, and which later he looked back on as his 'great snare'.[2] James Dowdle, a high officer who had come from a village in Wiltshire, was being himself, as well as showing that the ways of the Army were not those of the churches, when, with umbrella aloft, he would say to a man leaning on a public house: 'What are you propping that place up for, man? Come away, and let the devil prop his own house up.'[3] Another umbrella-waver, John Lawley ('the saved railway guard') used to tear his song book in shreds to show how the devil tears his victims, and dive from the platform making swimming motions, to demonstrate the sea of God's love and pardon.[4] These were people who themselves had failed to find nourishment for the imagination in church or chapel, and who believed that the form of religion they had found satisfying would similarly satisfy others. With minor exceptions they were the only group of Christian evangelists of their time who approached working-class non-worshippers at their own cultural

[1] H. Wallis, *op. cit.* p. 23.
[2] *War Cry*, 28 Aug. 1880.
[3] St J. Ervine, *God's Soldier: General William Booth* (1934), I. 357.
[4] *Ibid.* I. 360.

level. 'They can fall back in their appeals to the crowd on their OWN EXPERIENCE', Booth said of his supporters.[1] This, he believed, gave the Army an advantage over all other home missionary bodies.

Booth could not expect the vulgarity of his Army's methods to be wholly pleasing to respectable Christians. In extreme old age Lord Shaftesbury concluded that the Army was a trick of the devil, who having failed to make Christianity odious was now striving to make it ridiculous.[2] 'Their services', wrote a Wesleyan, 'are frequently a travesty of a music-hall entertainment.'[3] 'Laughter belongs not to our dispensation', wrote another evangelical critic.[4] The standard reply from the Army to charges of this sort was that certainly its methods were not those of refined people, that refined people were not its concern, and that in seeking the vulgar, vulgarity was necessary. Elijah Cadman had a simpler retort: 'They say I make a noise, but I tell them there will be a deal more in hell.'[5] *The Times* defended the Army's din more empirically. While not suggesting that its readers join the colours, it remarked that the noise made by converts sober was more tolerable than the noise previously made by the same people when unregenerate and drunk. 'Is there not a cause for some such movement?' asked *The Times* in 1882. 'Is there, or is there not, as alleged, a very large part of our population that the existing religious organizations have failed to make Christians, in any appreciable sense of the word?'[6]

Within the Church of England it was common by 1882 to admit a case for the Army. 'The shortcomings of the Church have been the occasion of the Salvation Army,' said one clergyman, 'and are the justification of its existence.'[7] Even the Archbishop of Canterbury, A. C. Tait, said that since there was 'a vast mass of persons who could not be reached by the more regular administration of the Church, it was not unlikely that much good might eventually result from the more irregular

[1] W. Booth, *How to Reach the Masses with the Gospel*, p. 77.

[2] St J. Ervine, *op. cit.* I. 596–7.

[3] *Methodist Times*, 19 Feb. 1885, p. 116.

[4] B. W. Newton, *Address respecting the Methods of the Salvation Army* (1882), p. 7.

[5] St J. Ervine, *op. cit.* I. 390.

[6] Quoted in *War Cry*, 27 April 1882.

[7] J. A. Atkinson, *The Salvation Army and the Church* (1882), p. 6.

action of the Salvationists.'[1] In 1882 the Queen herself gave the Army a benediction which was displayed prominently in the *War Cry* and read to cheering meetings. The Church of England's best tribute of all was the foundation of the Church Army in 1882; 'if the Army is going wrong,' said the *War Cry* with delight, 'the Church of England is coming after it as fast as it can march.'[2]

For a time it seemed that the Church might even enrol the Salvation Army. In 1882 E. W. Benson, then Bishop of Truro, wrote in a very friendly manner to Booth and persuaded the Canterbury Convocation to appoint a committee on the possibility of making the Army a Church organization. The committee comprised Benson, Canon B. F. Westcott, Dr Lightfoot and Randall Davidson (then Dean of Windsor and later Archbishop of Canterbury). At first Booth was impressed by 'the beautiful spirit of enquiry' in discussions between this committee and delegates from the Army. But the negotiations soon broke down, Booth said later, over the question of baptism and communion – which he believed inessential to salvation.[3] Booth's stand on the sacraments, however, was merely the point at which far wider disagreements met. The use of sacraments within the Army would have implied a notion of the priesthood, and of a formal distinction between sinners and saved, alien to the spirit of the movement. There were other differences between the Army's leaders and the Churchmen – above all, matters of taste – which were still less amenable to discussion. Davidson was repelled by the spiritual exhibitionism which, he believed, the Army encouraged in young children. From an Army journal for children, which appeared to him a 'really offensive little newspaper', he quoted the letter of Ada, aged ten: 'Thank God I am saved and on my way to Heaven. My two brothers, George and Teddy, are saved and baby May. I am sorry that my father and mother are not saved yet, but hope they will soon.'[4] The Army's leaders doubtless enjoyed having these talks at a time when they felt so keenly the need to be

[1] F. de L. Booth-Tucker, *op. cit.* II. 278.

[2] *War Cry*, 21 Sept. 1882.

[3] On this episode see H. Begbie, *op. cit.* I. 466; B. Booth, *Echoes and Memories*, p. 63.

[4] R. T. Davidson, 'The Methods of the Salvation Army', *Contemporary Review*, Aug. 1882, pp. 195–6.

tolerated; but real agreement demanded concessions that neither side could make. Having let the Methodists slip out of its fold the Church could not seriously hope to capture a movement which had begun as a protest, in turn, against the spirit of Methodism.

The Wesleyans greeted the Army with courtesy, inviting Booth to address their Conference in 1880. Mrs Booth, herself an expelled Wesleyan, was astonished. 'I should have thought it more probable for him to have addressed the House of Lords', she wrote, 'than those seven hundred ministers.'[1] It was indeed impressive that the Conference should listen with sympathy to a man whom they might have treated as a renegade. But his doctrines were their own ('we agree about Salvation', said the president of the Conference in 1881), and few Wesleyans were prepared to cast the first stone at a body of evangelists who were out to reach classes largely beyond their own ministry.[2] This was also true of other Nonconformists. 'I hear that Reverend Dale, of Birmingham, has been eulogizing us to the skies', wrote Mrs Booth in 1880.[3] Dale, we saw, believed that in a sense the Army absolved Congregationalists from recruiting the poor. Personally he was repelled by the Army's forms of expression; but he never doubted its orthodoxy. 'Let men hear "in their own tongue" ', he said in a sermon, '– that means in the intellectual forms which their minds can receive – the wonderful works of God.'[4] Among the Baptists, Charles Spurgeon disliked (as a Calvinist) parts of the Army's teaching, and he was critical of its methods. He spoke warmly, however, of Booth and his mission, and according to Bramwell Booth 'always recognized that souls were being brought to the truth. . . .'[5] John Clifford, who was, next to Spurgeon, the most prominent Baptist (and a man of far broader sympathies), helped the Army from the first, and allowed its officers to speak from his pulpit.[6]

The leader of the English Catholics, Cardinal Manning, feared that to encourage each man to judge his own spiritual condition, and to invite him to speak publicly about it, was to

[1] F. de L. Booth-Tucker, *op. cit.* II. 223.
[2] *War Cry*, 29 Dec. 1881.
[3] F. de L. Booth-Tucker, *op. cit.* II. 217.
[4] R. W. Dale, *General Booth's Scheme* (1890), p. 15.
[5] B. Booth, *Echoes and Memories*, p. 35.
[6] *Ibid.* p. 40.

invite the pride of the Pharisee. But because he believed that the Army was a judgment on all the churches (and because he liked Booth), he never smirked at it or damned it.[1] Some other Catholics were less tolerant of such an ultra-Protestant body – and might have been still less so had they peeped at the *Orders and Regulations* of the Army, which treated Romans, Mohammedans and Jews as roughly in the same class. A writer in the *Month* admitted that the Army's activities were symptoms of spiritual disease, but said also that they caused further deterioration.[2] Manning's successor Vaughan disagreed with him over the Army as on many other issues, believing that Manning saw only its philanthropic side and ignored its danger as a proselytizing agency.[3]

Although the Army gained support or toleration from leaders of all main denominations, many Christians in pulpit and pew remained hostile. There were people who could not approve preaching by women – a practice common in the Army, for Catherine Booth persuaded her husband that it was right. There were bishops who suspected that orgiastic meetings of the Army increased the numbers of illegitimate children.[4] There were devout Christians who feared that the doctrine of 'entire sanctification' taught by the Army implied a heretical perfectionism. And there were clergymen and worshippers who resented the din made by Army parades past their churches; for like a heavenly anthem, a Salvation Army brass band drowned all music but its own. The problem was recognized by Booth in an edict of 1883 forbidding any band to play near a church during a service. At other times officers were commanded to suppose the churches sincere, to emphasize points of agreement, never to argue, to keep to their own work and leave the churches to theirs. Whatever offence the Army gave was not calculated. 'We are not antagonistic to the Churches', Mrs Booth told an audience in the West End.[5] Providence had led Salvationists out of the churches, but not to fight them. Their one enemy was Sin,

[1] H. E. Manning, 'The Salvation Army', *Contemporary Review*, Sept. 1882, p. 336.
[2] G. R. Chichester, 'The Salvation Army', *Month*, April 1882, p. 480.
[3] J. G. Snead-Cox, *The Life of Cardinal Vaughan*, I. 478.
[4] Admiral Fishbourne, *A Calm Plea for the Enlargement of Salvation Army Work* (1882), p. 8.
[5] Catherine Booth, *op. cit.* p. 27.

a foe cunning and well-entrenched. The Booths wanted God's people to give all possible supplies and encouragement to the men and women who had dedicated themselves to be His shock troops.

Persecution by the ungodly, Booth said, was as inevitable for Christians who were carrying the fight to the heathen as it was for Christ Himself. It was a sign that one was fighting God's fight. Bramwell Booth noted in his diary a meeting held just before the mission became the Army, at which he and his friends were 'pelted in the open air with cabbages and turnip-tops, etc., and one woman came and smashed one of the brethren full on the face. He bore it. I had a good time. The Holy Spirit was at work.'[1] In 1882 Captain Tom Bull reported from Liverpool:

> The storm raged, the wind blew, rain and snow came down. Stones were thrown, a brickbat striking the head of Sergeant Fellowes, breaking his head, and causing the loss of a pint of blood. He was taken to the hospital, had his head bandaged, and came back leaping and praising God.[2]

The *War Cry* asked soldiers: 'Are you persecuted enough?'[3] Many could well have answered that they were. In 1882 alone, 642 soldiers were assaulted in the United Kingdom, one-third of them women and 23 of them children. Some were injured for life. Sixty army buildings were damaged. The only reply permitted to violence was: 'God bless you.' Even Elijah Cadman, the former champion boxer, never raised a hand against an attacker.[4]

Some of the worst onslaughts were conducted by the 'Skeleton Army', a band of pre-Edwardian Teddy Boys who parodied the Salvation Army's methods and symbols and broke up its meetings. George Lansbury, who had taken a pledge of teetotalism (which he kept all his life) at a meeting of Booth's mission, remembered the leader of the Skeletons as a man who jumped about like a dervish, slandered the Booths, and had about him the roughest characters in Whitechapel.[5] (Lansbury's pre-

[1] B. Booth, *These Fifty Years*, p. 80.
[2] *War Cry*, 5 Jan. 1882.
[3] *Ibid.*, 11 April 1883.
[4] H. Wallis, *op. cit.* p. 89.
[5] G. Lansbury, *My Life* (1928), p. 84.

decessor Ramsay MacDonald also attended an Army meeting as a young man, taking not the pledge but a pea-shooter.)[1] Brewers and publicans, alarmed at Booth's campaign against alcohol, probably helped to form the Skeleton Army, and perhaps to turn the eye of the law from its activities.[2] At Basingstoke in 1881, the mayor, a brewer, appears at least to have approved a banquet in the Corn Exchange given to some roughs who had beaten up Salvationists.[3] But their dislike of drink did not give Booth's people the illusion that they were mobbed solely at the will of its purveyors. The Devil they knew was a versatile fellow, who might attack them through the Irish labourer who hated a Protestant as cordially as he liked a brawl, or the brutalized slum-dweller who had nothing better to do. When the law appeared to offer them less than reasonable protection – as in 1881, when policemen in Whitechapel did nothing to restrain mobs from molesting the Army until John Morley moved in the Commons for an enquiry – Salvationists rarely alleged corruption. A ranting body of evangelists who blocked the streets and attracted toughs could easily seem a public nuisance. From time to time processions and street-meetings were dispersed by the police, and some officers went cheerfully to gaol for short sentences. Police and magistrates tended, however, to become more tolerant as they realized that the Army, whatever its eccentricities, was on the side of public order.

The Army quite early gained respectable friends. In financial terms, the most valuable supporters in the first years were wealthy Nonconformists or evangelical Churchmen who saw that Booth's message was essentially theirs and who admired his zeal to spread it among the poor. One of these men was the Congregationalist Samuel Morley, who had first given Booth money in the early days of the mission at Whitechapel, and whose last gift, £2,000, was made just before he died in 1886. The Wesleyan Lord Mayor of London, William McArthur, once gave Booth £1,000 when he wanted to buy a property for

[1] Lord Elton, *The Life of James Ramsay MacDonald (1866–1919)* (1939), pp. 37–8.

[2] 'The Siege of Whitechapel', *Saturday Review*, 5 July 1879, p. 20; F. P. Cobbe, 'The Last Revival', *Contemporary Review*, Aug. 1882, p. 189; H. Begbie, *op. cit.* I. 478; St J. Ervine, *op. cit.* I. 356.

[3] F. de L. Booth-Tucker, *op. cit.* II. 244; H. Begbie, *op. cit.* II. 7; St. J. Ervine, *op. cit.* I. 536.

the Army. In Yorkshire the Army was helped financially and personally by the ironfounder W. J. Armitage, M.P. A Lord Chancellor, Lord Cairns, was another eminent benefactor.[1] When such reputable support was given publicly, it must have encouraged the flow of smaller contributions which Booth said was necessary for the vast work in hand.

A New Strategy of Salvation

In 1883 the Army's journal the *War Cry* had a circulation of 350,000 copies a week in its English edition alone, and other editions were printed in Stockholm, San Francisco, Bombay, Dunedin, Sydney, Melbourne and Adelaide. France, Germany, Switzerland, South Africa and Canada had also been stormed. 'At this speed,' said Booth, 'the colours will soon be flying all over the world.'[2] Long reports appeared in the *War Cry* every week of new successes among the Zulus, the Indians or the Australians, and of fresh assaults on towns and villages in England. Expansion to the provinces had begun under Booth's own direction. The acquisition of an overseas empire probably surprised him at first. It began in the spontaneous activity of emigrants to the United States and Australia who had been in the ranks before they left England. Anxious that all should stay under his own command, Booth sent trusted officers to take charge abroad. They were ordered to learn the language and customs of other societies so that foreign sinners could be met as intimately as sinners at home. Army people in India wore Indian dress. But the teachings, the exhortations and the methods carried into new lands were exactly those with which Booth had begun. There was no sign, in the work overseas, of the remarkable change of direction which the Army was about to make.

In 1890 the *Methodist Times* exclaimed: 'here is General Booth turning Socialist. . . .' It was greeting his book, *In Darkest England and the Way Out*. 'General Booth', said the journal,

> is one of the most sagacious and fearless of religious leaders. He has discovered that men have bodies as well as souls, and that Christianity must save society as well as the individual. Having

[1] R. Sandall, *op. cit.* I. 256–8; II. 318–21.
[2] *War Cry*, 23 Dec. 1882.

accepted Social Christianity he has outstripped us all in the thoroughness of his proposals.[1]

In Darkest England was described by its author as a scheme of social salvation. The young preacher who had blamed intemperance for the poverty of Nottingham now declared: 'Gin is the only Lethe of the miserable. The foul and poisoned air of the dens in which thousands live predisposes to a longing for stimulant. . . .' The man who as late as 1886 had asked 'what is the fruitful source of poverty? Is it not sin?'[2] now said that a remedy for the social problem 'must change the circumstances of the individual when they are the cause of his wretched condition, and lie beyond his control.' He might have been interrogating himself when he asked:

> Why all this apparatus of temples and meeting-houses to save men from perdition in a world which is to come, while never a helping hand is stretched out to save them from the inferno of their present life?

What had persuaded Booth to sound like a socialist? There was only one way in which he could reach a view of poverty that would make him a social reformer. Radical economists would not have moved him, even if he had understood them; for the sources of his indifference to material destitution were moral and religious. He turned to social reform because he became convinced that poverty itself was a grave impediment to salvation.

Outside the Army it was widely said that the 'Darkest England' scheme was Booth's confession of failure. 'The most competent observers agree', said a clergyman, 'that his Army has failed most conspicuously in the East End as a spiritual agency, but he thinks that it may be made to succeed as a social agency.'[3] This was certainly the view of many clergymen actually competing with Booth's people in working-class London, several of whom now said in *The Times* that the Army, despite its claims, was not reaching the poorest.[4] These witnesses were partisan. Similar comments, however, came from friendly and

[1] *Methodist Times*, 18 Sept. 1890, p. 956.
[2] *War Cry*, 29 Feb. 1886.
[3] T. Hancock, *Salvation by Mammon* (1891), p. 3.
[4] *The Times*, 2 Jan., 11 and 13 March, 1891.

impartial sources. In 1888 the *British Weekly*, analysing the results of its own census of worship in London, noted the figures of attendance at Army meetings 'with amazement and keen disappointment.'[1] An intelligent American, Robert Woods, who was surveying English social movements when *In Darkest England* appeared, described its programme as an attempt to minister to social groups which neither the churches nor the Army itself had so far much influenced. 'It ought to be well understood,' wrote Woods,

> that before the Salvation Army took up definite social work it had little, if any, more success than other evangelistic agencies have among these people. The campaign of purely emotional religion in the East End of London was a failure.[2]

If the claims made on its behalf had been less grandiose, the Army's successes would have looked a little more impressive. The total attendance at all Army services in London on one Sunday in 1887, according to the *British Weekly*'s estimate, was 53,591. This was certainly a mere speck against the mass of non-worshippers among whom Booth and his followers claimed to be working so successfully; but it was a larger number (according to the same source) than any other evangelistic organization in London attracted to mission services.[3] Nor is there any reason to doubt the common admission by leaders of the churches that the people attracted to the Army tended to be from a social level unreached by other means. Nevertheless, there were depths to which the Army was not penetrating. The *War Cry* had warned Salvationists in 1880 not to forget the plight of London as a vaster field opened: 'It would never do amidst all the distressing calls that come from every quarter for us to forget great London, with its cities upon cities of working people, and its miles of public houses.'[4] Although the Army by no means ignored London in the next decade, reports of evangelistic work in the metropolis were not prominent in its literature. London appeared rather as the headquarters, where campaigns were organized and celebrated, than as part of the battleground. Much of the news from London was about meet-

[1] *British Weekly*, 13 Jan. 1888, p. 217.
[2] R. A. Woods, *English Social Movements* (2nd. ed., 1895), p. 170.
[3] *The Religious Census of London* (1888), p. 53.
[4] *War Cry*, 24 Jan. 1880.

ings in the Army's rallying points – the Clapton Congress Hall, the Eagle Tavern in City Road, and the Regent Hall in the West End. Stories of fresh conquests by the Army tended to come more from the provinces or from overseas.

According to Church of England witnesses, however, the Army was having less success in the provinces than many people imagined. The Bishop of Gloucester and Bristol, C. J. Ellicott, reported his clergy saying as early as 1885 that the energy of Salvationists in the diocese was declining; and when a committee of the York Convocation asked clergymen in the north of England about the Salvation Army in the late 'eighties, most of those who made any reply said 'either that little or no effect has been produced, or that the Army is losing in numbers and influence.'[1] This opinion that the Army was slowing down after its first few years can be supported by other evidence. English sales of the *War Cry* dropped from about 350,000 a week in 1883 to fewer than 290,000 in 1890.[2] Early in the 'eighties triumphal despatches would announce the 'capture' of a district if a good meeting had been held. By 1887, however, the Army was being warned against 'the continual neglect of back streets,' and against 'an habitual routine of service, leaving thousands as untouched as though there were no Salvation Army barracks within half a mile of them.'[3] The Army, in other words, must now work more intensively, cultivating patiently ground already 'captured'. It was Booth's anxiety about the Army's lack of penetrating power among slum-dwellers that turned him towards social reform.

In the earliest days of his mission in Whitechapel, Booth had given some charitable relief to the poor, but he abandoned it because it appeared to him that the recipients were pauperized.[4] In 1870 he opened shops to sell cheap meals, but this scheme – characteristically named 'Food for the Million' – had failed by 1874.[5] For the next ten years either there was no relief or it was

[1] Convocation of York, *Report of Committee of the Lower House on the Spiritual Needs of the Masses of the People* (1892), p. 8.

[2] *War Cry*, 17 May 1890.

[3] *Ibid.*, 2 July 1887.

[4] W. Booth, *How to Reach the Masses with the Gospel*, pp. 36, 80; J. R. Green, '"Soupers" in the East End', in his *Stray Studies* (2nd series, 1868); R. Sandall, *op. cit.* III (1955), p. 63.

[5] St J. Ervine, *op. cit.* I. 322.

given by stealth. A Rescue Home was opened in Whitechapel in 1884 to save women from prostitution, and in 1885 Bramwell Booth was associated with W. T. Stead in the 'Maiden Tribute' campaign which exposed trafficking in girls. A home for discharged prisoners was opened in 1884. Prostitutes and ex-prisoners were small, marginal groups among the distressed population of London, who were helped as sinners rather than on account of their poverty. Aid to them implied no real change in strategy. 'For many years after the commencement of my public work,' said Booth in 1911,

> during which time I had, as opportunity served, helped the poor in their distress, I was deterred from launching out to any great extent in this direction by the fear so commonly entertained that by relieving their physical necessities I should be helping to create, or at any rate to encourage, religious hypocrisy and pretence.[1]

Doubtless this fear was a restraint, but so also was his belief in the overwhelming importance – even the self-sufficiency – of pure evangelism.

The notion that poverty offered a peculiar problem to evangelists, and that slums might demand special techniques, began to appear in the *War Cry* after 1885. During the months of severe unemployment in 1886, its leading articles and reports were unusally attentive to social distress. An Army officer told a magistrate in 1887 that it was the duty of every officer 'to visit the poor and needy from door to door, and to help them body and soul.' The *War Cry* commented: 'One cannot help wondering how many Salvation Officers and Soldiers have learned this lesson, and put it into daily practice.'[2] It was still a novel lesson when these words were written. Slum posts were established in London in 1887, and in 1888 some Night Shelters. Officers in the slums, said a journalist in 1890, 'were soon reporting to Headquarters the starving condition of the people. "We can't go and talk to people about their souls while their bodies are starving," said one Slum lass. . . .'[3] Booth wrote similarly. Once food and shelter depots were provided, he said, his officers could put their arms around the necks of poor people

[1] G. S. Railton, *General Booth* (1912), p. 188.
[2] *War Cry*, 2 July 1887.
[3] *Daily News*, quoted in *Slum Evangels* (1890), p. 90.

and plead with them as brethren who had gone astray.[1] Of people helped in these depots, the *War Cry* wrote in 1889:

> better than anything that has been done in this way to assuage their bodily need is, that in the course of the year scores of the poor men who have been sheltered in this building have been led to the Saviour . . .[2]

Although the work was on a small scale, it was hailed in the Army as a triumph because it made accessible a social stratum previously out of reach. 'The Salvation Army Shelter Work', said an official account of it in 1891, 'reaches a class hitherto unapproachable by any of the ordinary means used by missions or even Salvation Army Corps. . . .'[3] 'The Army's recent interest in the temporal welfare of the poor', wrote Herbert Booth, one of the General's sons, 'has opened a way into thousands of hearts hitherto sealed with the signal of despair.'[4] In 1890 a Social Reform Wing was set up to conduct the new activities.[5] A few months later it was given orders to execute the plan laid down in Booth's *In Darkest England.*

Booth insisted that the social scheme was a purely spiritual enterprise, and had been blessed as such by his wife, who died just before the book appeared. In providing for the relief of temporal misery, he wrote, 'I am only making it easy where it is now difficult, and possible where it is now all but impossible, for men and women to find their way to the Cross of our Lord Jesus Christ.'[6] Secular utopias interested him as little as ever. What he had altered was his strategy of salvation.

'In Darkest England, and the Way Out'

Early in his book Booth explains that he is leaving the reconstruction of the social system to others. His plan is not for England but for Darkest England – the out-of-work, the homeless, the vicious, the criminals and the children of these groups. These people number some three millions, he estimates, or one-tenth of the population. They are 'the submerged tenth'. For

[1] W. Booth, *In Darkest England*, p. 104.
[2] *War Cry*, 5. Jan. 1889.
[3] Social News Supplement to *War Cry*, 14 Nov. 1891.
[4] F. C. Ottman, *Herbert Booth, Salvationist* (n. d.), p. 39.
[5] For a list of the social activities under way by the end of 1890, see R. Sandall, *op. cit.* III. 74.
[6] W. Booth, *In Darkest England*, preface.

the time being, he is not planning for those sections of the submerged who are supported by the State in Poor Law institutions, prisons or asylums: in a fashion they are cared for already; they must wait, since many are not cared for at all. At present he will solve only 'the Problem of the Unemployed'.

The plan is to form the unemployed into 'self-helping and self-sustaining communities, each being a kind of co-operative society, or patriarchal family, governed and disciplined on the principles which have already proved so effective in the Salvation Army.' There will be a City Colony, composed of institutions to gather, relieve, employ and uplift the destitute. Some of the occupants will be found permanent work outside or sent home to friends; the residue, once they have been passed as sincere, industrious and honest, will go to the Farm Colony, on an estate near enough to London for marketing and far enough from the nearest town for sobriety. Here, as in the City Colony, they will obey absolutely and learn industry, morality and religion. (No religious services at any stage of the scheme, however, were to be compulsory.) After training in the Farm Colony, some will go home, some will get work outside, some will be settled in cottages or on co-operative farms, and most will sail to the third community, the Oversea Colony – a vast tract of land in one of the British colonies, governed by the Army. When Booth was asked if his overseas colonists would have a vote in the elections of whatever country they were in, he replied: 'No, I don't think they should bother their heads about politics.'[1]

Booth also describes a series of small agencies, some of them already running and others proposed, for rescuing the submerged. Finally, he lays down sanctions. When all the help in the world has been offered to people, he says, some will disdain it. Sorrowfully but remorselessly, one must declare them moral lunatics and lock them up, treating them kindly and wrestling for their souls, but forbidding them for ever access to their fellow men. Elsewhere in the book Booth has expressed his dislike for charity, declaring that normally no benefits will be offered unless a return is made in labour. Now he asserts that once his scheme makes unemployment unnecessary, the soliciting of charity should become a punishable crime. 'Anyway, if a man would not work of his own free will I would

[1] *Age* (Melbourne), 17 Oct. 1891.

compel him.' Unlike the Charity Organization Society, Booth did not believe in distinguishing, in the existing state of society, between the deserving and the undeserving. He implies in his book that this distinction can be made only after all the submerged have been offered a way out. The 'lost souls' may then be segregated. It is a view at once more generous and more terrible than the view of the Charity Organization Society.

Although Booth insists that he defines the submerged 'not in a religious, but in a social sense,' it is plainly (as he says in the preface) their lack of religion that compels him to offer them social redemption. From the attention to be given at every stage of the scheme to reformation of character, moreover, it is obvious that he sees the submerged as not only workless and godless, but shiftless. He is farther than ever from denouncing them for being so, for to his natural compassion he has lately added the belief that social conditions are often the cause of a poor man's vices. But he expects that an unemployed man will need to be taught Christianity and morality as well as a trade.

Booth had not been used to thinking as a social planner. Before his sudden conversion to a social programme it was forty years since he had seen the problems of society in a secular light. When at last he was persuaded that it was good spiritual strategy to do so, he was not only content but compelled to draw on other minds. Among his own officers the man who contributed most to the social scheme was Frank Smith, a Commissioner in the Army at the time *In Darkest England* was published.[1] Smith was born of lower middle-class parents in Chelsea. He first heard of the Booths in 1879, when he became a part-time evangelist for the Army. After two years he gave up commerce to become an Army officer. 'My heart's cry,' he wrote in 1882, 'is, may I live fighting and die shouting under the flag of the Salvation Army.'[2] His talents as a preacher and organizer won him rapid promotion, until in 1884, when Booth was faced with a crisis in the American command, Smith was chosen to take charge.[3] Before he left for America, Smith had

[1] Commissioner was the highest rank below General. Smith's subsequent fall from grace has caused him to be neglected by writers sympathetic to Booth. Begbie does not mention him. Ervine mentions him once, in another context. Sandall mentions him once (*op. cit.* III. 101) but does not consider him important.

[2] *War Cry*, 21 Sept. 1882.

[3] *Ibid.* 29 May 1886.

spoken a purely evangelical language. He returned impressed by Henry George, and he mixed with such men as the trade union leader Ben Tillett.[1] When he addressed a meeting of unemployed men in Hyde Park in fiercely secular terms, the General was not pleased, and for a short time Smith laid down his Commissionership.[2] He soon convinced Booth, however, that his ideals were wholly spiritual. Early in 1890 Booth gave him command of all the Army's social work. The slum shelters and food depots, which had begun already, represented some change of approach for the Army; but Smith turned the screw farther towards social reform. It was he who organized the first labour bureau and the first factory.[3] Where the slum officers were giving relief to the workless, Smith began to offer them work. The title allowed for his new command – the Social Reform Wing – shows the extent of Booth's conversion to his methods.

The *War Cry* now printed articles by Smith with the unfamiliar heading of 'Sociology', containing some passages that might have appeared in one of the socialist journals. Why was there a starving multitude in England? Smith asked. 'Is it not because of the greed of the "Haves" shutting out from their patrimony the "Have nots"?'[4] Other parts of the articles were close in mood (and even sometimes in language) to the book that Booth was to publish later in the year.[5] When the book appeared, an anonymous writer in *The Times* suggested that the whole scheme was substantially Smith's, and accepted reluctantly by Booth.[6] Smith was actually in gaol for holding an illegal street procession when *In Darkest England* was published. W. T. Stead, commenting on the irony of this fact, described Smith as 'at present the most conspicuous of the Commissioners,' and 'one of the leading spirits of the new departure.'[7] Stead added that Smith had been urging the social scheme on Booth for three years.

Stead himself contributed largely to the book. His admiration

[1] E. I. Champness, *Frank Smith, M.P., Pioneer and Modern Mystic* (1943), p. 11.

[2] *Methodist Times*, 23 Oct. 1890, p. 1077; R. A. Woods, *op. cit.* p. 171.

[3] R. A. Woods, *op. cit.* pp. 171–2.

[4] *War Cry*, 29 Nov. 1890. This was the fifth of eight articles announced, and it was the last actually to appear.

[5] See *War Cry*, 5 July 1890, and following issues.

[6] *The Times*, 26 Dec. 1890.

[7] W. T. Stead, *The Salvation Army and its Social Scheme*, p. 15.

for the Army had begun in the first months of its life, when he was impressed by its effect on working-class morals in Darlington.[1] He shared with Booth a crusader's instinct and a simple conviction of divine guidance. The two men became allies and friends, and when Booth asked him to recommend a literary collaborator for *In Darkest England*, Stead offered himself.[2] Booth acknowledges in his preface the 'valuable literary help' of an unnamed friend. The help was more than literary. 'You will recognize my fine Roman hand in most chapters,' Stead wrote to Milner. He was not speaking of style alone. 'You will be delighted to see that we have got the Salvation Army not only for Social Reform but also for Imperial Unity. I have written to Rhodes about it and we stand on the eve of great things.'[3] It is probable, especially in the light of this remark about imperial unity, that Stead suggested the Oversea Colony to Booth. According to Stead, Booth added emigration to his scheme when somebody (not named) showed him W. L. Rees' *From Poverty to Plenty*. Since the view of empire embodied in this work was so very close to that shared by Stead and Rhodes, it seems reasonable to suppose that it was Stead who gave it to Booth.[4] In one passage of Booth's book Stead took over completely. The end of the first chapter was taken almost verbatim from the leading article in the *Pall Mall Gazette* on 16 October 1883 in which Stead hailed *The Bitter Cry of Outcast London*.[5]

The Farm Colony, according to Stead, was put into Booth's head by a friend – again unnamed – who gave him a book by Herbert Mills, a Unitarian minister who had been settling unemployed Londoners on the land in co-operative estates.[6] This is plausible, since the plan for the Farm Colony is quite like the one laid out in Mills' *Poverty and the State* – which was

[1] E. W. Stead, *My Father* (1913), pp. 81–4.

[2] F. Whyte, *The Life of W. T. Stead* (1925), II. 12.

[3] *Ibid.* p. 13. So much for Stead's public assertion in 1891 that he was 'only a scribe' for Booth. (See R. Sandall, *op. cit.* III. 326).

[4] See W. L. Rees, *From Poverty to Plenty: or, the Labour Question Solved* (1888), especially the passage on p. 7 beginning 'The colonies languish . . .'

[5] See F. Whyte, *op. cit.* II. 13.

[6] Stead said that the book shown to Booth was *Home Colonization*. There appears to be no work of that title by Mills (whose organization, like an earlier one of Robert Owen's, was called the Home Colonization Society). The book Stead meant was almost certainly Mills' *Poverty and the State* (1886). On Mills, see *Labour Annual* (1895), p. 180.

said by a sympathizer to be one of the few books Booth ever read.[1] Booth consulted Mills before *In Darkest England* appeared, and gained his co-operation so effectively that Mills transferred to the Army's scheme £25,000 he had raised for his own.[2] Pieces of the plan came from elsewhere. In his section on co-operative farming Booth acknowledged the precedent of an experiment at Ralahine in Ireland.[3] The emigration scheme, he said, drew partly on the experience of Arnold White, who had conducted parties of colonists to South Africa.[4] Some of the detailed proposals were patently Booth's own. It was a truly Boothian imagination which could 'see, as in a vision, barge loads upon barge loads of bones floating down the Thames to the great Bone Factory.' Boothian too, was the conviction that the scheme would work wonders. His piggery would 'dwarf into insignificance all that exist in Great Britain and Ireland.' His emigration scheme would transfer the entire surplus population of the country. 'The scheme, in its entirety, may aptly be compared to a Great Machine . . .' he wrote. Andrew Bell had spoken of his teaching system as the steam engine of the moral world, and Robert Owen called the principle of co-operation a railway to universal happiness. Booth said: 'What we have to do in the philanthropic sphere is to find something analogous to the engineer's parallel bars. This discovery I think I have made, and hence I have written this book.' Accordingly he called upon England for £100,000 to start the plan and £30,000 a year to keep it running.

The Social Scheme, the Public and the Army

Within two or three months, *In Darkest England* had provoked so many reviews, sermons, addresses and pamphlets that nobody with an interest in social questions could fail to know more or less what Booth was saying. 'Few books upon their first appearance have received so much attention . . .' said a writer in the *Contemporary Review*, who himself gave £1,500

[1] D. M. Stevenson, 'Darkest England: The Way Out and the Leader', *Westminster Review*, April 1891, p. 438.

[2] *Ibid.* pp. 435–6.

[3] See E. T. Craig, *History of Ralahine* (n. d.)

[4] The 'mutual friend' (*In Darkest England*, p. 144) who introduced Booth to White could have been Stead, who knew White well. See F. Whyte, *op. cit.* II. 74.

for the scheme.[1] After a year, according to one estimate, some 200,000 copies of the book had been sold.[2]

Among religious leaders the most cordial to Booth's plan were, naturally enough, those who had already expressed some sympathy with the Army. R. W. Dale told Independents that they should help Booth to get the money he was after, because the Salvation Army was 'a new instrument for social and moral reform,' and because 'by no other instrument could the scheme be worked so efficiently.[3] The president of the Wesleyan Conference wrote to Booth: 'No one can read your book without recognizing the claim which you have established on the sympathetic help of all Christian Churches.'[4] Cardinal Manning told Booth that the plan commanded his sympathy because it recognized the right of every man to work, but he noted elsewhere: 'He may have inherited a work which the neglect of his forefathers has put beyond his reach.'[5] In the Church of England the Bishops of Manchester (James Moorhouse) and Sodor and Man (J. W. Bardsley) commended the scheme; and the Bishop of Liverpool (J. C. Ryle), though a little reserved, allowed that the book had turned many people's minds to the condition of their fellow-creatures.[6] Twenty-two Nonconformist and Church of England ministers, most of them well known, addressed an open letter to their fellows declaring that Booth's proposals should be given a fair trial.[7] The two oracles of respectability, *The Times* and the Queen, took *In Darkest England* seriously. Long expository essays in *The Times* were followed by leading articles mixing praise and criticism. The Queen, caught between a bishop who detested the book and her chaplain who liked it, allowed the Army to be told:

> The Queen cannot of course express any opinion upon the details of a scheme with which she is not yet acquainted; but understanding that your object is to alleviate misery and suffering Her Majesty

[1] F. Peek, 'In Darkest England, and the Way Out', *Contemporary Review*, Dec. 1890, p. 796.

[2] R. A. Woods, *op. cit.* p. 173.

[3] R. W. Dale, *General Booth's Scheme*, pp. 4, 10, 11.

[4] *Methodist Times*, 13 Nov. 1890, p. 1153.

[5] H. Begbie, *op. cit.* II. 120; J. R. Shane Leslie, *Henry Edward Manning, his Life and Labours* (1921), p. 484.

[6] H. Begbie, *op. cit.* II. 121; *The Times*, 28 Jan. 1891 and 6 Feb. 1891.

[7] R. Sandall, *op. cit.* III. 88.

cordially wishes you every success in the undertaking you have originated.[1]

W. T. Stead helped Booth not only in the writing of the book but by putting it in his new *Review of Reviews*, a journal with a higher circulation than any of the monthly reviews. In two long articles Stead set out the argument of the book, concealed his own contribution, and praised the work as a revelation. 'I have read the manuscript . . .' he wrote. 'No such book, so comprehensive in its scope, so daring in its audacity, and yet so simple and so practical in its proposals, has appeared in my time.'[2] These articles were also sold as a separate pamphlet. The immediate financial response was encouraging. Booth had said that only if the public gave him the first £100,000 at once would he consider himself called to the work of social redemption. It would be a sign, just as the parting of the waters had been a sign for Moses. In a little over three months, subscriptions passed the prescribed figure. The children of Israel could begin to cross the sea.

Among the crowd of speakers and writers who greeted *In Darkest England*, however, there were many who believed that the destitute must be led to the promised land by other routes altogether. One common criticism was that Booth greatly exaggerated the scale of extreme poverty.[3] Another was that he had disparaged unfairly the work of existing charitable agencies, and would harm them financially by his competitive appeal for money.[4] A third charge was plagiarism.[5] On this score Booth would have been happy with the defence of a sympathizer who said that the novelty of his scheme was the *union* of separate projects, to be 'carried out by an army of Christian workers, obeying the orders of a master mind.'[6] But the role allotted to the master mind was itself a source of

[1] H. Begbie, *op. cit.* II. 122. See also H. D. A. Major, *The Life and Letters of William Boyd Carpenter* (1925), pp. 228–31.

[2] W. T. Stead, *The Salvation Army and its Social Scheme*, p. 2.

[3] 'Darkest England', *Church Quarterly Review*, April 1891, pp. 225–8; J. F. Kitto in *The Times*, 2 Jan. 1891; R. Eyton, '*A Rash Investment.*' *A Sermon on the Salvation Army Scheme of Social Reform* (1890), p. 18.

[4] '*General' Booth and Others: an Appeal for the Others* (n. d.); M. Jeune, 'General Booth's Scheme', *National Review*, Jan. 1891, pp. 708–9.

[5] *Ibid.*; H. M. Hyndman, *General Booth's Book Refuted* (1890), p. 3; *Church Quarterly Review*, April 1891, p. 239.

[6] F. Peek, *loc. cit.* p. 804.

anxiety: a pamphlet called *Pope Booth* closed with a vision of the year 1950, in which Pope Booth III, having banished all publicans and tobacconists to the North Pole, declares anybody whom he dislikes to be a publican. The scheme itself was declared by this critic to be 'Socialism in its most dangerous form.'[1] Socialists were not inclined, however, to welcome Booth as an ally. Perhaps the one who came nearest to doing so was 'Elihu' (Samuel Washington), who thought it within Booth's power to erect a reformed Christianity which would denounce and end social injustice; but 'Elihu' observed that Booth saw only the rotten surface, not the shameful sources under it.[2] H. M. Hyndman made a similar point, though more brusquely, expressing pleasure that Booth and his 'perfervid religionists' now admitted the need to change environment, but noting that Booth dealt only with the *symptoms* of social distress.[3]

This chorus of hostility was increased by the voices of evangelists and philanthropists who denied Booth's claim to have made a serious impression already in the slums, and by fastidious Christians whose dislike of the Army's vulgar methods had not waned. Some of the critics were too obscure or heterodox to have any influence on the 'sober, serious, practical men and women' to whom Booth was appealing for money.[4] But many of them were reputable people who could be supposed to know what they were talking about, and whose opposition was bound to affect public support for the scheme. Probably the most damaging of all hostile comments from outsiders were those made in a report issued by the London Charity Organization Society, and in a series of letters to *The Times* by T. H. Huxley.

The Charity Organization Society's report was a skilful attack on the plan in terms of its own widely-approved social principles. In the eyes of C. S. Loch and his colleagues of the Society, Booth – despite all his protests – was offering the poor a relief just as corrupting as alms. By relieving all who applied, without sorting out the deserving from the undeserving, he

[1] T. Hancock, *Salvation by Mammon*, p. 3.
[2] 'Elihu', *Is General Booth's Darkest England Scheme a Failure?* (n. d.), p. 29.
[3] H. M. Hyndman, *op. cit.* p. 4.
[4] W. Booth, *In Darkest England*, p. 17.

would merely increase the scale of the problem he was trying to solve. If Booth replied that he would make all his applicants work for what he gave them, the rejoinder was to question one of his basic assumptions about the social problem. He had spoken of his scheme as draining the bog, removing the sludge. This was to see society in falsely static terms, said the report. Society was in restless movement, up and down.

> It is not a mass that has to be moved or a bog that has to be drained. The problem is to be solved, if solved it can be, not by any process of carting and hauling, but by helping the moving atoms up as they rise, preventing them when they seem likely to fall, and drawing them up when they have fallen.[1]

If these truths were ignored, it was suggested, the 'bog' would fill as quickly as it was drained.

Thomas Huxley's many letters to *The Times* were written with the frank intention of discouraging people from giving Booth any money for the scheme. They were an attack less on the social theory of Booth's book than on the religious system of its author. Harlotry, intemperance and even starvation seemed to Huxley lesser evils than that 'the intellect of a nation' should be 'put down by organized fanaticism', and that political and industrial affairs should be at the mercy of a despot whose chief thought was to make his fanaticism prevail.[2] Nor was Huxley convinced that money contributed for the social scheme would not be used to make Salvationists. Even when an independent committee reported in 1892 that the Army was keeping its fund for social work quite separate, Huxley remained afraid that as long as power remained in the hands of one man, the use of funds would depend on his whim. Charles Bradlaugh shared this suspicion, and is said to have died muttering: 'General Booth's accounts, General Booth's accounts.'[3]

Among the authors of letters to *The Times* about the scheme was Frank Smith, the man who had been appointed to administer it. He wrote not to defend the enterprise but to say that

[1] *An Examination of 'General' Booth's Social Scheme, Adopted by the Council of the London Charity Organization Society* (1890), p. 4.

[2] T. H. Huxley, 'Social Diseases and Worse Remedies', in his *Evolution and Ethics, and Other Essays* (1894), pp. 58–9. The letters to *The Times* were published together, with an introduction, in 1891, and incorporated in this volume.

[3] H. Begbie, *op. cit.* II. 176.

he had resigned from the Salvation Army after a dispute with his leaders about how much independence he should have as commander of the Social Reform Wing.[1] Booth's despotism had begun to chafe Smith, as it had other senior officers. It was more than a clash of wills, however, that made Smith leave the Army. Some of Booth's followers were unhappy about the General's new passion for social activity. Stead noted that the food and shelter depots, and even the slum brigade, 'were regarded with grave misgivings by some members of the Army, but the General's authority sufficed to carry them through.'[2] George Railton feared, according to Bramwell Booth, that the social scheme was 'a turning aside from the highest to secondary things. . . .'[3] In May, when the Social Reform Wing was announced, an officer found it necessary to write in the *War Cry*: 'Let us . . . slay this bogie that stalks about, endeavouring to make believe that we are on any other side than the "spiritual side". . . .'[4] Elijah Cadman was stalked as closely as anybody by this bogie. When he spoke in favour of the social work he made the terms of his support clear:

> I am determined to know nothing among men, save Jesus Christ and Him crucified. He is the Physician for the world's woes, and until men yield their allegiance to Him, sin and misery will abound. It is only because this scheme helps me in this direction that we are so full of certainty and hope with regard to it.[5]

Alone among the high command of the Army, Frank Smith rested the case for social activity on secular as well as evangelistic grounds. In his articles on 'Sociology' (which stopped abruptly at the fifth of eight advertised) Smith attacked poverty not as an impediment to salvation but as an evil in itself. According to his friend Keir Hardie, Smith's experience at the head of the Social Reform Wing showed him 'that however godlike the work of saving the wreckage of our social system might be, it would be more godlike still to put an end to the causes which produced it.'[6] Men like Cadman and Railton

[1] *The Times*, 2 Jan. 1891.
[2] W. T. Stead, *The Salvation Army and its Social Scheme*, p. 18.
[3] E. Douglas and M. Duff, *op. cit.* pp. 61–4. Bramwell Booth added that Railton's enthusiasm was second to nobody's once the scheme was launched.
[4] *War Cry*, 23 May 1890.
[5] *Ibid.*, 16 May 1890.
[6] *Labour Prophet*, Sept. 1894, p. 113.

were prepared to take orders from their General, to accept a change of spiritual strategy; but they cannot have been happy that the new enterprise was under the command of a man with such socialistic notions. When Booth prevented Smith from having a free hand with either the finances or the management of the social work, it was probably on the advice of his most trusted deputies, Cadman, Railton and his own son Bramwell. The memoirs of Bramwell Booth leave his part in these events obscure, but Smith's biographer says it was he who told Smith that he could not have the independence he demanded.[1]

When Smith resigned it was Elijah Cadman, perhaps the least socially-minded of all high officers, who replaced him. 'When my appointment was announced,' Cadman said candidly, 'Officers and Soldiers asked me, "Why have they put you into this?" '[2] The Social Reform Wing was now re-named the Social Wing – a change which Cadman must have welcomed and possibly initiated. In 1892 a sympathetic student of the Army's social work observed that the officers in the field knew little about social problems. Their superiors, he said, seemed not to think such knowledge necessary.[3]

After the first months of 1891, subscriptions for the social scheme came slowly. Booth had calculated that if a million pounds were subscribed at once, the finances of this scheme would be assured; for this sum, invested, would yield the £30,000 a year needed for running expenses. But between February 1891, when £108,000 was in hand, and September 1892, he received only £20,000. Public opposition had doubtless discouraged many potential subscribers. Smith's resignation, and the consequent public controversy between him and his former colleagues, must have sown doubts in other minds. Booth himself later blamed apathy as much as opposition for the decline of public support. 'I have found,' he remarked sadly in 1911,

> that whilst the public will be ready – nay eager – to embrace a new thing, they soon get tired of it, run after some other novelty, and leave you largely to struggle for its continuance, as best you can.[4]

[1] E. I. Champness, op. cit. p. 16.
[2] H. Wallis, *op. cot.* p. 122.
[3] F. Peek, 'General Booth's Social Work', *Contemporary Review*, July 1892, p. 82.
[4] G. Railton, *General Booth* (1912), p. 123.

With its arresting and evocative title, its vivid folding chart in colour, and its supposed answer to one of the greatest questions of the day, *In Darkest England* had a great but brief success among the reading public. By the middle of 1891 references to it in print were rare. In the same year Booth made a remark which suggested that even he was tiring of the social scheme. 'We must have some more spiritual work up and down the country . . .' he said.[1] 'My dear boy,' he wrote to Bramwell in 1893,

> I cannot go in for any more 'campaigns' against evils. My hands and heart are full enough. And moreover, these . . . reformers of Society have no sympathy with the S.A. nor with Salvation from *worldliness and sin*. Our campaign is against Sin![2]

He remained thoroughly in favour of social work, but never again did it acquire the place in his imagination which it had occupied in 1890. In the long run Sin and Salvation, Hell and Heaven, the Devil and the Lord, were the only realities for Booth: Society was an abstraction which he held in his mind only for a moment. If the new strategy had paid striking and immediate spiritual profits, he and the Army might have remained more excited about it. But it did not. The Army, left now in the hands of younger men while Booth went on a series of triumphal tours around the world, incorporated social relief as one part of its work and forgot Booth's vast blueprint for uplifting one-tenth of the population.

Some of the more modest parts of the 'Darkest England' plan were realized. The social work which had been begun before the book appeared was continued and extended. Several minor agencies planned in the book were founded. A few factories – called 'elevators' – were opened. At Hadleigh, in Essex, a farm colony was formed, which had 260 men living in it by 1897.[3] The officers of the Army who engaged in social work helped thousands of unemployed people, especially in London, who might have found no aid elsewhere. There was no Oversea Colony. From 1905 the Army assisted emigration to

[1] H. Begbie, *op. cit.* II. 183.

[2] *Ibid.*

[3] Sir W. Besant, 'The Farm and the City', *Contemporary Review*, Dec. 1897, p. 795. For evidence of Herbert Mills' disappointment with this colony, see *Labour Prophet*, April 1892, p. 30.

Canada, but this was a self-contained enterprise, not part of any general plan for rehabilitation.

The Army and the Masses

Like other great practitioners of experimental religion, Booth discovered that enthusiasm was easier to kindle than to keep burning. In a detached survey of the Army written in 1891, W. J. Ashley gave the following account as typical oι the Army's history in any locality:

> Its arrival creates a great ferment; during the first few months it gains a band of adherents, and there are some wonderful instances, which cannot be gainsaid, of moral reform. But then the progress of the Army in this particular place comes to an end. Its services are still held; but adherents are now added one by one at long intervals, and the 'Corps' is as little likely to affect the regeneration of the 'residuum' in that district as any of the surrounding religious bodies. Hence the growth of the Army in numbers has not been a steady and sustained growth in their earlier fields of labour: it is the result of the constant establishment of fresh corps in new places.[1]

The Army's golden age had been those few years after 1880 when the excitement and energy of people already enlisted were fanned by accounts of fresh successes won by shock tactics up and down England and abroad.

It is difficult to know what proportion of Booth's recruits had attended no church before they came to the Army. 'As far as I can see,' said Hensley Henson in 1890, 'the members of the Salvation Army are, in the great majority of cases, ex-Dissenters.'[2] This was a common view. The various Methodist groups were usually thought to be the main sufferers. William Booth's namesake Charles found that in London the Army did make some 'genuine converts', but concluded that many, if not most, of its adherents came to it from some other religious body.[3] Of such people he noted, however, that the Army had

[1] W. J. Ashley, 'General Booth's Panacea', *Political Science Quarterly*, VI (1891), p. 550.

[2] *The Times*, 19 Nov. 1890.

[3] C. Booth, *Life and Labour of the People in London*, 3rd. series, *Religious Influences*, VII. 327.

bound them with new ties, strengthened their faith, and set them to work for the social and religious welfare of the world. Even if the numbers drawn from the churches were as great as some critics supposed, there were probably many among them who, but for the Army, would have lapsed. Joining the Army was at the very least a sign of discontent with existing opportunities for worship.

Despite Booth's declaration that he would never let his Army become one more sect, that was its destiny. What had once been sensational in its methods, preserved in the next generation, became old-fashioned. Henceforth it was to be run not by prophets but by administrators, and its ways became rather less different from those of other sects. Peculiarities remained. Its officers moved more easily than most ordained ministers through slums and into public houses, and they gained a reputation for dispensing social relief with a lack of condescension or inquisition forbidden by the Poor Law and rare, thanks to the Charity Organization Society, among voluntary philanthropists. As a religious community, moreover, the Army kept much of its original vigour through successive generations. Good Salvationists never forgot that their task was to win souls for Christ; and even if they won few, the sense of being a community set apart for this purpose contributed to the fellowship of an Army corps.

William Booth knew that he had affected the churches themselves. It was a proud day for the old man when Edward VII asked: 'How do you get on now with the Churches? What is their attitude towards you?' 'Sir,' Booth replied, 'they imitate me.'[1] The most direct imitation was the Church Army. The Wesleyans' Forward Movement, so Bramwell Booth believed, began as an attempt to create a respectable Salvation Army.[2] The Army's work was observed earnestly by Christians in every denomination, including Catholics. Some specific techniques, such as bold advertising, were copied widely. Nobody in Victorian England did more than Booth to put unconventional methods into the service of conventional Christianity. If he and his followers had not been so charged with a passion to fill the gap between the churches and the masses, they could

[1] H. Begbie, *op. cit.* I. 112.

[2] B. Booth, *These Fifty Years*, p. 186.

not have achieved the empire that was theirs by the time the founder died in 1912. It was clear long before then, however, that not even he had shown (in a phrase he loved) how to reach the masses with the gospel.

6

Labour Churches

The Beginning

John Trevor, the founder of the Labour Church movement, left his Unitarian pulpit for the same reason that William Booth had left the Methodists: because he could not reach poor people in the chapel. The social relief work of the Salvation Army impressed Trevor, although the Army's theology and economics seemed to him wrong. 'They taught me,' he said of Booth's people,

> that God can do nothing without love and self-sacrifice, and the witnessing spirit which may lead to martyrdom; that the 'Truth' taught comfortably, however reasonable it may appear, will never redeem society; indeed that, truth without self-sacrifice is not truth but a sham. . . .[1]

In this way the Army helped Trevor towards his decision in 1891 to leave the Upper Brook Street Free Church in Manchester and form the first Labour Church. The name was suggested by William Bailie, an anarchist, atheist and friend of Trevor's in Manchester, who described the enterprise as a Socialist Salvation Army.[2]

Like Booth, Trevor had been born in a provincial city, and into a family which, though poor, aspired to respectability. Booth's parents tried to push him into pawnbroking, and the

[1] *Great Thoughts*, 7 Nov. 1896, p. 90.
[2] *Ibid.*; J. Trevor, *My Quest for God* (1897), p. 242.

aunt who raised Trevor refused to let him become a builder or an engineer because she would not have him wear the clothes of a working man. Both men later developed a deep hatred of middle-class social values. Their religious pilgrimages, however, were in opposite directions. Not until adolescence did Booth take to his heart the doctrines of sin, conversion, justification by faith in a redeeming Christ, Hell and Heaven, which passed into the Salvation Army. Trevor, though born twenty-five years later, was subjected as a child to evangelical religion in a form quite naked and terrifying. Like many thoughtful people in the seventies and eighties he revolted against this gospel. The fear of hell pursued him as a child and scarred him permanently, but in his twenties he was an agnostic, and when he returned to a religious faith it was not one that he called Christian. The Salvation Army used novel methods to propagate doctrines of impeccable evangelical orthodoxy. Its programme of social reform, adopted in 1890, involved not the slightest lapse from this orthodoxy; and the vision of social regeneration expressed in Booth's book, though grandiose, troubled conservatives only when they did not understand it. The Labour Church challenged the social presuppositions of conventional Christianity far more boldly than the Salvation Army did, and it challenged Christian doctrines which Booth held as dearly as anybody.

In membership, organization, and circulation of literature, the Labour Churches had far less success than the Salvation Army. Probably there were never more than thirty churches at any one time; few of them were alive twenty years after the first was formed.[1] From a study of such a modest movement it would not be possible to confirm or refute any broad generalizations about the churches and the English working classes. The movement has a peculiar interest, however, as an attempt to give Labour a church of its own. It was by no means the only new church to appear in late Victorian England. From the religious turmoil of the age came an Ethical Church, a Church of Humanity, a Church of Our Father, and other bodies formed

[1] E. Hobsbawm, *Primitive Rebels* (Manchester, 1959), p. 144, underestimates the number that can be traced in the publications of the movement when he says that at its peak there were churches in 24 places. S. Pierson, 'John Trevor and the Labour Church Movement in England, 1891–1900', *Church History*, XXIX (1960), p. 478, says that the files of the *Clarion* and the *Labour Leader* disclose more than 120 churches, most of which died, however, in a few months.

by fugitives from orthodoxy who wanted to stop short of unbelief. But as an institution designed specifically for working-class people, the Labour Church appears to have had no predecessor in living memory other than the Chartist Churches which flourished for a while after 1840 and which were unknown to Trevor until his own movement was well under way.[1]

When members of the Labour Church explained why they could find no home in any existing church, what they said most often and most passionately was that the churches had been captured by the wealthy classes, who imposed on them both a social atmosphere in which the working man felt an alien, and social policies which denied his aspirations for justice. According to Trevor, the churches saw in slums a sign of God's anger at sin and a warning of its consequences; the working classes, knowing better, left the churches.[2] 'To whom must the workers look for guidance?' asked the writer of a prize essay in Trevor's paper, the *Labour Prophet*. 'To the churches, with their bishops and clergy, their sects and systems? No, no! They must get outside the existing institutions that are so much under the power of the capitalistic Pharoahs of this day.'[3] One of the merry men on the *Clarion*, A. M. Thompson, remarked that not until the Labour Church was formed did he think it possible to be associated with a religious body; 'for religion had become so identified within my observation with black clothes, kid gloves, tall silk hats, and long faces, that it and I appeared to have parted for ever.'[4]

It was above all the social conservatism of the existing churches that provoked Trevor to become an innovator. His acquaintance with socialists in Manchester shook him into doubting that he had any good reason for asking a working man to attend his chapel. 'It seemed to me that, in inviting him to come, I should be inviting him to desert his flag and neglect the true work of his life.'[5] He launched the new church after talking with a working man who had left the Upper Brook Street chapel because he could not stand the social climate of

[1] See H. U. Faulkner, *Chartism and the Churches* (1916), pp. 42–6.

[2] J. Trevor, *Theology and the Slums* (n. d.), p. 6.

[3] 'A Weaver', in *Labour Prophet*, Aug. 1892, p. 62. The subject of the essay was: 'Why is the Labour Movement a religious movement?'

[4] *Ibid.*, Nov. 1893, p. 105.

[5] J. Trevor, *My Quest for God*, p. 234.

the congregation. Trevor had also been lately to a Unitarian conference in London, where he heard two addresses which he described afterwards as almost prophesying the Labour Church. The addresses were by the Labour leader Ben Tillett and the Unitarian minister Philip Wicksteed, both of whom deplored antipathy in the churches towards ideas now filling the minds of class-conscious working men.

Tillett, riding on the reputation he had won in the dock strike of 1889, enjoyed nothing more than chance to harangue an audience of church-goers: preaching socialism at Christians was his recreation in the early 1890's. He became one of the most popular speakers at Labour Churches. In his socialist sermons Tillett never offered judgments about the doctrines expressed in the Christian creeds; he attacked the churches as strongholds of social reaction. When he heard Wicksteed at the Unitarian conference, Trevor had already been influenced by him. From November 1888 to June 1890 Trevor was his assistant-minister at the Unitarian chapel in Little Portland Street, London. 'In Philip Wicksteed,' he wrote in 1892, 'I found for the first time a man I could love.'[1] Trevor gained from Wicksteed not any specific ideas, but a general conviction that religion must be brought to bear on the problems of society, and an assurance that he was right to form the new church.[2] In a tract Wicksteed wrote for Trevor, *What does the Labour Church Stand for?* he gave no doctrinal reasons for having a Labour Church – partly because he found the newer Unitarianism theologically satisfying, and partly because the relation of religious thought to *social* problems seemed to him the most urgent problem of the day. It was the social attitudes of denominational churches, Wicksteed declared, that made a separate Labour Church necessary, 'No existing church is frankly and primarily based on the practical determination to re-organize society in the interests of unprivileged producers.' True, the worker was offered *religious* equality; but this was not enough:

> What workman can walk into a middle-class congregation with the consciousness that the underlying assumptions, both in the pew and

[1] *New Era*, Feb. 1892, p. 43. For a note on Wicksteed see H. M. Pelling, *The Origins of the Labour Party*, 1880–1900 (1954), p. 140.

[2] J. Trevor, *My Quest for God*, pp. 204–20.

in the pulpit, as to the proper organization of active industrial life and the justification of social and industrial institutions are in a militant sense his own? And if he cannot do that, then in asking him to join in the worship you are not asking him to express and nourish the religious aspects of his own higher life, but to suppress or suspend that life in order that he may share in the devotions of others, who cheerfully accept, and in many cases would stubbornly defend, the things against which it is his mission to fight.[1]

These attacks by Trevor and Wicksteed on the social values held in the churches were scarcely more vehement than many criticisms being made at assemblies of the Church of England and the larger Nonconformist bodies by people who never thought of seceding. Why then could not the energy about to be diverted into a Labour Church be used instead to support those who were trying already to convert the older churches from within?

One answer, inplicit in Wicksteed's tract, was that social reaction reigned so firmly in the churches, and its attackers were so relatively few, that conquest from within would be a long and possibly hopeless task. Tom Mann, it is true, indulged a brief fantasy of taking holy orders and capturing the Church of England. 'What attracted me to the Established Church,' he explained, 'was the fact that it was about the most perfectly organized body in this country. I love organization. I thought that instead of attacking the Church from outside it might be possible to direct it from within.' The vision of himself as archbishop faded before he did anything rash, even though his prospective vicar assured him that inability to accept the Thirty-Nine Articles was no obstacle.[2] But the view taken by Trevor and shared by the most prominent Labour and socialist leaders – whether or not they were Christians – was that while social reformers inside the churches could be admired for their courage and welcomed as allies, they had little chance of converting the bulk of respectable Christianity to a real sympathy with working-class aspirations.

To this argument Trevor added a quite different one. For him it was not only the churches' 'dependence on middle-class

[1] P. Wicksteed, *What does the Labour Church Stand For?* (n. d.), pp. 7–8.

[2] *Labour Prophet*, Jan. 1892, p. 11; June 1897, p. 81; *Tom Mann's Memoirs* (1923), pp. 119–20.

support' but also their being 'too muddled up with Theology and Christology,' that made a distinct Labour Church necessary.[1] 'The historic churches,' he wrote,

> mostly declare that God was on this earth nearly nineteen centuries back. The Labour Church was founded for the distinct purpose of declaring that God is at work, here and now, in the heart of the Labour movement; and that the religion of today consists in co-operating with the divine energy which is still operating on our planet.[2]

Even if a miracle made the older churches socialist, adherence to outworn religious dogma would still strangle their message; 'it is not in the least essential to bother our heads about what happened 1800 years ago, . . . we organize the Labour Church, because we protest against the assumptions of the other churches in religion' as well as against their social failings.[3]

In making a distinction between 'religion' and 'theology' Trevor was very much a man of his age. Many of the people who had surrendered their belief in Christian dogma – whether to the biblical scholarship of Tübingen, the positivism of Comte, the geology of Lyell and the biology of Darwin, or to some other of the Victorian solvents of orthodoxy – found it comforting to think that only the husk of formal doctrine must be abandoned, leaving a kernel of religious faith. It did not worry doubters who stopped short of agnosticism that this faith was vague: they gladly sacrificed the precision of belief which only dogma made possible, for they believed such precision to be illusory. They might or might not call themselves Christians. Their position was summed up by Robert Blatchford in 1885, when he described his religion as the Christianity of Abou Ben Adhem.[4] Once 'theology' was ruled out, differences over whether God was a person or a principle, whether Jesus was or was not divine, were matters of taste rather than subjects for discussion. It is true but it may be misleading to say that Keir Hardie was a Christian, for a more cordial response could be expected in the Labour Church than in any traditional church in his characteristic remark, 'The more a man knows about theology the less he is

[1] *Labour Prophet*, Jan. 1892, p. 11.
[2] *Ibid.*, Sept. 1894, p. 120.
[3] *Ibid.*, Feb. 1892, p. 12.
[4] A. M. Thompson, *Here I Lie* (1937), p. 54.

likely to know about Christianity.'[1] People who clung to 'theology' could join the Labour Church if they wished, but they must not expect to find there any recognition or discussion of theological doctrine. Dogmas were anathema.

But Trevor was quite serious when he called his movement a church. 'God in the Labour Movement – working through it, as he once worked through Christianity, for the further salvation of the world – that was the simple conception that I had been seeking, and which at last came to me. . . .'[2] Labour needed to be independent of the Church of England and the Nonconformists just as it needed to be independent of the Conservatives and the Liberals. In neither case, moreover, must it be content with mere emancipation: it must form an Independent Labour Party to win social justice, and a Labour Church to save its soul. It was the mission of the Labour Church, Trevor believed, 'to develop the religion of the Labour Movement into clearer self-consciousness.'[3] Trevor could only hope that the people who joined and who spoke for the Labour Church would agree with him about his purpose.

In 1891 Trevor drew up a set of principles on which he believed the Labour Church should be based. Less than two years later, delegates from his own and from sixteen other Labour Churches met in Manchester to form a Labour Church Union. Some delegates proposed amendments to the principles as Trevor had set them out, but none was carried. His original statement was then accepted. It read thus:

The Labour Church is based on the following Principles:

1. That the Labour Movement is a Religious Movement.
2. That the Religion of the Labour Movement is not a Class Religion, but unites members of all classes in working for the Abolition of Commercial Slavery.
3. That the Religion of the Labour Movement is not Sectarian or Dogmatic, but Free Religion, leaving each man free to develop his own relations with the Power that brought him into being.
4. That the Emancipation of Labour can only be realized so far as men learn both the Economic and Moral Laws of God, and heartily endeavour to obey them.

[1] *Labour Leader*, 10 Nov. 1894, p. 2.
[2] J. Trevor, *My Quest for God*, p. 241.
[3] *Labour Prophet*, Jan. 1892, p.4.

5. That the development of Personal Character and the improvement of Social Conditions are both essential to man's emancipation from moral and social bondage.[1]

Supporters

By the middle of 1895 the committee of the Labour Church Union could report that fourteen towns had churches affiliated with the Union, that in twenty others groups were 'carrying on Sunday work on our lines, and in many cases adopting our principles and title', and that there were good hopes of churches beginning in twenty-five more places.[2] The largest churches, at Manchester and Bradford, had over 300 members – people who had signed their acceptance of Labour Church Union principles – and several others had more than 100. Attendance of some hundreds at a Sunday meeting was common, and on a special occasion – an address by one of the leaders in the socialist movement – it could run into thousands. The Birmingham church normally met in its own premises, a former chapel seating 500; but if the speaker was a well-known visiting socialist, the Town Hall would be hired. At the first open-air meeting held by the Oldham church, Katharine Conway (later Mrs J. Bruce Glasier) spoke to over 3,000 people.[3] This progress was all the more pleasing to Trevor because it was spontaneous. Lacking a John Wesley's nervous energy, organizing genius and love of power, Trevor believed in letting new churches wait on local demand and activity. Apart from leading the Labour Church at Manchester, his main work for the movement was literary – editing the *Labour Prophet* and producing several tracts issued in its name. The first monthly issue of the *Labour Prophet* in January 1892 ran to 4,500 copies instead of the 2,000 which Trevor had expected to sell. In May 1893 the number of pages was increased from eight to twelve, and in January 1894 to sixteen; by the end of that year he was printing 6,000 copies.

One of the principles adopted by the Labour Church Union was that the religion of the Labour movement united members of all classes. This was said partly to forestall any charge of social exclusiveness or class animosity, and partly to encourage

[1] *Ibid.*, Aug. 1893, p. 76.
[2] *Ibid.*, June 1895, p. 95.
[3] *Ibid.*, April 1893, p. 32.

middle-class people who might be willing to help organize, subscribe to, or speak at Labour Churches. It is plain, however, both from the origins of the movement and from the policies of particular churches, that the real test of the Labour Church, in the minds of Trevor and his friends, was its power to recruit working-class members. 'A Labour Church is . . . a church of the workers', said a zealot in Hull. 'It is emphatically the poor man's church. . . .'[1] It was to attract working-class members that after its first few months the church at Manchester abandoned a compulsory fee as a condition of membership.[2] This practice was followed at other churches.

What evidence there is about Labour Church members and audiences suggests that they were mostly working-class people. 'They were of all classes,' Philip Wicksteed said of the people who attended an early meeting at Manchester, 'but the great bulk I took to be workmen.'[3] An Independent minister at Bradford in 1892 described a Labour Church meeting as crowded with workmen.[4] The Plymouth Church was founded in the same year by 'a number of working men', and at its first meetings the attendance was predominantly working-class.[5] At the Hull church in 1895, many of the people attending meetings were unemployed.[6] Among the rank and file the proportion of unskilled workers seems to have been smaller than Trevor had hoped. The *Workman's Times* described an early meeting of the Manchester and Salford Labour Church as composed mainly of well-to-do members of the working class.[7] An observer who attended several meetings in 1894 found a 'predominantly working-class' attendance that was 'respectable, responsible' and 'not to be confounded with one of the Salvation Army type . . . decently dressed artisans and mechanics, some of the highest grades. . . .'[8] Trevor confessed in 1898 that the problem of how to reach the very poorest people still troubled him, and James

[1] *Ibid.*, Jan. 1897, p. 1.
[2] *Ibid.*, April 1892, p. 32.
[3] *Manchester Guardian*, quoted in *ibid.*, Feb. 1892, p. 10.
[4] Dr Charles Leach at a meeting of the Congregational Union, quoted in *ibid.*, Nov. 1892, p. 84.
[5] *Ibid.*, Nov. 1892, p. 88; Jan. 1893, p. 8.
[6] *Ibid.*, March 1895, p. 47.
[7] L. Thompson, *Robert Blatchford: Portrait of an Englishman* (1951), p. 80.
[8] *Spectator*, 21 April 1894, quoted in S. Pierson, *loc. cit.* p. 468.

Sims, president of the Labour Church Union, said that the 'best material' for the movement were 'the self-respecting working-man, the shopkeeper, and the lower middle-class man.'[1]

Sims may not have meant 'man' to include 'woman'. On the platform, the Labour Church had a striking proportion of women: Margaret McMillan, Caroline Martyn, Enid Stacy, Eleanor Keeling, Fyvie Mayo, Ada Ward, Annie Jackson and Katharine Glasier were all Labour Church speakers. But in the body of a meeting the majority were male.[2] This was a characteristic of Labour meetings in general. It was explained variously. One female agitator thought that women were reluctant to attend Labour meetings because discussion were too materialistic: 'We must give her [woman] a religion, not mere economics.'[3] Another woman blamed men for making women stay home at the sink:

> They *do* care; they *do* want to know all about these unions or Eight Hours Bills, and competition and such like, and they want to have the chance of hearing your Tom Manns and Ben Tilletts, and if you'll let them come along, side by side with you, life will be ten times better. . . .[4]

The emancipation of women was a principle which received at least lip-service in the Labour Churches; but the committee of the Birmingham church refused (by four votes to three) to let women help take up the collection.[5] Until the granting of women's suffrage, politics was regarded as a business for men. The appearance of the New Woman on Labour – including Labour Church – platforms was a sign that this attitude was changing; but the change had not yet spread through the rank and file. Whether the excess of men over women at Labour Church meetings caused satisfaction or disappointment depended on the mood of the observer. The members of a Labour Church might hold a solemn discussion called 'How can we Reach the Women?' or they might congratulate themselves on being the

[1] *Labour Prophet*, June 1898, p. 186; Aug. 1898, p. 201.
[2] *Ibid.*, Feb. 1892, p. 10; Oct. 1894, p. 144; Feb. 1895, p. 28; Jan. 1897, p. 5.
[3] Isabella Ford in *Labour Prophet*, Dec. 1894, p. 162.
[4] 'Dorothy Scott' in *ibid.*, Feb. 1892, p. 10.
[5] Birmingham City Library, Birmingham Labour Church, minutes of executive committee meeting, 27 July 1894.

only church in the country which attracted as many men as women.

The geographical distribution of the movement can be described fairly precisely. Nearly all were in manufacturing towns. Most were in Lancashire and the West Riding of Yorkshire: here the churches were most vigorous as well as most numerous. In several midland towns the movement was comparatively active; but even at Birmingham, which had probably the largest church south of Sheffield, the secretary could write in 1894: 'The Labour movement here has not assumed anything like the proportions that it appears to have done in Lancashire and Yorkshire, and our success has only been relative.'[1] Farther south the churches were few and not prosperous. The editor of the *Labour Church Record* said in 1901 that 'in the south of England, the Labour Church has gained no foothold at all.'[2] Labour churches were founded in London from time to time, but none seems to have lasted long. In 1895 Trevor, now living in London and trying to start a church, called the metropolis 'the despair of the Labour movement.'[3]

The Labour Churches were associated closely with the political Labour movement. Trevor himself had initiated an Independent Labour Party in Manchester in May 1892, believing that Labour should have its own party and apprehensive that unless a distinct political organization was created alongside it, the Labour Church might occupy itself with political action at the expense of its spirituality.[4] One of Trevor's *Labour Prophet* Tracts was a plea for a national I.L.P., and he attended the conference at Bradford in 1893 which formed such a party. He had the satisfaction here of organizing a Labour Church service attended by some 5,000 people and addressed by speakers who included Keir Hardie and Bernard Shaw.[5] In Darlington and in Bolton, as in Manchester, the Labour Church was established before the I.L.P. branch and encouraged its foundation.[6] But the

[1] *Labour Prophet*, Sept. 1894, p. 128.

[2] *Labour Church Record*, Jan. 1901, p. 5. See also *Labour Prophet*, Feb. 1895, p. 28.

[3] *Ibid.*, May 1895, p. 73.

[4] *Ibid.*, April 1893, p. 28. For independent testimony to Trevor's part in forming the Manchester I.L.P., see C. H. Herford, *Philip Henry Wicksteed, his Life and Work* (1931), p. 227n.

[5] *Labour Prophet*, Feb. 1893, p. 16.

[6] *Ibid.*, Aug. 1892, p. 64; June 1894, p. 80.

opposite relationship was more usual. In Oldham (1893), the Spen Valley (1894), Southampton (1894), Paddington (1895) and elsewhere, I.L.P. branches were wholly or mainly reponsible for establishing Labour churches.[1] The churches often depended on the I.L.P. for accommodation, the two bodies often conducted joint meetings, and it was common for their membership to overlap considerably. In 1894 the administrative council of the I.L.P. (presumably in response to a request from the Labour Church Union) resolved: 'that Branches of the I.L.P., wherever practicable, should run a Sunday meeting on Labour Church lines.'[2] The *Labour Prophet* at once reported 'a tendency, if not a movement', to form twenty-three new churches.[3] The results were negligible, however: in March 1895 the Labour Church Union sent a circular to all I.L.P. branches reminding them of the resolution, but few replied.[4] Most I.L.P. branches, in fact, never had any association with a Labour church. In 1885 there were more than 260 branches in England.[5] Even if one makes a generous estimate of the number of Labour Churches, it is still plain that more than 200 of these branches had nothing to do with a Labour Church. In some I.L.P. branches, the general opinion was too secularist for sympathy with Labour Churches. Where this was so the Labour Church, if its existed at all, found the going hard.[6]

Some Labour Churches co-operated with branches of the Social Democratic Federation or the Fabians. The Birmingham Labour Church absorbed the local Fabian Society in 1895, worked closely with the S.D.F., supported I.L.P. candidates at municipal elections, planned joint outings with the Clarion Cycling Club which one of its members had founded, and favoured 'the Amalgamation of existing Socialist Bodies.'[7]

[1] *Ibid.*, Jan. 1893, p. 8; June 1894, p. 95; Oct. 1894, p. 143; Nov. 1895, p. 174.

[2] *Ibid.*, Sept. 1894, p. 124.

[3] *Ibid.*

[4] *Ibid.*, June 1895, p. 95.

[5] H. M. Pelling, *op. cit.* p. 172.

[6] See H. C. Rowe in *Labour Prophet*, Jan. 1896, p. 10, blaming the secularism of Labour men in Rochdale for the absence of a Labour Church there. See *ibid.*, June 1895, p. 95, for the split at Bolton between the I.L.P. and the Labour Church; and *ibid.*, April 1898, p. 171, for Trevor's explanation of the differences. On friction in Leeds, see *ibid.*, July 1896, p. 118. On 'the disintegrating policy' of the I.L.P. in Hull, see *ibid.*, June 1898, p. 191. On 'the sneers and vulgar words of the geniuses of the local I.L.P.' in Halifax, see *Labour Church Record*, Jan. 1901, p. 7.

[7] Birmingham Labour Church, minutes, passim.

Trevor blessed such activity. 'One of the great advantages of the Labour Church,' he wrote in 1895, 'is its unifying influence.'[1] It pleased him that the Labour Church should try to span the gulf in the socialist movement between moral enthusiasm and the hard cutting intellect – between Hardie and Shaw. But this was, after all, a merely political function. 'Labour Churches are formed too often from insufficient motives,' Trevor warned in 1895, 'and the whole movement will suffer from the thin soil in which a deal of it is rooted.'[2]

The Labour Church and the Churches

There is some evidence for the argument that the Labour Churches found support 'merely as a short-lived protest against the link which the Nonconformist churches had established with the middle class, and in particular against the alliance with the Liberal Party.'[3] Trevor's immediate motive in leaving the Unitarians at Manchester was to protest against this link. At Bolton, the oldest Congregational chapel in the town formed itself into a Labour Church, pastor and all, after a series of addresses in the chapel by Ben Tillett.[4] The most striking example of all is Bradford, where Tillett was again in the thick of it. It was his candidature for West Bradford in the parliamentary election of 1892 that occasioned the founding of a Labour Church. 'Mr Tillett and his followers,' wrote the correspondent of a Nonconformist journal, 'by a strange process of reasoning, came to the conclusion that the ministers and the churches were opposed to their labour movement.'[5] The Bradford Labour Union had chosen Tillett to fight West Bradford against the Liberal candidate, Alfred Illingworth. The political allegiance of Bradford Dissent was plain to all voters, since twelve Nonconformist ministers sat on the platform at a meeting held to support the Liberal. When Fred Jowett, president of the Bradford Labour Union, rose to move that the meeting support

[1] *Labour Prophet*, June 1895, p. 89.

[2] *Ibid.*, July 1895, p. 105.

[3] H. M. Pelling, *op. cit.* pp. 151–2. For a discussion of this point see K. S. Inglis, 'The Labour Church Movement', *International Review of Social History*, III (1958), 445–60, and correspondence from H. Pelling in *ibid.* IV (1959), 111.

[4] *Labour Prophet*, May 1892, p. 38.

[5] *Christian World*, 4 Aug. 1892, p. 38.

Tillett instead, the chairman – a Liberal Member of Parliament – at first refused to let him speak. The uproar caused by Jowett's friends made the chairman change his ruling. After denouncing the chairman as an enemy of the working classes, Jowett turned to the Nonconformist ministers. 'If you persist in opposing the Labour Movement,' he said, 'there will soon be more reason than ever to complain of the absence of working men from your chapels. We shall establish our own Labour Church.'[1] In political history the contest in West Bradford is notable for the shock given to the Liberals by the number of votes cast for Tillett.[2] In the social history of English religion it is interesting as a sign of working-class protest against the alliance between Nonconformity and Liberalism. After the election Tillett said that he had been forced to fight the pulpit as well as his Liberal opponents, and advised Bradford working men to do as Jowett had threatened and form a Labour Church.[3] They did so; and the Bradford Labour Church, which soon became the largest in the country, worked more closely with the political Labour movement than did any other.

But the Labour Churches were not a revolt against Nonconformity alone. In their ranks and their leadership were not only former Unitarians like Trevor, Quakers like Sam Hobson, Independents like the group at Bolton, and Wesleyans like Seth Ackroyd at Hull; there were also many people who had been members of the Church of England. R. A. Beckett, who edited the *Labour Prophet* for a time, had once been a Unitarian lay preacher; but he was the son of a clergyman in the Church of England, and he had been set on the path to socialism by reading F. D. Maurice. A. W. Hildreth, the first secretary of the Darlington Labour Church, was brought up in the Church of England. So was James Stott, secretary at Bradford. Tom Groom, secretary for some years of the Birmingham Labour Church, had been a member of Stewart Headlam's Guild of St Matthew. Another leader at Birmingham, J. A. Fallows, had been a clergyman. So, almost, had Fred Brocklehurst, the first general secretary of the Labour Church Union and next to Trevor the hardest of all workers for the movement. After leaving Cambridge, Brockle-

[1] F. Brockway, *Socialism over Sixty Years* (1946), p. 40.
[2] H. M. Pelling, *op. cit.* p. 112.
[3] *Christian World*, 4 Aug. 1892, p. 63.

hurst was on the point of taking holy orders when he turned instead to the Labour Church and the I.L.P.[1] Walter Morse, secretary of the Labour Church Union in 1896, had been a regular worshipper in the Church of England until he joined the Leeds Labour Church; he said that 'the very easy and ineffectual way' in which people in the Church of England dealt with social injustice, 'and their failure to understand what was the real evil, led me to embrace with greater zeal the religion of the Labour Church.'[2] The people named here contributed a high proportion of the energy that went into the Labour Churches. It is quite likely that recruits from Nonconformity contributed more.[3] It is possible, moreover, that people in the Labour Churches felt more bitterly towards Nonconformity, which purported to be the friend of the common people, than towards the Church of England, whose intimate association with the ruling classes had been long taken for granted by most radicals. But in the Labour Churches as in the political labour movement, attacks on the social attitudes of organized Christianity were made less often against this or that church than against the churches at large. 'The Church worships respectability,' wrote Keir Hardie, 'and puts its ban on poverty . . . I speak of no particular sect or denomination. I discern little to choose from in any of them.'[4] He was writing in the *Labour Prophet* and expressing the view predominant among its writers and (it seems reasonable to suppose) readers.

Where it gained attention within Christian churches, the Labour Church drew responses which varied widely, and which cut across denominational borders. When the Rev. G. S. Barrett, chairman of the Congregational Union in 1894, rebuked Trevor's movement for being doctrinally heterodox and socially exclusive, he was speaking for many ministers inside and outside his own sect. 'I cannot conceive of a Church of Christ', he declared, 'which makes no recognition of His Deity, of His atoning sacrifice, of the regenerating work of the Holy Spirit;

[1] *Labour Prophet*, Jan. 1893, p. 4; *Labour Annual* (1895), p. 163.

[2] *Labour Prophet*, Aug. 1896, p. 129.

[3] In a letter written in 1953, A. J. Waldegrave, who had been a leader of the movement in London, said: 'most of those I believe who took the initiative in forming . . . Labour Churches . . . were discontented Nonconformists'. S. Pierson, *loc. cit.* p. 468.

[4] *Labour Prophet*, Nov. 1892, pp. 85–6.

which has no place in it for the sacraments, and none for the authority of the Word of God. . . .' Even if its doctrines and religious practice were made sound, the movement was still unjustifiable: 'A Labour Church has no more right to be than a Capitalists' Church, or an educated man's Church.'[1] The doctrinal criticism could be made with confidence, for the Labour Churches were plainly and proudly opposed to creeds and sacraments. But to ministers who were aware of the gap between their own churches and the working classes, the criticism that a Labour Church was a contradiction in terms came less easily. Barrett himself admitted that 'if all the Churches of Christ had been true to the brotherhood of Jesus, this new movement could never have arisen. It is a rebuke as well as a warning to us.' He agreed with another leading Independent, Andrew Fairbairn, that the Labour Church was 'a creation more of despair than of hope, an attempt, as it were, to sanctify an evil rather than to cure it.'[2] But to admit that the evil existed was to agree that the Labour Churches had some claim on the sympathy of Christians.

A few Christians believed this claim to be overwhelming. When B. J. Harker turned his Independent chapel at Bolton into a Labour Church, he appears to have been rebelling against the social atmosphere of organized Christianity, not against any of its doctrines. 'It is the Capitalist Church', he declared, 'that necessitates the Labour Church.'[3] But in believing that allegiance to the Labour Church and to a Christian denomination were wholly compatible, Harker was unusual among ministers of religion. Such a view was common only in Unitarianism, which had become a halfway house between orthodox Christianity and agnosticism. Wicksteed was by no means the only Unitarian minister who felt free to give active support to the Labour Churches without putting in question his loyalty to Unitarianism. To some people the Labour Church was itself no more than 'a kind of milk-and-water Unitarianism, *plus* the same kind of socialism.'[4] But at least one Unitarian minister had to choose

[1] *Congregational Year Book* (1895), p. 42.

[2] A. M. Fairbairn, *Religion in History and in Modern Life* (New York, 1894), p. 62.

[3] B. J. Harker, *Christianity and the New Social Demands* (1892), p. 7.

[4] A. W. Hildreth, in *Labour Prophet*, Dec. 1896, p. 195.

between being a member of a Labour Church and having charge of a chapel: Joseph Wood resigned from the Birmingham Labour Church because, it was said, 'his Unitarian flock threatened to eject him if he remained a Socialist.'[1]

Most ministers who spoke at Labour Church meetings were Unitarians with a leaning to Socialism; but there were a number from more orthodox churches. Some spoke because they were socialists and willing to appear on any socialist platform; others, though not social radicals, believed that the churches were at least partly responsible for the Labour Church movement, and that ministers could lose nothing by agreeing to address its meetings. Although the clergyman James Adderley was a socialist, it was on other grounds that he advised fellow-parsons to accept invitations from Labour Churches. 'The Socialists at these places', he wrote, 'are most anxious to know the Christian position, and this being the case it seems to me good that clergy should go and tell them the truth rather than that they should have a perversion of it from other sources.'[2] Adderley and people like him – Stewart Headlam, Conrad Noel and Percy Dearmer, all of them ritualists and in some sense socialists – were the most popular Church of England speakers at Labour Church meetings. They did not always devote their addresses to explaining the claims of their own Church. At Manchester Dearmer argued that the Lord's Prayer should be interpreted as socialistic, and delighted his audience by his 'scathing but withal humorous references to some of our modern fathers in God. . . .'[3] Conrad Noel similarly pleased members of the Labour Church at Hanley; 'the truths he told his Christian brothers did us a treat.'[4] Perhaps these addresses contained more of orthodox Christianity, however, than the notes of them by Labour Church reporters indicate; Noel spoke later of having presented 'Socialism mingled with the Catholic Faith' at Labour Church meetings, and of having preached 'the whole gospel.'[5] Theologically, the ritualists were farther from the Labour Church than were any

[1] Birmingham Labour Church, pencilled note in minutes of members' meeting, 17 March 1898.

[2] *Goodwill*, Feb. 1897, p. 12.

[3] *Labour Prophet*, Jan. 1896, p. 12.

[4] *Ibid.*, Aug. 1896, p. 135.

[5] C. Noel, *An Autobiography* (1945), pp. 48–9.

Nonconformists. Collectivism and catholicism were, to their minds, two sides of a coin, and Scott Holland once remarked, with Trevor in mind: 'a religion that is individual can never be the religion of Socialism.'[1] But at least, so they believed, they were addressing at Labour Churches people who had a grasp on half the truth – which was more than Noel and Headlam would have admitted of many worshippers in the Church of England. They were the more willing to speak because it was often hard for them to find a platform in their own church.

In the Church of England, the clergyman farthest up in the hierarchy actually to speak in a Labour Church was probably J. M. Wilson, vicar of Rochdale and archdeacon of Manchester – the only man ever to have the same work published by both a Labour Church and the Society for Promoting Christian Knowledge.[2] When he spoke to the Bolton Labour Church, Wilson praised the movement for emphasizing aspects of Christianity which the Church and Nonconformity were neglecting; but he suggested that the older churches had preserved truths – above all 'that Christ is the Saviour of men' – which people in the Labour Churches should not overlook.[3] He delivered this address despite a letter from a churchman begging him 'for the sake of the Church in which he holds such a high position, for the sake of the churchmen of Bolton, and above all for the sake of truth, to cancel the engagement.'[4] When he spoke to the Manchester and Salford Labour Church in the following June, a similar letter, from a clergyman to a Manchester newspaper, suggested that people like the archdeacon 'might with advantage cease to unsettle the working men attending our churches and Bible classes. . . .'[5]

A few other clergymen, and several Wesleyans, Congregational and Baptist ministers, appear among the lists of speakers at Labour Churches; Birmingham even had a representative of the Salvation Army to address it. But a minister might speak at

[1] *Commonwealth*, Nov. 1896, p. 372.

[2] J. M. Wilson, *The Ethical Basis of the Labour Movement*, an address to the Bolton Labour Church and S.P.C.K. in Dec. 1894. It was published by the S.P.C.K. in 1895 and by the Bolton Labour Church in the same year – with a preface pointing out that the Labour Church did not accept the writer's theological views.

[3] J. M. Wilson, *op. cit.* p. 29.

[4] *Labour Leader*, 8 Dec. 1894, p. 3.

[5] *Labour Prophet*, Dec. 1895, p. 189.

a Labour Church and not be a supporter of the movement. A Baptist minister in Newcastle, Walter Walsh, known for his sympathy with the working classes, invited Trevor to take his services one Sunday while he himself preached in the Labour Church at Manchester.[1] One might infer from this gesture a keen sympathy with the Labour Church. But Walsh's experience convinced him that the movement was heading for secularism, and he wrote an able article in the *Contemporary Review* saying so.[2]

The presence of a few ministers as speakers no doubt helped to convince some waverers that the Labour Church was truly a religious movement. But inevitably, given the aims of the movement, any support from within the Christian churches was tentative, and hostility was more common. Possibly most ministers, and certainly most church-goers, ignored the movement altogether, either because it seemed to them not worth a thought or because they never heard of it.

The Labour Church as a Church

When the Rev. Walter Walsh predicted in the *Contemporary Review* that the movement would be secularized, one of his arguments was that it satisfied none of the criteria for a church. 'The three outward and visible signs of the historic continuity of the Churches', he wrote, 'are the ordinances, the Bible, and the historic Christ.' The Labour Church had no ordinance, no Bible ('it culls its public readings from all literature') and no Christ. Whether or not these were sufficient grounds for prophesying its failure as a church, Walsh's description was accurate. To his list of the traditional institutions which the Labour Church had denied itself, Walsh might have added a clergy; for each church had not a minister, but a chairman with no special status. The movement had no priesthood unless it could raise up a priesthood of believers.

Having decided what to abandon, the founders of the Labour Church had now to fashion their own system of worship. First of all, forms of service had to be worked out. The Nonconformist

[1] *Ibid.*, Dec. 1893, p. 128.

[2] W. Walsh, 'The New Secularism', *Contemporary Review*, Jan. 1895, pp. 117–29.

British Weekly described with faint amusement one of the first services at Manchester:

> The band 'played the people in,' and then followed a hymn. The lesson was taken from 'Looking Backward' – the parable about the rose bush being read, succeeded by a solo, 'Nazareth'. Then there was a hymn (?) of Sir G. Duff's. Ben Tillett spoke, and was listened to with breathless attention by his audience of 'all sorts and conditions of men'. Undoubtedly the most touching incident of the afternoon was the loud burst of applause which greeted the name of Christ when it was *first* mentioned in the afternoon service by Mr Tillett.[1]

Forms of service were usually similar to this one. Passages from suitable authors were printed in the *Labour Prophet* to be used as readings in the service. 'Unfortunately,' wrote Trevor, 'the Bible is so frightfully and falsely conventionalized that it is difficult to make a Bible reading a real and helpful thing to a Labour Church audience.'[2] The authors used instead were often those whose poetry appeared in Labour Church Hymn Books – among them Lowell, Emerson, Longfellow, Whittier, Matthew Arnold, William Morris, Carpenter and Kingsley. The first Labour Church Hymn Book, printed in 1892, contained some hymns found also in orthodox Christian hymnals, but none in which specifically Christian doctrine is proclaimed. Newman's 'Lead Kindly Light', was sung in the Labour Churches; but there is no word in that hymn to which an agnostic could object. Jesus was named only once in this collection, in a verse by Whittier. Some mentioned God; others spoke the language of secular radicalism, good cheer, or homely – even conservative – morality ('Be kind to thy father – for when thou wert young, Who lov'd thee more fondly than he?') Two of the hymns were clearly intended to be sung to the tune of the national anthem, one of them patriotic ('God bless our native land') and the other more class-conscious ('God save the working man').

[1] *British Weekly*, 5 Nov. 1891, p. 21. Cheers for Jesus were a common thing at Labour meetings in the nineties in Britain and elsewhere. They should perhaps be interpreted in the light of the following remark by 'a minister not a priest' in *Labour Leader*, 30 June 1894, p. 14: 'It was a sound instinct that made the Socialists of America at a recent meeting cheer every allusion to Christ, and hiss every reference to the church.'

[2] *Labour Prophet*, June 1895, p. 89.

Trevor recommended that three hymns should be sung at a service, and that the service should end with a benediction. 'Perhaps the Benediction will be deemed too formal a matter, and will be dispensed with; but when it is made a real thing, and when the audience keep their seats to the close, it should give an added sense of devotion.'[1] Some Christian critics noticed that Labour Church members tended to leave before a service ended. Trevor deplored the habit, and seems to have felt that a formal benediction could break it. At Manchester, the benediction was: 'May the strength and joy of God's presence be with all who love their brethren in sincerity. Amen.'[2]

The question of prayer was a delicate one. From the beginning usage varied, some churches having no prayers at all, and others wanting to keep them but finding them hard to compose. Trevor himself found in prayer 'an expression of my religious life . . . an intensely real thing.'[3] He did not think prayer incompatible with complete unbelief: 'We have heard even an Atheist regret deeply that there was no prayer at one of our Labour Church Services.'[4] Prayers, Trevor thought, were valuable not primarily for what was said in them, but for preventing the movement from losing its religious tone: 'the absence of prayer is so distinct a weakness in a religious service, that it should not be lightly abandoned.'[5] Lightly or not, many of the churches went on doing without it, despite Trevor's pleas. In some there might be prayer or no prayer, depending on the chairman's decision. Even if the chairman wanted prayer, the speaker might still prevent it. Sam Hobson was once alarmed when addressing the Bradford church by being asked to pray aloud. Remembering that he was by origin a Quaker, he explained that he could not pray unless the Spirit commanded. The Spirit bade silence. 'Thus at one stroke I saved myself from too obviously playing the hypocrite and acquired a reputation for piety.'[6]

The Labour Church might exist as a church without prayer, but it could not survive without the fellowship, the joy in cor-

[1] *Ibid.*
[2] *Ibid.*
[3] *Ibid.*, May 1893, p. 39.
[4] *Ibid.*, June 1895, p. 89.
[5] *Ibid.*
[6] S. Hobson, *Pilgrim to the Left* (1938), p. 41.

porate association, which so many recruits to the new church had failed to find in the older sects. Reports of some early services suggested that such a spirit had been achieved. When Wicksteed spoke to the Manchester and Salford Church he observed a freshness and gaiety which delighted him; and at Bolton, so the secretary of the Labour Church said in 1893, 'the heartiness and vigour with which Labour hymns are sung is in pleasing contrast to the conventional style of most churches and chapels. Enthusiasm and appreciation are capital substitutes for training and finish.'[1]

Trevor was not satisfied. 'Joy needs wedding to religion', he wrote in 1893. At least there was laughter – unheard now at Christian worship – in the Labour Churches. 'But even our services are horribly dull and gloomy compared with the bright joyousness of a sunny day in spring.'[2] 'There is a growing feeling among members of the Labour Church', wrote the secretary at Halifax in 1894, 'that something must be done to break the monotony of the cut-and-dried form of service to which we have been accustomed.'[3] When Herbert Casson, a former Methodist minister who had planted the Labour Church movement in America, inspected the English Labour Churches in 1897, he was depressed by the dinginess of the halls borrowed or hired for services, the dullness of the singing, and the introverted atmosphere in which a stranger could not feel welcome.[4] Coldness to strangers had been a constant criticism of respectable congregations in orthodox churches. It was ironical that it should be noticed so soon in the Labour Church. James Sims referred seriously to the problem in his presidential address to the Labour Church Union conference in 1898. 'Don't break up into little cliques after a meeting, perhaps looking at the strangers and saying you wonder who they are.'[5] He might have been speaking of Salem Chapel.

Sims spoke also of how the sense of fellowship between members could be heightened, suggesting in particular that a contributory fund should be established for helping members in

[1] *Labour Prophet*, Aug. 1893, p. 80.
[2] *Ibid.*, June 1893, p. 50.
[3] *Ibid.*, Feb. 1894, p. 32.
[4] *Ibid.*, Dec. 1897, p. 140.
[5] *Ibid.*, July 1898, p. 195.

need; but no such fund was begun. In some churches, other devices (such as bands) were tried in the hope that they would foster a congregational spirit. At Birmingham in 1895, when a member urged the necessity of 'developing a close bond of sympathy among L.C. members', the committee responded by holding a social 'at 6d. each to include Tea and Kiss in the Ring.'[1]

Among obvious sources of cohesion in Christian churches were the ceremonies of baptism, marriage and burial. At least one Labour Church, at Leeds, appears to have looked to such ceremonies as a way of binding the life of the family to the life of the association. Leeds had its first christening (this was the word used) in 1895.

> Our president officiated, who, in a little impressive speech, gave the child its name (Alice), hoping that when it grew so as to be able to take its place in the Battle of Life, she would be found in the ranks of the 'despised', if they be fighting for Love, Truth, and Justice.[2]

A similar service was reported from this church in 1897, called now 'an interesting ceremony equivalent to the orthodox baptism. . . .'[3] The Leeds church was also registered for solemnizing matrimony; but in this it was alone.[4] At Halifax in 1894 the members were 'most troubled' whether to perform baptisms, but 'managed to steer clear of such service.'[5] Burials and possibly baptisms were conducted occasionally at other churches. One observer noted an inability to give 'food for the heart' at times of death, for the 'newly bereaved would be missing from the Labour Church audiences week after week.'[6] It would have been hard to perform satisfying rites of passage without giving the celebrant, whether formally or not, a ministerial status incompatible with the deep anti-clericalism of the movement. The Labour Church ideal was an exacting one: to reject the forms and ceremonies of other churches while pre-

[1] Birmingham Labour Church, minutes of members' meeting, 25 Jan. 1895; minutes of executive committee meeting, 1 Feb. 1895.

[2] *Labour Prophet*, May 1895, p. 79.

[3] *Ibid.*, Dec. 1897, p. 140.

[4] *Ibid.*

[5] *Ibid.*, Sept. 1894, p. 128.

[6] P. Redfern, *Journey to Understanding* (1946), p. 78, quoted in S. Pierson, *loc. cit.* p. 475.

serving the fellowship and zest found in the liveliest of them. A. W. Hildreth, secretary of the Darlington church, spoke wistfully of the spirit animating some Nonconformist congregations:

> We may discard their ceremonies and denounce them for distorting the teachings of Christ; but until we become inspired with a faith in our mission like theirs, we shall be little better than 'children crying in the wilderness'.[1]

Nor could the doctrinal issue be dismissed as easily as Trevor had hoped. It was a noble vision that saw in the Labour Church 'the Great Catholic Church of Humanity';[2] but beyond a certain point catholicity of opinion could endanger the identity of the movement. Where should this point be fixed? What limits should be set to eclecticism? 'How can the Labour Church', as one member put it, 'be broad enough to embrace all, without being so infinite as to lose all cohesion and force? That is the real problem before us.'[3]

It was easier to say what the religion of the Labour Church was not than to say what it was. When a friendly critic suggested in 1896 that the Labour Church would attract sympathetic Christians if only it were more friendly to Christianity, there was no articulate dissent in the movement from Trevor's reply, firmly rejecting orthodoxy; as R. A. Beckett remarked, 'most of us have passed through the phase of Christianity. . . .'[4] Jesus was given a respected but not a crowning place in the pantheon of Humanity; 'we appreciate the good that can be got from all the great teachers and leaders,' wrote the secretary of the West Bromwich church, 'among whom Christ is prominent.'[5] Atheists, agnostics, deists and theists could sing, without compromising their belief, the Labour Church hymn which ended:

> When I survey the unrighteousness,
> Cause of all things that hurt, oppress,
> I feel, though I be sacrificed,
> That one must follow Buddha, Christ.[6]

[1] *Labour Prophet*, Sept. 1894, p. 128.
[2] *Ibid.*, June 1896, p. 90.
[3] *Ibid.*, March 1898, p. 162.
[4] *Ibid.*, Oct. 1896, p. 156. The critic was John Kenworthy, of the Brotherhood Church.
[5] *Labour Church Record*, April 1899, p. 8.
[6] *Ibid.*, Oct. 1901, p. 3.

But when they tried to affirm their beliefs more precisely, Labour Church members disagreed with each other; and these differences had important practical consequences for the movement.

Trevor, though discarding 'theology', believed in God; others, among whom Fred Brocklehurst was the most prominent, did not. In some ways Trevor was willing to make concessions to people with secularist ideas. The phrase 'God is our King' disappeared from the front page of the *Labour Prophet* after four issues, to be replaced by Mazzini's 'Let Labour be the basis of civil society.' But the name of God remained in the statement of principles adopted by the Labour Church Union in 1893, and Trevor was determined to keep it there. In 1894 it was saved by the narrowest possible margin, when nine out of twenty members of the Union's committee voted to substitute for the original statement of principles the following sentence drawn up by Brocklehurst: 'The Labour Church movement is a union of all those who, by organized or individual effort, are emphasizing or developing the moral and ethical aspect of the Labour Movement.'[1] Trevor and Brocklehurst argued this question so constantly that Sam Hobson's main task at Labour Church Union meetings, according to his autobiography, was to keep peace between the two men, 'both of whom were heavily inoculated with *odium theologicum*.'[2] The difference of opinion was wider than Brocklehurst's proposed statement of principle indicates. Brocklehurst really wanted the Labour Church to work in more practical ways for social justice, especially by harmonizing the different wings of the Labour movement. It appeared to Trevor that he was trying to turn the movement away from the very task which made it a church: the effort 'to satisfy the cravings of the human heart for God.'[3]

Trevor did not argue that this religious mission was incompatible with piecemeal practical activities. The church at Manchester under his chairmanship went in for a modest amount of philanthropic service to the sick and the poor; the 'Cinderella' activity of several churches – work among poor children, especi-

[1] *Labour Prophet*, Dec. 1894, p. 171.

[2] S. Hobson, *op. cit.* p. 40. Hobson does not say what they quarrelled about, but this is plain from reports of meetings.

[3] *Labour Prophet*, Oct. 1893, p. 100.

ally offering them holidays and entertainment – went on with his blessing; and he was not disturbed that the Bradford church should collect money for dockers on strike, or that the Hanley church should protest against poisonous working conditions in the potteries.[1] He welcomed, moreover, a large measure of secular oratory from the Labour Church platforms. But he was afraid that social reform might become an aim which the Labour Church pursued heedless of its spiritual life. 'The Labour Church', he wrote in 1894, 'is in danger of being too much immersed in the secularism and materialism necessarily and rightly attaching to a political movement.'[2] In the view represented by Brocklehurst, Trevor saw a grave threat not only to the spirituality of the Labour Churches, but tho their existence. 'Unless the Labour Church can do the work of the churches', he wrote, 'while it also carries out all the harmonizing effects which our General Secretary [Brocklehurst] presents to us, it cannot justify its existence. It will be no more than a Fabian Ethical Society, and will rightly cease to be.'[3]

Speakers and Missionaries

The committee of the Birmingham Labour Church once resolved 'that, in the event of Keir Hardie not being able to lecture, the Town Hall Meeting be dropped.'[4] Here is a clue towards understanding the success and failure of the whole movement. The Labour Churches gathered large audiences only when they could advertise a popular visiting speaker. Even the few active members who kept each church alive needed these visits, to reassure them that their work had some point and was making some progress.

The name of Robert Blatchford – 'Nunquam' – had drawn to the Manchester and Salford Labour Church its first large audience. 'I go few places', said John Trevor, 'where I am not met with the remark: "It was Nunquam converted me to Socialism." And it has not been to a new economic theory, merely, that these converts have been introduced. It has been to a new life. Their

[1] *Ibid.*, May 1898, p. 182.
[2] *Ibid.*, March–April 1894, p. 41.
[3] *Ibid.*, Oct. 1894, p. 100.
[4] Birmingham Labour Church, minutes of executive committee meeting, 21 Aug. 1896.

eyes shine with the gladness of a new birth.'[1] In Blatchford's case writing rather than speaking made eyes shine; it was his *Merrie England*, not his speeches from Labour Church or I.L.P. platforms, that won thousands to socialism. But the effect that Blatchford had in print, others had in person. Philip Snowden, whom many thought the most gifted speaker among the socialists of the 1890's, said later that their movement was 'something new in politics. It was politics inspired by idealism and religious fervour.'[2] The missionaries for socialism expressed, and kindled in others, an enthusiasm that contemporary Christian evangelists might well have envied. Ben Tillett, Tom Mann, Keir Hardie, Ramsay MacDonald, Philip Snowden, Edward Carpenter, J. Bruce and Katharine Glasier, J. R. Clynes, Margaret McMillan and Caroline Martyn – these were some of the people who carried the new gospel around Britain between 1890 and 1900. When they spoke at Labour Churches (as did all the people named here) they drew audiences ten and twenty times as great as could be gathered without them.

Since they had such power to attract and excite crowds, since they preached (in a phrase used by some of them) the religion of socialism, and since Labour Churches competed keenly to invite them, it might be concluded that the itinerant speakers were a source of unmixed strength to the Labour Church movement. Yet quite early in the history of the movement, Trevor was afraid that they were not; and within a few years his fear was shared by those who agreed with him about its purpose. One ground for his fear can be seen from a glance at the subjects of Labour Church addresses. The Drink Traffic; The Future Society; The Labour Problem; Municipal Workshops; The Coming Election; The Kingdom of God is Within You; Religion and Socialism; The Higher Life of a Vegetarian. Deep down, the people who spoke on these varied subjects might share the same vision; but the common denominator was not always easy to detect. 'On one Sunday', said a leading member of the Nottingham church, 'they would have an orthodox speaker, and perhaps on the next an aggressive secularist. People went away wondering what the Labour Church stood for.'[3]

[1] A. M. Thompson, *Here I Lie*, p. 101.
[2] Philip, Viscount Snowden, *An Autobiography* (1934), I. 71.
[3] E. Gutteridge, quoted in *Labour Church Record*, July 1899, p. 2.

Few of the addresses were on subjects which according to the traditional meaning of the word could be called religious. Many Socialists, of course, rejected the traditional meaning. A writer in the *Labour Leader* called Tillett's attack on the House of Lords, delivered at the Bradford Labour Church, a sermon.[1] 'I think our speakers do not understand this deepest need of the soul of man', Trevor complained.[2] 'Why is it that nearly all our speakers confine themselves almost entirely to questions concerning the conditions of life, and never approach the problem of how to live?[3] In 1895 the committee of the Labour Church Union, sharing Trevor's dissatisfaction, addressed a letter to all affiliated churches advising 'careful selection' of speakers, and urging them to invite 'only those who give prominence to the thoughts which underlie our movement and who embody them in personal conduct and life.'[4] But it was natural that a Labour Church should go on inviting the people who could best fill a hall, whatever their attitudes to religion. Three years later the secretary of the Halifax church wrote: 'There is a constant outcry against "economic materialism" as a sole theme in Labour Churches. Most of the present speakers are exponents thereof.'[5] At black moments Trevor could imagine the churches being drowned in a torrent of rhetoric, in

> the frightful flow of words that there is in our movement as compared with the very small amount of real upbuilding work that is being accomplished. One night I lay awake wondering whether it would not be possible to establish silent branches of the Labour Church. . . . We need to get face to face with our work rather than face to face with a speaker.[6]

He could even blame the speakers for corrupting the movement:

> You may get a large audience from Sunday to Sunday with a certain type of attractive speaker who flatters his audience and abuses his opponents; but you will never build up a Church in this fashion . . . such speakers are too frequent among us. They are a rotten foundation to build upon.[7]

[1] *Labour Leader*, 29 Dec. 1894, p. 4.
[2] *Labour Prophet*, Oct. 1893, p. 100.
[3] *Ibid.*, Oct. 1894, p. 136.
[4] Birmingham Labour Church, minute book.
[5] *Labour Prophet*, Sept. 1898, p. 216.
[6] *Ibid.*, July 1895, p. 105.
[7] *Ibid.*, June 1898, p. 188.

At first, Trevor admitted, the churches had needed rhetoric; but now they wanted organization and hard work, which the itinerant speakers neither offered on their own behalf nor encouraged in others.

It was this view of the speakers that made James Sims, who was just as anxious as Trevor that the movement should be literally a church, urge in 1896 that 'Keir Hardie, R. Blatchford, Miss McMillan, Mrs B. Glasier, and other prominent personages' be not asked to attend the next conference of the Labour Church Union. 'Can these "prominent personages," ' he asked, 'most of whom don't belong to any Labour Church, tell us of the difficulties, trials and obstacles each church has to contend with, and of the various methods adopted to make ends meet?'[1] Sims was right when he said that most of these people were not members of Labour Churches. It is an interesting experiment to search the autobiographies of men who were Labour Church speakers for references to the movement. Robert Blatchford, Edward Carpenter, J. R. Clynes, George Lansbury, Tom Mann, James Sexton, Philip Snowden, A. M. Thompson and Ben Tillett all spoke at Labour Churches, and most of them spoke often. Not one mentions the Labour Church in his autobiography: as a distinctive part of the socialist movement, it had made too little impression on each man's mind to be considered worth recalling when he looked back across his life. The Labour Church was simply a congenial and useful platform for them on Sundays. Some people, who would not have broken their Sabbath to listen to politics, could be got out to hear socialism at what purported to be a religious meeting. J. R. Clynes' remarks about Sabbatarianism among Labour leaders in the nineties suggest that some of the speakers themselves had easier consciences on Sundays when addressing a Labour Church than they would have had if speaking in exactly the same company at an I.L.P. rally.[2] The Labour Church label might even have seemed a protection against the law: Fred Brocklehurst was sent to prison for a month in 1896 for breaking the Sabbath when he spoke on a socialist pitch at Boggart Hole Clough, outside Manchester.[3]

The trouble with the speakers, said one member of the

[1] *Ibid.*, March 1896, p. 46.

[2] J. R. Clynes, *Memoirs* (1937), I. 85.

[3] *Labour Annual* (1898), p. 195; C. Noel, *op. cit.* pp. 54–5.

Nottingham church, was that, 'they did not build up the membership of the Church.' Nottingham had heard clever speakers, giving excellent addresses. 'But they never ended their addresses with pointing out to their hearers the nature of the work the Labour Church had to do, and gave no stirring appeal to the audience to join the Church and help forward its work.'[1] Why should they? Their eyes were fixed on a social millennium towards which all men would march together as brothers. They were not to be diverted into becoming evangelists for a mere sect, not even for a sect that called itself the Labour Church. Realizing this, Trevor searched for other ways of providing his movement with the roots which the speakers were not giving it.

In 1895 Trevor suggested for the first time that the Labour Churches form Sunday schools and thus prepare a second generation of members.[2] Others echoed his exhortation, and a few Sunday schools appeared.[3] Most Labour Churches, however, were unwilling or unable to found them. In any case, it was no use training children to take over the movement unless their parents could sustain it in the meantime. If the travelling speakers were not recruiting adult members and organizing them, not encouraging in them a sense of belonging together to a religious movement, how else could it be done? 'The Labour Church', Trevor decided, 'must raise its own speakers and send forth its own missionaries.'[4] As early as June 1892 he had announced in Manchester 'a missionary class for training workers and speakers to spread our message abroad.'[5] Eighteen months passed, and again he wrote about the missionary class, without being able to report any progress towards forming it. Four months later the class was given a new name – the Pioneer class – but there was still no evidence that it had any members. 'We want to build up individuals', Trevor now declared, '. . . who shall become living embodiments of the principles for which the Labour Church stands.'[6] Late in 1896 Trevor was telling an

[1] E. Gutteridge, quoted in *Labour Church Record*, July 1899, p. 7.

[2] *Labour Prophet*, July 1895, p. 105.

[3] *Ibid.*, July 1896, p. 119; Aug. 1896, p. 129; June 1898, p. 90. There were also a number of Socialist Sunday Schools run on similar lines but in association with I.L.P. branches rather than with Labour Churches.

[4] *Ibid.*, July 1898, p. 197.

[5] *Ibid.*, June 1892, p. 48.

[6] *Ibid.*, May, p. 56.

interviewer from a family newspaper that he was 'working for the development from within the churches of men on whose lips the Living Fire has been placed. . . .'[1] The first Labour Church missionary had still to begin his training.

In 1896 Trevor turned to social groups which so far had been almost entirely outside the range of the Labour Church, and invited 'educated people' to join what he called the Labour Church Brotherhood. There had been earlier signs in Trevor of a wish to find more helpers outside the working classes. In March 1894, for example, he had temporarily changed the name of his journal; the word 'Labour' was left out, and it appeared simply as the *Prophet*. But it was the *Labour Prophet* again next month, in an issue dated March-April. Trevor admitted that the change was 'almost universally condemned' and protested his loyalty to Labour.[2] In the following year he was reflecting that 'for the work we have in hand, the distinctive qualities of all classes are needed.'[3] He meant not that the Labour Church could satisfy the spiritual needs of educated people, but that educated people could supply the needs of the Labour Church. He was admitting that a church could not be built by working-class hands alone. The Labour Church Brotherhood was supposed to help finance the *Labour Prophet*. It was also to be a missionary body of educated people who would speak and teach in the churches and train others to do so; who would organize clubs, visit sick members, train choirs, and prepare slides for lantern lectures. The plan expressed a social principle similar to the one on which the settlement movement rested, with the difference that Trevor wanted the rich to act as servants of the working classes rather than as squires: 'my ideal of the relation of the classes to the masses is that the former should abandon all thought of leadership, and simply be satisfied to serve. . ..'[4] There was the further difference that nothing came of Trevor's plan, except a little money which helped to keep the *Labour Prophet* alive until 1898.

So far Trevor had called the hypothetical evangelists – what-

[1] *Great Thoughts*, 7 Nov. 1896, p. 90.

[2] *Labour Prophet*, March–April, 1894, p. 40.

[3] *Ibid.*, Aug. 1895, p. 119. See also J. Trevor, *The Labour Prophet Fund* (1896); J. Trevor, *The Labour Church Brotherhood* (1896).

[4] J. Trevor, *My Quest for God*, p. 260.

ever their social origin – missionaries and pioneers, carefully avoiding any suggestion that they would be like a clergy. He had remarked in 1893 that the problem of the Labour Churches was 'how to run a church without a minister. I know some of our Churches are feeling it a little difficult. I can only hope it won't be necessary to have anything like a minister.'[1] By 1899 he had changed his mind. When a paper was read to the Labour Church Union on the old problem, 'The Raising and Development of Speakers for the Labour Church', Trevor opened the discussion by asserting the 'necessity, if their movement was to become permanent and effective, of providing a trained body of men for speakers and workers, and especially in the pastoral work of the Labour Churches.' It was impossible, he said, to carry on the movement 'without setting apart those who were most suitable for such work, and providing them with the means of living.'[2] Every delegate who commented on Trevor's proposal saw it as a plan for a paid ministry and condemned it utterly. Trevor should not have been surprised, for he himself had encouraged a hostility to the clergy as an institution. Nor did he explain how the ministers were to be paid by a movement that was virtually bankrupt, or even how he expected to find any volunteers, when in seven years he had been unable to recruit any 'missionaries'.

This was Trevor's last serious attempt to shape the Labour Churches according to his own vision. In the first month of the new century he handed over the *Labour Church Record* – a small quarterly which had replaced the *Labour Prophet* in 1898 – to another editor, and retired to a chicken farm.[3] Although he remained friendly to the Labour Churches, he was reluctant to offer advice or criticism. 'We have a new religious message for the world,' he had said in 1899, 'but we have practically no messengers to deliver it. . . .'[4]

[1] *Labour Prophet*, May 1893, p. 41.

[2] *Labour Church Record*, July 1899, p. 6.

[3] *Ibid.*, Jan. 1901, p. 5.

[4] *Ibid.*, April 1899, p. 1. Privately this strange and unhappy man had another reason for withdrawing. 'I became increasingly convinced,' he wrote in 1909, 'that some day I should be compelled to deal seriously with the sex question and feared it would injure the cause.' (S. Pierson, *loc. cit.* p. 476). In 1909 he was appealing for people to form a community similar to the American Oneida experiment. Mr. Pierson comments: 'His thought thus culminated in an ideal of the unrepressed individual.'

The End

Trevor was not alone in his disappointment. 'I have seen with a considerable amount of dismay and sorrow', wrote Edwin Halford, of the Bradford church, in 1898, 'the rapid growth of a very materialistic spirit in our Churches. . . .'[1] At the Labour Church Union conference in the same year, several delegates complained that there was little religion left in the movement. In his address as president James Sims said that in most cases the church was active only when it joined the I.L.P. 'in some political struggle.'[2]

An inquest on the Labour Church as a religious institution was conducted by D. B. Foster when elected president of the Labour Church Union in 1902. Foster was a former Wesleyan in search of a gospel to satisfy both his concern for social justice and his need for a religious faith. He toured the churches, he explained later, 'to find if there was any indication of "God consciousness" amongst them, for without that I felt they could not meet the needs of the time.' He found 'loud and persistent' demands for economic change, but little interest in 'the development of the human soul.' At the end of a year's presidency Foster wrote to his friend Trevor, indicating his 'very keen disappointment at having thus to abandon any hope of these churches meeting the great religious call of the age.'[3]

The Labour Church movement faded rapidly after 1900. Most of the churches had been formed between 1892 and 1895, and few appeared after 1900. The *Labour Church Record* – smaller, less frequent and duller than the *Labour Prophet* – disappeared altogether in 1902, after the secretary of a church had written in one of the last issues: 'I find Labour Churches generally weak, unbusiness-like, and quarrelsome.'[4] The editor, Allen Clarke, fell back on Trevor's old idea of dropping the word 'Labour' as a way of widening the appeal of the movement. He offered 'Goodwill Church' instead, and seems to have had one reply to his call for other suggestions: Arthur Fallows of

[1] *Labour Prophet*, Aug. 1898, p. 207.
[2] *Ibid.*, July 1898, p. 195.
[3] D. B. Foster, *Socialism and the Christ* (1921), pp. 39, 50.
[4] *Labour Church Record*, April 1901, p. 4.

Birmingham offered 'Fellowship' or 'Brotherhood'.[1] Verbal ingenuity, however, could not give the movement a new zest.

Where Labour Churches survived it was because they performed some useful secular function locally. The Birmingham church lasted at least until 1914 by acting as a convenient mediator between other bodies. The committee at Birmingham stated its conception of the Labour Churches in 1909:

> As the common meeting ground of men and women representing all sections of the Socialist movement – where the S.D.F. lion may lie down with the I.L.P. lamb and receive the benediction of the Fabian – the Church fulfils an extremely useful purpose.[2]

In the same year a review of the movement at large suggested that its religious content had evaporated, leaving it a broad-front political body:

> For some years past it has stood as an avowedly Socialist organization – not political in the sense that the I.L.P. and S.D.F. are political, but rather in the sense of wakening a passion for reform to give strength to political movements. Labour Churches . . . have largely helped to increase and extend the influence of political Socialist organizations.[3]

Years before, Trevor had made his judgment on this view of the movement: 'If the aims of those who desire to start the work rise no higher than this, it will be wiser for them to abandon their intention.'[4]

Reflecting on the movement as a penniless old man in Hampstead, Trevor probably believed that the secularizing impulse had killed it. Yet if the Labour Churches had been more exactly what he wanted, it is unlikely that they would have survived as long as they did. They could draw large audiences, or they could embody and keep pure Trevor's eclectic but distinctive form of religious faith. The demand for that faith was never strong enough for them to do both things at once. By 1900 the large audiences were rarer, and would have been so even if Trevor had not given up; for the appeal of Snowden's sort of

[1] *Ibid.*

[2] Birmingham Labour Church, annual report of executive committee, 14 Nov. 1909.

[3] *Reformers' Year Book* (1909), p. 153.

[4] *Labour Prophet*, June 1895, p. 88.

'politics inspired by . . . religious fervour' had begun to wane before the century was out.[1] Not many people, even within Labour Churches, were ever interested in them except as a means towards a united Labour movement; and once the Labour Party was firmly established they were anachronisms. The Labour Party did not satisfy all socialists after World War I. But by that time, those who wanted to unite the Left thought of the Labour Churches, if they thought of them at all, as a quaint piece of Victoriana.

[1] See H. M. Pelling, *op. cit.* p. 189.

7

The Churches and Social Reform

The Spirit of the Age

IN different societies and generations, Christians have come to very different conclusions about the attitude to poverty required of them by their religion. Biblical maxims on the subject, although they may serve as general guides, rarely have self-evident applications. To the socialist, 'Love thy neighbour' has appeared to be a manifesto of his own social faith; but a Christian may well doubt it. 'Love' may not mean 'treat as an equal': do we not speak of loving animals? Even if Luke's 'Blessed are the poor' is an accurate report and Matthew's 'Blessed are the poor in spirit' is not, it is one thing to pronounce blessing and another to recommend any change in social arrangements. True, Jesus spoke harshly of the rich and ordered them to perform acts of self-sacrifice and philanthropy so extreme that few rich Christians have ever taken the command literally; but the recorded sayings of Jesus about riches and poverty are ambiguous. It is not surprising, therefore, that the secular circumstances of Christians have affected their responses to poverty, or that the New Testament has provided texts for the social revolutionary and for his enemies.

'A man's eyes', says one of Charles Kingsley's characters in a discussion of poverty, 'can only see what they've learnt to see.'[1] For most of the nineteenth century, Englishmen looked

[1] Tregarva in *Yeast* (1897 ed.), p. 38, paraphrasing a remark in Carlyle's *The French Revolution*, where it appears in quotation marks. *Yeast* first appeared in 1848.

at poverty and found it morally tolerable because their eyes were trained by evangelical religion and political economy. A preacher could spend his life surrounded by the squalor of a manufacturing town without feeling any twinge of socially radical sentiment, when he believed that many poor people were suffering for their own sins, and that the plight of the rest was the result of spiritual ordinances which it would be impious to question and of economic laws which it was foolish to resist; charity could alleviate the suffering caused by these laws, but in any case the poor had only to wait until death for the end of all temporal hardships and distinctions. Many men who believed these things were humane; but pity alone would never provide them with an alternative social theory.

This vision of poverty was shared by many who would not have admitted that evangelical religion influenced them. The Tractarians, despite their theological revolt against evangelicalism, still saw the poor as individual souls to be saved and not as members of a society to be transformed. Drastic mental changes were necessary before the eyes of a Christian could learn to see poverty differently. Social reform could not interest him until he valued the mortal world more highly than theologians who condoned temporal misery as a short prelude to eternal joy, until he stopped believing in iron laws of economics, and until he began to think of poverty and personal sin, circumstance and character, as separable notions. If his mind changed in these respects he could become a social reformer; and if further he rejected the notion that God had made men high and lowly and ordered their estate, he might become a thorough-going socialist demanding a classless society.

Towards the end of the century, and especially after 1880, social reformers could expect a more friendly hearing within the churches than they had ever before enjoyed. People with very different attitudes to religion agreed in noticing this increase of sympathy. *The Times* remarked in 1890 that the clergy of another age would have 'stood aghast' to hear the range of social questions talked about at the current Church Congress.[1] Socialism was still dismissed as wicked or utopian by many Christians, but it was by no means the bogey it had been to their predecessors in the days of Robert Owen; 'the time is past, I

[1] *The Times*, 2 Oct. 1890, p. 7.

think,' said a canon of Canterbury in 1888, 'when socialism would be spoken of merely as an enemy.'[1] Only a minority of professing Christians declared themselves converts to socialism, but many more were ready to take seriously the principles and the protest embodied in the word. Some thirty years after the death of the Wesleyan leader Jabez Bunting – the man who had said 'Methodism is as much opposed to democracy as to sin' – Hugh Price Hughes was publishing a book called *Social Christianity* which urged on Christians an enthusiasm for social reforms, and was declaring that attitudes in the pulpit to 'irresponsible wealth' had changed greatly.[2] Andrew Fairbairn, intellectual leader of the Congregationalists, observed in 1894 that ministers of all churches were expressing a new view of the state and the claims of labour.[3] 'From no ignoble motive,' wrote the *British Weekly* in 1893, 'but in direct obedience to the Master, all the Churches are considering earnestly their relation to the poor.'[4]

When described in these words the concern might not sound new, for Christians had traditionally recognized a duty to be compassionate towards the poor. Throughout the nineteenth century the Church of England had its charities; the Nonconformists had their Dorcas meetings at which ladies of the chapel met to drink tea and make clothes for the needy; the Catholic priest gave alms. After 1860 some people (including keen Christians) began to discourage gratuitous relief, but not because they were misanthropists. The founders of the Charity Organization Society believed, rightly or wrongly, that charity degraded the recipient unless it was morally rationed; they wanted to reform philanthropic aid to the poor, not to remove it, and although they often blamed the clergy for giving without discrimination, they had no fundamental objection to the association of religion and charity.

Later in the century arose two drastic criticisms of this association. The first applied more particularly to the Church of England, where 'the charities' were a normal part of the

[1] W. H. Fremantle, *The Present Work of the Anglican Communion* (1888), p. 27.

[2] H. P. Hughes, 'Irresponsible Wealth', *Nineteenth Century*, Dec. 1890, p. 890. Bunting's dictum is quoted in T. P. Bunting and G. S. Rowe, *The Life of Jabez Bunting*, II. 112.

[3] A. M. Fairbairn, *Religion in History and in Modern Life*, p. 10.

[4] *British Weekly*, 19 Oct. 1893, p. 401.

parochial structure. 'So great is the evil of "Church and Charity" ', wrote a future Bishop of London in 1896,

> and so seared is it into the minds of the self-respecting working men that 'people go to Church for what they can get', and that therefore if they are to keep their self-respect they must neither come themselves nor let their wives come, that I am feeling convinced more every year, except in cases of sickness, there ought to be an entire severance between the pastoral work of the Church and relief work. . . .[1]

Whether or not its charitable activities discredited the Church among the working classes as widely as this clergyman believed, there is no doubt that the memory of charitable aid given by the clergy on certain conditions could be a searing one. Joseph Arch remembered bitterly the parson in Warwickshire who demanded that labourers and their families who were granted charity should give deferential thanks and stay away from the dissenting chapel.[2]

The other criticism of religious philanthropy applied to all sorts of help, given by different sects, with or without strings, to the 'deserving' or the 'undeserving'. Among Christian social reformers towards the end of the century it was common to compare charity with an ambulance which picked up the wounded but did nothing to attack the sources of injury. In an essay on *The Christian Church and the Problem of Poverty* published in 1894, a socialist clergyman argued that although the church has always seen a duty to relieve the poor she was now called to a new task: 'She must go on to inquire what influences have combined to make men poor, and how these influences should be dealt with.'[3] A clerical friend of this writer summed up the distinction nicely when he said, to Churchmen at large: 'we appeal to you with reference to the evils of poverty, not that they may be alleviated by Christian charity, but that they may be prevented by Christian justice.'[4] Although these two clergymen were far to the left of most people in the Church of England, on this particular issue they had the support of a wide

[1] A. F. Winnington-Ingram, *Work in Great Cities*, pp. 72–3.

[2] J. Arch, *The Story of His Life*, pp. 8, 18, 21–2.

[3] H. C. Shuttleworth, 'The Christian Church and the Problem of Poverty', in A. Reid, ed., *Vox Clamantium* (1894), p. 10.

[4] S. Headlam, *The Guild of St Matthew, an Appeal to Churchmen* (1890), p. 13.

range of Christian opinion. The Wesleyan Conference, not the most sensitive barometer to changes in intellectual and social climate, admitted in its annual address for 1890 that in the past activities relating to the material welfare of the people had been directed largely towards effects, often overlooking causes. 'But at length we are widening the scope of our policy,' the Conference announced, 'so as to embrace, not only the constitutional needs but also the environment of the people.'[1] A warning followed about the danger of trespassing into politics, and an exhortation that social problems 'should be discussed from a Christian standpoint, and in a spiritual temper.' But it was a novelty for the Conference to recommend that they should be discussed at all.

The change in the social temper of the churches was not sudden or spectacular. Before 1850, Chartists and co-operators had a few clerical sympathizers, and although the first Christian socialists were mostly not democrats, their thinking about social questions was unorthodox. Conversely, the voice of William Wilberforce could be heard quite late in the century declaring through ministers of religion that social inequality was the will of God, and that the poor had as many blessings as the rich. Many other Christians, without using this sort of argument, still believed that social reform had nothing to do with religion. Nevertheless, the change in the opinion of representative Christians – those chosen as members of the various denominational assemblies – was substantial. H. H. Champion was invited to address the Church Congress in 1887, and Keir Hardie spoke to the Congregational Union in 1892. Such events were reported widely. 'The time is one of universal publicity,' said a Catholic journal in 1885 (speaking of the 'new passion of pity' for the suffering poor), 'and by means of an omnipotent press, we seem almost to hear one another's unspoken thought. And in this way our good impulses become contagious.'[2] Non-Christian social radicals were admitted to the religious press. One day in 1895 Beatrice Webb noted in her diary: 'Sidney spending all his morning writing articles for all sorts of papers – especially the religious organs, such as the *Guardian*, the *Church Times*, the *Christian World*, the *Methodist*

[1] *Wesleyan Conference Minutes* (1890), pp. 346–7.
[2] *Tablet*, 31 Jan. 1885, p. 163.

Times, etc.'[1] The churches had been deeply affected by the spirit of the age, whose activities Beatrice Webb herself described so vividly in *My Apprenticeship*.

The 'great depression', the exhaustion of Liberal thought, the fatigue of a ruling class, the influence of a widened electorate, the literary influence of Ruskin, George, Marx and other prophets: these are some of the factors which singly and in various combinations have been nominated to explain why in England between 1880 and 1895 socialist organizations flourished, windows were broken by unemployed marchers in Pall Mall, the Prince of Wales sat on a Royal Commission on the Housing of the Poor, London dockers staged the first successful mass strike of unskilled labour, and the Independent Labour Party emerged to federate a wide range of grievance and hope. When a historian gives a satisfying account of this watershed in the evolution of English social relationships, he will also – whether explicitly or not – account in large part for the filtration into the churches of new ideas about poverty and citizenship. English churches were not monasteries protected from contact with the surrounding society and having a mental history separate from that of the nation: the clergy of all sects – as the names of Creighton, Dale, Price Hughes and Manning remind one – were involved in secular discussion and action, and each tended to bless some existing party or policy rather than offer a contribution purporting to be specifically Christian. In 1905 a Wesleyan minister, observing the greater tolerance for social radicalism now shown in his own church, remarked: 'the Zeitgeist has had much to do with it.'[2] A member of any other church might have said the same.

On the crucial matter of the ethics of poverty, the dependence of Christian social attitudes on fashions of secular thought (in this case, economic theory) was clear. Of all the arguments against a sort of social reform which would benefit not just the worst casualties in the struggle for existence but the whole army of the deprived, one was more powerful than any other. 'Why do we sit still,' asked Arnold Toynbee, 'and quietly behold degradation worse than that from which we have rescued women and children in mines and factories? Why are we

[1] B. Webb, *Our Partnership* (1948), pp. 69–70.
[2] S. E. Keeble, Note-book, 1905. (In possession of Mr G. W. Keeble).

content to see the sources of national life poisoned? I believe it is because we think this condition of things inevitable.'[1] A tract on *Capital and Wages* issued by the Society for Promoting Christian Knowledge was only expressing an opinion widespread in the churches when it informed the working classes that they 'might as well try to stop the wind or the tide or to alter day and night' as combine to push up wages.[2] Those who hoped to see a Christian crusade against social injustice had to persuade the churches at large that economic laws were not immutable. They had first to convince themselves. 'We live as shuttlecocks,' wrote the radical clergyman Henry Scott Holland in 1890, 'bandied about between our political economy and our Christian morality.'[3]

Long before the name of Karl Marx was widely known in England, some writers suggested replies which Christian and other social radicals might make to the expositors of political economy. John Stuart Mill argued that some economic laws were not at all like the law of gravity, although he also allowed that under certain conditions the law of wages was inevitable; 'and in saying this,' Toynbee complained, 'he undid the chief benefit of his treatises.'[4] In *Unto This Last* (1862), Ruskin defined wealth to incorporate the notion of justice and declared that although in a sense both natural and economic laws were immutable, man was not helpless to control either natural or economic phenomena. Many readers found in Ruskin an escape from the conflict between social morality and economic theory. But despite examples of legislative interference with economic relationships, the laws of economics were still accepted as immutable by many humane people whose deference to orthodox theorists inhibited them from protesting against social distress. Those who did protest were still likely to be rebuked by defenders of the established social order for resisting the irresistible. When the Bishop of Durham, B. F. Westcott, said at the Church Congress in 1890 that Christians should en-

[1] A. Toynbee, 'Are Radicals Socialists?', in his *Lectures on the Industrial Revolution*, p. 217.

[2] *Capital and Wages: What are They?* (n. d.), p. 24. This tract was published well after 1850.

[3] S. Paget, ed., *Henry Scott Holland, Memoir and Letters* (1921), p. 172.

[4] A. Toynbee, 'Wages and Natural Law', in his *Lectures on the Industrial Revolution*, p. 158.

courage steps towards social equality, *The Times* lectured him on the facts of life:

> It is, unfortunately, a truth from which there is no escape, though generous minds find it hard not to revolt against it, that, in spite of any conceivable social reforms, under any and every ideal scheme of human organization, economic laws will continue to operate and will often produce painful results.[1]

As Emile de Laveleye observed, 'for the orthodox economy there is, in truth, no social question.'[2]

Arnold Toynbee won the attention of Christian social radicals partly because, from motives like theirs, he had set out to offer a professional challenge to the older economics. 'For the sake of religion,' wrote his friend Alfred Milner, 'he had become a social reformer; for the sake of social reform he became an economist.'[3] The land tax of Henry George was seized by other Christians, including Stewart Headlam and his friends in the Guild of St Matthew, as a device for circumventing the economists without overturning society. Alfred Marshall was a liberator of the more cautious. Christians worried by the relation of economics to social justice found in him a thinker more systematic than Toynbee (whom he succeeded at Balliol) and more respectable than George (with whom he debated publicly at Oxford) – an economist who asserted in the preface to his *Principles of Economics* (1890) that 'ethical forces are among those of which the economist has to take account,' and who suggested in its closing pages that extreme poverty could be removed. When the *Principles* appeared Benjamin Jowett wrote to Marshall: 'It answers implicitly the question so often asked: "What is the relation of political economy to ethics?" '[4] A Wesleyan minister noted that the book was 'more humane than the general run of economic works. The Socialist and other criticisms have told on the orthodox economy.'[5] Whether or not they read Marshall in detail, Christians with a desire for social justice but a respect for the body of professional opinion could reassure themselves and

[1] *The Times*, 2 Oct. 1890, p. 7.
[2] *Methodist Times*, 13 May 1886, p. 310.
[3] A. Milner, *Arnold Toynbee: a Memoir*, p. 39.
[4] E. Abbott and L. Campbell, *The Life and Letters of Benjamin Jowett*, II. 378
[5] S. E. Keeble, Note-book, 1891.

others that here was an eminent and orthodox economist who blessed efforts to remove social misery, whose notion of economic theory was quite friendly to what Scott Holland called 'the unfaltering assertion of moral as supreme over mechanical laws.'[1] When Scott Holland and other High Churchmen attempted to reconcile their faith and their age in *Lux Mundi*, they invited an economist, J. K. Ingram, to contribute an appendix on 'Some Aspects of Christian Duty.' 'The most significant fact perhaps of our time,' he wrote, 'is the process of transition from (so-called) political to ethical economics.'[2] *Lux Mundi* appeared in 1889. A year later, William Booth permitted a blast against 'economic laws' to go out under his name. Since *In Darkest England* contained no idea which was not already common coin, Booth's onslaught may be cited as evidence of a growing confidence among Christians that it was possible to interfere with economic arrangements in the interest of social reform. The only people whom his book would disappoint, Booth declared, were

> those anti-Christian economists who hold that it is an offence against the doctrine of the survival of the fittest to try to save the weakest from going to the wall, and who believe that when once a man is down the supreme duty of a self-regarding Society is to jump upon him.[3]

Among Christians even faintly touched by the spirit of social reform, timidity before the once mighty laws of economics was now becoming old-fashioned. The Congregational Union held a conference in 1895 on a subject once unimaginable – 'Christian economics.'[4] In 1897 the *Methodist Times* quoted with warm approval from Bellamy's *Equality*: 'Any economic proposition which cannot be stated in ethical terms is false.'[5]

There were still Christians in the England of 1900 who

[1] Quoted by J. Adderley in H. Martin, ed., *Christian Social Reformers of the Nineteenth Century* (2nd. ed., 1933), p. 208. See also the dedication to Marshall in W. Moore Ede, *The Attitude of the Church to some of the Social Problems of Town Life* (1896).

[2] C. Gore, ed., *Lux Mundi* (5th ed., 1890), p. 523.

[3] W. Booth, *In Darkest England*, p. 18. As evidence that the 'anti-Christian economists' still carried some weight, however, see also p. 44: 'In the struggle of life the weakest will go to the wall, and there are so many weak.'

[4] *Congregational Year Book* (1896), p. 13.

[5] *Methodist Times*, 19 Aug. 1897, p. 573.

believed that it was impossible to improve the circumstances of the poor as a class. At the end of the century Beatrice Webb's sister was telling her young son, who had been horrified by a first sight of East London: 'the iron laws of economics necessitate that many of our fellow-countrymen should live like this. . . .'[1] But the arguments available against this view – from the case of the Social Democratic Federation, through those of the Fabian Society, Henry George and Arnold Toynbee to that of Alfred Marshall – were now plentiful enough for all but the most exacting taste. It now required as much pure faith in dogma to defend the old view as, not so long before, it had taken to oppose it.

Social Reform and Christian Prudence

If the churches had been more successful in getting the working classes to worship, they might have been affected less deeply by new currents of secular opinion on social questions: a leader who is popular may be bored to hear arguments about the nature of discontent. The leaders of English Christianity knew that the Churches were far from popular. Prudence, therefore, opened the ears even of some Christians who otherwise might never have listened to the prophets and the planners who claimed to interpret the will of the masses; and it strengthened the conviction of others who were sympathetic already.

William Booth was the most spectacular example of a Christian converted into a social reformer by what appeared to him the dictates of strategy. Others before him, however, had concluded that the social environment of the poorest made them inaccessible to the gospel; and in the few years before Booth's conversion a number of Christians were thinking like the writer in the *Methodist Times* who said in 1886; 'the duty of the Evangelist is not simply to preach the Gospel, but if the condition of his hearer is unfavourable for his reception, it becomes his duty also to improve those conditions. . . .'[2] *In Darkest England* dramatized this notion, and helped to make it a commonplace after 1890 among Christians of all persuasions. Prudence like Booth's would not make a Christian an ally of the Social

[1] S. Hobhouse, *Forty Years and an Epilogue*, p. 47.
[2] J. J. Findlay, in *Methodist Times*, 2 Sept. 1886, p. 588.

Democratic Federation, the Independent Labour Party or even the Fabian Society. Its object was simply the lowest stratum of the working classes, the people whose circumstances were wretched and corrupting – in Booth's word, the submerged. Booth and others believed that the submerged could be brought into the range of Christian missionaries without any other change in the social structure. For this reason socialists had a point when they argued that Booth was offering merely a gigantic engine for old-fashioned relief. In Booth and in others, the view that social reform was strictly necessary to evangelism could sound remarkably like an appeal for more and more charity.

The argument from prudence could take a subtler and potentially more radical form. By William Booth, the story of Jesus feeding the multitude would be read as an exercise in divine compassion, and as a recognition that the hungrier a man gets the less alertly can he listen to a sermon. But the miracle might also be interpreted as an answer to mental doubts as well as physical pangs, an assurance that Christianity would have a social message no less than a spiritual one. Towards the end of the nineteenth century, some people who were anxious about the gulf between the churches and the masses argued that the churches should show, by demonstrating their support for social reform, that they were truly for the common people. Not that a sense of strategy converted Christians from the assumptions of Adam Smith to those of Hyndman, Shaw or Hardie. The social concern shown in the name of prudence might be very tentative indeed, involving only a belief that the churches should shake off capitalist associations and stand outside the social conflict as benevolent neutrals. Moreover, Christians who advanced the argument from prudence were quite likely to favour social reform already on other grounds. 'The great question of the twentieth century is the Social Question,' wrote the Wesleyan minister Samuel Keeble.

> Young Christians especially should study it, for in their hands, humanly speaking, lies the future of the Christian Church. According to their interest in it will be the influence of that Church upon the working classes of this country. . . .[1]

[1] S. E. Keeble, *Industrial Day-Dreams* (1896), p. 3.

Although Keeble believed this sincerely, his own interest in social problems had been kindled first by *Unto This Last*, and was powerful quite apart from any judgment about ways of recruiting working-class worshippers. He was writing 'to popularize ideas which would not otherwise reach certain of the religious section of society,' and he was well aware that he was more radical than most Methodists.[1] The safest argument, the argument from prudence, he therefore put first. Exhortations were common in which a social concern was urged on Christians as both expedient and a duty. Thus a chairman of the Congregational Union said that social reform demanded attention 'in the truest interest of the people, and in the truest interest of the Churches themselves'; and the *British Weekly*, warning the churches that a final cleavage would be disastrous for them, also concluded that when the poor arraigned English Christianity for not declaring the whole counsel of Christ upon wealth, they were speaking the truth.[2]

The argument from prudence sometimes took a broader form, expressing an anxiety about the mood in which the coming rulers of England would rule. The victory of the common people was inevitable, it was said by some radicals in both the Church of England and Nonconformity; Christians must decide whether their reign was to be religious in spirit or not. The first Christian Socialists had seen the alternatives similarly. During the Paris revolution of 1848 J. M. Ludlow wrote to his friend F. D. Maurice saying that unless socialism were Christianized it would shake Christianity to its foundation. Maurice remarked that this letter awakened thoughts in his mind which 'conspired with some that had been working there for a long time.'[3] Some of these thoughts were about the necessity of taming socialism by bringing Christianity to bear on it, and others concerned social implications of Christianity which were largely invisible to most of his contemporaries in the churches. Like men of the next generation who learned from him, Maurice was both anxious about the future of Christianity and eager to mend society.

[1] S. E. Keeble, Note-book, 1895.

[2] A. Spicer in *Congregational Year Book* (1894), p. 38; *British Weekly*, 12 Sept. 1890, p. 305; 13 Oct. 1892, p. 395.

[3] F. Maurice, *The Life of Frederick Denison Maurice* (1884), I. 458.

Christian Socialism

If Sir William Harcourt had been a minister of religion and not a minister of state, he might well have said: 'We are all Christian Socialists now.' The term which shocked so many Christians when F. D. Maurice, Charles Kingsley and J. M. Ludlow first used it fell from sight when their own experiments under the name ended, and appeared again by 1880, to become so respectable that Ludlow, still alive in 1908, could tell the Lambeth Conference that true Christian Socialism was the faith of all present.[1] When Christians late in the century discussed the sources of their interest in social problems, the name of F. D. Maurice was mentioned second only to Ruskin's. Stewart Headlam, founder of the socially radical Guild of St Matthew, had sat under Maurice at Cambridge and was inspired by his lectures to take holy orders. Headlam's right-hand man Thomas Hancock was a friend and disciple of Maurice. Henry Scott Holland, who was at the centre of the movement to make the Church of England aware of its social mission, believed that after 1880 clergymen confronted with the challenge of socialism 'woke up to Maurice,' through whose teaching 'Christian doctrine showed itself as the heart of a Social Gospel.'[2]

Those out of sympathy with him found Maurice's mind obscure. 'He was misty and confused,' said Benjamin Jowett, 'and none of his writings appear to me worth reading.'[3] The greatest admirer of Maurice could not call his writing limpid. As a boy he had been forced to live with mental complexity: his father was a radical Unitarian minister, his mother became a Calvinist with a Byronic conviction that she was not among the elect, one sister joined the Baptists, and another the Church of England. Every story which his son could gather about Maurice's youth suggested 'a boy puzzled into silence by the conflicting influences around him. . . .'[4] He remained always open to new stimuli, from the ideas of Coleridge which impressed him greatly at Oxford to the moral philosophy of

[1] G. C. Binyon, *The Christian Socialist Movement in England* (1931), p. 177.
[2] M. Reckitt, *Maurice to Temple* (1947), p. 121.
[3] E. Abbott and L. Campbell, *op. cit.* II. 45.
[4] F. Maurice, *op. cit.* I. 33.

Comte, to whom he acknowledged 'unspeakable obligations' in his last work, published in 1869.[1] A mind so sensitive and absorbent could in turn affect very diverse people. Maurice was acknowledged as a master not only within his own church but by the Wesleyans Hugh Price Hughes and J. Scott Lidgett (who believed him 'the greatest prophet of the nineteenth century'); and a Congregational minister suggested that his most abiding influence was on Independents.[2]

Some Christians who found Maurice stimulating as a theologian or moral philosopher were not impressed by his social ideas. In his own professional life Maurice got into more trouble for his views about eternal punishment than for his Christian Socialism. But a patient student of Maurice could discover that his ideas about hell and about working-men's co-operatives were parts of a single maze. 'The desire for *Unity* has haunted me all my life through,' he wrote in a fragment of autobiography.[3] His tract *Christian Socialism* (1849) had at the heart of its argument an attack on evangelical theology. Maurice here declared that the only form of Christianity compatible with the evil economic doctrine of competition was one that made religion a 'scheme for bribing or terrifying men into compliance with certain rules and maxims. . . .' He believed that Christianity had become unsound 'as men have ceased to connect it with the whole order of the world and of human life, and have made it a scheme or method for obtaining selfish prizes which men are to compete for, just as they do for the things of the earth. So it has become mingled with the maxim of selfish rivalry which is its deadly opponent.' This, obviously the evangelical form of Christianity, he contrasted with an 'older view of the Church, as a fellowship constituted by God Himself, in a divine and human Person, by Whom it is upheld, by Whom it is preserved from the dismemberment with which the selfish tendencies of our nature are always threatening it.'[4] Maurice believed that this view of the church had been restored by the Tractarians. In the first phase of the Tractarian movement

[1] F. D. Maurice, *Social Morality* (1869), p. 416.

[2] Alexander Mackennal, quoted in D. Macfadyen, *Alexander Mackennal, Life and Letters* (1905), p. 25.

[3] F. Maurice, *op. cit.* I. 41.

[4] F. D. Maurice, *Christian Socialism* (Christian Social Union ed., 1893), pp. 10–3.

Maurice was an exhilarated supporter. Even after he broke with the party because he disliked Pusey's tracts on baptism, Maurice could thank them for recovering 'the great principle of a social faith, the principle that we exist in a permanent communion which was not created by human hands, and cannot be destroyed by them.'[1] This principle became central to his own account of society.

The church, in this account, was an expression of the permanent fellowship which God had given His creatures, and which was there even when men could not see it. Having taken over the Tractarians' reminder that the church was co-operative in nature, Maurice believed it his task to help Christians recognize the co-operative nature of the whole of society. The order which secular socialists such as Owen, Fourier and Blanc wanted to *introduce* into society, Maurice found existing already, most strongly in the family and the Church – institutions reflecting the fatherhood of God – and more faintly elsewhere. Once this order was *seen*, the spirit of competition would be routed, men would be treated as men and not as members of castes, and the spirit of co-operation, which was the spirit of the Bible and the creeds, would reign.

This element in Maurice's social theory becomes more intelligible, if not more cogent, when it is read in the context of his other writings, especially his last work, *Social Morality* (1869). To Maurice's own satisfaction the belief that he was advocating not change but re-discovery removed any tension between his socialism and his conservatism. 'Our object,' he tried to reassure the worried principal of King's College, London, in 1851,

> 'has been to separate, in what seemed to us the most effectual way, that Socialism, which Mr Southey and other eminent Conservatives believed to be the best solution of the practical difficulties of England, from Communism, Red Republicanism, or any anarchical opinion whatsoever.'[2]

Christian socialism then, as set out by Maurice, was a very different faith from the socialism of Continental reformers.

[1] F. D. Maurice, *On the Right and Wrong Methods of Supporting Protestantism* (1843), p. 10.

[2] F. Maurice, *op. cit.* II. 92.

Equally, however, it cut loose from the evangelical view of social problems. Maurice took doctrines which the Tractarians had used to show the corporate nature of the church, and argued that these doctrines applied to the social as well as the ecclesiastical order. The consequent notion of poverty was quite unlike that of evangelical Christianity. 'Our Church,' he wrote, 'must apply herself to the task of raising the poor into men; she cannot go on . . . treating them merely as poor.'[1]

Although Maurice's social theory involved an application of Tractarian doctrines, it was one which none of the Tractarians themselves made. It is true that when Newman in his sermons attacked the worship of Mammon – 'avarice, fortune-getting, amassing capital, and so on – 'and when Keble described England as 'By Mammon's touch new moulded o'er and o'er', the Tractarians could sound like Disraeli and his friends of Young England.[2] The villains of *Sybil* – Lord Mowbray, Shuffle and Screw – are Newman's and Keble's villains. But unlike Disraeli, who offered what he called the baronial principle, neither Newman nor Keble was moved by hatred of Mammon to work out any social programme; although alarmed at the moral influences acting on the first of England's two nations, they did not turn their minds to the plight of the second. The task they saw before them was to increase the power and dignity of the church. They denounced the pursuit of gain as part of a rival religion that weakened and corrupted Christianity. Newman confessed late in life that 'he had never considered social questions in their relation to faith, and had always looked upon the poor as objects for compassion and benevolence.'[3] Those Tractarians who remained in the Church of England could have said much the same.

Pusey, the most highly born of all the Tractarians, had the most acute distaste for the social atmosphere of towns. Like Newman and Keble he deplored the rule of Mammon, and he went farther in his anxiety about the spiritual and moral condition of the masses. He was not interested in social reform,

[1] F. D. Maurice, *Christian Socialism*, p. 15.

[2] Newman is quoted in W. G. Peck, *The Social Implications of the Oxford Movement* (1933), p. 66, and Keble ('The One Way') by H. Scott Holland in his introduction to *Lyra Apostolica*, reprinted in his *Personal Studies* (1905), p. 66.

[3] M. Reckitt, *op. cit.* p. 35.

however. When he awakened his young disciples to the challenge which the industrial working classes offered to the Church, Pusey was only seeing what Evangelicals had seen already. Moreover, he was seeing it just as they did, and echoing men whose religious principles were repugnant to him. No less than Wesley and Wilberforce, Pusey conceived destitution as a spiritual condition.[1] Although he encouraged his followers to serve the church where poverty was deepest, he gave them no special notion of its causes and remedies. If some of them began to see poverty and spiritual destitution as two different problems, they cannot be said to have learned the distinction from Pusey. Of all the Tractarians W. G. Ward seems to have been alone in realizing that having rejected the assumptions of a *laissez-faire* society, the movement should work out social ideas of its own.[2] As Ward realized and as the case of Pusey shows, theological doctrines do not produce social corollaries of their own accord; and since none of the leaders at Oxford was more than casually interested in social problems it was left to their followers to decide for themselves what attitudes they would take towards social inequalities and distress.

When they had cast off old habits of thought, those who took up the Oxford doctrines might discover ideas startling to the authors of the Tracts. Taught by the Tractarians that a solemn duty lay upon them, young clergymen advanced towards whatever they imagined to be the front line in the Church's battle with the forces of evil, and on their march sometimes came to conclusions unlike those of their masters: 'as the clergy came in contact with this neglected world,' says G. M. Trevelyan, 'it naturally did not appear to successive generations of High Churchmen exactly as the distant prospect of it from Oriel windows had looked at the time of the first Reform Bill.'[3] The Tractarians' disciples had acquired a crusading zeal, and a stern judgment of both evangelical and secular individualism, which made it likely that some of them, especially those who heard a call to evangelize the masses, would become dissatisfied by orthodox notions about poverty. If they did, it was possible that

[1] See E. B. Pusey, *Churches in London* (1837), pp. 9–10; *The Councils of the Church* (1857), pp. 4–6.

[2] W. G. Peck, *op. cit.* pp. 74–6.

[3] G. M. Trevelyan, *British History in the Nineteenth Century and After*, p. 281,

they would find in their doctrines implications which could help them to become social radicals. But only as they listened to other teachers.

Maurice was by far the most important of these teachers, for his Christian socialism was founded explicitly on doctrines of God and the church which the Tractarians had taught him. Towards the end of the century those social radicals in the Church of England who belonged also to the wing called Catholic, or ritualist, believed that Maurice was peculiarly their own. But Maurice had tried to avoid being identified with any one faction, and partly on that account his memory could be cherished by Christians in other parties than the Anglo-Catholic. Even some people reared in the Evangelical tradition found his case against it impressive; for he understood it well, exposed it severely but without spite at its most vulnerable points, and in his own theology was just as preoccupied as Evangelicals with the problem of right conduct.[1] It would have delighted Maurice, since his passion for unity was intense, to know that such a variety of people took him seriously.

For the next generation of Christians Maurice and his friends had also a symbolic importance. Although of their practical efforts only the educational experiments survived, they were remembered as a group of Christians who had shown an unusual sympathy with the ambitions of working-class reformers. When social radicals displayed a new energy in England after 1880 and people in the churches had to decide whether to approve of them or not, the precedent of the Christian socialists was recalled. The *Life* of Maurice by his son, packed with his remarkable letters, was published in 1884 and gave those to whom he had been only a name their first chance to know him more intimately. What was most important in Maurice, as an influence on Christian social attitudes, was not the particular method he recommended for achieving a harmonious society but the fact that he had given a theological justification for trying to replace the spirit of competition in society by the spirit of co-operation.

[1] For an example of the influence of Maurice's theological and social thinking on a Christian brought up in the evangelical tradition, see J. Llewelyn Davies. 'The Social Doctrine of F. D. Maurice', in W. H. Hunt, ed., *Sermons on Social Subjects* (1904), pp. 179–80.

There was no Christian in late Victorian England to whom one can point as a pure disciple of Maurice: his mind was too idiosyncratic, the world had changed too much, and there were too many other pressures on the mind of anybody wondering what to think and do about social reform. But among the specifically Christian influences tending to make people in the churches sympathetic towards a general reduction in social inequalities, Maurice was the most important.

Maurice was no State socialist. 'Christian socialism,' he wrote to Ludlow,

> is to my mind, the assertion of God's order. Every attempt to hide it under a great machinery, call it Organization of Labour, Central Board, or what you like, I must protest against as hindering the gradual development of what I regard as a divine purpose, as an attempt to create a new constitution of society, when what we want is that the old constitution should exhibit its true functions and energies.[1]

His dislike of State interference helped to make Christian Socialism an acceptable notion to many people in the churches who were apprehensive about the designs of the men who called themselves Socialists. If this element alone were taken from Maurice, the name of Christian Socialism could be given to a doctrine quite compatible with the views of Herbert Spencer. 'Christian Socialism is an obedience to the Law of Christ,' wrote a clergyman in 1884,

> not compliance with the ordinance of State. The cry for State intervention is often nothing more than a cowardly or indolent resource of people who think thus to throw on impersonal shoulders the weight of obligation which they secretly feel and openly shirk.

Christian Socialism could 'ease that pressure upon Government which threatens to push us over the abyss of State Socialism. . . .'[2] This contrast between Christian Socialism and a socialism implied to be less Christian was a common one. One's definition of Christian Socialism could become so airy as to take it quite out of the arena of actual political and social problems, or so homely that it could provoke nobody: one writer said that Christian Socialism was 'the duty of the farmer to pay good

[1] F. Maurice, *op. cit.* II. 44.

[2] T. P. Forsyth, *Christian Socialism and State Socialism* (1884), pp. 5, 8.

wages, and the duty of the labourers to do their work.'[1] It could even be a useful debating trick to say: 'Of course, I am a *Christian* Socialist' and to leave it at that, hoping that right and left would make different estimates of how much water the speaker was adding to the pure spirit of socialism.

Some Christian Socialists believed that the name stood for a special view of society and took up more of Maurice than his dislike of the state. H. C. Shuttleworth, a clergyman who once spoke at Hyde Park with Hyndman, had a Mauricean conviction that Christianity offered crucial insights to social reformers. 'Of one thing I am sure,' he wrote,

> that the gospel of Jesus Christ is the only power that can cast out the devils that oppress our society; and that of the unsolved social problems which perplex us all, *the Church still holds the key*. If this is to be a Christian socialist – and I think it is – then I am not ashamed of the name.[2]

But those Christian Socialists who were exploring their theology for paths to social justice, like those who were opposing the Christian variety to more radical types of reform, usually seemed rather mild in their opinions compared with socialists at large.

In a different and rather less common sense, Christian Socialism was not a distinct position but was the faith of those who agreed with Keir Hardie that socialism was simply 'the embodiment of Christianity in our industrial system,' and with Lansbury that although a socialist might not be a Christian, it was the duty of a Christian to be a socialist.[3] This position was defended in the *Christian Socialist*, a monthly paper published from 1883 until 1891 by a very mixed band who included members of the Social Democratic Federation and the Fabian Society, followers of Henry George, and a few clergymen and Nonconformist ministers of varying shades of social and theological radicalism. 'In our view,' an early issue announced, 'Christianity and Socialism are almost interchangeable terms.'[4]

[1] (Anon.), *In Darkest Ecclesiastical England* (1893), p. 8.

[2] H. C. Shuttleworth, 'The Christian Church and the Problem of Poverty', in A. Reid, ed., *Vox Clamantium*, p. 45.

[3] *British Weekly*, 18 Jan. 1894, p. 202; R. Postgate, *The Life of George Lansbury* (1951), p. 60.

[4] *Christian Socialist*, Nov. 1883, p. 81. For a history of the journal and an account of its support, see *ibid.*, Dec. 1891, pp. 129–30.

Why bother then to add 'Christian' at all? The answer was given candidly by John Glasse, a socialist minister from Edinburgh. 'The adjective "Christian" is not . . . adopted as a sign of antagonism [to non-Christian socialists], but for purposes of propagandism' among Christians.[1]

One of the editors complained in 1887, however, that the position of the journal, and of the new Christian Socialist Society which had lately adopted it as an organ, was 'very much misunderstood, both by friends and opponents. . . .'[2] In the Social Democratic Federation and the Socialist League, some sneered at the journal's faith.[3] In the churches there was suspicion of any attempt to dress socialist propaganda in holy robes. Joseph Parker, chairman of the Congregational Union in 1884, had a stark image for the danger. 'Let us,' he warned, 'be on our guard lest the word Christian be only the handle with which the knife "socialism" is worked.'[4] With Christians and socialists both on guard, this group of Christian Socialists remained, as one of its leaders said, 'a small and uninfluential body. . . .'[5] When a meeting of members was called in 1887 to consider dissolving the Christian Socialist Society, twelve turned up and six of them voted for dissolution, only the chairman's casting vote saving the society.[6] By 1891 there were small branches in Bristol, Leicester and Glasgow as well as the original group in London; but the entire membership was only 116, of whom fifty were 'not always in direct connexion with the society. . . .'[7]

When the journal ran out of money and disappeared in 1891, some members turned to the Labour Church movement and some joined a new body, the Christian Socialist League. This was a slightly more respectable organization than the Christian Socialist Society, having as its president the distinguished Baptist minister John Clifford, who was unique among the leaders of orthodox Nonconformity in supporting Fabian socialism: his address to the annual meeting of the Christian

[1] *Ibid.*, Feb. 1887, p. 25.
[2] *Ibid.*, Sept. 1887, p. 137.
[3] *Ibid.*, Oct. 1887, pp. 149–50.
[4] *Congregational Year Book* (1885), p. 91.
[5] W. H. P. [Campbell], in *Christian Socialist*, June 1889, p. 87.
[6] *Ibid.*, Oct. 1887, p. 156.
[7] *Ibid.*, May 1891, p. 60.

Socialist League in 1895 was printed as a Fabian tract.[1] It was also less specific in its social ambitions. The Christian Socialist Society had called in 1886 for 'Public control of Land, Capital, and all means of production, distribution, and exchange, involving the abolition of all Interest.'[2] Although this policy was given a more Fabian dressing in 1889 ('Public control of Land and Capital to be gradually assumed'), it was still more concrete than that of the League, which was open to all who agreed 'that the principles of Jesus Christ are directly applicable to all social and economic questions, and that such application to the conditions of our time demands the reconstruction of society upon a basis of association and fraternity.'[3] Like its predecessor, the League remained small, and it seems to have attracted even less public notice. James Adderley, a clergyman who described himself as a socialist, said that at this time the name Christian Socialist 'gave people the idea that this was a special brand of Socialism, not quite orthodox from the I.L.P. or Fabian point of view.'[4]

Such bodies as the Christian Socialist Society and the Christian Socialist League represented an alliance, often precarious, between people in different churches and in none. The church-affiliated members were active also within their own denominations, trying to arouse and organize there an interest in what late Victorians called 'the social question'. In general, as we have seen, ecclesiastical opinion towards social radicals grew rather more benign late in the century. It remains to inspect this change more closely, church by church.

The Church of England

Many clergyman had a high notion of the Church's duty to society. 'The Church of Christ,' said one of them, 'ought to be the main instrument for the social as well as the spiritual regeneration of the people.'[5] A very few found in the Social Democratic Federation the principles which the Church should

[1] J. Clifford, *Socialism and the Teaching of Christ* (1897).
[2] *Christian Socialist*, May 1886, p. 190.
[3] *Ibid.*, July 1889, p. 109; *Labour Annual* (1895), p. 111.
[4] J. Adderley, *In Slums and Society*, p. 234.
[5] R. R. Dolling, quoted in C. E. Osborne, *Life of Father Dolling*, p. 79.

support; others saw a more conservative role for her, as 'Christ's instrument for inspiring and softening those great social changes that lie before us.'[1] However they differed in shades of radicalism, they believed, as Maurice had, that it was the Church's mission to be 'the healer of all privations and diseases, the bond of all classes, the instrument for reforming abuses, the admonisher of the rich, the friend of the poor, the asserter of the glory of that humanity which Christ bears.'[2] Scores of individual clergymen helped strikers, offered to mediate between strikers and employers, expressed sympathy with trade unions and Labour Leagues and urged the Church to respond more earnestly to demands for social reform. Reformers also founded two societies, the Guild of St Matthew and the Christian Social Union, as vehicles for their concern.

The Guild of St Matthew was formed in 1877 by Stewart Headlam, then curate of St Matthew's Bethnal Green.[3] At first its purpose was mainly apologetic – to meet the case against the Church put by secularist lecturers. In encounters with Charles Bradlaugh and his friends (whom he respected greatly) Headlam used to accept many of their charges, and argue that the good secularist was virtually an unconscious Christian.[4] This part of the Guild's work absorbed it less after the first few years. When Bradlaugh died in 1891 and Annie Besant turned to theosophy, the Guild lost its strongest opponents. Well before this time, however, it had been spending more energy in trying to convert Churchmen to an interest in social problems than in trying to convert secularists to a sympathy with Christianity. Headlam's response to *The Bitter Cry* in 1883 was to say: 'I cannot think that the mere building of churches, or organizing missions, or starting philanthropic agencies, can be any adequate answer. . . .'[5] To those in the Church who contrasted Christian Socialism with State socialism, Headlam replied that the State was a sacred organism to be used for righteous ends, and that it was a Christian duty to work for such things as land nationalization, a progressive

[1] T. C. Fry in C. Gore, ed., *Essays in Aid of the Reform of the Church*, p. 319.

[2] F. D. Maurice, quoted in C. F. G. Masterman, *Frederick Denison Maurice* (1907), p. 234.

[3] S. Headlam, *The Guild of St Matthew, an Appeal to Churchmen*, p. 4.

[4] F. G. Bettany, *Stewart Headlam* (1926), p. 217.

[5] *Church Reformer*, Nov. 1883, p. 3.

income tax, universal suffrage, and the abolition of a hereditary House of Lords.[1] Nor did Headlam agree that Christian social reformers should refuse to co-operate with socialists who called themselves atheists. 'We Christians are rather bigger than that: the eagerness of these men for Social reform, we know is inspired by GOD: it is in Him they live and move and have their being: Him, without knowing it, they worship.'[2] It was Headlam who preached the funeral sermon over Alfred Linnell, run down by police during a demonstration of the unemployed in 1887 and hymned in a Death Song by the non-Christian socialist William Morris.

Headlam was one of those reformers, common in late Victorian England, who could be described as 'socialist-but.' 'Yes, I am a Socialist,' he remarked once, 'but I thank God I am a Liberal as well.'[3] The words 'socialist' and 'socialism' never appeared in the stated objects of the Guild. Like all decisions of the Guild this expressed the will of the founder, who believed that it would be misleading to include either word.[4] In party politics Headlam was a Fabian who favoured the radical wing of the Liberals, and in social policy he was first and last a land reformer. The social reformist organization which best expressed his own views was the English Land Restoration League, of which Headlam himself was treasurer. 'The weakness of the guild,' said Conrad Noel, a clergyman for whom it was not radical enough, 'was that beyond a general support of the working-class movement it confined itself to land reform, and was dominated by the teachings of Henry George.'[5]

Next to Headlam, the man who did most to keep the Guild going was its secretary Frederick Verinder, secretary also of the English Land Restoration League.[6] With Verinder's help Headlam produced a monthly paper, the *Church Reformer*, which he took over from another radical curate, R. H. Hadden, at the end of 1883. It was the unofficial organ of the Guild, ever urging the Church to reform itself by adopting new social policies and by accepting internal democracy. Apart from writing in the *Church*

[1] G. C. Binyon, *The Christian Socialist Movement in England* (1931), p. 144.
[2] *Church Reformer*, Jan. 1884, p. 2.
[3] F. G. Bettany. *op. cit.* p. 136.
[4] A. V. Woodworth, *Christian Socialism in England* (1903), pp. 122–3.
[5] C. Noel, *An Autobiography* (1945), p. 60.
[6] *Labour Annual* (1895), p. 191.

Reformer, the active members of the Guild produced some pamphlets, held occasional open-air demonstrations, and preached sermons when they could find a pulpit open to them. Most of them were young clergymen who, like Headlam, believed that they had inherited the traditions both of the Tractarians and of Maurice.[1] Although there were about three lay members to every clergyman, the Guild depended very much on the zeal of its clergy. Membership appears to have been highest early in 1895, when there were 99 clergymen and 265 laymen. Later in that year the *Church Reformer* disappeared after losing £1,200.[2] Numbers in the Guild fell steadily until Headlam decided in 1909 to dissolve it. 'The Guild,' wrote G. P. Gooch in 1903, 'has made but little headway among the clergy or adherents of the Established Church. . . .'[3] One of its members, James Adderley, said later: 'the G.S.M. was not destined to convert the Church of England to Socialism or anything like it.'[4]

The Guild of St Matthew had no life apart from its leader, whose personal programme was an unusual combination of crusades. He was a ritualist so extreme that he was called before a Royal Commission on Ecclesiastical Discipline on suspicion of papistry, and this put off some who were otherwise in sympathy with his ideas. Headlam was also a dedicated enemy of Puritanism, founding a Church and Stage Guild as well as the Guild of St Matthew, and putting up the bail for Oscar Wilde in 1895. Adderley believed that Headlam's anti-Puritan activities cost the Guild of St Matthew some popularity, and C. L. Marson, though no friend of Mrs Grundy, objected in 1895 that lecturers for the Guild were talking too much about the Empire Promenade and the ballet.[5] Again, Headlam's proposal for the entire abolition of patronage in the Church may have lost him the alliance of people who would have supported him on other grounds. Much of his reputation as a wild man, then, arose from controversies which had nothing to do with social reform. We should therefore be cautious about concluding

[1] For a list of some clerical members see F. G. Bettany, *op. cit.* pp. 81–2.
[2] *Ibid.* pp. 110, 112.
[3] *Reformers' Year Book* (1903), p. 38.
[4] J. Adderley, *In Slums and Society*, p. 204.
[5] F. G. Bettany, *op. cit.* p. 89.

that the Guild failed to influence the Church greatly because its social principles were too radical. Nevertheless the milder Christian Social Union grew at the expense of the Guild, and Headlam, at least, believed that it was the very moderation of its social doctrines which gave it the advantage. To many socialists, Headlam and his Guild appeared a gradualist, even timid, band. But they did commit themselves clearly to one side in the social contest, even if they wanted it to be conducted peaceably and by strict rules. Within the Church of England there was more demand for an organization which concerned itself about social problems without making such a clear gesture of committal.

The Christian Social Union was formed in Oxford in 1889. Like the Guild of St Matthew, it was open to clergy and laity and had on it the marks of the Tractarian movement and of F. D. Maurice. As theologians, however, the leaders of the Christian Social Union worried more than Headlam about reconciling Catholic doctrine with contemporary thought; as students of society they were less ready to identify themselves with social reformers at large; and as members of the Church they were a good deal more respectable. The chairman at its first meeting was a Canon of Christ Church and the president until 1900 was the Bishop of Durham. Between 1889 and 1913, 16 out of 53 episcopal appointments went to members of the Christian Social Union.[1] The Guild of St Matthew probably had only one member, C. W. Stubbs, who became a bishop.

The founder of the Christian Social Union, Henry Scott Holland, and its intellectual leader, Charles Gore, were men who believed that they were at the very heart of the Church, and were responsible for keeping it alert to the needs of the time. In 1889, the year in which the Christian Social Union was formed, Gore, Holland and others had published *Lux Mundi*, a series of essays in a spirit which has been described as liberal Catholicism, designed to end antagonism between intellectual freedom and the tradition of the Oxford movement, by showing, in effect, that God intended the new secular knowledge of the century to bring out the essential truth of incarnational religion. It was a remarkable book, for these followers of Pusey and Keble were also pupils of Jowett and Green. Although *Lux*

[1] M. Reckitt, *op. cit.* p. 138.

Mundi contained some evidence of a concern about social problems, its first task was to arm the Church to meet the mental challenge of the age. The Christian Social Union was the response of essentially the same group to the social challenge.

If social reformers can be divided into rebels and repenters, Gore and Holland and their friends were repenters. The founding of the Christian Social Union was described by Gore himself as 'a tardy act of repentance' in the Church.[1] When the Christian Social Union was first in the air, Scott Holland wrote: 'For the first time in all history, the poor old Church is trying to show the personal sin of corporate and social sinning.'[2]

In its first term, the Oxford branch of the Christian Social Union had over 100 resident members; most of the dons in it were clergymen, and many of the undergraduates were later to be ordained.[3] They discussed social theories in general, profit-sharing, co-operative production, the poor law, arbitration and other matters. They also believed it their duty to go beyond academic study and encourage reforms: in February 1890 a resolution was passed urging state interference to house the poor, the cost to be met by a tax on the unearned increment of landowners. They showed some interest in local affairs. A list of 'fair employers' received from the Oxford Trades Council was read at one meeting, and on another occasion in 1890, the society wrote to a Mr Lillingstone in Cornmarket Street, Oxford, offering to intercede between him and his employees in a dispute over unionism, and assuring him 'that we have been studying recently the subject of working men's Labour Organization and so perhaps might be able to give some little assistance.'[4] A London branch was formed in the same month as the founding meeting at Oxford. Although many other branches appeared after 1890, the Union remained at its most vigorous in Oxford and London. The central executive, under the Bishop of Durham (B. F. Westcott) as president, was virtually a joint committee of the Oxford and London branches.

The literature produced officially and unofficially on behalf

[1] S. Paget, ed., *Henry Scott Holland*, p. 241.

[2] *Ibid.* p. 169.

[3] Pusey House Library, Oxford, Christian Social Union, Oxford Branch, Minutes.

[4] *Ibid.*

of the Christian Social Union was considerable. In 1891 the Oxford branch began to publish a serious quarterly journal, the *Economic Review*, whose main purpose was to encourage Christian discussion of economic morality. Scott Holland's the *Commonwealth*, a more popular magazine dealing with social questions at large, first appeared in 1897. James Adderley launched *Goodwill*, a bright little paper meant to be sold with parish magazines, in 1894; its policy was declared to be Catholic and to involve an interest in the aspirations of the working classes. Within two years Adderley was claiming a circulation of 28,000. Although *Goodwill* had no official connexion with the Christian Social Union, its contributors were often leading members, its editorial notes advertised the Union's activities, and some of its articles were based on Christian Social Union pamphlets. Another shot in Adderley's personal campaign to influence Church opinion was *Stephen Remarx* (1893), a novel about a socially-conscious parson, which ran to twelve editions after twenty publishers had rejected it.[1] Courses of sermons during Lent were given for several years in London churches on behalf of the Union and published later as books. Propaganda informally representing it was delivered nearly every year by members speaking at the Church Congress.

Among the more practical activities of the Christian Social Union were 'white lists' of manufacturers who paid and treated their employees well and whose products, it was suggested, Christians could buy with a clear conscience. Publicity was given in journals and pamphlets to industrial processes, especially in the making of pottery, which endangered the health of workers. In 1897 the central executive wrote to the Home Secretary on this subject, suggesting 'that the primary object of the Factory Acts is the protection of the workpeople and not of the manufacturers.'[2] The other main enterprise of the Christian Social Union before 1900 was Maurice Hostel (1898), a small settlement in Hoxton which the secretary of the London branch, Percy Dearmer, described in 1901 as 'the most arduous and expensive of our efforts.'[3]

[1] J. Adderley, *op. cit.* pp. 170–1.

[2] Copy of letter in Pusey House Library.

[3] P. Dearmer, 'The Christian Social Union', in W. J. Hocking, ed., *The Church and New Century Problems* (1901), p. 171.

To some Churchmen the social attitudes found in the Christian Social Union appeared too radical. The *Church Times*, organ of the more conservative among High Churchmen, named Gore, Holland, Adderley and others as Christian Socialists who needed reminding 'that the spiritual and the material are distinct spheres. . . . Nor is the Church the Church of the poor only, but of the rich also.'[1] The president, Westcott, may have alarmed such critics when he defended socialism in an address to the Church Congress of 1890 which the Christian Social Union (and also, independently, the Guild of St Matthew) published as a pamphlet, and which the general executive of the Union later accepted as expressing its general principles. What Westcott meant by socialism, however, had 'no necessary affinity with any forms of violence, or confiscation, or class selfishness, or financial arrangement.' It was simply a principle, the spirit of co-operation as against the spirit of competition.[2] Gore said later that the Christian Social Union was socialist only in so far as socialism expressed the antithesis of *laissez-faire* individualism, and that any Churchman, High, Low or Broad, was welcome in it who believed that the Church needed to be awakened to the social implications of Christianity and who agreed on the need for 'fundamental social reconstruction . . . whether they called themselves Conservatives or Liberals or Radicals, whether they accepted or refused the name of Socialist.'[3] Nevertheless, the theological sympathies of most members were undeniably with the attitudes of *Lux Mundi*. Were there also social principles on which members broadly, if unofficially, agreed?

They were divided into two groups. Scott Holland noted in 1894 the difficulty of holding a balance in the Christian Social Union between the 'Respectables' and an 'extreme' group, 'partly cracky, party fervid.'[4] It was partly on account of differences between members who wanted it to be cautious and reflective, and others who believed in a more positive engagement on the side of social reform, that the arguments and actions of the Christian Social Union sometimes expressed ambiguous social principles.

[1] 'The New Christian Socialism', *Church Times*, 27 July 1894, p. 801.
[2] B. F. Westcott, *Socialism* (1890), pp. 3–4.
[3] S. Paget, ed., *op. cit.* pp. 242–3. [4] *Ibid.* pp. 203–4.

Scott Holland meant by 'Respectables' people who agreed that the Union should stand for social reform so long as it was of a piecemeal, gradual and not very controversial kind. The 'partly cracky, partly fervid' wing was stronger in London than at Oxford, and contained people who were also members of the Guild of St Matthew. Percy Dearmer, the author of a *Clarion* pamphlet and a Fabian Tract, was one of its leaders. He could discern in Christian teaching consequences which were a socialist's delight. 'If you are a Christian,' he wrote, 'and love your rich neighbour as yourself, you will do all you can to help him to become poorer.'[1] By 1900 the Christian Social Union was uneasily divided between sympathizers with Dearmer's views and people who believed them too drastic. There were times when only the skilful conciliation of Scott Holland kept the Union together. Tension persisted until 1908, when a number of the radicals including Dearmer, C. L. Marson, F. L. Donaldson and James Adderley, signed a manifesto declaring that their Christian Socialism involved public ownership of the means of production and exchange, and was therefore 'essentially the same Socialism as that which is held by Socialists throughout the world.'[2] This set off a serious conflict in the Union.

By some tests the Christian Social Union failed. It did not attract working-class members. One historian has suggested that it never intended to do so;[3] but Gore was writing in 1892: 'I do desire that the Christian Social Union shall become a widely ramifying league, through all classes . . .' and in 1921, when the Union no longer existed, Gore expressed regret that it had not raised enough trade-unionist Churchmen to make an impression on the labour movement.[4] A deliberate effort was begun in 1897 to establish a working-class organization alongside the Christian Social Union. 'It was felt for various reasons,' wrote Adderley in February 1898, 'many working-men could not join the Christian Social Union.'[5] After a correspondence in his paper *Goodwill* about providing some alternative, the Christian Fellowship League was formed,

[1] P. Dearmer, *Socialism and Christianity* (Fabian Tract 133, 1907), p. 8.
[2] Leaflet in Pusey House Library.
[3] M. Reckitt, *Faith and Society* (1932), p. 91.
[4] S. Paget, ed., *op. cit.* p. 250.
[5] *Goodwill*, Feb. 1898, p. 29.

with Gore as president and Dearmer and Adderley on the committee. It was laid down that the executive committee must be members of the Christian Social Union. The chairman was H. A. Colville, a former Salvation Army officer who had founded the Lichfield Evangelist Brotherhood. *Goodwill* offered regular space to the League; but after noting the formation of a few branches and the holding of quarterly meetings, the paper apparently found nothing to report. The League seems to have disappeared by the end of 1899. It was the only attempt to make up for the inability of the Christian Social Union to recruit working-class members.

Gore admitted in retrospect that the Christian Social Union had failed in another way. 'It has not succeeded,' he said, 'in stirring-up what it believes to be the right spirit in the mass of those who preach in the pulpits or sit in the pews of the Anglican churches.' As represented locally, said Gore, the Church was still seen as alien by the Labour man and the social reformer.[1] On the other hand it had not satisfied the left wing of social reformers in the Church. To Conrad Noel it was a 'mild and watery society', and its radical members found a more congenial home in the Church Socialist League, founded on 1906.[2] The views expressed by the Christian Social Union were 'watery' not only because they represented a compromise but because some of its spokesmen themselves had vague opinions about society. This was especially true of the president, Westcott. 'With every word almost of Canon Westcott's general propositions,' remarked the *British Weekly* in 1887 of his *Social Aspects of Christianity*, 'partisans of all schools will agree. The difficulty is in the application.'[3] Conrad Noel found a love of generalities throughout the Union: 'It glories in its indefiniteness, and seems to consider it a crime to come to any particular economic conclusion. . . .'[4]

The achievement of the Christian Social Union was nevertheless substantial. 'I thank God,' wrote a radical clergyman in 1894, 'that an increasing number of our younger Church

[1] S. Paget, ed., *op. cit.* p. 250.
[2] C. Noel, *op. cit.* p. 71.
[3] *British Weekly*, 17 June 1887, p. 1.
[4] C. Noel, *Socialism in Church History* (1910), quoted in M. Reckitt, *Faith and Society*, p. 91.

folk, especially the clergy, are banding together in branches of the Christian Social Union.'[1] It was exaggerating to say as Dearmer did that by 1900 the Union 'might almost be described as an informal committee of the English Church upon social questions,' but when he said this there were nearly fifty branches and 4,060 members including 1,436 clergymen.[2] A clergyman has said of his experience at Jarrow, where he became vicar in 1897:

> I came to the conclusion that, as a member of the Christian Social Union, my first urgent task was to blazon abroad the nature of the housing conditions in St Peter's parish, and the shameful evils to moral and physical health to which they inevitably lead.[3]

J. W. C. Wand, who was to become Bishop of London, found that at Oxford just after 1900 the Christian Social Union 'opened one's eyes for the first time to the implications of Christianity in the whole industrial field.'[4] Even if it was only to a small minority that membership brought such a sense of responsibility, the leavening could in the long run be significant. The less active members were at any rate plied with literature on social problems, and the clergy who were not members were likely to meet advocates of the Union at the Church Congress, at diocesan conferences or in Church papers.

The interest of Churchmen in social questions after 1890 cannot, of course, be attributed entirely to the propaganda of the Christian Social Union. As Dearmer observed, it found 'a Church that was ready to listen, a public that was touched with some measure of social compunction.'[5] Adderley modestly put down the success of his novel *Stephen Remarx*

> to the simple fact that it dealt with a subject which was in everybody's mind at the time. . . . *Stephen Remarx* came out just when slumming was the fashion among religious people of the upper classes, and Socialism of a very mild type was beginning to be indulged in even by duchesses.[6]

[1] Canon E. L. Hicks, in *Labour Prophet*, July 1894, p. 86.
[2] Christian Social Union, *Annual Report* (1900), p. 1.
[3] Father Holmes in *Church Times*, 26 Aug. 1955.
[4] J. W. C. Wand, in Sir J. Marchant, ed., *What I believe* (1953), p. 170.
[5] P. Dearmer, 'The Christian Social Union', in W. J. Hocking, ed., *The Church and New Century Problems*, p. 160.
[6] J. Adderley, *op. cit.* p. 170.

The Christian Social Union exploited and focused this tolerance for 'socialism of a very mild type' more skilfully than the Guild of St Matthew, and encouraged it to spread in the Church of England.

For some time before the Christian Social Union appeared, an interest in social questions was being displayed at sessions of the Church Congress. At each of its annual meetings between 1880 and 1900 (except in 1891) the Congress had at least one session on social problems. Some of the discussions were about such traditional subjects as pauperism, thrift, and parochial relief; but nearly every year (the exceptions are 1882 and 1883) there was also a debate which raised in some form the relationship of the Church to fundamental social reforms. When H. H. Champion was invited to address the Congress in 1887, a fairly friendly reception was given to his remarks about the duty of the church to sympathize with socialism. Since no vote was ever taken one cannot judge the balance of opinion at Church Congresses. Even the reports of discussions may be misleading; 'a programme heavily weighed with invited readers and speakers,' said the editor of the *Year-Book of the Church of England* in 1900, '. . . kills free discussion in impromptu speech.'[1] Addresses by members of the Christian Social Union and the Guild of St Matthew, moreover, may not have been taken seriously by hearers who believed, as one Churchman put it, that the Congress was useful mainly as 'a safety valve for the vagaries of the crank.'[2] But many of the addresses on social reform were given by clergymen whom nobody could describe as cranks, and the Church Congress platform gave them a large audience. The Congresses were fully reported in Church journals. Each Congress between 1880 and 1900 had between 2,000 and 4,500 members, not including those people, mainly residents of the Congress town, who took tickets for particular sessions. There was also the Working Men's Meeting, at which social problems were often discussed before a supposedly working-class audience. After 1898, however, this meeting was called simply 'for men'.

Opinion in high places of the Church was expressed at the

[1] *Year-Book of the Church of England* (1900), p. viii.

[2] *Goodwill*, Aug. 1899, p. 171. For a similar comment see *Saturday Review*, 5 Sept. 1891, p. 267.

gatherings of bishops known as Lambeth Conferences. The Conference of 1888 considered socialism. A committee of ten bishops submitted a report on the practical work of the Church in relation to socialism, defining it as 'any scheme of reconstruction which aims at uniting labour and the instruments of labour (land and capital), whether by means of the State, or of the help of the rich, or of the voluntary co-operation of the poor.'[1] Between socialism thus defined and Christianity, the committee suggested, there was no necessary contradiction; but the Christian church could form no alliance with socialists who were atheists, who would murder and rob, or who believed that 'the very possession of private property is a usurpation and a wrong to the community.' The committee recommended that private property should be regarded as neither fit to be abolished nor permanently owned by anybody, but 'a trust to be administered for the good of humanity'. The State was described by the committee as an instrument which could help to preserve the poor against the effects of competition, so long as its protection was not strong enough to undermine thrift and self-restraint. This report was formally received by the Conference and submitted to the Churches of the Anglican Communion with the observation that no more important problem than socialism could occupy the attention of clergy and laity. The drift of the report was summed up thus by a writer in the *Christian Socialist*: 'The bishops accept Socialism and reject it in the same breath.'[2]

At the next Lambeth Conference, in 1897, socialism as such was not on the agenda. The choice of subjects annoyed James Adderley, who wrote:

> It is disappointing to find only two very 'safe' social subjects placed on the agenda, 'The unemployed' and 'Co-operation'. Surely if the Bishops wished to deal with these matters they should have selected serious moral questions, such as '*Commercial Morality*', '*Sweating*'. Of course these questions might bring us into conflict with the average plutocrat who subscribes to our Church expenses. But are we afraid of him? God help us if we are! What a glorious thing a really courageous Lambeth Conference would be.[3]

The committee of bishops reporting on the unemployed and

[1] Lord Davidson of Lambeth, ed., *The Six Lambeth Conferences* (1929), p. 137

[2] *Christian Socialist*, Sept. 1888, p. 138.

[3] *Goodwill*, Oct. 1896, p. 223.

co-operation did mention sweating, but probably in terms too general to satisfy Adderley.[1] Their report also advised the Church not to identify itself with any one social system and rebuked the 'numberless Christians' who never thought of applying their religious principles to social situations. Without even a backward glance at the iron laws of economics, the committee urged that moral standards be applied to industrial affairs, and in particular that the principle of brotherhood be embodied in economic relationships.

Both in the report and in the general encyclical letter which commended it warmly to Christians, there remained clear signs of an older view of 'the poor'. The bishops were worried about the temptation faced by the poor 'to throw off their burdens and expect to obtain aid without any exertion on their own part. . . . It is character that they need.'[2] A reader of the Lambeth reports does well, moreover, to remember the warning that 'it is easy to exaggerate the importance of the admirable generalizations in which they are commonly, and perhaps inevitably, phrased.'[3] At the Lambeth Conferences of 1888 and 1897, the bishops admitted that Christians had a responsibility for the condition of society and that many contemporary social arrangements were unjust; they did not pronounce judgment on, or even make recommendations about, any of the actual policies which socialists and their critics were debating.

In their individual pronouncements on social problems, bishops were often little more specific than the legendary preacher who was against sin. The Bishop of Peterborough, W. G. Magee (who became Archbishop of York in 1891), virtually raised this vagueness into a principle when he said in 1889 that the Church ought to 'try to make labour just towards capital and capital towards labour, and yet not to attempt to define what in every particular case was the precise amount of justice due on one hand or the other.'[4] Social reformers could nevertheless find something to please them in a number of bishops between 1880 and 1900. Joseph Arch was grateful

[1] Lord Davidson, ed., *op. cit.* p. 269.

[2] *Ibid.* p. 185.

[3] M. Reckitt, *Faith and Society, p.* 93.

[4] J. C. Macdonnell, *The Life and Correspondence of William Connor Magee,* II. 278.

to James Fraser, Bishop of Manchester, for supporting the Agricultural Labourers' Union during a lock-out, saying of him when he died in 1885 that 'he was deeply and sincerely mourned by thousands of poor in his diocese.'[1] At Durham, J. B. Lightfoot presided over a Co-operative Congress in 1880.[2] His successor, Westcott, besides blessing a mild sort of socialism mediated successfully in a coal strike and was proud that he was trusted by the miners.[3] As Bishop of London, Mandell Creighton won the respect of the Webbs; 'during his reign in London,' wrote Mrs Webb, 'the Church was encouraged to throw itself bodily on the side of good, and even progressive government in all local concerns.'[4] E. S. Talbot, Bishop in turn of Rochester, Southwark and Winchester, was a friend of the Webbs and expressed sympathy with the labour movement in his published sermon *The Religious Aspirations of Labour* (1895). C. W. Stubbs was an ardent supporter of Joseph Arch in the 'seventies and called himself a socialist while Bishop of Truro.[5]

Some bishops stayed clear of industrial disputes, agreeing with the economist Archdeacon Cunningham that 'Our Lord distinctly declined the part of an arbitrator between brethren, and no bishop can claim on account of his office to be competent to arbitrate between capital and labour in any dispute.' Cunningham named also an expediential consideration which may have occurred to some bishops:

> If, as is likely to be the case, he assumes the maintenance of existing society in some modified form he will appear, to those who are advocating an entire reconstruction of society, as a half-hearted creature who is content to advocate some temporary and unsatisfactory patchwork.[6]

Walsham How found as Bishop of Wakefield that the attempt to end a strike could make an unsuccessful mediator unpopular; when he urged both sides to arbitrate in a glassblowers' strike

[1] J. Arch, *The Story of his Life*, p. 222.

[2] H. M. Lynd, *England in the Eighteen-Eighties* (New York, 1945), p. 247.

[3] See W. Moore Ede, *The Attitude of the Church to some of the Social Problems of Town Life*, p. 72; E. Welbourne, *The Miners' Unions of Northumberland and Durham* (1923), pp. 283–6, 306–7.

[4] B. Webb, *Our Partnership*, p. 207.

[5] E. H. Sedding, *Charles William Stubbs* (1914), p. 31.

[6] W. Cunningham, *The Function of the Clergy in Regard to Economic Life* (1908), p. 4.

the men refused, and in a subsequent mining dispute he declined to take sides but criticized the miners for violence. 'My lord of Wakefield has lately issued a feeble pastoral bleat to the locked-out miners in his diocese,' wrote C. L. Marson. 'He is shocked that they have destroyed some property; but confesses that he does not know the rights and wrongs of the strike.'[1]

Indiscretions of this sort encouraged the survival of the old radical conviction that a bishop was an enemy of the people, a belief made all the more resilient by the continued presence of bishops in the House of Lords. Bishops were often attacked for voting as they did on particular issues; but their real crime, in the eyes of social radicals, was membership of an institution regarded as the home of privilege. 'This alliance with the comfortable classes,' wrote the editor of the *Daily Chronicle* in an essay on the Church of England, 'is typified to the workmen by the presence of our leaders in the House of Lords.'[2]

At the end of the century, those of her clergymen who considered the matter undoubtedly believed that the Church of England was less unpopular than she had been sixty and seventy years earlier. They were right, at least in the sense that social radicals did not now think of the clergy as a practically unanimous block of opponents.

Gore, Adderley, Headlam and Holland were less isolated than Maurice and his fellow Christian socialists had been. In the forums of the Church their arguments were taken seriously, and their right to raise questions of social policy in ecclesiastical assemblies was almost universally conceded. The resolutions of such assemblies on social questions were often too vague, or too high-mindedly neutral, to satisfy the radicals; but they sensed that the initiative was with them, and that they were making slow progress. By 1897 Scott Holland was saying that 'a fair proportion' of the clergy supported boards of conciliation, shorter working hours, the principle that wages are the first charge in determining price, increased communal control of land 'wherever public purposes require it,' regular absorption of unearned increment, and a number of other reforms which,

[1] F. D. How, *Bishop Walsham How*, pp. 305–11; C. L. Marson, 'Churchmen and their Politics', *Westminster Review*, Feb. 1894, pp. 182–3.

[2] A. E. Fletcher in A. Reid, ed., *Vox Clamantium*, p. 121.

not so long ago, nearly all clergymen would have resisted sternly.[1] But the most optimistic radical could not believe that this 'fair proportion' made up anything like a majority of the 25,000 clergymen in the nation. Among the clergy at large were many who, thinking social arrangements tolerably just or not thinking about them at all, ignored the publications of the Christian Social Union and the Guild of St Matthew in favour of works like the Rev. John Gritton's *Dangers Attending the Use of Painted Windows in Churches* (1882). Among the laity there was proportionately less ardour for social reform. 'Church newspapers still take it for granted,' wrote Adderley in 1916, 'that the vast majority of their readers have little interest in politics beyond wishing and praying for the downfall of Liberal governments.'[2] The radicals were a not ineffective vanguard of the Church; but they had not yet carried with them the average vicar, and still less the average worshipper.

Nonconformity

In no Nonconformist sect was there by 1900 a body resembling the Christian Social Union or the Guild of St Matthew. It does not follow, however, that a zeal for social reform was rarer among Methodists and Congregationalists than among Anglicans; for in the Church of England it was an established custom for a group of people with a programme to form a society, and they could do so with impunity so long as they offered no serious challenge to doctrinal orthodoxy or to ecclesiastical authority. Methodist organization, on the other hand, was too rigid and all-embracing to allow such procedures. A connexional society, for whatever purpose, could be formed only if the Conference authorized it; it could not, therefore, represent the will of a minority. The polity of Congregationalism raised a different obstacle. The difficulty of achieving *any* common organization between members of the self-governing churches was notorious. Radical Wesleyans and Congregationalists tended to act separately from each other except at the annual Conference and the biannual assembly of the Union. To judge the popularity

[1] H. Scott Holland, 'The Church of England and Social Reform', *Progressive Review*, Jan. 1897, p. 324.

[2] J. Adderley, *op. cit.* pp. 204–5.

of social reform among Nonconformists it is therefore necessary to look at individual campaigners, and to study the resolutions of each central body relating to social problems. Nor should one overlook the role of the *British Weekly* and the *Methodist Times*, which performed functions broadly like that of the Christian Social Union. Each carried the word 'social' in its sub-title. Without standing for any particular detailed programme of reform, each tried to persuade its readers (most of whom were Nonconformists) to consider the social implications of their faith. And the papers offered a better forum than existed elsewhere for Nonconformists who wished to discuss in public what those implications might be. The names of William Robertson Nicoll and Hugh Price Hughes, founders and editors of the two journals, must therefore stand high on any list of individual Nonconformists who contributed to a general awareness of social problems.

Among leaders of Wesleyan Methodism, Hughes' was the most powerful voice raised in favour of social reform. It was heard in other journals as well as his own, in addresses from pulpit and platform, and in *Social Christianity*, a collection of sermons published in 1889. This book was the manifesto of a man who had rejected altogether the old dogma that Methodists should have 'no politics,' who saw that behind this slogan stood Toryism, and who declared that evangelical Christians should abandon their vision of the world as an aggregation of individual souls. 'Jesus Christ came into this world to save human society as well as to save individuals,' he wrote, 'indeed, you cannot effectually save the one without saving the other.' Challenging the notion that poverty was the fruit of sin, Hughes asked Christians to think about people who, although in no way vicious, suffered terribly on account of unemployment. He denounced legal injustice with a vigour which many a secular socialist could well admire. 'The one deadly charge I have to bring against the law of England,' he said, 'is this, that crimes against the *person* are regarded as almost trivial in comparison with crimes against *property*. The law, he concluded, reflected 'the current opinion of the ruling classes of the past.'[1]

[1] H. P. Hughes, *Social Christianity* (1889), pp. 54, 145, 153.

The vehemence of these remarks is a little misleading, for Hughes was by no means as radical as some Anglican clergymen. In a review of *Social Christianity* Annie Besant wrote: 'Mr Hughes has not, apparently, obtained the same intellectual grip on the poverty problem visible in some of his brethren of the Establishment.'[1] Given her own views at the time (she was in her Fabian phase), Mrs Besant was right to be dissatisfied. For Hughes put more trust in personal compassion than in communal interference as a solution for social distress. 'In answer to the employer's question: "What must I do to be saved?" ' wrote the *Methodist Times*, 'might we not say, "Believe on the Lord Christ Jesus and adjust your wages sheet?"'[2] This appeal to the conscience of the rich would have pleased Ruskin or Toynbee; but it divided Hughes sharply from those reformers who believed in State socialism. The crucial difference was well expressed by J. Scott Lidgett, the founder of the Bermondsey Settlement and one of the few Wesleyan ministers who thought Hughes too conservative. Lidgett said later of his dissatisfaction with the Forward Movement in the 1880s: 'I could not be content with appeals that sought rather to palliate existing evils by charitable help than radically to reconstruct the existing organization of society on the basis of righteousness and the comradeship of brotherly love.'[3] M. L. Edwards describes Lidgett's *The Fatherhood of God* (1902) as the first work by a Wesleyan whose social theory can be called fully collectivist.[4]

No Wesleyan minister thought harder about social and economic relationships than Samuel Keeble. Like many sensitive contemporaries (he was born in 1853), Keeble found Ruskin a mental liberator in these matters; and like some of them, he went farther than his master. In 1889 Keeble spent three months reading *Capital* and summarizing its argument in 200 closely-written octavo pages. The book seemed to him 'a piece of massive, virile reasoning . . . a masterly study of the economic development of human society.'[5] Keeble never became a Marxist: at first reading and on reflec-

[1] *Pall Mall Gazette*, 11 June 1889.
[2] *Methodist Times*, 12 Feb. 1885, p. 102.
[3] J. Scott Lidgett, *My Guided Life*, p. 61.
[4] M. L. Edwards, *Methodism and England*, pp. 91–3.
[5] S. E. Keeble, Note-book, 1889.

tion, he was sceptical. 'I believe there are huge fallacies,' he said, 'yet I can see great truth.' The great truth, it seemed to him, was a vindication in economic terms of Ruskin's moral protest against – in Keeble's phrase – 'the immorality, the barbarism and the unscrupulousness of modern masters and men in trade.'[1]

Just before discovering Marx, Keeble had published his first article in the *Methodist Times* – a warm review of Hughes' *Social Christianity*. Soon, as 'Labour Lore,' he was writing a regular column for Hughes on social and industrial affairs. The gap between contributor and editor was clear in 1891, when Keeble sent Hughes an article on Marx which was neither published nor returned. In 1895 the column ended. 'H. P. Hughes has long been restive over it,' Keeble noted privately. 'He does not like my advanced ideas on economic subjects. . . .' Occasional articles and reviews by Keeble appeared later in the *Methodist Times*, and not until the Boer War did Keeble – a pacifist – believe that the gulf between them was complete. When Hughes died in 1902 Keeble's summary of his influence was not bitter. 'Hugh Price Hughes had reactionary tendencies,' he wrote, 'which came out with fearful force at times. But on the whole, he has been the leader of the progressive forces in Methodism and Nonconformity.'[2]

About his own book, *Industrial Day-Dreams* (1896), Keeble was modest. His opinions, he wrote in his note-book, were mainly derivative: 'The only thing is they are novel in a Christian minister alas – such rarely touch the industrial question – proper – not even P. Hughes. . . .' His method was to introduce readers to the leading figures and ideas in the history of socialism, and to suggest temperately that on certain terms Christians should agree with them: 'if Socialism will only eliminate all morally obnoxious features, as well as all economic fallacies, from its programme, Christianity will clasp hands with it; for a purified Socialism is simply an industrially-applied Christianity.'[3] Between *Industrial Day-Dreams* and Hughes' *Social Christianity* there were two substantial differences. First, Keeble tried to convince the reader by close

[1] *Ibid.* 1882–4.

[2] M. L. Edwards, *Samuel Keeble, Pioneer and Prophet* (1949), p. 57.

[3] S. E. Keeble, *Industrial Day-Dreams*, p. 105.

argument, while Hughes, who had seen his subject only from the air, wrote with a preacher's rhetoric. Second, Keeble was far more interested in systematic, collectivist reform. On a map of socialism his place would be somewhere between the Fabians and the Independent Labour Party, for he was rather more preoccupied than the former with problems of moral principle and rather more cerebral than the latter.

Opinion on social questions, as on matters of doctrine, was more diverse in Congregationalism than in Methodism. Unlike the Wesleyans mentioned here, a number of Congregational ministers combined social radicalism with extreme liberalism in theology. Of R. J. Campbell, for example, who had left the Church of England, a fellow Congregational minister said in 1898: 'I gather he is advanced in all his views, political, social, educational, and theological.'[1] Early in the present century Campbell was well known both for his modernist 'new theology' and as a champion of socialism. In his case, the search for a true faith ended in a return to the Church of England. Some other ministers whose religious and secular opinions were like Campbell's travelled in a less orthodox direction. Two such men were B. J. Harker, the pastor at Bolton who persuaded his congregation to form themselves into a Labour Church, and J. Bruce Wallace, founder of the Brotherhood Church, an organization which stood, as the Labour Church did, for socialism and untheological religion.[2] This combination of heterodoxies was not unusual in Congregationalism, whose border with the Unitarians had been crossed many times.

There were other social reformers in the Independent ministry who correspond to Hugh Price Hughes – men more conservative theologically than Harker or Wallace, prominent in denominational affairs, and earnestly arguing the case for reforms which, although considerable, would involve no upheaval of the existing social order. One such man was John Brown Paton, the Nottingham minister who hoped that interdenominational councils would study social problems in the light of Christianity, and that church reunion and Christian

[1] C. S. Horne, quoted in W. B. Selbie, *The Life of Charles Sylvester Horne* (1920), p. 166.

[2] See *Labour Annual* (1895), pp. 47, 191; (1896), p. 44; *Reformers' Year Book* (1901), p. 42.

[3] See J. F. Laun, *Social Christianity in England* (1929), pp. 90–1, 136.

social reform would thus advance together.[3] Another was Andrew Mearns, promoter of *The Bitter Cry of Outcast London.* A third minister of this type was C. Fleming Williams, a member of the London County Council who seemed, to a correspondent of the *British Weekly*, one-eyed in his defence of the workers in any industrial dispute.[1] When Williams himself wrote on social reform in the *British Weekly*, however, he asked no more of Christians than a broad sympathy with socialists.[2] This was an attitude endorsed by the editor, W. Robertson Nicoll, and by a number of ministers who wrote in the journal, including Andrew Fairbairn, the first principal of Mansfield College, Oxford. The churches, Fairbairn once said, had 'allowed the industrial classes to grapple, almost unaided, with their problems, to fight, unhelped, their way into their liberties and rights.'[3] The writer who calls Fairbairn 'a pompous windbag',[4] is too harsh, for he could see more clearly than many of his colleagues where the greatest threats to Nonconformity lay; but it is true that when he exhorted Christians to help the masses to gain social justice he did so in the broadest of terms, offering no judgment on concrete policies.

A more specific social concern was shown by R. F. Horton. In his church at Lyndhurst Road, Hampstead, Horton lectured on such subjects as the Unemployed, the Eight Hours' Day, and the Housing Question. He formed the men who heard these lectures into a Social Reform League which campaigned for sanitary improvements in the neighbourhood, and which was responsible for introducing the Adult School movement into Hampstead and Kentish Town. During one of his lectures Horton spoke of Jesus as the leader of the labour party (or Labour Party – reports differed). His use of this phrase was criticized by the *British Weekly* as likely to encourage the 'socialist humanitarian view of Jesus.'[5] Horton was happy to accept all but the anti-theological implications of such a view; from the time he left Oxford, he said later, he had been eager

[1] *British Weekly*, 12 Oct. 1893, p. 386.
[2] *Ibid.*, 1 March 1894, pp. 297–8.
[3] *Congregational Year Book* (1884), p. 100.
[4] W. B. Glover, *Evangelical Nonconformists and the Higher Criticism in the Nineteenth Century* (1954), p. 154.
[5] *British Weekly*, 10 March 1892, p. 324.

'to make the Church the champion of the people and the leader in economic progress.'[1]

Many Nonconformists believed that a church should be no such thing. To the head of a Wesleyan mission in Liverpool, it appeared reasonable that evangelists as such should relieve social hardship only if the recipient was a likely convert. 'Of course we have helped thousands of people who have been in distress,' he told an interviewer, 'but never until we have assured ourselves that their religious professions or intentions were sincere.'[2] To Edward White, a keen evangelist who was once chairman of the Congregational Union, social Christianity and the like seemed unnecessary because of the 'self-acting machinery of civilized society, by which capital is compelled to minister to the necessities of labour and poverty, irrespective of goodwill.'[3] Another chairman of the Union, Thomas Green, gave an anxious address in 1890 on 'the secular element in our church life,' which he believed was threatening 'to hide Jesus Christ by confounding the Gospel with a comprehensive but material benevolence.'[4] When Hughes received a letter asking him to 'preach the Gospel' in his sermons and stay off the social question, he described the viewpoint of the writer as 'one of the most dangerous ever entertained by Christian men,' but admitted that it was held by thousands of 'the best Christians in England.'[5] There is no way of knowing *how many* thousands of Nonconformists shared this (or any other) belief about the right relations of Christianity and social reform. The policies of the Wesleyan Conference and the Congregational Union provide, however, a useful index to the balance of articulate opinion.

When the Wesleyan Conference turned its attention to the plight of central urban chapels in 1885, it resolved 'that more practical interest should be shown in the domestic and social well-being of people in the neighbourhood of such Chapels.'[6] For the Conference, this was a novel interest in the *environment*

[1] R. F. Horton, *An Autobiography*, p. 81.
[2] Charles Garrett, in *Methodist Times*, 29 April 1886, p. 278.
[3] *British Weekly*, 31 Oct. 1895, p. 20.
[4] *Congregational Year Book* (1891), p. 70.
[5] H. P. Hughes, *Social Christianity*, *pp*. 19–20.
[6] *Wesleyan Conference Minutes* (1885), p. 265.

of working-class people. Many of the ministers who voted for this resolution doubtless took it as no more than a warning, of the sort which William Booth was soon to thunder, that the poorest needed temporal aid to lift them within reach of the gospel. In its address to the Wesleyan Societies for 1887, however, the Conference spoke a little more boldly, recommending a sympathy towards 'legitimate efforts' of the working classes 'to ameliorate their condition.'[1] In 1891 the Conference again asserted the social responsibilities of Methodism, saying: 'Let us . . . help those who are trying to relieve the physical necessities of the poor.'[2] A year later the Conference said:

> We all regard with deep sympathy the lot of the toiling multitudes; we desire for them more leisure, a larger share of comforts and refinements. Let us make the fullest use of our influence and power to obtain for them these important conditions of a higher life.[3]

Each of these passages expressed the social consciousness of the Forward Movement. Elsewhere in the annual addresses, a more traditional attitude broke through. 'Our great work is to save the soul from sin,' the Conference declared in 1894; 'and if we can accomplish this, all other evils will naturally and necessarily disappear. It is through the individual we must work upon society.'[4] Such a remark breathed the spirit not of Hughes and his friends but of older men like James Harrison Rigg, to whom Hughes was 'our Methodist firebrand.'[5] Certain other references to social questions, in which the tone was of engaged impartiality, must have been more acceptable to Hughes than to the minority on his left. 'Let us protest . . . against trade oppression, by master or by man,' said the Conference in 1891.[6] A man who believed, as Samuel Keeble did, that the economic system was permanently unjust to labour, must have been dissatisfied by this refusal to take sides. Keeble had other reminders that most Wesleyans were far less radical

[1] *Ibid.* (1887), p. 304.
[2] *Ibid.* (1891), quoted in R. F. Wearmouth, *Methodism and the Struggle of the Working Classes, 1850–1900*, p. 149.
[3] *Ibid.* (1892), quoted in *ibid.*
[4] *Ibid.* (1894), p. 379.
[5] J. Telford, *The Life of James Harrison Rigg*, p. 325.
[6] *Wesleyan Conference Minutes* (1891), quoted in R. F. Wearmouth, *op. cit.* p. 149.

than himself. Only 208 copies of *Industrial Day-Dreams* had been sold when, under an agreement drawn up by his canny publisher, Keeble had to buy the remaining 267. (Eventually he sold the rest.) At the Conference of 1899 a motion of Keeble's that the study of social problems be included in the training of theological students got no further than to a committee. In 1902 he took over the *Methodist Weekly*, the only Wesleyan journal more radical than the *Methodist Times*. The paper kept losing money and had to be stopped in 1903 because too few Methodists wanted to read it.

It was nevertheless a heartening day for Wesleyan social reformers when, at the Conference of 1898, Hugh Price Hughes was elected president, receiving 369 out of 505 votes cast. Hughes interpreted his election as a triumph for 'Social Christianity.'[1] As expressed at the Conference, Wesleyan opinion was not prepared to be identified with the politics of the poor; but it now recognized that Christians as such should be interested in problems of social welfare. Keeble was convinced, moreover, that the current of denominational opinion was flowing, however gradually, in his own direction.[2]

The attitudes to social questions expressed at assemblies of the Congregational Union of England and Wales were very similar to those of the Wesleyan Conferences. General statements of the Congregational Union on social policy, like those of the Wesleyan Conference, often represented a compromise between more and less radical views. In 1885, for example, it was resolved:

> That this Assembly, while deprecating all action that would lessen the sanctions of the rights of property, and recognizing the condi-

[1] See D. P. Hughes, *The Life of Hugh Price Hughes*, p. 510.

[2] In 1905 his agitation for what he called 'a Sociological Society' was successful, when the Wesleyan Methodist Union for Social Service was formed. In the same year he was asked to write a leading article for the official weekly, the *Methodist Recorder* – on a social subject if he chose. 'It is a pleasant little victory', he wrote in his note-book, '. . . the rest of the world – including the *Recorder* – is coming to see that the views that I, in common with others, have advocated in reference to social righteousness are bound to be heard and destined to be influential.' A second edition of *Industrial Day-Dreams* was published by the Wesleyan Book-room in 1907, and in 1909 his proposal about social training for theological students was finally passed. Keeble never gained, however, the recognition which his ability would almost certainly have earned if it had been exercised in supporting more conventional attitudes.

> tions which at the present time control the markets both of labour and material, affirms it to be the duty of every Christian citizen to seek by all means in his power to diminish the inequalities which unjust laws and customs produce in the condition of those who are common members of the State, to endeavour to bring about such changes in the modes of property in land as shall lead to a fairer distribution of it among the people, to the better housing of the poor, and the relief of the overcrowding of the cities; and, further, it calls upon every Christian man and woman to remember that the so-called laws of trade and economics are not the only rules which should direct the transactions of manufacturers, traders, labourers, and purchasers.[1]

This resolution followed discussions, sometimes heated, in which a few socialistically-minded ministers competed with such conservatives as Joseph Parker, who was chairman of the Union in 1884 and whose lack of sympathy for social reform was illustrated by the remark: 'I cannot but feel that the world would be poorer but for its poverty. . . .'[2] The moderate majority was able to pass a statement which did not venture from the level of principle to the hazards of particular cases, and which recognized both that the existing social order was basically valid and that injustices occurred within it.

In 1890 the mental challenge of socialism was considered at some length in an anxious debate about the failure of recent evangelistic activity among the working classes. As a result of this discussion a Social Questions Committee of the Union was formed, and working-class leaders were invited to address subsequent assemblies. At a session of the Union in Bradford in 1892 on 'The Church and the Labour Problem', Keir Hardie was an unannounced speaker in what proved to be the Congregationalists' most lively debate on social problems. Charles Leach, a minister from Birmingham, said during an attack on the Labour Churches that he had recently heard a member of parliament declare at one of them 'that Christianity was dead, and that he was glad of it. . . .' He was obviously referring to Keir Hardie, who happened to be present during Leach's address and who jumped up at once demanding to be heard. ('I fairly lost control of myself,' he wrote later, '. . . and what

[1] *Congregational Year Book* (1886), p. 17.
[2] *Ibid.* (1885), p. 63.

I said or what I did remains to this day unknown to me, save in so far as newspapers have revealed it.')[1] Permitted to speak by a vote of the meeting, Hardie gave a milder account of what he had said at the Labour Church service, and proceeded to tell the Congregationalists what he thought of their attitude to social relationships. His remarks, and the responses to them, were reported thus in the *British Weekly*:

> The reason the Labour party had turned its back on the Church was because the Church had turned its back upon them. ('No, no.') They got respectable congregations on Sunday, and preached to please respectability (Cries of 'No, No.') But they did. (Loud cries of 'No, no,' and 'It is false'.) They forgot the writhing and suffering mass of humanity outside the walls of their churches. (Voices, 'No, no'.) He knew what they had done. He had listened to their teaching. In the slums of the cities men and women and children, made in the image of God, were being driven down into hell for all eternity, and they had no helping hand stretched out for them. (Cries of 'It is false,' and interruption.) It was a disgrace to the Christian ministry of England. (Loud cries of dissent.)

Finally, 'amid some confusion Mr Keir Hardie left the platform'.[2]

In the discussion that followed, some speakers repudiated Hardie's charges and others agreed that they were true. The *British Weekly* warned the churches that they were 'dangerously near a permanent cleavage with the leaders of the new democracy. A word just now might precipitate it, and once effected, it would be the task of generations to bring together what had been rent asunder.'[3] Sympathy for Hardie among the delegates increased when it was proved by a shorthand account of his Labour Church address that Leach had misinterpreted him, and when Leach offered only, in the words of the *British Weekly*, 'a mean and shabby apology'.[4] As a consequence of this incident Leach was converted from a severely evangelical view of society to such keen sympathy with social reform that he joined the Independent Labour Party and began to advocate nationalization of railways, mines and land.[5] The encounter with Hardie

[1] *Labour Prophet*, Nov. 1892, p. 85.
[2] *British Weekly*, 13 Oct. 1892, p. 401.
[3] *Ibid.* p. 395.
[4] *Ibid.*, 20 Oct. 1892, p. 411.
[5] *Ibid.*, 1 Nov. 1894, p. 24.

also helped Congregational leaders to take a less academic interest in poverty. A few weeks after the Bradford meeting, the committee of the Union and the Social Questions Committee arranged a conference between Congregational and Labour members of parliament (including Hardie). After this conference the committee of the Union issued to the Congregational churches a statement which not only proclaimed a general duty to see that righteousness prevailed in industrial disputes, but made practical recommendations about sweating, sanitation and housing.[1] In 1893 an assembly of the Union agreed to open a fund for the relief of distress among workers' families caused by the prolonged and bitter dispute between coal miners and their employers. This meeting also carried by a large majority a resolution (moved by Fleming Williams and seconded by Bruce Wallace) saying that 'the rights of humanity must always take precedence of those of property,' and that 'mining royalties and profits made out of the labours of men receiving wages inadequate for the support of themselves and their families are obviously inconsistent with righteousness and fraternity. . . .'[2] This statement and the relief fund (for which £1,247 was collected) constituted the most positive gesture of sympathy with working-class demands which the Union had ever made.

In the remaining years of the century social questions were neither ignored at assemblies of the Union nor discussed as fully as in 1893. The chairman in 1894 told Independents that they should assert the authority of Christ's law over the conscience of society, but reminded them that the church's first duty was to save the soul, not the body. In 1897 a resolution urged both parties in industrial disputes to go to arbitration, and in 1899 F. H. Stead, a minister who was playing a leading part in the national campaign for old age pensions, successfully introduced a resolution declaring it 'the duty of all Christian citizens to endeavour to secure more honourable provision than is now made for the support of the aged poor.'[3] In 1904 the chairman of the Union observed a widespread belief among Congregationalists that one mission of the churches was 'the producing of conditions, economic and social, which are just

[1] A. Peel, *These Hundred Years*, p. 333.
[2] *Congregational Year Book* (1894), p. 25.
[3] *Ibid.* (1900), p. 8.

and favourable to godly and righteous life, the establishing of the Kingdom of God wherein are political righteousness, social peace and religious joy.'[1]

Ordinary Nonconformist worshippers, belonging mostly to those middle classes who had every reason to believe in self-help, were perhaps unlikely to attend to their pastor as closely as he would wish when he talked about the duty of Christians to support efforts to remove social inequalities. Among ministers zealous for reform, there must have been many who could say, as Keeble did of his congregation at Chester: 'the people are . . . hard to "enthuse", lukewarm discontented and reactionary. They have no care for social Christianity.'[2]

It has sometimes been argued that the relationship between laity and ministry in Nonconformity made it peculiarly difficult for a Nonconformist preacher to express social attitudes which were not acceptable to middle-class worshippers. According to Halévy, the law which made dissenting congregations put their places of worship in the hands of trustees helped the chapel to become a plutocracy; for the trustees, Halévy suggests, were normally chosen from the influential members of the congregation, and the pastor could not easily risk offending them.[3] When a minister's income depended largely on the size of his congregation and the generosity of its richer members, the danger of antagonizing his flock was plain. Even Edward Miall, the most staunch defender of voluntaryism in religion, admitted that the fear of losing goodwill tempted preachers 'to proffer palatable rather than salutary doctrine,' and allowed that there was some truth in the anti-Nonconformist squib:

> The pulpit's laws the pulpit's patrons give,
> And men who live to preach must preach to live.[4]

'Mark Rutherford' showed how powerful a deacon could be in the Congregational polity, and described one who wrote (anonymously) to a newspaper: 'I fail to see how a minister's usefulness can be stimulated if he sets class against class. Like

[1] A. Goodrich, quoted in J. W. Grant, *Free Churchmanship in England, 1870–1940*, p. 173.
[2] S. E. Keeble, Note-Book, 1891.
[3] E. Halévy, *A History of the English People in the Nineteenth Century*, I. 409.
[4] E. Miall, *Views of the Voluntary Principle* (1845), p. 109.

the widows in affliction of old, he should keep himself pure and unspotted from the world.'[1]

The control which the laity could exercise over their minister was a source of pride to many Nonconformists. A Wesleyan minister offered it as a criticism of the Church of England that 'the clergy are independent of the people, being neither nominated nor supported by them.'[2] He was not referring to the *secular* opinions of ministers; but the formal and actual authority which Nonconformist systems of government gave the laity might be invoked on any issue, and might be expected to inhibit a minister from expressing advanced secular opinions as well as to keep his behaviour spotless and his doctrine sound. A Labour politician recalling his experience of agitation in a suburb of London late in the century said that the labour movement had public support from several Church of England clergymen but none from Nonconformist ministers. 'The clergymen of the Church of England,' he suggested, 'were in a position of independence compared with that of Nonconformist ministers, whose livelihood might depend upon the approval of a few perhaps intolerant and uninformed chapel notables.'[3] There were indeed Nonconformist ministers who resigned, or were forced to retire, on account of difference of political and social opinion with their congregations. In 1896 Richard Westrope left his Congregational pulpit in Leeds because some leading laymen found him too radical.[4] Richard Roberts, another Congregational minister, was reported in 1901 to be unable to get a church because of his socialistic views.[5] Some other ministers had small congregations as a punishment for radicalism. A Nonconformist reported with pleasure in 1896 that in a certain large town there were two young dissenting ministers, one who 'preached Christ and Him crucified' and the other who 'adopted and proclaimed almost exclusively the views and demands of the new Trades Unionism': one chapel was now filled and the other almost empty. 'The preacher of

[1] [W. H. White], *The Autobiography of Mark Rutherford* (15th ed., n. d.), p. 43. The novel was first published in 1881.

[2] T. Jackson, *Recollections of my Own Life and Times* (1873), p. 503.

[3] Lord Snell, *Men, Movements and Myself* (2nd. ed., 1938), p. 117. For a similar judgment see H. M. Pelling, *op. cit.* p. 132.

[4] *Labour Prophet*, April 1896, p. 58.

[5] *Labour Church Record*, Jan. 1901, p. 1.

Jesus Christ has large congregations, and the preacher of Socialism has small congregations.'[1] Radical Nonconformists complained that their brothers with orthodox social principles could fill sermons with conservative propaganda and never be rebuked, while the few who expressed advanced views were accused of bringing secular politics into the House of God. R. F. Horton found in the 1890s that some of his flock at Hampstead objected to his mild social radicalism. 'Every time I pleaded the cause of the people,' he said,

> the wealthy employers and successful professional men charged me with introducing politics into the pulpit. It had no effect in silencing me, but it constantly depleted the Church of that class which used to be the support of suburban Christianity.[2]

At about the same time Charles Leach, the minister who had followed his attack on Keir Hardie by joining the I.L.P., was persuaded by pressure of his deacons to leave it again. 'And so we have lost our only D.D.,' said Hardie wryly.[3]

There may well have been other radicals who were silenced by the prospect of a dwindling congregation, and incipient rebels who convinced themselves that their congregations had the right not to hear sermons on secular affairs. 'I had a feeling,' wrote J. Guinness Rogers, 'that those who came expecting to be instructed in the Gospel of Christ, had some right to complain if they were treated to a political harangue.' Rogers himself dreaded 'the conversion of the pulpit into a rostrum for any schemes for political or social reforms,' and believed that a minister was seldom penalized by any congregation on account of his opinions, 'except by some compromising action of his own.'[4] The exception rather weakened his point. Many congregations might use their authority judiciously, but if they chose to exercise it arbitrarily the minister could not stop them.

In the connexional organization of Methodism a minister was less at the mercy of a particular congregation than his Independent brother. But as R. F. Wearmouth remarks: 'Laymen always comprised the majority in quarterly meetings,

[1] *British Weekly*, 10 Sept. 1896, p. 322.

[2] R. F. Horton, *op. cit.* p. 83.

[3] *Labour Leader*, 15 Dec. 1894, p. 2. In 1910 Leach defeated Victor Grayson and became M.P. for Colne Valley.

[4] J. G. Rogers, *An Autobiography* (1903), pp. 132, 134.

trustee meetings, and leaders' meetings; regardless of the authority of the chairman of the meeting (the Superintendent Minister) the verdict of the laymen predominated.'[1] Samuel Keeble was advised by his superintendent minister at Sheffield in the 1890's to convey his message more moderately because wealthy trustees were alarmed by his preaching on social questions. The itinerancy rule, moreover, meant that a prudent Wesleyan minister had to consider the effect of his preaching not only on his present congregation but on the stewards of those who might be wondering whether to ask him for his next three years. A steward from Highgate decided after an evening's conversation with Keeble that he was too radical to be invited.

But if the experience of Keeble illustrates some of the pressures acting on a Nonconformist minister, it shows also that they could be resisted. To the superintendent at Sheffield Keeble said simply: 'My message has been entrusted to me.' 'Well, if you feel like that, dear brother,' the senior minister replied, 'you must fulfil your trust and deliver your message. God bless you.'[2] Although his opinions put off one congregation and possibly others from asking him to be their minister, Keeble never lacked a choice of invitations when his three years in a circuit were up. Horton's experience among Congregationalists suggests that a minister whose social opinions shocked pew-holders might go on expressing them and even gain moral support from colleagues elsewhere: the London Congregational Union elected him to its chair in 1896, and so did the Congregational Union of England and Wales in 1903. Not many of those Nonconformist ministers who ignored or opposed social radicals did so because the laity intimidated them. Most of them were expressing their own genuine convictions.

Nor was the contrast between Nonconformity and the Church of England on this score as vivid as it has appeared to some observers. 'I wish I could say that the security of church incumbents made them visibly more independent,' wrote a clergyman who went around campaigning on behalf of the Agricultural Labourers' Union. Clergymen used to applaud

[1] R. F. Wearmouth, *Methodism and the Struggle of the Working Classes, 1850–1900*, p. 116.

[2] M. L. Edwards, *Samuel Keeble, Pioneer and Prophet*, p. 25.

him stealthily, he said, and explain that they shrank from public expressions of sympathy with social radicalism 'for the sake of parish and of poor on whom their independence would be visited.'[1] They were afraid, in other words, that wealthy parishioners would stop contributing to the church. In country parishes there was a long tradition of deference to the opinions of the squire. In certain town churches too, one layman had the authority of a squire and might use it if the clergyman's attitude to social relationships appeared offensive. A devout Anglican in 1901 told the story of a proprietary chapel in Mayfair whose incumbent asked his richest parishioner whether she could manage with fewer footmen and give what she saved in wages to a fund for the sick and poor. The lady stopped contributing to the expenses of the chapel, and the incumbent was forced to resign.[2] In towns, it was unusual for one worshipper to have such power. But in thousands of parishes a single layman had, quite officially, the right to choose the incumbent. The patron of a living had in his own hands much of the power held by a Nonconformist congregation, and it is a safe guess that most individual patrons – who together had the right of presentation to more than half the livings in England – were Tories. A clergyman who believed that his social views may have kept him out of a living had of course no redress; and as the biographer of the rebellious Stewart Headlam remarked, 'Livings are not usually the reward of the unsubmissive. . . .'[3]

Most clergymen in the Church of England were not incumbents, but curates with far less security. When Conrad Noel was a fiery young curate in Cheshire in 1894 his socialist lectures on Sunday afternoons led the churchwardens to complain to the bishop and the bishop to ask: 'Are you prepared to make yourself acceptable to your congregation?' Noel replied that he was not, and found himself unemployed.[4] It was clear that the bishop had interfered here to execute the will of worshippers. In other cases, it was difficult to say whether a bishop or a rector who dismissed a curate was acting on his own initiative or at the request of parishioners. The bishop could

[1] W. Tuckwell, *Reminiscences of a Radical Parson* (1905), p. 27.
[2] G. W. E. Russell, *An Onlooker's Notebook* (1902), p. 178.
[3] F. G. Bettany, *op. cit.* p. 5.
[4] C. Noel, *op. cit.*, p. 45.

dismiss a curate at will, as Stewart Headlam complained. Headlam lost four curacies, the fourth for 'being political.'[1] Neither Noel nor Headlam was silenced by being removed. But curates in general were situated no better than Nonconformist ministers to escape penalties for radical opinions.

There were curates and vicars and even bishops who in varying degrees were friendly to the forces of social radicalism; and if it was true, as some people said, that such friendliness was commoner in the Church of England than among Nonconformists, the difference cannot be accounted for in terms of differences in the relationship between clergy and laity, or in terms of other variations in formal structure. It could be imprudent for clergymen in the Church of England to support radical schemes for social reform, and it was by no means impossible for Nonconformist ministers to do so.

The Evangelical Schism

The crucial distinction within English Christianity on social questions was not denominational but doctrinal: it was evangelicalism, not Nonconformity, that offered a peculiar resistance to social radicalism. The sternest Christian opponents of reform were those who believed most completely that body and soul were antithetical, and that the duty of a Christian was to reject the world, not to sanctify it. This was the religion of 'Mark Rutherford's' 'Reverend Broad' who believed:

> we are so constituted, with a body, and with fleshly appetites, that we must be in the world; but we must be separate from it and its controversies, which are so unimportant compared with our eternal welfare.[2]

The heart of Joseph Parker's objection to social Christianity was essentially the same notion. 'We shall never get right by socialistic theories, anarchical programmes, and a certain power of befooling the trustful classes,' he told his congregation: 'we can only get right by "Jesus Christ, and Him crucified." '[3] This last phrase was a popular one among Christians who believed

[1] Headlam's words, quoted in *ibid.* p. 63.

[2] [W. H. White], *The Revolution in Tanner's Lane* (4th ed., n. d.), p. 336. The novel was first published in 1887.

[3] *British Weekly*, 4 Oct. 1889, p. 370.

that social reform was one thing and spiritual religion another. The evangelical schism between soul and body, between the spirit and the world, appeared in the Church of England as well as in Nonconformity. Readers of the *Record* and the *Rock*, and supporters for the Church Pastoral-Aid Society, adhered to doctrines no different from those of evangelical Nonconformists. Indeed, it was R. W. Dale's opinion that to extreme evangelicals, theology mattered far more than denomination. 'They own no allegiance to the Church to which they happen to belong,' said Dale. '. . . They are conscious of nearer kinship to men of other communions who share their special religious "views" or who are engaged in similar religious work.'[1] Christians of this sort, some taking communion in the Church of England and others in Nonconformist churches, had founded (in 1835) and were still conducting the London City Mission, whose missionaries, according to its official magazine in 1888, were doing good work 'battling with Socialism, in its violent as well as in its more moderate and constitutional form.'[2]

In the Church of England, however, evangelicalism was less mighty than in Nonconformity. Many Churchmen believed that the evangelical tradition denied the true role of the priesthood and sacraments, and that it exalted the Bible unduly at the expense of church tradition; others found evangelical doctrines crude and anti-intellectual. However else men of Broad and High opinions differed, they could agree that the Evangelicals, preoccupied with the salvation of the individual soul, neglected cardinal truths of Christianity. Many of them, having listened eagerly when Maurice told them that Christian Socialism was a corollary of non-evangelical religion, went on to crusade for social reform in the name of Christianity believing (if Broad) that any service to humanity was a truly religious act or (if High) that a sacramental faith knew no gulf between spirit and matter. Broad or High Church principles did not necessarily make a man sympathetic with the campaign for social reform, but they insulated his mind against it far less effectively than evangelical principles. As always in the Church of England, moreover, there were many clergymen who were not committed wholly

[1] J. W. Grant, *op. cit.* pp. 99–100.

[2] *London City Mission Magazine*, Jan. 1888, quoted in *Christian Socialist*, Feb. 1888, p. 26.

to any one theological party, and who were prepared to find that the truth lay in more than one direction.

In Nonconformity, on the other hand, evangelicalism was not one of several respectable traditions: it was synonymous with orthodoxy. Nobody could honestly call himself a follower of Wesley who disavowed the doctrines of the evangelical revival; nor could a Congregationalist or a Baptist reject them either, unless he was prepared to ally himself theologically with Unitarians. It was a common and reasonable feeling among Nonconformists that as spiritual communities they owed too much to the evangelical revival to tolerate any disloyalty to it. Any apparent denigration of evangelicalism could appear a lethal threat: for where else were Nonconformists to find inspiration?

This fear was illustrated at an assembly of the Congregational Union in 1890, when a special committee appointed to study the condition of Congregationalism submitted its report. It considered the difficulty of reconciling an evangelical faith with a proper concern for social justice, and in the course of this discussion made the following judgment:

> It was the defect of the honoured leaders of the Evangelical Revival, as it has remained the defect of that great movement, that it disparaged and belittled the life on earth, except so far as it was a preparation for the life above. . . . It was not sufficiently considered that the life which Christ gives . . . being a Divine power . . . is to rule and transform every relation in which its possessor stands to his fellow man. When this sacred leaven is boldly and thoroughly mixed with the whole mass, it will not be said that religion is on the outside of practical life.[1]

Although its tone was far more respectful, this passage expressed much the same criticism of evangelical Christianity as Maurice had offered. The whole passage was deleted by a vote of the Congregational Union assembly before the report was circulated to the churches, because the majority were unwilling to agree that they must revise the doctrines of the revival in order to reduce the tension between evangelicalism and socialism.

Those Nonconformists who were conspicuously keen for social reform had usually exposed themselves to mental in-

[1] *Congregational Year Book* (1891), p. 33.

fluences outside the evangelical tradition. In the Church of England, the revolt against evangelicalism had been initiated by the theological conservatives of Oxford. In Nonconformity theological radicals were in the vanguard. The spectacle, late in the century, of near agnostic pastors and ritualist parsons speaking to the same Labour Church or writing together in the *Christian Socialist* is an odd one, until it is realized that each group was anti-evangelical, and that by different routes, each had come to adopt religious principles which made the material world seem important, and which could therefore lie easily alongside some degree of socialism. The liberal and the Catholic in theology could each believe far more readily than the evangelical that his faith was congruous with social radicalism.

Many of the Nonconformist social radicals – Hughes, Horton, Lidgett, and Keeble, for example – were by no means close to agnosticism or even to Unitarianism. Each of these men, however, assimilated ideas hitherto foreign to the evangelical tradition. 'It is humiliating,' said the *Methodist Times* in a revealing essay on 'A Cultured Ministry', 'that we should have to resort to the literature of other communities for our theological food.'[1] Hughes himself had a remarkably rich mental diet. Maurice and Westcott had both impressed him, and an accident of pastoral appointment brought him to the Oxford circuit in time to hear the lectures given by T. H. Green just before the philosopher died. Green's last public lecture was to a small society of Methodists. Hughes once remarked that the words of Green had sunk into his soul.[2] Of few Nonconformists could it be said, as Scott Holland said of Hughes: 'Everything that told upon the generation of Churchmen who grew up in Oxford in the 'Sixties told upon him also'[3] Horton, the Hughes of Independency, was rare among Nonconformist ministers in having been educated at Oxford; and his zeal for social reform can be traced to his years at the university, 'where Toynbee', as he said in his autobiography, 'was held to be the herald of a better day. . . .'[4] A. M. Fairbairn, another Congregational

[1] *Methodist Times*, 5 Feb. 1885, p. 84.
[2] D. P. Hughes, *op. cit.* p. 134.
[3] H. Scott Holland, *A Bundle of Memories*, p. 145.
[4] R. F. Horton, *op. cit.* p. 81.

leader who recommended a greater tolerance for working-class aspirations, had been first interested in economics by reading *Unto This Last.*[1] An education at University College, London, introduced Lidgett to a wider intellectual world than the theological colleges knew. His tribute to Maurice has been quoted already. He also acknowledged a debt to Green, and from 1887 to 1890, the years immediately before his foundation of the Bermondsey Settlement, he was a minister at Cambridge, having close relationships with undergraduates and teachers. Keeble, to his great regret, attended no university; but his resolute self-education led him to the untheological Ruskin and the unchristian Marx.

These men and others represented what was sometimes called 'the new evangelicalism' – an attempt within Nonconformity to come to terms with secular thought (on scientific, historical and moral matters as well as on social relationships) while standing firmly behind the essential evangelical affirmations about sin and salvation. The task required a delicate compromise. Moreover, Hughes and Horton and those who stood with them had to contend with traditionalists who agreed with the intelligent, anti-intellectual Charles Spurgeon that the battle of the age was 'the truth of God *versus* the inventions of men.'[2] Neither the dialogue between old and new within the minds of 'new evangelicals', nor the debate between them and their less radical opponents, had ended by 1900.

The Catholics

Of all Catholics in England, the one most deeply involved in efforts to improve the material circumstances of the working classes was the Cardinal Archbishop, Manning. His successor Cardinal Vaughan and Lytton Strachey agreed in interpreting Manning's alliance with social reformers as a sign of senile decay.[3] This is a facile view. Nor does it take the matter much further to explain it simply as the fruit of compassion. There

[1] J. W. Grant, *op. cit.* p. 173.

[2] W. B. Glover, *op. cit.* p. 164.

[3] For Vaughan's opinion see *Nineteenth Century*, Feb. 1896, p. 252. Strachey's interpretation is not explicit, but it is unmistakable. See *Eminent Victorians* (Penguin, 1948), p. 122.

were many compassionate Christians in every denomination who did not defend trade unions or arbitrate in strikes. Certainly Manning showed compassion; but why in just this way?

Manning had seen his church gain tolerance, and towards the end of his life his great hope was that it would also gain popularity. In 1890, when it was obvious that Vaughan would be the next archbishop, Manning wrote to him, reflecting on the lessons of the dock strike: 'Is it not plain that if only we are prudent and serve the Commonwealth, everything is open? . . . The people are not against us if only we are with them. . . . Go on boldly and mix with the English people.'[1] In the same year he wrote, in a memorandum on the failings and opportunities of the church in England, that Catholics must be 'prompt and foremost in working with all who are labouring to relieve every form of human suffering, sorrow and misery. If we come forward gladly and usefully the people of this country are visibly glad to receive us among them.' These gestures, he believed, should be made in the spirit of Catholicism but not necessarily in its name: 'Our faith must go with us and govern us everywhere, but except on the rarest occasions it need not be proclaimed.'[2]

Manning's attitude and activities were part of a general movement among Catholics in many countries. Ketteler in Germany, Meyer in Austria, De Mun in France, Gibbons in the United States and Moran in Australia all wished to identify the Church with the suffering classes. An early historian of this tendency suggested that Catholics were especially inclined to sympathize with social radicalism in those countries where Protestant opposition to them was strongest, and where a popular alliance was seen therefore as a shrewd form of ecclesiastical competition.[3] Nevertheless, Manning's desire for such an alliance in England owed little or nothing to overseas example. Few English Catholics were interested in the work of such men as Ketteler.[4] Manning expressed sympathy with De Mun,

[1] J. G. Snead-Cox, *The Life of Cardinal Vaughan*, II. 476.

[2] E. S. Purcell, *Life of Cardinal Manning*, II. 775–6.

[3] F. S. Nitti, *Catholic Socialism* (1895), esp. p. 314.

[4] None of Ketteler's social writings were translated into English. Among English Catholics only one writer, C. S. Devas, showed much familiarity with the Catholic Socialist movement in Europe; there were references to Ketteler and others in his *Groundwork of Economics* (1883). There was a favourable, though unexcited, review in the *Month*, Jan. 1896, pp. 144–5, of Kannengieser's *Ketteler et Organisation Sociale en Allemagne* (1894).

approved of the Swiss Catholic Socialist Decurtius, and supported Cardinal Gibbons at Rome in his defence of the Knights of Labour;[1] but his zeal to co-operate with the suffering was not learned abroad: it was his own response to English conditions.

Unlike Ketteler, Meyer and De Mun, Manning tried to draw up no specifically Catholic programme of social reform. He was content to offer his support to whatever programme, originated by secular radicals, seemed to him worthy. Socialism as a creed he deplored; but he disliked the use of the word 'socialism' to discredit proper and moderate attempts at reform. 'When the Corn Laws were to be abolished,' he said, 'it was called robbery! When the Irish Church was to be disestablished it was called confiscation! When the world of labour is to be protected by law it is called Socialism!'[2] Among English social radicals, Manning believed, were many who were not really socialists, who wanted reasonable reforms which the church could bless, and who might in return look at the church with a new sympathy.

'They will trust you,' Manning told Vaughan, 'but not my brother Benson.'[3] He was alluding in particular to the Archbishop of Canterbury's unhappy role in the dock strike, and more generally to his conviction that the Catholic Church, partly on account of its historic isolation from English society, now had an advantage over all others in competing for popular allegiance. The Church of England, he believed, was so entangled with the state, and with wealth and privilege, that its every appeal to the masses rang hollow. Nor was Nonconformity, as he saw it, in any better position:

> The public feeling of the country is not and never will be with either Anglicanism or Dissent. It is not irreligious, the leaders of the Labour Unions are religious men; but its Unionism and public action is outside of all religion. It therefore is ready to listen and even to be led by a Catholic, if only he has their confidence; and that confidence is created by what we *are* chiefly, and by what we *do* in sympathy with the people.[4]

[1] Manning to De Mun, *Catholic Times*, 6 Feb. 1891, p. 5; F. S. Nitti, *op. cit*. p. 251; E. S. Purcell, *op. cit.* II. 651.

[2] *Tablet*, 17 Jan. 1891, p. 100.

[3] J. G. Snead-Cox, *op. cit.* I. 476.

[4] E. S. Purcell, *op. cit.* II. 637.

Manning's social policy was the fruit not only of compassion and calculation, but of a personal sensitivity to the common prejudice that a servant of Rome was not quite an Englishman. Newman had been similarly sensitive: nothing in the onslaught by Charles Kingsley which provoked his *Apologia* caused more pain than the charge that Newman had abandoned his national identity when he forswore the national religion. A newspaper thought it worth noting that Cardinal Wiseman, although a Catholic, was 'thoroughly English in feature and in accent. . . .'[1] The view that Catholics were aliens was expressed most tersely by Archibishop Benson, who described the Catholic church in England as 'the Italian mission'. The charge had just enough truth in it to hurt many Catholics – and especially converts, who had passed, in Manning's own words, 'from the broad stream of the English Commonwealth into the narrow community of English Catholics . . .' a community which in some ways was *not* English.[2] 'What a number there are,' wrote Manning's successor at Westminster, 'who every day enter the fold of the Catholic Church and find themselves shy and self-conscious, as foreigners in a strange land.'[3] For Manning, to participate in social controversy was to make a personal return to England. 'No man,' he wrote in 1881, 'could have been more exiled and shut out of English life private and public than I was thirty years ago. I have returned to it in some remote ways; but if I have any hold on the English people it will be only as I have gained it by mixing among them in their good works, and by writing.'[4] When Manning was asked, during the dock strike: 'How did you feel when the men cheered you?' he is said to have replied: 'An Englishman.'[5]

Among Catholic leaders only E. G. Bagshawe, Bishop of Nottingham, was close to Manning in his attitude to social questions. In a series of pastoral letters during 1883 and 1884, Bagshawe invoked Christian doctrines to denounce the cruelty of English society. He blamed the Reformation for beginning the age of pauperism by its plunder of religious agencies which

[1] W. Ward, *The Life and Times of Cardinal Wiseman* (1897), II. 49.
[2] E. S. Purcell, *op. cit.* II. 631.
[3] H. Vaughan, preface to Anon., *The Catholic Church from Within* (1901), p. vi.
[4] E. S. Purcell, *op. cit.* II. 677.
[5] *New Era*, 15 Feb. 1892, p. 29.

had provided social relief and by its failure to offer any adequate substitute. Once the authority of the true church had been overthrown, he said, the way was clear in England for the inhuman laws of political economy to rule unchallenged by 'the Divine precepts of justice and mercy. . . .' Bagshawe declared that the state had 'a duty to foster, regulate, and protect the industry of its subjects, and to defend the poor from being ruined by the tyrannous caprices of wealth.'[1] This was the tone of voice which Manning hoped would make the masses more sympathetic to Rome.

But to an eminent layman, Edwin de Lisle, Bagshawe's ideas seemed 'socialistic and subversive.' In a published attack on the Bishop's pastoral letters, de Lisle declared that he was expressing no mere private anger, but

> the intense feeling of many of the most learned, devoted, and public-spirited men of this diocese, who are beginning, against their wills and against the highest instincts which they have inherited together with the Catholic Fatih, to perceive in the modern disloyal sentiments of some of their co-religionists in these Islands, an apostacy from the Christian frame of mind. . . .

Bagshawe's sympathies, according to de Lisle, lay 'with men whose covetous eyes and longing hearts are fixed upon acquiring their neighbours' property at home . . .' and his remarks constituted 'an attack upon the landlords and tradesmen of England. . . .' At a public meeting of protest, de Lisle even hinted that if priests were to turn radical, the laity – 'we, at least we who are Tories' – might revolt.[2] Yet Bagshawe's views were no more extreme than those of his Cardinal Archbishop. Here was a great obstacle to Manning's plan for a popular alliance. In approving policies which were designed to benefit the poor, he was not increasing his popularity among those upper-class Catholics who disliked him already on other grounds.

The main Catholic journals generally stood for social attitudes more conservative than Manning's. The *Tablet*, which in principle he controlled, but which in practice often expressed opinions

[1] E. G. Bagshawe, *Mercy and Justice to the Poor* (1885), pp. 5, 7, 12, 21. This was made up of three pastoral letters issued in 1883 and 1884. See also his Lenten pastoral of 1891, summarized in the *Catholic Times*, 13 Feb. 1891, p. 5.

[2] E. de Lisle, *Pastoral Politics* (1885), pp. 4–6.

different from his own (especially on Home Rule), from time to time paid lip-service to Manning's vision of a church united with the masses; and once it was even prepared to write cordially of H. M. Hyndman as a man who loved the poor.[1] But when it considered social questions at length, the *Tablet* exposed a philosophy very different from Manning's. During riots in the West End in February 1886, the *Tablet* noted not that the demonstrators were out of work, but that they were a godless mob.[2] 'The poor we have always with us: and shall have always,' said the journal in 1885. 'But here comes in Christianity declaring the blessedness of poverty, of hunger, of thirst, of all the ills of life, as the instruments of perfection in this world, to be crowned by supreme rewards in the world to come.'[3] This note was familiar also to readers of the *Month* and the *Dublin Review*. When a priest in the former journal reflected on *The Bitter Cry of Outcast London*, it was to suggest as a solution that England should 'reinstate the Vicar of Christ in his rightful place. . . .'[4] In the *Dublin Review*, the author of an essay entitled 'Social Disturbances – their cause and cure' declared that inequality was a law more universal than gravity, that true Christians who suffered would always remember that Christ suffered far more, and that the hope of immortality was the one sure protection against revolutionary violence.[5] There were Catholic journals more radical than these – notably the *Catholic Times* and the *Weekly Herald* – but none that campaigned for Manning's grand alliance. Despite his high authority, Manning appeared to be having little success in communicating his social enthusiasm.

In 1891, less than two years before Manning died, there came a proclamation on the social question from a higher authority still. Pope Leo XIII's encyclical *Rerum Novarum* was written by a man who had begun his tenure of the papal throne by issuing an encyclical condemning socialism, communism and nihilism, and who now (responding to pleas from social reformers of immaculate orthodoxy, including Manning) agreed

[1] *Tablet*, 27 Jan. 1883, p. 121.
[2] *Ibid.*, 13 Feb. 1886, p. 000.
[3] *Ibid.*, 10 Jan. 1885, p. 43.
[4] A. J. Christie, 'Catholic Reform', *Month*, Jan. 1884, p. 41.
[5] J. S. Vaughan, in *Dublin Review*, Oct. 1886, pp. 335–51.

to bless some sorts of reformist activity, yet without withdrawing anything in his earlier statement. Moreover, the universal church addressed in *Rerum Novarum* faced a different political and social situation in each country. Every general remark about the State must be applicable where Catholicism was the established religion, where it faced a hostile secular arm, and where the government was indifferent. Every broad reference to working-class organizations must cover Marxist bodies in Germany, Catholic trade unions in Belgium, and the American Knights of Labour. For these reasons the argument of *Rerum Novarum* could not be simple. The Pope's method at the most delicate points was to state a thesis and an antithesis and to leave it at that. To suffer and endure, he observed, was the lot of humanity; but a remedy must be found for the wretchedness of the poor. The state should protect the poor from exploitation by the rich; but on the whole the duty of a rich man to give what he did not need to the poor was a duty of Christian charity, not of justice. Strikes injured a society; but they were often caused by bad working conditions. Not for nothing did Pius XI, in an encyclical celebrating and restating *Rerum Novarum*, call Leo XIII 'the prudent pontiff'.

The encyclical was not intended, despite what some of its Catholic and non-Catholic readers said, to provide a set of rules from which a specific Catholic policy on detailed issues could be deduced. Its purpose was rather to proclaim limits within which the church was prepared to tolerate social controversy, and outside which lay forbidden country. Unbridled capitalist exploitation was condemned, and so at the opposite extreme was community of goods. Above all, the world was warned against revolutionary and anti-Christian associations. Within the boundaries set by his prohibitions, Leo XIII was concerned less with programmes than with the principles that should be recognized if the two broad classes in modern industrial society were to realize their proper, symmetrical relationship. The principle mentioned most often in *Rerum Novarum* was the necessity of true religion as a foundation for any right relationship between capital and labour.

Interpretations of *Rerum Novarum* could differ greatly from each other without contradicting anything in it. In America, according to one historian, Catholics 'stressed, even exaggerated, its condemnation of Socialism, but largely ignored its positive programme of Christian social reform.'[1] In Australia Cardinal Moran hailed it as a papal blessing for the young labour movement and an indictment of the excesses of capital ism.[2] Clearly the manner in which the encyclical was received in a country depended on the degree and direction of interest among the Catholics of that country in the situation of the working classes.

In England, all Catholic journals printed the encyclical in full or paraphrased it at length during May and June 1891. This was rather a tribute to the authority of *any* papal encyclical than a clue to opinions about the message of this one. Next came essays by English Catholics on the encyclical. Manning, in the *Dublin Review*, followed carefully the arguments and the actual words of the Pope, introducing the encyclical rather than interpreting it. The Bishop of Newport and Menevia, J. C. Hedley, who had translated *Rerum Novarum* into English, wrote about it at length in the *Tablet*. He described it as 'a proclamation of Individualism', and declared: 'there are few documents in which the note of true Conservatism is more firmly sounded than in this Encyclical.'[3] Apart from Hedley's article, the most prominent interpreter in the *Tablet* was a writer who contributed a series of letters over the name 'A Liberal', and who found it pleasing and significant that the Pope said nothing about votes for the working classes.[4] From the Pope's words about keeping the Sabbath holy he inferred that Catholics must oppose any strike begun on a Sunday, and from various other remarks he concluded that to approve strikes on any week-day was equally incompatible with reverence to the Holy Father. In the whole of *Rerum Novarum*, he concluded, 'It is impossible to discover any space which the Labour Movement could occupy.'[5] This view of the encyclical was not challenged in the editorial or correspondence columns of the *Tablet*.

A rather different view was taken by Bishop Bagshawe, who

[1] A. J. Abell, 'The Reception of Leo XIII's Labor Encyclical in America, 1891–1919', *Review of Politics*, VII (1945), p. 481.

[2] P. F. Moran, *The Rights and Duties of Labour* (Sydney, 1891).

[3] *Tablet*, 6 June 1891, p. 885.

[4] *Ibid.*, 15 Aug. 1891, p. 261.

[5] *Ibid.*, 5 Sept. 1891, p. 381.

held up the encyclical as a confirmation from 'the universal teacher' of the very principles which he himself had been abused for holding a few years earlier.[1] In the *Catholic Times*, a weekly which often found the *Tablet* reactionary, the task of interpretation rested mainly on Dr W. Barry, a priest who wrote widely on social questions in Catholic journals. Barry denied that the Pope intended to bless individualism, and suggested that the sort of socialism condemned in *Rerum Novarum* was Continental communism, not the ameliorative movement which went by the name of socialism in England.[2] In the Jesuit journal the *Month* a priest wrote similarly, arguing that the Pope had rejected *laissez-faire* economics and had raised the subsistence of the worker above the free action of economic laws.[3] Another Catholic journal, the *Weekly Herald*, saw the encyclical as an impartial address to both sides in the social contest, a demonstration that 'neither side is wholly right nor wholly wrong'.[4] But it leaned a little to one side when it said: 'there is but slight difference, if any, between the ideas laid down by the Holy Father in his encyclical, and the views advanced by the author of "Progress and Poverty".'[5] The most enthusiastic and most radical reception given to *Rerum Novarum* by any Catholic journal was that of the Preston *Catholic News*, which declared that the Pope's words were a simple, lucid and irrefutable response to the lamentations of the oppressed. 'The amount of food for reflection which it provides is almost infinite,' said the journal, 'and we propose to devote a considerable space from time to time in discussing its chief heads, all-important as they are to Catholics everywhere.'[6] No such discussion ever appeared.

Among English Catholics, then, *Rerum Novarum* was all things to all men. With odd exceptions like the Catholic who was bold enough to say in Keir Hardie's paper that his Holiness did not know what he was talking about, none wished to challenge the limits which the Pope set to discussion of the

[1] *Catholic News*, 5 Dec. 1891, p. 2.
[2] *Catholic Times*, 19 June 1891, p. 5.
[3] H. Lucas, 'The Encyclical and the Economists', *Month*, July 1891, pp. 305–20.
[4] *Weekly Herald*, 5 June 1891, p. 5.
[5] *Ibid.*, 24 July 1891, p. 4.
[6] *Catholic News*, 6 June 1891, p. 4.

condition of the working classes.[1] On the right, Catholic Tories – contemporaries of Salisbury – were happy to agree that the State should alleviate the worst sufferings in an industrial society. On the left, there was no group of Catholics extreme enough to be discomfited by the Pope's words about revolutionary socialism. Nothing in the rest of the encyclical related precisely enough to English conditions to be taken as laying down a concrete policy which would guide the church in its relations with working-class movements. Barry and Hedley, Bagshawe and 'A Liberal', could each be satisfied that the Pope was with him.

Nor can it be argued that by 1900 the publication of *Rerum Novarum* aroused among Catholics in England previously unconcerned an interest in the condition of the poor. The encyclical was not mentioned once in Purcell's biography of Manning (1895), in Snead-Cox's life of Vaughan (1910), in the official short history of the Catholic Church in England issued by the Catholic Truth Society in 1895, or in Thureau-Dangin's *The English Catholic Revival in the Nineteenth Century* (first published in French, 1899). Purcell's omission alone might mean little, for his interest in social questions was slight. But it would be strange if the encyclical greatly stimulated among Catholics an interest in the working classes which was not noticed by the authors of *any* of the works named. Where *Rerum Novarum* was quoted, it was to support views held already. Possibly it strengthened the conviction with which these views were held; but some of these views were not easily compatible with each other. At the turn of the century, flatly conflicting interpretations were still being offered, one Catholic writer arguing that the Pope had rejected social democracy and another saying that he had justified a Fabian-type collectivism.[2]

Among social radicals *Rerum Novarum* seems to have caused no greater stir than it did in the secular press at large, where it was treated as less newsworthy than a concurrent baccarat case involving the Prince of Wales. Ben Tillett deplored the Pope's remarks on socialism, but found his argument in general more wholesome than could ever be expected from 'our Pro-

[1] J. J. H. Quinn in *Labour Leader*, 8 Dec. 1894, p. 11.

[2] C. S. Devas, *Social Questions and the Duty of Catholics* (1902), p. 25; R. E. Dell, *The Catholic Church and the Social Question* (1899), pp. 55–61.

testant prelates'.[1] The most sustained and probably the most widely read commentary on the encyclical written for working-class readers was by Robert Blatchford. 'In writing his Encyclical,' said Blatchford,

> the Pope seems to have been in two minds. He had evidently a desire to help the poor; but he had just as evidently a reluctance to interfere with the rich. . . . He pins his faith to the old rotten method of preaching mercy to the rich and patience to the poor. This method has been tried for nineteen centuries without success. Robbery and justice cannot be reconciled; the wolf and the sheep cannot be preached into amity. The Pope means well, but he is timid, and he does not understand the subject.

Although he was unimpressed by the Pope's statement, Blatchford admitted to having a soft spot for Catholic priests. 'I have met them in the slums engaged in works of mercy,' he wrote; 'I have met them in Ireland fighting for the people. I am satisfied that they are the most devoted and the most unselfish of all clergymen. . . .'[2] Tillett, moved by Manning's intervention in the dock strike, sensed in the Cardinal an 'authority which seems to attach to the priestly office only when it is exercised by Roman Catholics.'[3] Keir Hardie's paper the *Labour Leader* observed in 1894: 'there are many who think that the Roman Catholic is the most democratic of all the orthodox churches. . . .'[4] In so far as a feeling of this sort was common among labour leaders, Manning had certainly helped to arouse it – though it also had origins in a radical sympathy for Ireland and a romantic socialist image of the medieval church.

Radical sympathy with Rome never approached the enthusiasm of which Manning had dreamed. His successor, Vaughan, made no serious effort to stimulate it. 'Cardinal Vaughan,' said a critic not unfairly in 1894, 'thinks we can only enter the haven of social salvation in the bark of St Peter of Rome.'[5] The immediate problem of preserving the faith of working-class

[1] G. P. McEntee, *The Social Catholic Movement in Great Britain* (New York, 1927), p. 87.

[2] R. Blatchford, *Socialism: a Reply to the Encyclical of the Pope* (1893), pp. 9, 19.

[3] B. Tillett, *Memories and Reflections*, p. 147.

[4] *Labour Leader*, 22 Sept. 1894, p. 12.

[5] W. R. Sullivan, 'The Key to the Social Problem', *Westminster Review*, Feb. 1894, p. 128.

Catholics occupied him far more than the vague possibility of wooing their non-Catholic workmates. To this narrower task, however, Manning's social activities may have contributed more than Vaughan realized. His demonstration of sympathy with the poor may well have helped to check the leakage of Catholics even if it had no great effect on the working classes outside the church. Almost half the dockers involved in the strike of 1889 were Irishmen or the sons of Irishmen: and it is at least plausible to suggest that Manning's 'untiring devotion to the improvement of conditions for the working classes infused into the mass of the poor Irish Catholics . . . a sense of real confidence in the rulers of the English Church.'[1]

Social Reformers and the Churches

Among Labour and socialist leaders in 1900 it was normal to speak of the churches severely. To churchgoing Christians who were in sympathy with social radicalism, and who had seen general Christian opinion grow more tolerant towards it, the intensity of the criticism often seemed unfair. A Wesleyan suggested to Charles Booth that memory kept hostility alive even when present experience gave no cause for it. 'Working men are prejudiced,' he said, 'thinking of the churches as they were, not as they are.'[2] There was some evidence for this view. The constant attacks on formal Christianity in the *Labour Leader*, for example, had behind them a bitterness planted in Keir Hardie's soul long before, by a pillar of the church in Glasgow who had been cruel to him and his family when he was a child.

No Christian could deny, however, that a wary radical might still find in the churches plenty for his prejudice to feed on. The news that the Congregational Union had set up a fund for miners' families might not stick in his memory as long as the report that Joseph Parker had called Ben Tillett 'a man who has been accustomed to have it all his own way among the fools he was gulling. . . .'[3] He might be less stirred by seeing a few

[1] D. R. Gwynn, *A Hundred Years of Catholic Emancipation*, p. xviii.

[2] C. Booth, *Life and Labour of the People in London*. 3rd. series. *Religious Influences*, VII. 152.

[3] *British Weekly*, 4 Oct. 1889, p. 370.

clergymen on socialist platforms than by knowing that when some unemployed men entered St Paul's Cathedral, a detachment of police was sent to wait in the crypt.[1] If he attended the Working Men's Meeting of the Church Congress in 1898 expecting to hear speeches sympathetic to social reform, he heard the Archbishop of Canterbury say: 'forgive me if I have taken the opportunity of calling you to something higher than the mere conflict with the employing class.'[2] And if he wanted to be ribald at the expense of what he liked to call 'Churchianity' he could recite to himself the remark made by a curate at the Canterbury Diocesan Conference in 1886: 'We all of course have a natural bias towards that which is wrong, but this bias is greater and stronger in the lower orders than in the better educated.'[3] Such a radical might be grateful for the support of people in the churches who spoke up for social reform, but genuinely believe them to be exceptions. 'He was a wonderfully liberal man,' said Joseph Arch of James Fraser, Bishop of Manchester, 'considering his cloth and his lawn sleeves.'[4]

It is unlikely that the motions passed by denominational assemblies expressing an impartial concern about matters of social controversy won the churches much respect among their critics. After the Congregational Union passed one such resolution during an industrial dispute, a minister wrote angrily to the *British Weekly*:

> 'When two countries are at war, is it a friendly action on the part of a neighbouring power to send a vote of sympathy to both sides? . . . We mistake the working man if we think he can be taken in by such palpable expedients as were resorted to last week to run with the hare and hunt with the hounds. If we cannot side with him we had better leave him to fight his own battle.'[5]

To the thorough-going socialist it could easily appear that a lofty neutrality was the most radical attitude which could ever be expected from the churches, since the majority of people in them, both leaders and followers, were attached profoundly

[1] *Ibid.*, 7 April 1892, p. 383.
[2] *Church Congress Report* (1898), p. 181.
[3] J. B. Parker, *The Spiritual Work of the Church amongst Domestic Servants*, (1886), p. 4.
[4] J. Arch, *op. cit.* p. 222.
[5] 'A Younger Minister', in *British Weekly*, 18 May 1893, p. 50.

to capitalism. 'For the Christian,' said Archdeacon Cunningham, '. . . the property of his neighbours, rich or poor, is *sacred*, because these neighbours are God's stewards, and their possessions have been entrusted to them by Him.'[1] Some such statement would have been acceptable to most members of the Church of England. For the minority in the Church who opposed capitalism root and branch, Hensley Henson had an ironic reminder: they belonged, he pointed out, to a church endowed with tithes – a form of rent – and with a great accumulation of landed property. As members of the Church, Henson suggested, they were committed to the principle of private property.[2]

Mentally if not materially, Wesleyans and Congregationalists as a whole were committed no less deeply than members of the Church of England to maintaining private property. 'Let the working man and the capitalist be taught that they are "members of one another",' said a chairman of the Congregational Union,

> and let the relation between them be based on brotherly consideration of the common needs of life, and there will then be no cause to invite the rich man to 'howl', or the poor man to conspire and confiscate, under pretence of 'Social Equality'.[3]

As in this remark, so in every statement of the Congregational Union and the Wesleyan Conference on the relations between capital and labour, it was assumed that capitalism and social justice were wholly compatible. The churches could not therefore expect their policies to satisfy people who thought otherwise.

[1] *The Church of the People* (1894), p. 26.
[2] D. O. Wagner, *The Church of England and Social Reform since* 1854 (New York, 1930), p. 291.
[3] E. White, in *British Weekly*, 31 Oct. 1895, p. 20.

Epilogue

A CENTURY ago an Englishman casually referred to the 'upper and middle classes (those whom we term church-goers)'.[1] Charles Booth, comparing middle-class and working-class behaviour, wrote of 'the remarkable influence of class on religious observance in England'.[2] He did not find that every middle-class Englishman who went to church or chapel was an enthusiast; indeed, he could see on the faces of many worshippers 'blank indifference'. Such faces suggested that custom rather than inclination brought many people to church. 'The middle classes of England are most distinguished for church-going habits,' reflected a Congregational minister in 1867:

> It is one of their traditional proprieties to be associated with some place of worship. But there are not wanting indications that many come into all our churches who would not be found there, were they less influenced by the respectabilities; that many are there rather from habit and regard for appearances, than from real respect for Christ's ordinance of social worship and real desire for Christian edification.[3]

A lady who remembers upper-middle-class Edwardian Manchester has confessed: 'I would not like to say how many were assiduous because churchgoing was still a normal and mannerly activity of society and how many for more relevant reasons.'[4] Nevertheless, normal and mannerly it was. Since 1900 it has become less so, until the differences of religious behaviour between

[1] 'A Layman', *Why are Our Churches Closed?* (1858), p.23.

[2] C. Booth, *op. cit.* VII. 47.

[3] A. Mackennal, in A. P. Stanley and others, *Sermons Preached to Working People* (1867), p. 90.

[4] K. Chorley, *Manchester Made Them*, p. 171.

classes, though still discernible, are less striking than they were in Charles Booth's day. Interpreters of the decline often look now for explanations common to all social groups: such as the industrializing of pleasure through the cinema and its allies, the secularizing of the public mind by popular science, or the demoralizing effect of two world wars. The authors of such hypotheses do not realize that in the case of the working classes, any recent decline in attendance at worship has only accentuated a pattern that was clear long before 1900. In the modern urban environment, the act of worship did not become customary among most working-class people. The bishop who was in charge of the Church of England in East London said in 1880 that Churchmen should ask themselves 'how the very self-same motives which in the East keep people *from* Church, in the West bring them *to* Church'. The people of east London, he said, thought of religion 'as belonging to a wholly different class from themselves. . . .'[1] Estrangement of classes and popular indifference to religious practice had possibly gone farther in East London than anywhere else. Certainly there were northern and midland towns where social relations were more harmonious and the range of worshippers was far wider. But even in such places, the majority did not attend worship. W. D. Maclagan, the future Archbishop of York, was speaking of the whole nation when he observed that social convention kept working-class people from worshipping; it was the fashion among higher classes to go to church, but among the poorer classes 'the marked men are those who go to church – not those who stay away.'[2] That is an over-simplication, but it shows an insight not shared by those authors of evangelistic strategy who proceeded, decade after decade, in apparent ignorance of the fact that popular abstinence from worship was an inherited custom. Its hereditary character was noticed by some. As long ago as 1876 F. W. Farrar interpreted the absence of poor people from worship as 'the result of habit' which arose from 'generations of neglect . . .';[3] and a generation earlier, the incumbent of a church in Sheffield built under the 'Million' Act of 1818, observing that the free seats provided for the poor

[1] Walsham How, in *Church Congress Report* (1880), pp. 94–5.
[2] W. D. Maclagan, *The Church and the People* (1882), p. 11.
[3] F. W. Farrar, *Free and Open Churches* (1876), p. 5.

were 'too often thinly tenanted', asked: 'To what shall we attribute this indifference to Divine ordinances?' and answered: 'The prevailing reason, I am assured, is the *force of inveterate habit* . . . they tread in the steps of their fathers. . . .'[1] Yet it is always easy for people who are anxious about the souls of their fellows to believe that in father's day the world was a rather more wholesome place and that in grandfather's it was quite godly. In this case retrospective fantasy may even have been encouraged by the sensible practice – common since the 1840s – of asking people why they do not attend church. Just as a Protestant who is asked why he is not a Catholic rarely answers: 'Because I happened not to be born in a Catholic country,' so the non-worshipper interrogated about his religious practice is less likely to reply that he is behaving as his parents did, and as his friends do, than to advance reasons for his own absence. A Christian sociologist finds it 'of much value to the Christian mission in Britain that people still feel obliged to justify their failure to participate in the worship of the churches. Historically too related to feel the churches completely foreign to themselves, and finding the churches, at periodic times, and solemn ones, the appropriate agents of their needs and yet disassociated for historical and sociological reasons unknown to them, they feel obliged to proffer their pathetic reason, when the fact is – they do not really know.'[2] Whether pathetic or cogent, their reasons may be historically misleading.

Historians and sociologists have done little to dispel the evangelist's illusions. Some ecclesiastical historians, believing all too literally that the kingdom of God is not of this world, or that 'the history of the Church is neither more nor less than the history of its theology,'[3] give little attention to the relationship between the act of worship and its social environment. Even when an ecclesiastical historian does discuss religion in its social context, it is more often to advertise the achievements of a particular body than to explore the encounter between the churches as a whole and the society. General historians of modern Britain have written of the churches primarily in the

[1] E. R. Wickham, *Church and People in an Industrial City*, p. 87.
[2] *Ibid.* p. 181.
[3] R. Lloyd, *The Church of England in the Twentieth Century* (1946), I. 3.

context of secular national politics. Those with a Marxist orientation have here differed little from the rest. Marx and Engels themselves nowhere investigated religious phenomena in detail. Each of them made occasional assertions specific enough to be provocative, as when Engels, in *Socialism, Utopian and Scientific*, argued that the British ruling classes were so terrified by the events of 1848 that they began to pour vast sums into the Church; but piecemeal remarks of this sort do not much more than embellish the aphorism that religion is the opium of the people. Like other children of the Enlightenment, the founders of Marxism thought it too obvious to need serious argument that religion would disappear from a properly organized society. Religion was part of the superstructure of all societies in which nature was imperfectly controlled; it remained part of the superstructure of capitalism, though weakened and changed; it could be left to topple of its own accord. Putting first things first, they gave most of their intellectual attention to economics and politics. The challenge which Weber threw out to Marx when he examined the origins of the association between Protestant Christianity and capitalism has proved stimulating to historians of Tudor and Stuart England, thanks above all to the work of R. H. Tawney; but the later phenomenon, the estrangement of the industrial working classes from formal Christianity, awaits its Weber.[1] Many sociologists of religion have until lately been less interested in interpreting phases of particular religions in particular countries than in trying to discover laws about religion in general; and they have shown a related tendency to prefer their evidence to come from primitive societies. Some sociologists, sensibly aware that their elders used historical evidence recklessly, have drawn the less sensible conclusion that they had better avoid it altogether. In England, of course, sociology of any kind has been rare; but even in America, where it flourishes, illuminating studies of the changing incidence of religious practice are not numerou[s.] The situation is different in France, where a group of 'religious sociologists' around Gabriel Le Bras has been at work for thirty years reconstructing in painstaking detail the history of religious behaviour, mapping it with technical ingenuity,

[1] M. Weber, *The Protestant Ethic and the Spirit of Capitalism* (translated by Talcott Parsons, 1930); R. H. Tawney, *Religion and the Rise of Capitalism* (1926).

and discussing with care the interaction of environment and worship.[1] One of Le Bras' colleagues, writing in 1958 of religion among the French working classes in the middle of the nineteenth century, observed that knowledge of the subject is still terribly imprecise and impressionistic.[2] Yet it is vast, alongside what we know about the situation in England at the same time.

On the history of religious practice in modern England there is so far only one study, by E. R. Wickham, which deserves comparison with those of the French group.[3] Like the French scholars Mr Wickham was led into sociological history by pastoral concern. It was because he wanted, as director of an industrial mission, to understand 'the weakness and collapse of the churches in the urbanized and industrialized areas of the country', that he began his microcosmic study of Sheffield and England. 'The reasons popularly given,' he found, '. . . betray ignorance of the process of history through which the churches have passed since urbanization and industrialization in the modern sense began some seven or eight generations ago.' His survey begins in the seventeenth century, when probably a high proportion of Sheffield's few thousand inhabitants went to church; they could be fined if they did not. By the middle of the eighteenth century church accommodation in the town was lagging so far behind population that many people must have been unable to attend worship even if they wanted to. The Dissenters were now well established; but the common people were no more likely to worship in Nonconformist chapels than in the parish church. Many seats in church and chapel were leased to individual laymen. 'Such arrangements hardly suggest that the poor were expected to "belong" in an age when they were many.' Methodism burst on the town after John Wesley visited in 1742. The social composition of its adherents was uncommonly broad; by taking their faith outside the normal

[1] For introductions in English, see Eva J. Ross, 'Modern Studies in the Sociology of Religion in France and Belgium', *American Catholic Sociological Review*, XV (1954), pp. 115–40; F. Boulard, *An Introduction to Religious Sociology. Pioneer Work in France* (translated and introduced by M. J. Jackson, 1960). Work in progress is reported and reviewed in the *Revue de l'Eglise de France* and the *Archives de Sociologie des Religions*.

[2] F. Isambert, 'L'Attitude religieuse des Ouvriers Français au milieu du XIXe Siècle', *Archives de Sociologie des Religions*, VI, July–Dec. 1958, p. 9.

[3] *op. cit.*

institutions and by proclaiming it among the people, Mr Wickham writes, the Methodists brought the gospel to people 'rude, poor and even brutish'. But not to *most* of the rude and poor. The early Methodists of Sheffield were a minority despised both by the well-to-do and by the masses. In the nineteenth century the Methodists, now split into three, still failed to penetrate the mass of the poor. The evangelical revival aroused earnest dedication in all denominations to the task of saving souls, but most souls in the town remained outside the churches.

Taking Sheffield as his base Mr Wickham explores the nation and argues, from solid evidence, that 'the broad generalizations and conclusions that emerge are substantially those of any large industrial city of the country. . . .' In the England of 1850 he discerns 'a return to the church on the part of the upper classes . . . continued religious habits of the growing middle classes with some of the superior, more respectable and individualistic of the artisan class . . . and the labouring class, itself capable of cultural subdivision, generally outside all the religious institutions'. The picture hardly altered by 1900. 'Great social change took place in the century, but the pattern of religious habit in the second half of the century, certainly of the middling and labouring classes, is basically determined by the habits of the first half; so strong is the law of social habit, a "law" to which churches have paid virtually no attention.'

This work has been welcomed by a reviewer of the French group, who notes that its conclusions are remarkably similar to those of the sociography of French Catholicism.[1] The findings derive much of their value from resting on a precise use of statistics and a clear awareness of social complexity. Contemporary students of late nineteenth-century English society knew that 'there were significant divisions *inside* what were conventionally regarded as classes, and these divisions were often more significant than divisions *between* the classes'.[2] Mr Wickham reminds us that within the great social aggregate known as the working classes, patterns of practice could vary substantially: 'There was that fraction of the poor in the parish

[1] H. Desroche, in *Archives de Sociologie des Religions*, VI, July–Dec. 1958, pp. 197–8.

[2] A. Briggs, 'The Language of "Class" in Early Nineteenth Century England', in A. Briggs and J. Saville, eds., *Essays in Labour History* (1960), p. 70.

churches, respectable and socially conservative; that fraction of the skilled craftsmen and superior mechanics at home in the liberal Nonconformist chapels, amongst whom would be men active in the world of the Unions, the Benefit Societies, and political affairs, and there were the reclaimed poor in the Salvation Army and the Workmen's Missions. There would be greater numbers of active trade unionists critical of all the religious bodies, and the masses without any serious social interests, preoccupied with the job of living from day to day, from week to week, and with their sport, drinking, racing and gambling.'

It is to be hoped that Mr Wickham's study will provoke examination of changing religious practice in other regions. The more we have of such studies, the less will historians be tempted to document conclusions about nineteenth-century England by citing evidence which may not be applicable from another time and place.[1] It would also be useful to have detailed maps of the distribution of support for particular denominations at different times. Such a study would be especially valuable in the case of the Primitive Methodists, who have been the subject of so much generalizing and so little sociographic investigation. In Sheffield, Mr Wickham reports, the Primitives contributed little to religious life before 1850 but later enjoyed an 'astonishing awakening and growth', which are 'indicative

[1] E. Hobsbawm, *Primitive Rebels* (1959), p. 131, draws on L. Pope, *Millhands and Preachers* (Yale, 1942), a study of Gaston County, North Carolina, in writing about the religious life of people in the industrial areas of nineteenth-century England. Mr Hobsbawm says that Pope's work is the best account he knows 'of working-class religion under early industrialism', and writes: 'Though my account is based on British conditions, the religion of these mountain poor-whites turned millworkers is so strikingly like that of nineteenth-century sectarians, that I shall from time to time use Pope to illustrate it.' The following differences between nineteenth-century England and twentieth-century North Carolina make this approach risky: (1) The people in Gastonia were not typically 'poor-whites' but 'chiefly . . . descendants of small independent farmers . . . who had fallen on evil days and lost their land'. (L. Pope, *op. cit.* p. 10). (2) Most of the mill workers were not living in large or even in small towns, but were isolated geographically and socially into separate villages, living lives half-rural and half-urban. (3) The community was divided into three clearly distinguishable classes – mill workers, farmers, and 'uptown' bourgeoisie – who formed a structure not normally found in England. (4) A majority of the population of Gastonia attended public worship. (5) The population of the region increased more than seventy-fold in the fifty years from 1880 (thus making it unlike most other parts of the U.S.A. as well as most parts of England).

not only of the religious habits of the lower middle classes, but also of the social elevation and newly-acquired religious habits of some part at least of the superior working class'. Why was it that, in Mr Wickham's words, 'Primitive Methodism in Sheffield embraced more of the artisan class than any other church in the second half of the century . . . ?' But why, too, did it not embrace more? For the study of popular abstinence from public worship it is no less necessary to ask why the Primitive Methodists were confined as they were than to investigate their spread. Why, moreover, were they losing strength elsewhere while gaining it in Sheffield? In the last two decades of the century, more and more working men were having their political and industrial interests represented by such people as William Crawford, the leader of the Durham Miners' Association who was one of five Primitives elected to Parliament in 1885, and who spoke for many others when he declared that he 'attributed his position, socially and spiritually, largely to Primitive Methodism'.[1] Yet as the lay preachers stepped forward in their secular capacities, the movement behind them was attracting a declining proportion of the population. 'It is a sign that something is wrong,' remarked the *British Weekly* in 1892, 'when a church of so aggressive a type loses ground in this way.'[2] This phenomenon has been noticed by a number of writers but mapped by none. It could well be studied by methods used so pertinaciously across the Channel.

Positive infidelity, like Primitive Methodism, failed to attract a large proportion of the working classes. There was wide agreement with the author of the report on the religious census of 1851 that the masses could be described as 'unconscious Secularists', and that a dislike for the particular vessels of Christianity seldom became a generalized, fundamentalist rejection of the religion itself. Half a century later, despite the efforts of Bradlaugh, Holyoake and other evangelists of unbelief, it was still thought to be uncommon; in 1900, people friendly and unfriendly to religion agreed that among the working classes indifference to the churches was normal, moral and political hostility to them was common, and cosmological objections to their message were rare – rarer, as many observers

[1] *Methodist Times*, 11 March 1886, p. 171.
[2] *British Weekly*, 16 June 1892, p. 117.

noted, in England than on the continent of Europe. Why this should have been so must remain a puzzle to the reader who finds Methodist historians attributing it to Methodism, historians of Christian socialism giving the prize to Maurice and Ludlow, Sir Philip Magnus insisting that it was Gladstone's work, and a Catholic writer concluding that 'the coherence and strength of the Catholic Church [in England] has been shown in the elimination of any anti-religious character from the trade-union movement.'[1] Clearly, a student who took up this question would have an opportunity for careful thinking as well as for original research in comparative history.

He would be helped if there were adequate studies of the temperance movement and the Sunday schools. Although the crusade against alcohol began outside the churches and for a time had to face ecclesiastical opposition, people in every church eventually contributed to it; by 1882 a writer could say that teetotalism was 'at this moment the common ethical ground of all the sects, from that of General Booth to that of Cardinal Manning.'[2] Quite apart from its association with churches, the movement was itself quasi-religious: agents of the United Kingdom Alliance were in a strict sense missionaries, and it is no architectural accent that Temperance Halls look like chapels. Charles Booth judged at the end of the century that the temperance movement had failed.[3] Perhaps it had; but if only because of its association with religion on one side and with radical politics on the other, the movement deserves examination as a means by which the churches may have exerted some indirect influence on working-class people. In the case of the Sunday schools, there is evidence that they were attended mostly by working-class children, that for most of the century more children attended them than attended day schools, and that they enrolled hundreds of thousands who belonged later in life to no church. A Wesleyan said in 1890 that the teaching given in childhood stuck for life, that people 'would retain the impressions that were then made, and cherish a grateful remembrance of the hymns they sung, and a few of the lessons.'[4] The

[1] D. R. Gwynn, *A Hundred Years of Catholic Emancipation*, pp. 282–3.
[2] F. P. Cobbe, 'The Last Revival', *Contemporary Review*, Aug. 1882, p. 184.
[3] C. Booth, *op. cit.* VII. 21.
[4] *Wesleyan Methodist Magazine*, Feb. 1890, p. 108.

matter seems worth investigating more fully. It would also be interesting to know why Sunday schools, as was generally admitted, lost much of their attractive power by the end of the century. Was it simply that as weekday education improved, fewer parents thought them necessary? Was it partly that parents objected to the increasingly close association of the Sunday schools with particular churches? Such questions would take the student to the border of that great and neglected subject, the history of the English family. One wonders how many non-worshipping parents in the nineteenth century, as now, regarded Sunday schools as useful vehicles of moral instruction for their children, and how effectively the schools provided it. The evidence probably allows only conjecture; but all in all, it seems likely that the Sunday schools were, as Mr Wickham suggests in a brief survey of their role in Sheffield, 'a major working-class institution in the nineteenth century, and the source of an indefinable, no doubt slight, but pervasive influence upon the people at large.'[1] They were evangelical in origin and flourished best under evangelical auspices; and they may well have been the most important single means by which evangelical Christianity was brought to bear mildly on people who were otherwise out of reach of the churches.

On behalf of the interdenominational missionary societies and other fruits of Evangelicalism, as on behalf of Sunday schools, it was sometimes claimed that Christianity was affecting more people than were ever drawn to public worship. 'Evangelical religion,' said a Congregational minister in 1849,

> is, we contend, the chief cause of the improvement so manifest in the great masses of English society. We do not mean that great numbers are converted to God, but we do mean that great numbers are, more or less (and now, far more than ever), under the indirect influence of the Christian religion. There may be more of religious feeling than we imagine, if we form our estimate only from the numbers who attend the public ministrations.[2]

According to evangelical belief, this sort of 'indirect influence', falling short of conversion, was not quite the same thing as saving souls; but it must indeed have been the case that

[1] E. R. Wickham, *op. cit.* p. 155.

[2] *Congregational Year Book* (1849), p. 76.

'religious feeling' of varying intensity and at varying distances from Christian orthodoxy was experienced by many people without issuing in any visible act. Whether there is less of such 'religious feeling' now than in the 1840s is impossible to say; but recent studies, and especially Geoffrey Gorer's *Exploring English Character* (1955), show that it has been hardier than Engels expected it to be. After observing among the workers 'a total indifference to religion, or at the utmost, some of Deism too undeveloped to amount to more than mere words, or a vague dread of the words infidel, atheist, etc.' Engels predicted that 'necessity will force the working-men to abandon the remnants of a belief which, as they will more and more clearly perceive, serves only to make them weak and resigned to their fate, obedient and faithful to the vampire property-owning class.'[1]

Certain religious acts, short of attending worship, did remain customary among the working classes. Ministers of religion married and buried all but the most doctrinaire unbelievers, and baptized millions who might never enter a church until it was time for the next rite of passage to be conducted. How often, and how profoundly, the participants derived from these ceremonies joy, hope or solace, we shall never know. We do know that today many people without religious affiliation believe in some sort of personal immortality. We know that when they are old or in mortal danger, people are more inclined to entertain religious belief than at other times, though they may be no more inclined to attend worship.[2] We know that although the incidence of baptism has declined steadily for generations and that of civil marriage has risen, it is still unusual in England for a body to be buried or cremated without a Christian ceremony. The ritual has been steadily secularized, it is true, as the undertaker has become a funeral director and the role of the minister has correspondingly diminished; but a religious ceremony it remains. Some aspects of the history of death await study, others defy it. But it may be that for many people in Victorian England who felt no need or obligation to attend public worship, the message and ministry

[1] F. Engels, *The Condition of the Working Class in England in* 1844, pp. 126, 238, quoted in E. R. Wickham, *op. cit.* p. 111.

[2] See M. Argyle, *Religious Behaviour* (1958), pp. 152–3.

of the churches helped to assuage grief at the death of loved ones and fear at the prospect of their own. Whether a person thus comforted was brought any closer to heaven is a matter on which Christians would disagree.

Why, finally, did every religious body attract more women to worship than men? Whether this disparity was greater among working-class worshippers than other classes is difficult, on present evidence, to say; but Mayhew's informant was certainly right when she said: 'We poor gals ain't very religious, but we are better than the men.'[1] The difference was explained confidently, but diversely. 'Women, as a whole, have fewer temptations,' said a Wesleyan, 'and seem to have an innate disposition toward godliness more than have men.'[2] Young East Londoners, said a clergyman,' associate religion with weakness . . . and . . . think that Christianity is only fit for women and children.'[3] Another clergyman blamed 'hat spoiling'. Unlike women, he pointed out, men had to hold their hats during a service, and to risk having them dirtied or sat upon; many of them therefore stayed away, and would be coaxed back only if hooks were provided on each seat.[4] It would be fairly easy to add to these hypotheses. A student wanting to pick his way through them might begin by asking whether the proportion of women among worshippers was higher in some churches, in some social groups, in some regions, and in some types of community, than in others; and he might try out the hypothesis that in its communal aspect, the church provided for many women the only regular formal opportunity to get out of the house and meet each other, serving them in this respect as the public house served men. The student of women, like the student of Primitive Methodists, should be careful not to explain too much; he must remember the millions who were not drawn to church by whatever psychic and social forces attracted some.

By 1900 there was in the churches a far more acute awareness than in 1820 or in 1850 that in evangelizing the masses they were trying to overcome not merely the reluctance of a great

[1] H. Mayhew, *op. cit.* I. 46.
[2] E. Smith, *The Great Problem of the Times* (1883), p. 30.
[3] A. F. Winnington-Ingram, in *The Church of the People* (1894), p. 180.
[4] G. Venables, *Thoughts at the Eventyde* (1899), pp. 41–2.

number of separate individuals but a deeply-rooted social habit. It appeared that no body of evangelists, whether orthodox or heterodox in message, and however militant and vulgar in manner, could alter the habit. This growing understanding of the problem did not, however, make missionary enterprise any more successful. Nor is there any reason to think that it should have done so. For insofar as the differences of religious behaviour reflected social divisions, efforts to change religious habits without changing their social basis were bound to fail. A Presbyterian minister in London argued his way to such a conclusion in a letter to the *British Weekly*. 'It seems to me,' he wrote, 'that the chief cause of the alienation of working men from the Church is one which cannot be effectually dealt with by ecclesiastical agency. The social cleavage is far deeper than any spiritual division.' The only solution he could suggest was 'a redistribution of residences'.[1]

Failing this, or some yet more radical social transformation, the churches could do little more than enrol those working-class people who were prepared to adapt themselves to middle-class ways. A Nonconformist observed in 1888 that recruits to mission-hall services changed so much in manner and dress as to be mistaken easily for people who had come from churches and chapels.[2] 'The nature of our work helps to promote migrations,' said a Methodist missionary in central London, 'for, as soon as a man rises a little in the social scale, his first thought is to get out of the slums.'[3] Charles Booth summed up the point with his usual shrewdness:

> The great section of the population, which passes by the name of the working classes, lying socially between the lower middle class and the 'poor', remains, as a whole, outside of all the religious bodies, whether organized as churches or as missions; and as those of them who do join any church become almost indistinguishable from the class with which they then mix, the change that has really come about is not so much *of* as *out of* the class to which they have belonged.[4]

Booth did not try to estimate how often the act of joining a

[1] *British Weekly*, 1 Dec. 1892, p. 92.
[2] *Ibid.*, 20 Jan. 1888, p. 230.
[3] *Ibid.*, 27 Dec. 1894, p. 161.
[4] C. Booth, *op. cit.* VII. 399.

religious body may have been accompanied by ascent to a middle-class style of life. Insofar as the working-class recruit became socially invisible, people who judged the success of evangelism mainly by inspecting worshippers could be misled. Possibly the climb was performed only by those who were on some criteria middle-class already. Certainly it did not happen often enough to diminish perceptibly the proportion of non-worshippers in the nation. To some people farther below the line between gentility and poverty, an invitation to attend worship could seem like an incitement to betray their class. This was perceived by the clergyman who detected among working-class people a feeling 'that they compromise themselves in some way by going to a church'.[1]

Charles Booth noticed that the conflict between ways of life when evangelist met working man expressed itself partly in moral terms. There was, he said, 'an incompatibility of moral temper. The average working man of today thinks more of his rights or of his wrongs than of his duties and his failures to perform them'.[2] To the minds of at any rate the most articulate and class-conscious working men, the Christian missionary was a representative not only of a faith but of groups which were defending an unjust set of social arrangements. In political and industrial affairs, the sense of injustice led to positive demands, in the one case for a share of power and in the other for better conditions. But since there were no advantages to be gained from participating in the affairs of churches comparable with those to be derived from voting or belonging to a trade union, the appeal to attend worship was met simply by indifference. With rare exceptions like the Anglican George Lansbury, working-class leaders denounced the churches – and often in the name of Christianity – but made no effort to enter and change them.

As many Christians observed, competition from other vehicles of fellowship diminished whatever chance the churches might otherwise have had of attracting working-class non-worshippers. The trade union, the friendly society and the political party were given an allegiance denied to the churches. Charles Booth doubted, however, whether the most popular substitutes for

[1] *Church Congress Report* (1881), p. 215.
[2] C. Booth, *op. cit.* VII. 427.

churches among the working classes were the serious ones: 'pleasure, amusement, hospitality and sport', he suggested, may have done more to take 'a place which might have been otherwise occupied by religious interests. . . .'[1] Booth offered this judgment tentatively. Whether he described the balance between them accurately or not, he saw that in the twentieth century the crucial contest for the attention and allegiance of the English working classes would be conducted between politics and pleasure, with religion offering no serious challenge to either.

[1] *Ibid.* p. 425.

Index